Introduction to Networks v6
Labs & Study Guide

Allan Johnson
Cisco Networking Academy

Cisco Press

800 East 96th Street

Indianapolis, Indiana 46240 USA

Introduction to Networks v6 Labs & Study Guide

Allan Johnson

Cisco Networking Academy

Copyright© 2017 Cisco Systems, Inc.

Cisco Press logo is a trademark of Cisco Systems, Inc.

Published by:
Cisco Press
800 East 96th Street
Indianapolis, IN 46240 USA

Printed in the United States of America

2   17

Library of Congress Cataloging-in-Publication Number: 2016949729

ISBN-13: 978-1-58713-361-9
ISBN-10: 1-58713-361-X

Editor-in-Chief
Mark Taub

Product Line Manager
Brett Bartow

Alliances Manager, Cisco Press
Ronald Fligge

Executive Editor
Mary Beth Ray

Production Manager
Sandra Schroeder

Development Editor
Ellie Bru

Project Editor
Mandie Frank

Copy Editor
Paula Lowell

Technical Editor
Rick Graziani

Editorial Assistant
Vanessa Evans

Designer
Chuti Prasertsith

Composition
Tricia Bronkella

Proofreader
Debbie Williams

Trademark Acknowledgments

All terms mentioned in this book that are known to be trademarks or service marks have been appropriately capitalized. Cisco Press or Cisco Systems, Inc., cannot attest to the accuracy of this information. Use of a term in this book should not be regarded as affecting the validity of any trademark or service mark.

Warning and Disclaimer

This book is designed to provide information about networking. Every effort has been made to make this book as complete and as accurate as possible, but no warranty or fitness is implied.

The information is provided on an "as is" basis. The author, Cisco Press, and Cisco Systems, Inc. shall have neither liability nor responsibility to any person or entity with respect to any loss or damages arising from the information contained in this book or from the use of the discs or programs that may accompany it.

The opinions expressed in this book belong to the author and are not necessarily those of Cisco Systems, Inc.

Special Sales

For government sales inquiries, please contact governmentsales@pearsoned.com.

For questions about sales outside the U.S., please contact intlcs@pearson.com.

Feedback Information

At Cisco Press, our goal is to create in-depth technical books of the highest quality and value. Each book is crafted with care and precision, undergoing rigorous development that involves the unique expertise of members from the professional technical community.

Readers' feedback is a natural continuation of this process. If you have any comments regarding how we could improve the quality of this book, or otherwise alter it to better suit your needs, you can contact us through email at feedback@ciscopress.com. Please make sure to include the book title and ISBN in your message.

We greatly appreciate your assistance.

Americas Headquarters
Cisco Systems, Inc.
170 West Tasman Drive
San Jose, CA 95134-1706
USA
www.cisco.com
Tel: 408 526-4000
800 553-NETS (6387)
Fax: 408 527-0883

Asia Pacific Headquarters
Cisco Systems, Inc.
168 Robinson Road
#28-01 Capital Tower
Singapore 068912
www.cisco.com
Tel: +65 6317 7777
Fax: +65 6317 7799

Europe Headquarters
Cisco Systems International BV
Haarlerbergpark
Haarlerbergweg 13-19
1101 CH Amsterdam
The Netherlands
www-europe.cisco.com
Tel: +31 0 800 020 0791
Fax: +31 0 20 357 1100

Cisco has more than 200 offices worldwide. Addresses, phone numbers, and fax numbers are listed on the Cisco Website at **www.cisco.com/go/offices**.

About the Author

Allan Johnson entered the academic world in 1999 after 10 years as a business owner/operator to dedicate his efforts to his passion for teaching. He holds both an MBA and an M.Ed in occupational training and development. He taught a variety of technology courses to high school students and is an adjunct instructor at Del Mar College in Corpus Christi, Texas. Since 2006, Allan has worked full time for Cisco Networking Academy in several roles. He is currently engaged as Curriculum Lead.

About the Technical Reviewer

Rick Graziani teaches computer science and computer networking courses at Cabrillo College in Aptos, California. Prior to teaching Rick worked in the information technology field for Santa Cruz Operation, Tandem Computers, Lockheed Missiles and Space Corporation, and served in the U.S. Coast Guard. He holds an M.A. in Computer Science and Systems Theory from California State University Monterey Bay. Rick also works as a curriculum developer for the Cisco Networking Academy Curriculum Engineering team. When Rick is not working, he is most likely surfing at one of his favorite Santa Cruz surf breaks.

Dedication

For my wife, Becky. What a year! I couldn't ask for a better partner in life.

Acknowledgments

When I began to think of whom I would like to have as a technical editor for this work, Rick Graziani immediately came to mind. With his instructor and industry background, as well as his excellent work building the new Cisco Networking Academy curriculum, he was an obvious choice. Thankfully, when Mary Beth Ray contacted him, he was willing and able to do the arduous review work necessary to make sure that you get a book that is both technically accurate and unambiguous.

The Cisco Network Academy authors for the online curriculum and series of Companion Guides take the reader deeper, past the CCENT exam topics, with the ultimate goal of not only preparing the student for CCENT certification, but also for more advanced college-level technology courses and degrees, as well. Thank you to the entire Curriculum and Assessment Engineering team.

Mary Beth Rey, executive editor, you amaze me with your ability to juggle multiple projects at once, steering each from beginning to end. I can always count on you to make the tough decisions.

As for development editor, Ellie Bru, her dedication to perfection pays dividends in countless, unseen ways. Thank you again, Ellie, for providing me with much-needed guidance and support. This book could not be a reality without your persistence.

Contents at a Glance

Contents

Reader Services

Register your copy at www.ciscopress.com/title/9781587133619 for convenient access to downloads, updates, and corrections as they become available. To start the registration process, go to www.ciscopress.com/register and log in or create an account*. Enter the product ISBN 9781587133619 and click Submit. Once the process is complete, you will find any available bonus content under Registered Products.

*Be sure to check the box that you would like to hear from us to receive exclusive discounts on future editions of this product.

Command Syntax Conventions

The conventions used to present command syntax in this book are the same conventions used in the IOS Command Reference. The Command Reference describes these conventions as follows:

- **Boldface** indicates commands and keywords that are entered literally as shown. In actual configuration examples and output (not general command syntax), boldface indicates commands that are manually input by the user (such as a **show** command).

- *Italics* indicate arguments for which you supply actual values.

- Vertical bars (|) separate alternative, mutually exclusive elements.

- Square brackets [ ] indicate optional elements.

- Braces { } indicate a required choice.

- Braces within brackets [{ }] indicate a required choice within an optional element.

Introduction

This book supports instructors and students in Cisco Networking Academy, an IT skills and career building program for learning institutions and individuals worldwide. Cisco Networking Academy provides a variety of curricula choices including the very popular CCNA curriculum. It includes four courses oriented around the topics of the Cisco Certified Entry Networking Technician (CCENT) and Cisco Certified Network Associate (CCNA) certifications.

Introduction to Networks v6, Labs & Study Guide is a supplement to your classroom and laboratory experience with the Cisco Networking Academy. To be successful on the exam and achieve your CCNA certification, you should do everything in your power to arm yourself with a variety of tools and training materials to support your learning efforts. This Labs & Study Guide is just such a collection of tools. Used to its fullest extent, it will help you gain the knowledge as well as practice the skills associated with the content area of the *Introduction to Networks v6* course. Specifically, this book will help you work on these main areas:

- Understand and describe the devices and services used to support communications in data networks and the Internet.

- Understand and describe the role of protocol layers in data networks.

- Understand and describe the importance of addressing and naming schemes at various layers of data networks in IPv4 and IPv6 environments.

- Design, calculate, and apply subnet masks and addresses to fulfill given requirements in IPv4 and IPv6 networks.

- Explain fundamental Ethernet concepts, such as media, services, and operations.

- Build a simple Ethernet network using routers and switches.

- Use Cisco command-line interface (CLI) commands to perform basic router and switch configurations.

- Utilize common network utilities to verify small network operations and analyze data traffic.

Labs & Study Guides similar to this one are also available for the other three courses: *Routing and Switching Essentials, Labs & Study Guide*; *Scaling Networks, Labs & Study Guide*; and *Connecting Networks, Labs & Study Guide.*

Goals and Methods

The most important goal of this book is to help you pass the 100-105 Interconnecting Cisco Networking Devices Part 1 (ICND1) exam, which is associated with the Cisco Certified Entry Network Technician (CCENT) certification. Passing the CCENT exam means that you have the knowledge and skills required to manage a small, enterprise network. You can view the detailed exam topics any time at http://learningnetwork.cisco.com. They are divided into five broad categories:

- Network Fundamentals
- LAN Switching Fundamentals
- Routing Fundamentals
- Infrastructure Services
- Infrastructure Maintenance

Although the *Introduction to Networks v6* course covers some material in all the categories, the primary focus is the first two bullets. The next course, *Routing and Switching Essentials v6*, covers the remaining content.

Each chapter of this book is divided into a Study Guide section followed by a Lab section.

The Study Guide section offers exercises that help you learn the concepts, configurations, and troubleshooting skills crucial to your success as a CCENT exam candidate. Each chapter is slightly different and includes some or all of the following types of exercises:

- Vocabulary Matching Exercises
- Concept Questions Exercises
- Skill-Building Activities and Scenarios
- Configuration Scenarios
- Packet Tracer Exercises
- Troubleshooting Scenarios

The Labs and Activities sections include all the online course labs and Packet Tracer activity instructions. If applicable, this section begins with a Command Reference that you will complete to highlight all the commands introduced in the chapter.

Packet Tracer and Companion Website

This book includes the instructions for all the Packet Tracer activities in the online course. You will need to be enrolled in the *Introduction to Networks v6* course to access the Packet Tracer files.

However, four Packet Tracer activities have been created exclusively for this book. You can access these unique Packet Tracer files at this book's companion website.

To get your copy of Packet Tracer software and the four unique files for this book, please go to the companion website for instructions. To access this companion website, follow these steps:

1. Go to www.ciscopress.com/register and log in or create a new account.
2. Enter the ISBN: 9781587133619.
3. Answer the challenge question as proof of purchase.
4. Click on the Access Bonus Content link in the Registered Products section of your account page to be taken to the page where your downloadable content is available.

Audience for This Book

This book's main audience is anyone taking the Routing and Switching Essentials course of the Cisco Networking Academy curriculum. Many Academies use this Labs & Study Guide as a required tool in the course, whereas other Academies recommend the Labs & Study Guide as an additional resource to prepare for class exams and the CCENT certification.

The secondary audiences for this book include people taking CCENT-related classes from professional training organizations. This book can also be used for college- and university-level networking courses, as well as anyone wanting to gain a detailed understanding of routing. However, the reader should know that the content of this book tightly aligns with the Cisco Networking Academy course. It may not be possible to complete some of the Study Guide sections and Labs without access to the online course. Fortunately, you can purchase the *Introduction to Networks v6.0 Companion Guide* (ISBN: 971587133602).

How This Book Is Organized

Because the content of the *Introduction to Networks v6 Companion Guide* and the online curriculum is sequential, you should work through this Labs & Study Guide in order beginning with Chapter 1.

The book covers the major topic headings in the same sequence as the online curriculum. This book has 11 chapters, with the same names as the online course chapters.

- **Chapter 1, "Exploring the Network":** This chapter provides vocabulary and concept exercises to reinforce your understanding of network components, LANs, WANs, and the Internet. You will also practice classifying network architecture requirements.

- **Chapter 2, "Configure a Network Operating System":** The exercises in the first part of this chapter are devoted to accessing Cisco devices, navigating the IOS, and learning about command structure. In the second half, you practice configuring and verifying a switch for basic connectivity.

- **Chapter 3, "Network Protocols and Communications":** This chapter's exercises are devoted to protocols, standards, and the two main reference models we use in networking: TCP/IP and OSI. You will also complete activities that focus on data encapsulation and addressing as information moves across a network.

- **Chapter 4, "Network Access":** This chapter is all about how computing devices physically connect to the network. You will complete exercises that focus on physical access including copper, fiber, and wireless media. Then, moving up the OSI model to Layer 2, you will engage in activities that focus on the data link layer protocols and concepts.

- **Chapter 5, "Ethernet":** This chapter continues with the data link layer with exercises devoted to Ethernet concepts and operation, including the Ethernet frame, the MAC address, and ARP. In addition, you will complete activities focused on the operation of the main Layer 2 device: the switch.

- **Chapter 6, "Network Layer":** This chapter starts off with exercises for understanding the operation of the Internet Protocol, both version 4 and version 6. Then the activities move on to routing operations, including how hosts determine a gateway of last resort, and identifying the parts of a routing table. Next, you will engage in exercises that focus on router components and the boot-up process. Finally, you will practice basic router configuration and verification.

- **Chapter 7, "IP Addressing":** With the growing adoption of IPv6, networking students now need to be competent in both IPv4 and IPv6. The activities in this chapter focus on the operation, configuration, and verification versions of the Internet Protocol.

- **Chapter 8, "Subnetting IP Networks":** Segmenting IP addresses into logical subnets is the focus of the exercises, activities, and scenarios in this chapter. You will practice subnetting for fixed-length and variable-length subnet masks. In addition, you will practice subnetting IPv6 addresses.

- **Chapter 9, "Transport Layer":** Continuing the journey up the OSI model, this chapter's activities focus on the operation of the transport layer, including TCP, UDP, and the three-way TCP handshake.

- **Chapter 10, "Application Layer":** This chapter focuses on the layer at which the end user interacts with the network. Exercises are devoted to reinforcing your understanding of common application layer protocols.

- **Chapter 11, "Build a Small Network":** In this chapter, we step back and see how to assemble these elements together in a functioning network that can be maintained. Activities include small network design considerations, network security concerns, securing remote access with SSH, and verifying basic network performance.

CHAPTER 1

Exploring the Network

The Study Guide portion of this chapter uses a combination of matching, fill-in-the-blank, multiple-choice, and open-ended question exercises to test your knowledge and skills of basic router concepts and configuration. The Lab and Activities portion of this chapter includes all the online curriculum labs and Packet Tracer activities to ensure that you have mastered the hands-on skills needed to understand basic IP addressing and router configuration.

As you work through this chapter, use Chapter 1 in *Introduction to Networks v6 Companion Guide* or use the corresponding Chapter 1 in the Introduction to Networks online curriculum for assistance.

Study Guide

Globally Connected

In today's world, we are connected like never before. People with ideas can communicate instantly with others—next door or halfway around the world. Networks are rapidly transforming our planet into a global village.

Vocabulary Exercise: Matching

Match the definition on the left with a term on the right. This exercise is a one-to-one matching.

Definitions	Terms
a. Gives anyone a means to communicate their thoughts to a global audience without technical knowledge of web design.	_____ collaboration tools
b. Enables instant real-time communication between two or more people.	_____ social media
c. Web pages that groups of people can edit and view together.	_____ blogs
d. Enables people to share files with each other without having to store and download them from a central server.	_____ P2P file sharing
e. Interactive websites where people and communities create and share user-generated content.	_____ podcasting
f. Allows people to deliver their recordings to a wide audience.	_____ IM/texting
g. Gives people the opportunity to work together without the constraints of location or time zone, often across real-time interactive video.	_____ wikis

Completion Exercise

_____ come in all sizes. They can range from simple configurations consisting of two computers to complex topologies connecting millions of devices. Simple networks installed in _____ enable the sharing of resources, such as printers, documents, pictures, and music, among a few local computers. Home networks also allow a connection to the Internet.

In businesses and large organizations, networks can be used to provide access to information centrally located on network _____. In addition to the many internal organizational benefits, companies often use their networks to provide products and services to customers through their connection to the _____, which is the largest network in existence.

All computers connected to a network that participate directly in network communication are classified as _____ or end _____. They can act as a _____, a _____, or both. The software installed on the computer determines which role the computer plays. _____ are hosts that have software installed that enables them to provide information, like email or web pages, to other hosts on the network. _____ are computer hosts that have software installed that enables them to request and display the information obtained from servers.

The simplest peer-to-peer network consists of _____ using a wired or wireless connection. Multiple PCs can also be connected to create a larger peer-to-peer network, but this requires a network device, such as a _____, to interconnect the computers.

In Table 1-1, list the advantages and disadvantages of peer-to-peer networking.

Table 1-1   Advantages and Disadvantages of Peer-to-Peer Networking

Advantages	Disadvantages

LANs, WANs, and the Internet

The path that a message takes from source to destination can be as simple as a single cable connecting one computer to another or as complex as a network that literally spans the globe. LANs, WANs, and the Internet provide the basic framework for that interconnectedness.

Completion Exercise

The network infrastructure contains three categories of network components: devices, media, and services. _____ and _____ are the physical elements, or hardware, of the network. Hardware is often the visible components of the network platform. Some components may not be so visible, such as _____ media. _____ are the communication programs, called software, that run on the networked devices.

The network devices that people are most familiar with are called _____. These devices form the interface between users and the underlying communication network.

List at least five examples of end devices:

_____

_____

_____

_____

_____

An end device is either the _____ or destination of a message transmitted over the network. Each end device on a network is identified by an _____ .

_____ devices connect the individual end devices to the network and can connect multiple individual networks to form an _____ . These devices use the destination end device _____ to determine the path that messages should take through the network.

List three examples of intermediary network devices:

_____

_____

_____

_____

_____

_____

List at least three of the main functions of intermediary devices:

_____

_____

_____

_____

Communication across a network is carried on a _____ (singular form of the word *media*), which provides the channel over which the message travels from source to _____ .

List the three types of media used to interconnect devices:

_____

_____

_____

On metallic wires, the data is encoded into _____ that match specific patterns. Fiber-optic transmissions rely on _____ . In a wireless transmission, patterns of _____ depict the various bit values.

List the four criteria for choosing network media:

_____

_____

_____

_____

When conveying complex information such as displaying all the devices and medium in a large inter-network, it is helpful to use visual representations known as _____ diagrams. They provide visual maps of how the network is connected.

There are two types of _____ diagrams:

_____ identify the physical location of intermediary devices, configured ports, and cable installation.

_____ identify devices, ports, and IP addressing schemes.

Classify and Identify Network Components

In Figure 1-1, label the three major classifications of network components. Then, underneath each icon, label the network component.

Figure 1-1   Common Network Component Icons

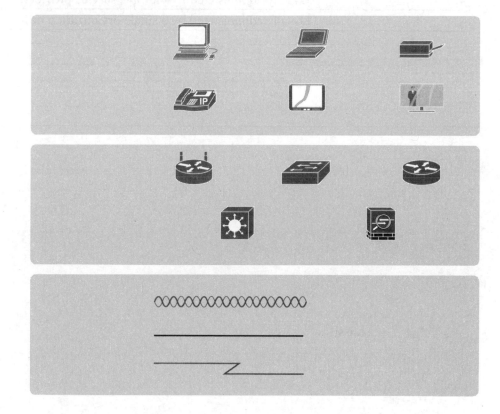

Compare LANs and WANs

In Table 1-2, indicate whether the feature is a LAN feature or a WAN feature by marking the appropriate column.

Table 1-2   LAN and WAN Features

LANs	WANs	LAN or WAN Feature
		Interconnect end devices in a limited area such as a home, a school, an office building, or a campus
		Typically provide slower speed links between networks
		Provide high-speed bandwidth to internal end devices and intermediary devices
		Interconnect networks over wide geographic areas such as between cities, states, provinces, countries, or continents
		Usually administered by multiple service providers
		Usually administered by a single organization or individual

Vocabulary Exercise: Matching

Match the definition below with the terms at the bottom of the page. This exercise is a one-to-one matching.

Definitions

a. Similar to a LAN but wirelessly interconnects users and endpoints in a small geographic area.

b. Requires a clear line of sight, installation costs can be high, and connections tend to be slower and less reliable than its terrestrial competition.

c. Also called a LAN adapter, it provides the physical connection to the network at the PC or other host device.

d. Available from a provider to the customer premise over a dedicated copper or fiber connection providing bandwidth speeds of 10 Mbps to 10 Gbps.

e. The availability of this type of Internet access is a real benefit in those areas that would otherwise have no Internet connectivity at all, or for those constantly on the go.

f. Provide the interface between users and the underlying communication network.

g. A network infrastructure that provides access to users and end devices in a small geographic area.

h. These devices interconnect end devices.

i. Reserved circuits that connect geographically separated offices for private voice and/or data networking. In North America, circuits include T1 (1.54 Mbps) and T3 (44.7 Mbps); in other parts of the world, they are available in E1 (2 Mbps) and E3 (34 Mbps).

j. A private connection of LANs and WANs that belongs to an organization—basically an internetwork that is usually only accessible from within the organization.

k. An inexpensive, very low-bandwidth option to connect to the ISP and should only be considered as a backup to other higher-speed connection options.

l. Data signal is carried on the same coaxial media that delivers the television signal. It provides a high-bandwidth, always-on connection to the Internet.

m. Provides secure and safe access to individuals who work for different organizations but require access to the company's data.

n. A network infrastructure that is larger than a LAN but smaller than a WAN and is usually operated by a single organization.

o. Provides the channel over which the message travels from source to destination.

p. A network infrastructure that provides access to other networks over a wide geographic area.

q. Provides a high-bandwidth, always-on connection that runs over a telephone line, with the line split into three channels.

r. A network infrastructure designed to support file servers and provide data storage, retrieval, and replication.

Terms

_____ DSL	_____ intranet
_____ medium	_____ storage-area network (SAN)
_____ metropolitan-area network (MAN)	_____ cellular
_____ network interface card	_____ dial-up telephone
_____ Metro Ethernet	_____ cable
_____ wireless LAN (WLAN)	_____ local-area network (LAN)
_____ dedicated leased line	_____ end devices
_____ satellite	_____ intermediary devices
_____ wide-area network (WAN)	_____ extranet

The Network as a Platform

The converged network is capable of delivering voice, video streams, text, and graphics between many different types of devices over the same communication channel and network structure. This platform provides access to a wide range of alternative and new communication methods that enable people to interact directly with each other almost instantaneously.

The converged network must support a wide range of applications and services, and must operate over many different types of cables and devices that make up the physical infrastructure. As networks evolve, we are discovering that the underlying architectures need to address four basic characteristics to meet user expectations:

- Fault tolerance
- Scalability
- Quality of service (QoS)
- Security

Classify the Requirements for a Reliable Network

In Table 1-3, select the appropriate column to classify each of the requirements for a reliable network.

Table 1-3   Reliable Network Requirements

Requirement	Characteristic			
	Fault Tolerance	Scalability	Quality of Service	Security
Preventing unauthorized access to the management software that resides on network devices.				
Common network standards allow hardware and software vendors to focus on product improvements and services.				
The fewest number of devices are impacted by a network outage.				
Networks can grow or expand with minimal impact on performance.				
Protecting the information contained in packets as they are transmitted over the network.				
Priority queues are implemented when demand for network bandwidth exceeds supply.				
Data can travel through more than one route for delivery from a remote source.				
The primary mechanism for managing congestion and ensuring reliable delivery of content.				
Includes the goals of confidentiality, integrity, and availability.				

The Changing Network Environment

Before the Internet became so widely available, businesses largely relied on print marketing to make consumers aware of their products. Compare that to how consumers are reached today. Most businesses have an Internet presence where consumers can learn about their products, read reviews from other customers, and order products directly from the website. As new technologies and end-user devices come to market, businesses and consumers must continue to adjust to this ever-changing environment.

Completion Exercise

The concept of any device, to any content, in any way is a major global trend that requires significant changes to the way devices are used. This trend is known as _____.

_____ tools give employees, students, teachers, customers, and partners a way to instantly connect, interact, and conduct business, through whatever communications channels they prefer, and achieve their objectives.

_____ calls and _____ conferencing are proving particularly powerful for sales processes and for doing business.

_____ computing is the use of computing resources (hardware and software) that are delivered as a service over a network. A company uses the hardware and software in the _____, and a service fee is charged.

There are four primary types of clouds: _____ clouds, _____ clouds, _____ clouds, and _____ clouds.

_____ networking uses existing electrical wiring to connect devices. Although it is not designed to be a substitute for dedicated cabling for data networks, it is an alternative when data network cables or wireless communications are not a viable option.

Although many homes connect to the Internet either through a cable or DSL service provider, wireless is another option. Briefly describe two types of wireless (not satellite) options for the home:

_____

_____

_____

_____

_____

_____

Network Security Terminology

Provide the security term that matches the definition.

_____ refers to a network attack on the first day that the vulnerability becomes known.

_____ is malicious software and arbitrary code running on user devices.

_____ block unauthorized access to your network.

_____ is an attack that slows down or crashes equipment and programs.

_____ filter network access and data traffic.

Labs and Activities

1.0.1.2 Class Activity–Draw Your Concept of the Internet

Objectives

Demonstrate that networks are made of many different components.

Background/Scenario

Draw and label a map of the Internet as you interpret it now. Include your home or school/university location and its respective cabling, equipment, devices, and so on. Some items you may want to include:

- Devices or equipment
- Media (cabling)
- Link addresses or names
- Sources and destinations
- Internet service providers

Upon completion, save your work in a hard-copy format; it will be used for future reference at the end of this chapter. If it is an electronic document, save it to a server location provided by your instructor. Be prepared to share and explain your work in class.

For an example to get you started, please visit: http://www.kk.org/internet-mapping.

Note: This webpage requires Adobe Flash.

Required Resources

- Internet access
- Paper and pencils or pens (if students are creating a hard copy)

Reflection

1. After reviewing your classmates' drawings, were there computer devices that you could have included on your diagram? If so, which ones and why?

   _____

2. After reviewing your classmates' drawings, how were some of the model designs the same or different? What modifications would you make to your drawing after reviewing the other drawings?

   _____

3. In what way could icons on a network drawing provide a streamlined thought process and facilitate your learning? Explain your answer.

   _____

1.1.1.8 Lab–Researching Network Collaboration Tools

Objectives

Part 1: Use Collaboration Tools

Part 2: Share Documents with Google Drive

Part 3: Explore Conferencing and Web Meetings

Part 4: Create Wiki Pages

Background/Scenario

Network collaboration tools provide people with the opportunity to work together efficiently and productively without the constraints of location or time zone. Collaborative tools include document sharing, web meetings, and wikis.

Required Resources

Device with Internet access

Part 1: Use Collaboration Tools

Step 1.   List at least two collaboration tools that you currently use.

_____

_____

Step 2.   List at least two reasons for using collaboration tools.

_____

_____

Part 2: Share Documents with Google Drive

In Part 2, you will explore the document sharing functions by using Google Drive to set up document sharing. Google Drive is a web-based office suite and data storage service that allows users to create and edit documents online while collaborating in real time with other users. Google Drive provides 15 GB of storage with every free Google account. You can purchase additional storage if needed.

Step 1.   Create a Google account.

To use any of Google's services, you must first create a Google account. This account is used with any of Google's services, including Gmail.

    a.   Browse to www.google.com and click **Sign in** (located at the top-right corner of the web page).

b. On the Google Accounts web page, if you already have a Google account, you can sign in. If you do not have an account, click **Create an account**.

c. On the Create your Google Account web page, fill out the form to the right. Provide all the required information. The name you enter in the **Choose your username** field becomes the account name. It is not necessary to supply your mobile phone or current email address. You must agree to the Google Terms of Service and Privacy Policy before clicking **Next step**.

d. The next web page allows you to add a profile photo. Click **Create your profile** to complete the account creation process.

e. You have successfully created your Google account when the Welcome screen appears.

Step 2.   Create a new document.

    a.   Click the Apps (⚏) icon to access a list of Google Services. Use the credentials you created in Step 1 to sign in to all of the Google services.

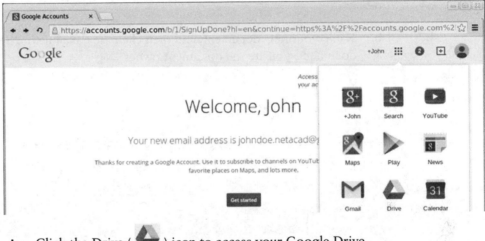

    b.   Click the Drive (◭) icon to access your Google Drive.

    c.   Click **New** to display a drop-down menu that allows you to select the type of document to create. Choose **Google Docs** to create a word document.

d. The new document displays. Many of the functions of the Google editor work similarly to Microsoft Word.

Step 3.   Share a Google document.

a. After the blank Google document opens, you can share it with others by clicking the Share button (at the top-right corner of the web page).

b. Name your new document, and then click the Save button. Because you created the document, you are the document owner.

Name before sharing

Give your untitled document a name before it's shared:

Untitled document

Save   Skip

c. In the **Share with others** dialog box, enter the names, groups, or email addresses with whom to share this document. You can choose to allow others to view, comment, or edit the document.

Share with others   Get shareable link ⊖

People

Enter names or email addresses...   ✏ Can edit ▾

Done   Advanced

d. When you start entering information into the **Share with others** dialog box, you may also add a note.

e. Click the **Send** button. This will navigate you back to the open document.

f. All users can see who currently has the document open. Users currently viewing the document are represented by the icons at the top-right corner. You can determine where the other users are making changes by locating the other users' cursors in the document.

g. This new document is automatically saved on the Google Drive. You can close the document by closing the associated browser window or tab.

Note: You can navigate directly to the Google Drive using https://drive.google.com and view the list of documents created by you or shared with you.

Part 3: Explore Conferencing and Web Meetings

Web meetings combine file and presentation sharing with voice, video, and desktop sharing. Cisco WebEx Meeting Center is one of the leading web meeting products available today.

In Part 3 of this lab, you will watch a video produced by Cisco that reviews the features contained within WebEx Meeting Center. The video is located on YouTube at the following link: http://www.youtube.com/watch?v=fyaWHEF_aWg

Part 4: Create Wiki Pages

"Wiki" is a word from the Hawaiian language. It means fast. In networking terms, a wiki is a web-based collaboration tool that permits almost anyone to post information, files, or graphics to a common site for other users to immediately read and modify. A wiki provides access to a home page that has a search tool to assist you in locating the articles that interest you. A wiki can be installed for the Internet community or behind a corporate firewall for employee use. The user not only reads wiki contents, but also participates by creating content within a web browser.

Although many different wiki servers are available, the following common features have been formalized into every wiki:

- Any web browser can be used to view or edit pages or create new content.

- Edit and auto links are available to edit a page and automatically link pages. Text formatting is similar to creating an email.

- A search engine is used for quick content location.

- Access control can be set by the topic creator, which defines who is permitted to edit content.

- A wiki is a grouping of web pages with different collaboration groups.

In this part of the lab, you will use the Google account that you created in Part 2 and create a wiki page in Google Sites.

Step 1.   Sign in to Google Sites.

Navigate to http://sites.google.com and sign in using the Google account that you created in Part 2. Click **CREATE** to create a new Google site.

Step 2.   Name your new wiki site.

In the **Name your site** field, type in a name for your new wiki site. You will need to use a unique name for your site. Google also requires that you enter the code (displayed at the bottom of the screen) to prevent automated scripts, called web robots, from creating multiple sites. After you have entered your site name, click the **CREATE** button. If someone has used your site name already, you are prompted to enter another name. You may need to re-enter the code at the bottom of the page and click **CREATE SITE** to continue.

Step 3.   Edit the look of your new wiki site.

    a.   Google provides templates to customize the look of your new wiki site. Click the More Action (⚙▾) icon for the drop-down menu, and then click Manage site.

b. Click Themes, Colors, and Fonts at the bottom of the left sidebar.

c. Currently, the site is using the Base theme. Click **Browse more themes** to select a Wiki site template.

d.   Search and select a wiki template for your site. Click **Select** to continue.

Select a Site Template

Public	wiki 🔍
Featured	
Business collaboration	**Project wiki**
	Pull all your project information together in one place and stay connected wi...
Activities & events	
Schools & education	**Wiki**
	provide important information to your MMORPG
Clubs & organizations	
Personal & family	

e.   The preview of your home page appears. You can also customize the colors and fonts on your home page. Click **Edit Colors and Fonts**. When you are satisfied with your new home page, click **Save** to accept the changes.

f.   After you have saved your theme selection, click your site name under **Manage Site**.

Manage Site   [SAVE] [Cancel] [Clear all customizations]   [Browse more themes] [⚙ ▾]

‹ John Smith's Wiki Site

⚠ Below is a preview of your site. You must save the changes for the site appearance to take effect.

Edit Colors and Fonts

Recent site activity

Pages

John Smith's Wiki Site

Step 4.   Update the Home page.

a.   The Home page is the first page visitors see when they navigate to your website. Click the Edit page (✏) icon to edit the content of this page. You can add text, pictures, and so on to this page.

johnsmith.netacad@gmail.com ▾

Home Updated 4 hours ago   [✏] [📄] [⚙ ▾] [Share]

John Smith's Wiki Site   [Search this site]

Home
Sitemap   Home

b. Click Save to save the changes and exit the page edit mode.

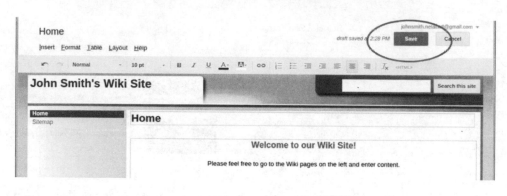

Step 5. Create a wiki page.

a. Click the Create page ( ) icon to create a new page for posting.

b. In the Name your page field, enter a page name. In the example below, the name Routers is used as the topic for this page.

c. Click the **Web Page** drop-down menu and select **Announcements**. Google uses this term to indicate a wiki page.

> Create a page in Site: John Smith's Wiki Site
>
> **Name your page:**
>
> Routers
>
> Your page URL: /site/johnsmithswikisite/routers change URL
>
> **Select a template to use** (Learn more)
>
> Web Page
> Announcements
> File Cabinet
> List

d. Click **CREATE** to create your new wiki page.

> Sites   CREATE   Cancel
>
> Create a page in Site: John Smith's Wiki Site
>
> **Name your page:**
>
> Routers
>
> Your page URL: /site/johnsmithswikisite/ change URL
>
> **Select a template to use** (Learn more)
>
> Announcements ↕

e. Your new wiki page, called Routers, displays. The new page has a **New post** menu option that allows information to be added to the page. (Notice that the left sidebar has a new link to allow your site visitors access to this page.)

> johnsmith.netacad@gmail.com ▾
>
> Routers   ✎   📄   ⚙▾   🔗 Share
>
> **John Smith's Wiki Site**   Search this site
>
> Home
> **Routers**   **Routers**
> Sitemap
>   New post   📶 Subscribe to posts
>
>   There are currently no posts. Create one now by clicking the "New post" button.
>
> Recent Site Activity | Report Abuse | Print Page | Remove Access | Google Sites

Step 6.   Share your web site.

A wiki site is not really a wiki site unless other people can contribute. There are a number of ways to share your new site.

a.   On your wiki site, click Share.

b.   You can invite specific individuals to view or edit this website. You may also grant ownership to others.

c.   You can specify how to notify people about the wiki by entering their email address. Click **Send** to share the wiki with others.

d. The **Manage Site** page displays the people who have access to your site. Notice Jane Smith was added to the list of people with access. Click your site name to return to your home page.

Step 7. Provide the URL of your site.

You can provide the URL to your new site by adding your site name to the end of the Google site URL, as shown here: http://sites.google.com/site/(sitename).

Step 8. Find additional information.

You can find a quick overview of how a wiki works at http://www.youtube.com/watch?v=-dnL00TdmLY.

Other examples of wikis and their web sites include:

- Wikipedia—http://www.wikipedia.org/

- Atlassian Confluence (a popular business wiki)—http://www.atlassian.com/software/confluence/

- Wikispaces (another free wiki)—http://www.wikispaces.com/

Reflection

1. Can you think of other collaboration tools used in the business world today?

_____

2. What collaboration tools do you see as useful to a network administrator?

_____

1.2.4.4 Packet Tracer–Help and Navigation Tips

Topology

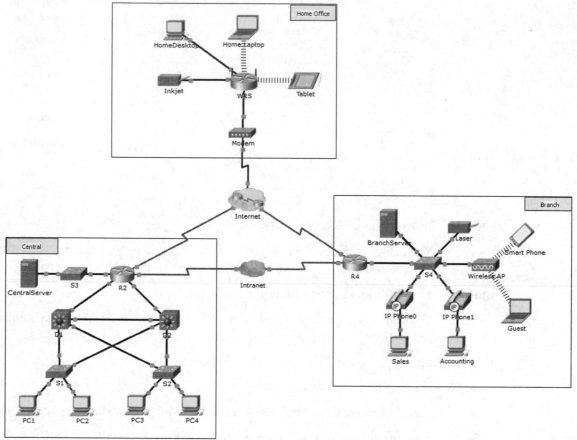

Objectives

Overview of the Packet Tracer program

Background

Packet Tracer is a fun, take-home, flexible software program that will help you with your Cisco Certified Network Associate (CCNA) studies. Packet Tracer allows you to experiment with network behavior, build network models, and ask "what if" questions.

In this activity, you will explore a relatively complex network that highlights a few of Packet Tracer's features. While doing so, you will learn how to access Help and the tutorials. You will learn how to switch between various modes and workspaces. You may need to adjust the window size of Packet Tracer to see the full network. If necessary, you can use the zoom in and out tools to adjust the size of the Packet Tracer window.

Note: It is not important that you understand everything you see and do in this activity. Feel free to explore the network on your own. If you wish to proceed more systematically, follow the steps below. Answer the questions to the best of your ability.

Step 1. Access the Packet Tracer Help pages, tutorial videos, and online resources

    a. Access the Packet Tracer Help pages in two ways:

- Click the **question mark icon** in the top, right-hand corner of the menu toolbar.

- Click the **Help** menu, and then choose **Contents**.

    b. Access the Packet Tracer tutorial videos by clicking **Help > Tutorials**. These videos are a visual demonstration of the information found in the **Help** pages and various aspects of the Packet Tracer software program. Before proceeding with this activity, you should gain some familiarity with the Packet Tracer interface and Simulation mode.

        1) View the **Interface Overview** video in the **Getting Started** section of Tutorials.

        2) View the **Simulation Environment** video in the **Realtime** and **Simulation Modes** section of **Tutorials**.

    c. Find the "Configuring Devices Using the Desktop Tab" tutorial. Watch the first part of the tutorial and answer the following question: What information can you configure in the IP Configuration window?

_____

_____

Step 2. Toggle between Realtime and Simulation modes.

    a. Find the word **Realtime** in the bottom right corner of the Packet Tracer interface. In Realtime mode, your network is always running like a real network, whether or not you are working on the network. Your configurations are performed in real time, and the network responds in near real time.

    b. Click the tab directly behind the **Realtime** tab to switch to **Simulation** mode. In Simulation mode, you can watch your network run at a slower pace, observing the paths that data takes, and inspecting the data packets in detail.

    c. In the Simulation Panel, click **Auto Capture / Play**. You should now see data packets, represented as envelopes of various colors, traveling between the devices.

    d. Click **Auto Capture / Play** again to pause the simulation.

    e. Click **Capture / Forward** to step through the simulation. Click the button a few more times to see the effect.

    f. In the network topology on the left, click one of the envelopes on an intermediary device and investigate what is inside. Over the course of your CCNA studies, you will learn the meaning of most everything inside these envelopes. For now, see if you can answer the following questions:

- Under the **OSI Model tab**, how many **In Layers** and **Out Layers** have information?

_____

- Under the **Inbound PDU Details** and **Outbound PDU Details** tabs, what are the headings of the main sections?

_____

■ Click back and forth between the **Inbound PDU Details** and **Outbound PDU Details** tabs. Do you see information changing? If so, what?

_____

_____

    g. Click the toggle button above **Simulation** in the bottom right corner to return to **Realtime** mode.

Step 3.   Toggle between Logical and Physical views.

    a. Find the word **Logical** in the top left corner of the Packet Tracer interface. You are currently in the Logical workspace where you will spend the majority of your time building, configuring, investigating, and troubleshooting networks.

Note: Although you can add a geographical map as the background image for the Logical workspace, it does not usually have any relationship to the actual physical location of devices.

    b. Click the tab below **Logical** to switch to the **Physical** workspace. The purpose of the Physical workspace is to give a physical dimension to your Logical network topology. It gives you a sense of scale and placement (how your network might look in a real environment).

    c. During your CCNA studies, you will use this workspace on occasion. For now, just know that it is available for you to use. To learn more about the Physical workspace, refer to the Help files and tutorial videos.

    d. Click the toggle button below **Physical** in the top right corner to return to the **Logical** workspace.

Challenge

Now that you have had an opportunity to explore the network represented in this Packet Tracer activity, you may have picked up a few skills that you would like to try out. Or maybe you would like the opportunity to explore this network in more detail. Recognize that most of what you see and experience in Packet Tracer is currently beyond your skill level. However, here are some challenges you might want to attempt. Do not worry if you cannot do them all. You will be a Packet Tracer master user and network designer soon enough.

■ Add an end device to the topology and connect it to one of the LANs with a media connection. What else does this device need to send data to other end users? Can you provide the information? Is there a way to verify that you correctly connected the device?

■ Add a new intermediary device to one of the networks and connect it to one of the LANs or WANs with a media connection. What else does this device need in order to serve as an intermediary to other devices in the network?

■ Open a new instance of Packet Tracer. Create a new network with at least two LANs connected by a WAN. Connect all the devices. Investigate the original Packet Tracer activity to see what else you might need to do to make your new network functional. Record your thoughts and save your Packet Tracer file. You may want to revisit your network later after you have mastered a few more skills.

Suggested Scoring Rubric

Question Location	Possible Points	Earned Points
Step 1c	4	
Step 2f	6	
Total Score	10	

Packet Tracer
☐ Activity

1.2.4.5 Packet Tracer–Network Representation

Topology

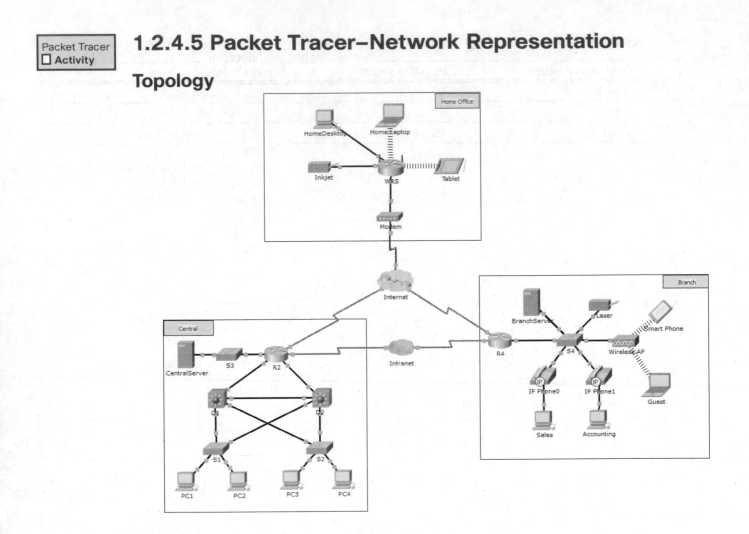

Objectives

The network model in this activity incorporates many of the technologies that you will master in your CCNA studies. It represents a simplified version of how a small to medium-sized business network might look. Feel free to explore the network on your own. When you are ready, proceed through the following steps and answer the questions.

Note: It is not important that you understand everything you see and do in this activity. Feel free to explore the network on your own. If you wish to proceed more systematically, follow the steps below. Answer the questions to the best of your ability.

Step 1. Identify common components of a network as represented in Packet Tracer.

   a. The icon toolbar at the bottom left hand corner has various categories of networking components. You should see categories that correspond to intermediary devices, end devices, and media. The **Connections** category (with the lightning bolt icon) represents the networking media supported by Packet Tracer. There is also an **End Devices** category and two categories specific to Packet Tracer: **Custom Made Devices** and **Multiuser Connection**.

   b. List the intermediary device categories.

---

  c. Without entering into the Internet cloud or Intranet cloud, how many icons in the topology represent endpoint devices (only one connection leading to them)? _____

  d. Without counting the two clouds, how many icons in the topology represent intermediary devices (multiple connections leading to them)? _____

  e. How many end devices are **not** desktop computers? _____

  f. How many different types of media connections are used in this network topology? __

Step 2. Explain the purpose of the devices.

  a. In Packet Tracer, only the Server-PT device can act as a server. Desktop or Laptop PCs cannot act as a server. Based on your studies so far, explain the client-server model.

_____

_____

_____

_____

_____

_____

  b. List at least two functions of intermediary devices.

_____

_____

_____

_____

_____

  c. List at least two criteria for choosing a network media type.

_____

_____

_____

Step 3. Compare and contrast LANs and WANs.

  a. Explain the difference between a LAN and a WAN. Give examples of each.

_____

_____

_____

_____

_____

  b. In the Packet Tracer network, how many WANs do you see?

_____

    c.   How many LANs do you see?

    _____

    d.   The Internet in this Packet Tracer network is overly simplified and does not represent the structure and form of the real Internet. Briefly describe the Internet.

    _____

    e.   What are some of the common ways a home user connects to the Internet?

    _____

    f.   What are some common methods that businesses use to connect to the Internet in your area?

    _____

Challenge

Now that you have had an opportunity to explore the network represented in this Packet Tracer activity, you may have picked up a few skills that you would like to try out. Or maybe you would like the opportunity to explore this network in more detail. Realizing that most of what you see and experience in Packet Tracer is currently beyond your skill level, here are some challenges you might want to attempt. Do not worry if you cannot do them all. You will be a Packet Tracer master user and network designer soon enough.

- Add an end device to the topology and connect it to one of the LANs with a media connection. What else does this device need to send data to other end users? Can you provide the information? Is there a way to verify that you correctly connected the device?

- Add a new intermediary device to one of the networks and connect it to one of the LANs or WANs with a media connection. What else does this device need to serve as an intermediary to other devices in the network?

- Open a new instance of Packet Tracer. Create a new network with at least two LANs connected by a WAN. Connect all the devices. Investigate the original Packet Tracer activity to see what else you might need to do to make your new network functional. Record your thoughts and save your Packet Tracer file. You may want to revisit your network later after you have mastered a few more skills.

Suggested Scoring Rubric

Question Location	Possible Points	Earned Points
Step 1b	5	
Step 1c	5	
Step 1d	5	
Step 1e	5	
Step 1f	5	
Step 2a	5	
Step 2b	5	
Step 2c	5	
Step 3a	5	
Step 3b	5	
Step 3c	5	
Step 3d	5	
Step 3e	5	
Step 3f	5	
Total Score	70	

1.3.1.3 Lab–Researching Converged Network Services

Objectives

Part 1: Survey Your Understanding of Convergence

Part 2: Research ISPs Offering Converged Services

Part 3: Research Local ISPs Offering Converged Services

Part 4: Select Best Local ISP Converged Service

Part 5: Research Local Company or Public Institution Using Convergence Technologies

Background/Scenario

Convergence in the context of networking is a term used to describe the process of combining voice, video, and data communications over a common network infrastructure. Technology advances have made convergence readily available to large, medium, and small businesses, as well as for the home consumer. In this lab, you will research the converged services available to you.

Required Resources

Device with Internet access

Part 1: Survey Your Understanding of Convergence

Step 1.   Describe convergence as you understand it and provide examples of its use in the home.

Write a definition of convergence and list at least two examples.

_____

_____

_____

_____

_____

_____

_____

Part 2: Research ISPs Offering Converged Services

In Part 2, you will research and find two or three ISPs who offer converged services for the home, regardless of geographical location.

Step 1.   Research various ISPs that offer converged services.

List some of the ISPs that you found in your search.

_____

Step 2.   Fill in the following form for the ISPs you selected.

Internet Service Provider	Product Name of Converged Service

Part 3: Researching Local ISPs Offering Converged Services

In Part 3, you will research and find two or three local ISPs that offer converged services for the home in your geographic area.

Step 1.   Research various ISPs that offer converged services.

List at least two of the ISPs that you found in your search.

Step 2.   Fill in the following form for the ISPs you selected.

Internet Service Provider	Product Name of Converged Service	Cost per Month	Download Speed

Part 4: Select Best Local ISP Converged Service Offering

Select your top choice from the list of local ISPs that you selected and provide reasons why you chose that particular one.

Part 5: Research Local Companies or Public Institutions Using Convergence Technologies

In Part 5, you will research and locate a company in your area that currently uses convergence technologies in its business.

Step 1.   Research and find a local company using convergence.

In the following table, list the company, industry, and convergence technologies used.

Name of Company	Industry	Convergence Technologies

Reflection

1.   Identify at least two advantages of using convergence technologies.

2.   Identify at least two disadvantages of using convergence technologies.

1.4.4.3 Lab–Researching IT and Networking Job Opportunities

Objectives

Part 1: Research Job Opportunities

Part 2: Reflect on Research

Background/Scenario

Jobs in Information Technology (IT) and computer networking continue to grow. Most employers require some form of industry standard certification, degree, or other qualifications from their potential employees, especially those with limited experience. The Cisco CCNA certification is a known and established entry-level networking certification that is respected in the industry. There are additional levels and kinds of Cisco certifications that one can attain, and each certification may enhance employment opportunities as well as salary range.

In this lab, you will complete targeted job searching on the web to find what types of IT and computer networking jobs are available; what kinds of skills and certifications you will need; and the salary ranges associated with the various job titles.

Required Resources

Device with Internet access

Part 1: Research Job Opportunities

In Part 1, you will use a web browser to visit the popular job listing websites monster.com and salary.com.

Step 1. Open a web browser and go to a job listing website.

In the URL address bar type http://monster.com and press Enter.

Note: For job listings outside of the U.S., use the following link to search for your country: http://www.monster.com/geo/siteselection/

Step 2. Search for networking related jobs.

a. Type the word *Network Administrator* in the job title box. Click **SEARCH** to continue.

b. Notice the search results:

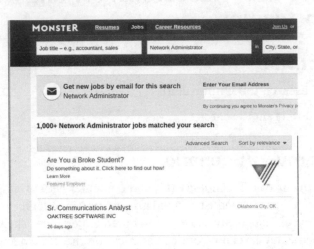

c. Now, focus your search by adding terms to the search for Network Administrator. Try terms like Cisco CCNA, CCNP, CCNA Security, CCNA Voice, and so on.

d. Now try refining your search by adding different geographical locations. Did you find jobs in the locations you entered?

_____

e. Try searching a different website. Go to http://salary.com and click the **Job Search** menu bar button.

Note: For salary listings outside of the U.S., use the following link to search for your country: http://www.payscale.com/rccountries.aspx

f. Add a search term like _Information Technology_ to the job title field box and click **Submit.**

g. In the image below, note the large number of matching search results. Additional tools for refining your search are available in the left column.

h. Spend time searching for jobs and looking through the search results. Take note of what skills are required for different job titles and the range of starting salaries.

Part 2: Reflect on Research

In Part 2, answer these questions based on your research findings.

a. What job titles did you search for?

_____

_____

b. What skills or certifications were required?

_____

_____

c. Did you find any jobs that you previously did not know existed? If so, what were they?

_____

_____

d. Did you find any jobs that you are interested in? If so, which ones and what skills or certifications do they require?

_____

_____

_____

1.5.1.1 Class Activity–Draw Your Concept of the Internet Now

Objectives

Identify the common components of a network.

Background/Scenario

In this activity, you will use the knowledge you have acquired throughout Chapter 1, and the Modeling Activity document that you prepared at the beginning of this chapter. You may also refer to the other activities completed in this chapter, including Packet Tracer activities.

Draw a map of the Internet as you see it now. Use the icons presented in the chapter for media, end devices, and intermediary devices.

In your revised drawing, you may wish to include some of the following:

- WANs
- LANs
- Cloud computing
- Internet Service Providers (tiers)

Save your drawing in hard-copy format. If it is an electronic document, save it to a server location provided by your instructor. Be prepared to share and explain your revised work in class.

Required Resources

- Beginning of chapter Modeling Activity drawing
- Packet Tracer (may be optional if students sketch their own drawing)
- Paper and pencils or pens

Reflection

After completing Chapter 1, are you more aware of the devices, cabling, and physical components of a small-to-medium size network? Explain your answer.

_____

_____

Modeling Activity Graphic Representation

CHAPTER 2

Configure a Network Operating System

The Study Guide portion of this chapter uses a combination of matching, fill-in-the-blank, multiple-choice, and open-ended question exercises to test your knowledge and skills of basic router concepts and configuration. The Lab and Activities portion of this chapter includes all the online curriculum labs and Packet Tracer activities to ensure that you have mastered the hands-on skills needed to understand basic IP addressing and router configuration.

As you work through this chapter, use Chapter 2 in *Introduction to Networks v6 Companion Guide* or use the corresponding Chapter 2 in the Introduction to Networks online curriculum for assistance.

Study Guide

IOS Bootcamp

The user can interact with the shell of an operating system using either the command-line interface (CLI) or graphical user interface (GUI). For many Cisco routers and switches, using the CLI is the preferred method for configuring and managing the devices.

Completion Exercise

When a computer is powered on, it loads the operating system into _____ (acronym). When using the _____ (acronym), the user interacts directly with the system in a text-based environment by entering commands on the keyboard at a command prompt. The _____ (acronym) allows the user to interact with the system in an environment that uses graphical images, multimedia, and text.

In Table 2-1, identify the term for the description of each part of an operating system.

Table 2-1   Three Major Parts of an Operating System

Term	Description
	Communicates between the hardware and software and manages how hardware resources are used to meet software requirements
	The user interface that allows users to request specific tasks for the OS, either through the CLI or GUI
	The physical part of the computer, including underlying electronics

The operating system on home routers is usually called _____ware. The most common method for configuring a home router is using a _____ to access an easy-to-use _____ (acronym).

The network operating system used on Cisco devices is called the Cisco _____. The most common method of accessing these devices is using a _____ (acronym).

Accessing Devices

You can access the CLI environment on a Cisco IOS device in several ways. In Table 2-2, indicate which access method is described for the given scenario.

Table 2-2   Methods for Accessing a Cisco IOS Device

Console	SSH	Telnet	Scenario
			You physically cable access to the switch, are not prompted for a password, and can access the IOS. This is the default operation.
			You access the IOS by using another intermediary device over an unsecure network connection.
			Your manager gives you a rollover cable and tells you to use it to configure the switch.
			You are in the equipment room with a new switch that needs to be configured.
			You use a password-encrypted connection to remotely access a device over a secure network connection.

Navigating the IOS Matching Exercise

Match the definition on the left with a term on the right. This exercise is a one-to-one matching. Each definition has exactly one matching term.

Definitions

a. Scrolls down through the commands in the history buffer.

b. Privileged EXEC mode.

c. Moves the cursor to the beginning of the command line.

d. Interface configuration mode.

e. Has the same effect as using the key combination Ctrl+Z.

f. When in any configuration mode, ends the configuration mode and returns to privileged EXEC mode.

g. User EXEC mode.

h. Returns the user to the previous configuration mode. Can also end the console session.

i. Moves the cursor to the end of the command line.

j. All-purpose break sequence. Use to abort DNS lookups.

k. Completes a partial command name entry.

l. global configuration mode.

m. Scrolls up through the commands in the history buffer.

Terms

_____ Switch

_____ up arrow

_____ down arrow

_____ Ctrl+A

_____ Switch(config-if)#

_____ end

_____ Ctrl+Shift+6

_____ Tab

_____ exit

_____ Router(config)#

_____ Ctrl+E

_____ Ctrl¡Z

_____ Router#

Hotkeys and Shortcuts

The IOS CLI provides hot keys and shortcuts that make configuring, monitoring, and troubleshooting easier. In Table 2-3, record the hotkey or shortcut that is described.

Table 2-3   CLI Hotkeys and Shortcuts

Hotkey or Shortcut	Description
	At the "----More----" prompt, display the next screen.
	Moves the cursor one character to the left.
	Completes a partial command name entry.
	Moves the cursor to the beginning of the line.
	Recalls command in history buffer, beginning with the most recent commands.
	When in any configuration mode, ends the configuration mode and returns to privileged EXEC mode.
	Moves the cursor to the end of the line.
	Moves the cursor one character to the right.
	All-purpose break sequence. Use to abort DNS lookups, traceroutes, pings.

Basic Device Configuration

Now that we have reviewed accessing and navigating the IOS, we are ready to review initial switch configuration, including setting a name for the switch, limiting access to the device configuration, configuring banner messages, and saving the configuration. We will also review configuring the switch for remote management by adding IP addressing and the default gateway.

Apply a Basic Configuration

First, enter global configuration mode for the switch:

```
Switch> _____
Switch# _____
```

Next, apply a unique hostname to the switch. Use S1 for this example:

```
Switch(config)# _____
```

Now, configure the encrypted password that is to be used to enter privileged EXEC mode. Use **class** as the password:

```
S1(config)# _____
```

Next, configure the console and vty lines with the password **cisco**. The console commands follow:

```
S1(config)# _____
S1(config-line)# _____
S1(config-line)# _____
```

The vty lines use similar commands for Telnet access:

```
S1(config-line)# _____
S1(config-line)# _____
S1(config-line)# _____
```

Return to global configuration mode:

```
S1(config-line)#_____
```

From global configuration mode, encrypt all plaintext passwords:

```
S1(config)# _____
```

Configure the message-of-the-day banner. Use the following text: Authorized Access Only. A delimiting character such as a # is used at the beginning and at the end of the message:

```
S1(config)# _____
```

What is the purpose of the message of the day?

_____

_____

What is the command to enter VLAN interface configuration mode for S1?

```
S1(config)# _____
```

Enter the command to configure the IPv4 address 10.1.1.11 and subnet mask 255.255.255.0:

```
S1(config-if)# _____
```

Enter the command to activate the VLAN interface:

```
S1(config-if)# _____
```

Configure S1 with the default gateway address 10.1.1.1:

`S1(config)#` _____

Return to the privileged EXEC prompt:

`S1(config)#` _____

What command saves the current configuration?

`S1#` _____

What command displays the current configuration?

`S1#` _____

Packet Tracer
☐ **Activity**

Packet Tracer Exercise 2-1: Basic Switch Configuration

Now you are ready to use Packet Tracer to apply your documented configuration. Download and open the file LSG01-0201.pka found at the companion website for this book. Refer to the Introduction of this book for specifics on accessing files.

Note: The following instructions are also contained in the Packet Tracer Exercise.

In this Packet Tracer activity, you will configure a switch with its basic settings. Use the commands you documented in the section "Apply a Basic Configuration." You will then verify the switch has connectivity to the default gateway.

Requirements

Configure the switch with the following settings:

- Name the switch **S1**.
- The privileged EXEC password is **class**.
- The line password is **cisco**.
- All plaintext passwords should be encrypted
- Users must log in to the console and vty lines.
- The message of the day is **Authorized Access Only**.
- Configure and activate the VLAN 1 interface with the IPv4 address 10.1.1.11 and subnet mask 255.255.255.0.
- Configure R1 as the default gateway at 10.1.1.1.
- Save the configuration.
- Verify connectivity to the default gateway.

Your completion percentage should be 100%. All the connectivity tests should show a status of "successful." If not, click **Check Results** to see which required components are not yet completed.

Labs and Activities

Command Reference

In Table 2-4, record the command, including the correct router or switch prompt, that fits the description. Fill in any blanks with the appropriate missing information.

Table 2-4   Commands for Chapter 2, Configure a Network Operating System

Command	Description
	Enter privileged EXEC mode.
	Exit privileged EXEC mode.
	Enter global configuration mode.
	Configure S1 as the hostname for the switch.
	Enter line configuration mode for the console.
	Configure the console password to be "cisco123."
	Require a password for user EXEC mode.
	Encrypt all plaintext passwords.
	Configure "Authorized Access Only!" as the message of the day. Use $ as the delimiting character.
	View the configuration currently stored in RAM.
	Save the configuration to NVRAM.
	Erase the configuration stored in NVRAM.
	Reboot the switch.
	Enter interface configuration mode for VLAN 1.
	Configure the IPv4 address 192.168.1.1 255.255.255.0 on interface VLAN 1.
	Activate the interface.
	Describe the interface as "Management VLAN."
	Use the "brief" command to verify IP addresses configured on the switch.
	Test connectivity to another switch at IPv4 address 192.168.2.1.

2.0.1.2 Class Activity–It Is Just an Operating System!

Objectives

Describe the command structure of Cisco IOS Software.

Background/Scenario

Imagine that you are employed as an engineer for a car manufacturing company. The company is currently working on a new car model. This model will have selected functions that can be controlled by the driver giving specific voice commands.

You must design the set of commands used by this voice-activated control system.

Some of functions of the car that can be controlled by voice commands are:

- Lights
- Wipers
- Radio
- Telephone set
- Air conditioning
- Ignition

Your task is to devise a simple set of spoken commands that will be used to control these systems and identify how they are going to be executed.

Required Resources

- Paper and pencils or pens, or computer

Reflection

How can devising a set of voice commands assist in operating a vehicle? How could these same commands be used on a computer or network operating system?

_____

_____

_____

_____

_____

_____

_____

_____

_____

_____

2.1.4.6 Packet Tracer–Navigating the IOS

Packet Tracer
☐ Activity

Topology

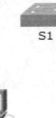

S1

PC1

Objectives

Part 1: Establish Basic Connections, Access the CLI, and Explore Help

Part 2: Explore EXEC Modes

Part 3: Set the Clock

Background

In this activity, you will practice skills necessary for navigating the Cisco IOS, such as different user access modes, various configuration modes, and common commands used on a regular basis. You will also practice accessing the context-sensitive Help by configuring the **clock** command.

Part 1: Establish Basic Connections, Access the CLI, and Explore Help

In Part 1 of this activity, you will connect a PC to a switch using a console connection and explore various command modes and Help features.

Step 1.   Connect PC1 to S1 using a console cable.

   a.   Click the **Connections** icon (the one that looks like a lightning bolt) in the lower left corner of the Packet Tracer window.

   b.   Select the light blue console cable by clicking it. The mouse pointer will change to what appears to be a connector with a cable dangling from it.

   c.   Click **PC1**. A window displays an option for an RS-232 connection.

   d.   Drag the other end of the console connection to the S1 switch and click the switch to access the connection list.

   e.   Select the **Console** port to complete the connection.

Step 2.   Establish a terminal session with S1.

   a.   Click **PC1** and then select the **Desktop** tab.

   b.   Click the **Terminal** application icon. Verify that the Port Configuration default settings are correct.

   What is the setting for bits per second? _____

c. Click **OK**.

d. The screen that appears may have several messages displayed. Somewhere on the screen there should be a `Press RETURN to get started!` message. Press ENTER.

What is the prompt displayed on the screen? _____

Step 3.   Explore the IOS Help.

a. The IOS can provide help for commands depending on the level accessed. The prompt currently displayed is called **User EXEC**, and the device is waiting for a command. The most basic form of help is to type a question mark (**?**) at the prompt to display a list of commands.

`S1> ?`

Which command begins with the letter 'C'? _____

b. At the prompt, type **t** and then a question mark (**?**).

`S1> t?`

Which commands are displayed? _____

c. At the prompt, type **te** and then a question mark (**?**).

`S1> te?`

Which commands are displayed? _____

This type of help is known as **context-sensitive** Help. It provides more information as the commands are expanded.

Part 2: Explore EXEC Modes

In Part 2 of this activity, you will switch to privileged EXEC mode and issue additional commands.

Step 1.   Enter privileged EXEC mode.

a. At the prompt, type the question mark (**?**).

`S1> ?`

What information is displayed that describes the **enable** command?

_____

b. Type **en** and press the **Tab** key.

`S1> en<Tab>`

What displays after pressing the **Tab** key? _____

This is called command completion (or tab completion). When part of a command is typed, the **Tab** key can be used to complete the partial command. If the characters typed are enough to make the command unique, as in the case of the **enable** command, the remaining portion of the command is displayed.

What would happen if you typed **te<Tab>** at the prompt?

_____

_____

_____

c. Enter the **enable** command and press ENTER. How does the prompt change?

_____

d. When prompted, type the question mark (**?**).

```
S1# ?
```

One command starts with the letter 'C' in user EXEC mode. How many commands are displayed now that privileged EXEC mode is active? (**Hint:** you could type c? to list just the commands beginning with 'C'.)

_____

Step 2. Enter global configuration mode.

a. When in privileged EXEC mode, one of the commands starting with the letter 'C' is **configure**. Type either the full command or enough of the command to make it unique. Press the <**Tab**> key to issue the command and press ENTER.

```
S1# configure
```

What is the message that is displayed?

_____

b. Press Enter to accept the default parameter that is enclosed in brackets [**terminal**].

How does the prompt change? _____

c. This is called global configuration mode. This mode will be explored further in upcoming activities and labs. For now, return to privileged EXEC mode by typing **end**, **exit**, or **Ctrl-Z**.

```
S1(config)# exit
S1#
```

Part 3: Set the Clock

Step 1. Use the clock command.

a. Use the **clock** command to further explore Help and command syntax. Type **show clock** at the privileged EXEC prompt.

```
S1# show clock
```

What information is displayed? What is the year that is displayed?

_____

_____

b. Use the context-sensitive Help and the **clock** command to set the time on the switch to the current time. Enter the command **clock** and press ENTER.

```
S1# clock<ENTER>
```

What information is displayed? _____

c. The "% Incomplete command" message is returned by the IOS. This indicates that the **clock** command needs more parameters. Any time more information is needed, help can be provided by typing a space after the command and the question mark (**?**).

```
S1# clock ?
```

What information is displayed? _____

d. Set the clock using the **clock set** command. Proceed through the command one step at a time.

```
S1# clock set ?
```

What information is being requested? _____

What would have been displayed if only the **clock set** command had been entered, and no request for help was made by using the question mark? _____

e. Based on the information requested by issuing the **clock set ?** command, enter a time of 3:00 p.m. by using the 24-hour format of 15:00:00. Check to see if more parameters are needed.

```
S1# clock set 15:00:00 ?
```

The output returns a request for more information:

```
<1-31>  Day of the month
MONTH   Month of the year
```

f. Attempt to set the date to 01/31/2035 using the format requested. It may be necessary to request additional help using the context-sensitive Help to complete the process. When finished, issue the **show clock** command to display the clock setting. The resulting command output should display as:

```
S1# show clock
*15:0:4.869 UTC Tue Jan 31 2035
```

g. If you were not successful, try the following command to obtain the output above:

```
S1# clock set 15:00:00 31 Jan 2035
```

Step 2.   Explore additional command messages.

a. The IOS provides various outputs for incorrect or incomplete commands. Continue to use the **clock** command to explore additional messages that may be encountered as you learn to use the IOS.

b. Issue the following command and record the messages:

```
S1# cl
```

What information was returned? _____

```
S1# clock
```

What information was returned? _____

```
S1# clock set 25:00:00
```

What information was returned?

_____

_____

_____

```
S1# clock set 15:00:00 32
```

What information was returned?

_____

_____

_____

Suggested Scoring Rubric

Activity Section	Question Location	Possible Points	Earned Points
Part 1: Establish Basic Connections, Access the CLI, and Explore Help	Step 2b	5	
	Step 2d	5	
	Step 3a	5	
	Step 3b	5	
	Step 3c	5	
	Part 1 Total	25	
Part 2: Explore EXEC Modes	Step 1a	5	
	Step 1b	5	
	Step 1c	5	
	Step 1d	5	
	Step 2a	5	
	Step 2b	5	
	Part 2 Total	30	
Part 3: Set the Clock	Step 1a	5	
	Step 1b	5	
	Step 1c	5	
	Step 1d	5	
	Step 2b	5	
	Part 3 Total	25	
	Packet Tracer Score	20	
	Total Score	100	

2.1.4.7 Lab–Establishing a Console Session with Tera Term

Topology

Objectives

Part 1: Access a Cisco Switch Through the Serial Console Port

Part 2: Display and Configure Basic Device Settings

Part 3: (Optional) Access a Cisco Router Using a Mini-USB Console Cable

Note: Netlab users or other remote access equipment should complete only Part 2.

Background/Scenario

Various models of Cisco routers and switches are used in all types of networks. These devices are managed using a local console connection or a remote connection. Nearly all Cisco devices have a serial console port to which you can connect. Some newer models, such as the 1941 Integrated Services Router (ISR) G2 used in this lab, also have a USB console port.

In this lab, you will learn how to access a Cisco device via a direct local connection to the console port, using the terminal emulation program called Tera Term. You will also learn how to configure the serial port settings for the Tera Term console connection. After you have established a console connection with the Cisco device, you can display or configure device settings. You will only display settings and configure the clock in this lab.

Note: The routers used with CCNA hands-on labs are Cisco 1941 ISRs with Cisco IOS Release 15.2(4)M3 (universalk9 image). The switches used in the labs are Cisco Catalyst 2960s with Cisco IOS Release 15.0(2) (lanbasek9 image). Other routers, switches, and Cisco IOS versions can be used. Depending on the model and Cisco IOS version, the commands available and the output produced might vary from what is shown in the labs. Refer to the Router Interface Summary Table at the end of the lab for the correct interface identifiers.

Note: Make sure that the switch and router have been erased and have no startup configuration. If you are unsure, contact your instructor.

Required Resources

- 1 Router (Cisco 1941 with Cisco IOS software, release 15.2(4)M3 universal image or comparable)

- 1 Switch (Cisco 2960 with Cisco IOS Release 15.0(2) lanbasek9 image or comparable)

- 1 PC (Windows 7 or 8 with a terminal emulation program, such as Tera Term)
- Rollover (DB-9 to RJ-45) console cable to configure the switch or router via the RJ-45 console port
- Mini-USB cable to configure the router via the USB console port

Part 1: Access a Cisco Switch Through the Serial Console Port

You will connect a PC to a Cisco switch using a rollover console cable. This connection will allow you to access the CLI and display settings or configure the switch.

Step 1. Connect a Cisco switch and computer using a rollover console cable.

  a. Connect the rollover console cable to the RJ-45 console port of the switch.

  b. Connect the other cable end to the serial COM port on the computer.

Note: Serial COM ports are no longer available on most computers. A USB-to-DB9 adapter can be used with the rollover console cable for console connection between the computer and a Cisco device. USB-to-DB9 adapters can be purchased at any computer electronics store.

Note: If using a USB-to-DB9 adapter to connect to the COM port, you may be required to install a driver for the adapter provided by the manufacturer of your computer. To determine the COM port used by the adapter, please see Part 3, Step 4. The correct COM port number is required to connect to the Cisco IOS device using a terminal emulator in Step 2.

---

  c. Turn on the Cisco switch and computer.

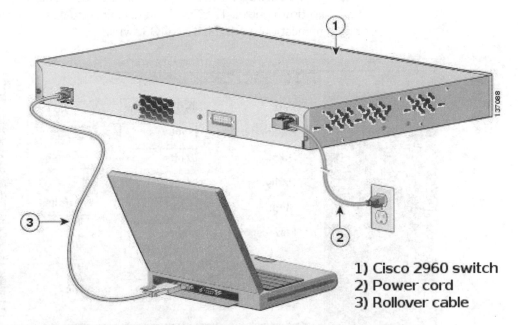

1) Cisco 2960 switch
2) Power cord
3) Rollover cable

Step 2. Configure Tera Term to establish a console session with the switch.

Tera Term is a terminal emulation program. This program allows you to access the terminal output of the switch. It also allows you to configure the switch.

  a. Start Tera Term by clicking the **Windows Start** button located in the task bar. Locate **Tera Term** under **All Programs**.

Note: If the program is not installed on the system, Tera Term can be downloaded from the following link by selecting Tera Term:

http://logmett.com/index.php?/download/free-downloads.html

b. In the New Connection dialog box, click the **Serial** radio button. Verify that the correct COM port is selected and click **OK** to continue.

c. From the Tera Term **Setup** menu, choose the **Serial port...** to verify the serial settings. The default parameters for the console port are 9600 baud, 8 data bits, no parity, 1 stop bit, and no flow control. The Tera Term default settings match the console port settings for communications with the Cisco IOS switch.

d. When you can see the terminal output, you are ready to configure a Cisco switch. The following console example displays the terminal output of the switch while it is loading.

```
COM1:9600baud - Tera Term VT                                           _ |□| x|
File  Edit  Setup  Control  Window  Help
Rights clause at FAR sec. 52.227-19 and subparagraph
(c) (1) (ii) of the Rights in Technical Data and Computer
Software clause at DFARS sec. 252.227-7013.

              cisco Systems, Inc.
              170 West Tasman Drive
              San Jose, California 95134-1706


Cisco IOS Software, C2960 Software (C2960-LANBASEK9-M), Version 15.0(2)SE, RELEA
SE SOFTWARE (fc1)
Technical Support: http://www.cisco.com/techsupport
Copyright (c) 1986-2012 by Cisco Systems, Inc.
Compiled Sat 28-Jul-12 00:29 by prod_rel_teamInitializing flashfs...
Using driver version 3 for media type 1
mifs[4]: 0 files, 1 directories
mifs[4]: Total bytes      : 3870720
mifs[4]: Bytes used       : 1024
mifs[4]: Bytes available  : 3869696
mifs[4]: mifs fsck took 1 seconds.
mifs[4]: Initialization complete.
```

Part 2: Display and Configure Basic Device Settings

In this section, you are introduced to the user and privileged executive modes. You will determine the IOS version, display the clock settings, and configure the clock on the switch.

Step 1.   Display the switch IOS image version.

   a.   After the switch has completed its startup process, the following message is displayed. Enter **n** to continue.

   ```
   Would you like to enter the initial configuration dialog? [yes/no]: n
   ```

Note: If you do not see the above message, please contact your instructor to reset your switch to the initial configuration.

   b.   While you are in the user EXEC mode, display the IOS version for your switch.

   ```
   Switch> show version
   Cisco IOS Software, C2960 Software (C2960-LANBASEK9-M), Version 15.0(2)SE,
   RELEASE SOFTWARE (fc1)
   Technical Support: http://www.cisco.com/techsupport
   Copyright (c) 1986-2012 by Cisco Systems, Inc.
   Compiled Sat 28-Jul-12 00:29 by prod_rel_team

   ROM: Bootstrap program is C2960 boot loader
   BOOTLDR: C2960 Boot Loader (C2960-HBOOT-M) Version 12.2(53r)SEY3, RELEASE
   SOFTWARE (fc1)

   Switch uptime is 2 minutes
   System returned to ROM by power-on
   System image file is "flash://c2960-lanbasek9-mz.150-2.SE.bin"
   <output omitted>
   ```

   Which IOS image version is currently in use by your switch?

Step 2.   Configure the clock.

As you learn more about networking, you will see that configuring the correct time on a Cisco switch can be helpful when you are troubleshooting problems. The following steps manually configure the internal clock of the switch.

   a.   Display the current clock settings.

```
Switch> show clock
*00:30:05.261 UTC Mon Mar 1 1993
```

   b.   The clock setting is changed from within the privileged EXEC mode. Enter the privileged EXEC mode by typing **enable** at the user EXEC mode prompt.

```
Switch> enable
```

   c.   Configure the clock setting. The question mark (?) provides help and allows you to determine the expected input for configuring the current time, date, and year. Press Enter to complete the clock configuration.

```
Switch# clock set ?
  hh:mm:ss  Current Time


Switch# clock set 15:08:00 ?
  <1-31>  Day of the month
  MONTH   Month of the year


Switch# clock set 15:08:00 Oct 26 ?
  <1993-2035>  Year


Switch# clock set 15:08:00 Oct 26 2012
Switch#
*Oct 26 15:08:00.000: %SYS-6-CLOCKUPDATE: System clock has been updated from
00:31:43 UTC Mon Mar 1 1993 to 15:08:00 UTC Fri Oct 26 2012, configured from
console by console.
```

   d.   Enter the **show clock** command to verify that the clock setting has updated.

```
Switch# show clock
15:08:07.205 UTC Fri Oct 26 2012
```

Part 3: (Optional) Access a Cisco Router Using a Mini-USB Console Cable

If you are using a Cisco 1941 router, or other Cisco IOS device with a mini-USB console port, you can access the device console port using a mini-USB cable connected to the USB port on your computer.

Note: The mini-USB console cable is the same type of mini-USB cables that are used with other electronics devices, such as USB hard drives, USB printers, or USB hubs. These mini-USB cables can be purchased from Cisco Systems, Inc., or other third-party vendors. Please verify that you are using a mini-USB cable, not a micro-USB cable, to connect to the mini-USB console port on a Cisco IOS device.

Note: You must use either the USB port or the RJ-45 port. Do not use both ports simultaneously. When the USB port is used, it takes priority over the RJ-45 console port.

Step 1.   Set up the physical connection with a mini-USB cable.

    a.   Connect the mini-USB cable to the mini-USB console port of the router.

    b.   Connect the other cable end to a USB port on the computer.

    c.   Turn on the Cisco router and computer.

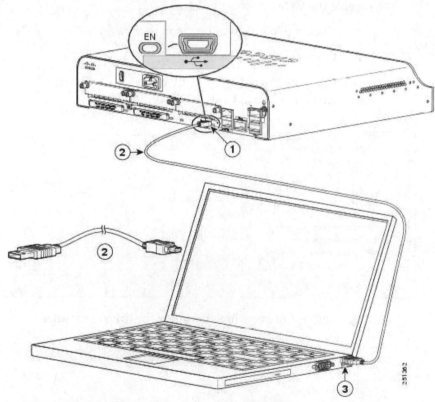

1) USB 5-pin mini Type-B console port
2) USB 5-pin mini Type-B to USB Type-A Console Cable
3) USB Type-A connector

Step 2.   Verify that the USB console is ready.

If you are using a Microsoft Windows-based PC and the USB console port LED indicator (labeled EN) does not turn green, please install the Cisco USB console driver.

A USB driver must be installed prior to connecting a Microsoft Windows-based PC to a Cisco IOS device with a USB cable. The driver can be found on www.cisco.com with the related Cisco IOS device. The USB driver can be downloaded from the following link:

http://www.cisco.com/cisco/software/release.html?mdfid=282774238&flowid=714&softwa reid=282855122&release=3.1&relind=AVAILABLE&rellifecycle=&reltype=latest

Note: You must have a valid Cisco Connection Online (CCO) account to download this file.

Note: This link is related to the Cisco 1941 router. However, the USB console driver is not Cisco IOS device-model specific. This USB console driver works only with Cisco routers and switches. The computer requires a reboot after finishing the installation of the USB driver.

Note: After the files are extracted, the folder contains instructions for installation, removal, and the necessary drivers for different operating systems and architectures. Please choose the appropriate version for your system.

When the LED indicator for the USB console port has turned green, the USB console port is ready for access.

Step 3. (Optional) Enable the COM port for the Windows 7 PC.

If you are using a Microsoft Windows 7 PC, you may need to perform the following steps to enable the COM port:

a. Click the **Windows Start** icon to access the **Control Panel**.

b. Open the **Device Manager**.

c. Click the **Ports (COM & LPT)** tree link to expand it. Right-click the **USB Serial Port** icon and choose **Update Driver Software**.

d. Choose **Browse my computer for driver software.**

e.   Choose **Let me pick from a list of device drivers on my computer** and click **Next**.

f. Choose the **Cisco Serial** driver and click **Next**.

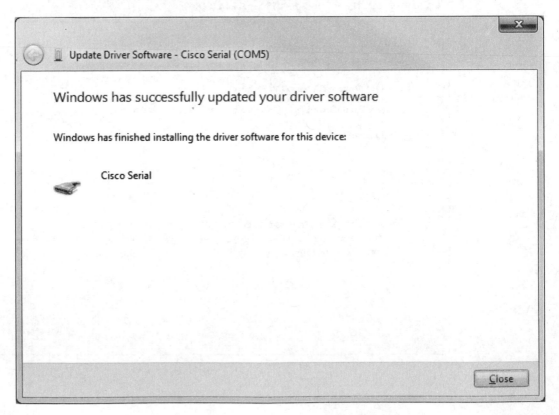

g. Note the port number assigned at the top of the window. In this example, COM 5 is used for communication with the router. Click **Close**.

h. Open Tera Term. Click the **Serial** radio button and choose the appropriate serial port, which is **Port COM5: Cisco Serial (COM 5)** in this example. This port should now be available for communication with the router. Click **OK**.

Reflection

1. How do you prevent unauthorized personnel from accessing your Cisco device through the console port?

   _____

   _____

2. What are the advantages and disadvantages of using the serial console connection compared to the USB console connection to a Cisco router or switch?

   _____

   _____

Router Interface Summary Table

Router Interface Summary				
Router Model	Ethernet Interface #1	Ethernet Interface #2	Serial Interface #1	Serial Interface #2
1800	Fast Ethernet 0/0 (F0/0)	Fast Ethernet 0/1 (F0/1)	Serial 0/0/0 (S0/0/0)	Serial 0/0/1 (S0/0/1)
1900	Gigabit Ethernet 0/0 (G0/0)	Gigabit Ethernet 0/1 (G0/1)	Serial 0/0/0 (S0/0/0)	Serial 0/0/1 (S0/0/1)
2801	Fast Ethernet 0/0 (F0/0)	Fast Ethernet 0/1 (F0/1)	Serial 0/1/0 (S0/1/0)	Serial 0/1/1 (S0/1/1)
2811	Fast Ethernet 0/0 (F0/0)	Fast Ethernet 0/1 (F0/1)	Serial 0/0/0 (S0/0/0)	Serial 0/0/1 (S0/0/1)
2900	Gigabit Ethernet 0/0 (G0/0)	Gigabit Ethernet 0/1 (G0/1)	Serial 0/0/0 (S0/0/0)	Serial 0/0/1 (S0/0/1)

Note: To find out how the router is configured, look at the interfaces to identify the type of router and how many interfaces the router has. There is no way to effectively list all the combinations of configurations for each router class. This table includes identifiers for the possible combinations of Ethernet and Serial interfaces in the device. The table does not include any other type of interface, even though a specific router may contain one. An example of this might be an ISDN BRI interface. The string in parentheses is the legal abbreviation that can be used in Cisco IOS commands to represent the interface.

2.2.3.4 Packet Tracer–Configuring Initial Switch Settings

Topology

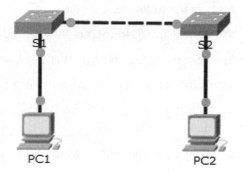

Objectives

Part 1: Verify the Default Switch Configuration

Part 2: Configure a Basic Switch Configuration

Part 3: Configure a MOTD Banner

Part 4: Save Configuration Files to NVRAM

Part 5: Configure S2

Background

In this activity, you will perform basic switch configurations. You will secure access to the command-line interface (CLI) and console ports using encrypted and plain text passwords. You will also learn how to configure messages for users logging into the switch. These banners are also used to warn unauthorized users that access is prohibited.

Part 1: Verify the Default Switch Configuration

Step 1.   Enter privileged EXEC mode.

You can access all switch commands from privileged EXEC mode. However, because many of the privileged commands configure operating parameters, privileged access should be password-protected to prevent unauthorized use.

The privileged EXEC command set includes those commands contained in user EXEC mode, as well as the **configure** command through which access to the remaining command modes is gained.

    a.   Click **S1** and then the CLI tab. Press Enter.

    b.   Enter privileged EXEC mode by entering the **enable** command:

```
Switch> enable
Switch#
```

Notice that the prompt changed in the configuration to reflect privileged EXEC mode.

Step 2.   Examine the current switch configuration.

    a.   Enter the **show running-config** command.

```
Switch# show running-config
```

    b.   Answer the following questions:

      1)   How many FastEthernet interfaces does the switch have? _____

      2)   How many Gigabit Ethernet interfaces does the switch have? _____

      3)   What is the range of values shown for the vty lines? _____

      4)   Which command will display the current contents of non-volatile random-access memory (NVRAM)? _____

      5)   Why does the switch respond with `startup-config is not present`?

_____

Part 2: Create a Basic Switch Configuration

Step 1.   Assign a name to a switch.

To configure parameters on a switch, you may be required to move between various configuration modes. Notice how the prompt changes as you navigate through the switch.

```
Switch# configure terminal
Switch(config)# hostname S1
S1(config)# exit
S1#
```

Step 2.   Secure access to the console line.

To secure access to the console line, access config-line mode and set the console password to **letmein**.

```
S1# configure terminal
Enter configuration commands, one per line. End with CNTL/Z.
S1(config)# line console 0
S1(config-line)# password letmein
S1(config-line)# login
S1(config-line)# exit
S1(config)# exit
%SYS-5-CONFIG_I: Configured from console by console
S1#
```

Why is the **login** command required?

_____

Step 3.   Verify that console access is secured.

Exit privileged mode to verify that the console port password is in effect.

```
S1# exit
Switch con0 is now available
Press RETURN to get started.


User Access Verification
Password:
S1>
```

Note: If the switch did not prompt you for a password, then you did not configure the login parameter in Step 2.

Step 4. Secure privileged mode access.

Set the **enable** password to **c1$c0**. This password protects access to privileged mode.

Note: The 0 in c1$c0 is a zero, not a capital O. This password will not grade as correct until after you encrypt it in Step 8.

```
S1> enable
S1# configure terminal
S1(config)# enable password c1$c0
S1(config)# exit
%SYS-5-CONFIG_I: Configured from console by console
S1#
```

Step 5. Verify that privileged mode access is secure.

a. Enter the **exit** command again to log out of the switch.

b. Press **Enter** and you will now be asked for a password:

```
User Access Verification
Password:
```

c. The first password is the console password you configured for **line con 0**. Enter this password to return to user EXEC mode.

d. Enter the command to access privileged mode.

e. Enter the second password you configured to protect privileged EXEC mode.

f. Verify your configurations by examining the contents of the running-configuration file:

```
S1# show running-config
```

Notice how the console and enable passwords are both in plain text. This could pose a security risk if someone is looking over your shoulder.

Step 6. Configure an encrypted password to secure access to privileged mode.

The **enable password** should be replaced with the newer encrypted secret password using the **enable secret** command. Set the enable secret password to **itsasecret**.

```
S1# config t
S1(config)# enable secret itsasecret
S1(config)# exit
S1#
```

Note: The **enable secret** password overrides the **enable** password. If both are configured on the switch, you must enter the **enable secret** password to enter privileged EXEC mode.

Step 7.   Verify that the enable secret password is added to the configuration file.

    a.   Enter the **show running-config** command again to verify the new **enable secret** password is configured.

Note: You can abbreviate **show running-config** as
S1# `show run`

---

    b.   What is displayed for the **enable secret** password?

    _____

    c.   Why is the **enable secret** password displayed differently from what we configured?

    _____

Step 8.   Encrypt the enable and console passwords.

As you noticed in Step 7, the **enable secret** password was encrypted, but the **enable** and **console** passwords were still in plain text. We will now encrypt these plain text passwords using the **service password-encryption** command.

```
S1# config t
S1(config)# service password-encryption
S1(config)# exit
```

If you configure any more passwords on the switch, will they be displayed in the configuration file as plain text or in encrypted form? Explain.

_____

Part 3: Configure a MOTD Banner

Step 1.   Configure a message of the day (MOTD) banner.

The Cisco IOS command set includes a feature that allows you to configure messages that anyone logging onto the switch sees. These messages are called message of the day, or MOTD banners. Enclose the banner text in quotations or use a delimiter different from any character appearing in the MOTD string.

```
S1# config t
S1(config)# banner motd "This is a secure system. Authorized Access Only!"
S1(config)# exit
%SYS-5-CONFIG_I: Configured from console by console
S1#
```

    a.   When will this banner be displayed?

    _____

    b.   Why should every switch have a MOTD banner?

    _____

    _____

    _____

Part 4: Save Configuration Files to NVRAM

Step 1.   Verify that the configuration is accurate using the show run command.

Step 2.   Save the configuration file.

You have completed the basic configuration of the switch. Now back up the running configuration file to NVRAM to ensure that the changes made are not lost if the system is rebooted or loses power.

```
S1# copy running-config startup-config
Destination filename [startup-config]?[Enter]
Building configuration...
[OK]
```

What is the shortest, abbreviated version of the **copy running-config startup-config** command? _____

Step 3.   Examine the startup configuration file.

Which command will display the contents of NVRAM? _____

Are all the changes that were entered recorded in the file?

Part 5: Configure S2

You have completed the configuration on S1. You will now configure S2. If you cannot remember the commands, refer to Parts 1 to 4 for assistance.

Configure S2 with the following parameters:

a.   Name device: **S2**

b.   Protect access to the console using the **letmein** password.

c.   Configure an enable password of **c1$c0** and an enable secret password of **itsasecret**.

d.   Configure a message to those logging into the switch with the following message:

Authorized access only. Unauthorized access is prohibited and violators will be prosecuted to the full extent of the law.

e.   Encrypt all plain text passwords.

f.   Ensure that the configuration is correct.

g.   Save the configuration file to avoid loss if the switch is powered down.

Suggested Scoring Rubric

Activity Section	Question Location	Possible Points	Earned Points
Part 1: Verify the Default Switch Configuration	Step 2b, q1	2	
	Step 2b, q2	2	
	Step 2b, q3	2	
	Step 2b, q4	2	
	Step 2b, q5	2	
	Part 1 Total	10	
Part 2: Create a Basic Switch Configuration	Step 2	2	
	Step 7b	2	
	Step 7c	2	
	Step 8	2	
	Part 2 Total	8	
Part 3: Configure a MOTD Banner	Step 1, q1	2	
	Step 1, q2	2	
	Part 3 Total	4	
Part 4: Save Configuration Files to NVRAM	Step 2	2	
	Step 3, q1	2	
	Step 3, q2	2	
	Part 4 Total	6	
	Packet Tracer Score	72	
	Total Score	100	

2.3.2.5 Packet Tracer–Implementing Basic Connectivity

Packet Tracer
☐ Activity

Topology

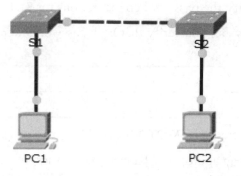

Addressing Table

Device	Interface	IP Address	Subnet Mask
S1	VLAN 1	192.168.1.253	255.255.255.0
S2	VLAN 1	192.168.1.254	255.255.255.0
PC1	NIC	192.168.1.1	255.255.255.0
PC2	NIC	192.168.1.2	255.255.255.0

Objectives

Part 1: Perform a Basic Configuration on S1 and S2

Part 2: Configure the PCs

Part 3: Configure the Switch Management Interface

Background

In this activity, you will first perform basic switch configurations. Then, you will implement basic connectivity by configuring IP addressing on switches and PCs. When the IP addressing configuration is complete, you will use various **show** commands to verify configurations and use the **ping** command to verify basic connectivity between devices.

Part 1: Perform a Basic Configuration on S1 and S2

Complete the following steps on S1 and S2.

Step 1.   Configure S1 with a hostname.

    a.   Click S1 and then click the **CLI** tab.

    b.   Enter the correct command to configure the hostname as **S1**.

Step 2.   Configure the console and privileged EXEC mode passwords.

    a.   Use **cisco** for the console password.

    b.   Use **class** for the privileged EXEC mode password.

Step 3.   Verify the password configurations for S1.

How can you verify that both passwords were configured correctly?

_____

_____

_____

Step 4.   Configure an MOTD banner.

Use an appropriate banner text to warn unauthorized access. The following text is an example:

Authorized access only. Violators will be prosecuted to the full extent of the law.

Step 5.   Save the configuration file to NVRAM.

Which command do you issue to accomplish this step?

_____

_____

Step 6.   Repeat Steps 1 to 5 for S2.

Part 2: Configure the PCs

Configure PC1 and PC2 with IP addresses.

Step 1.   Configure both PCs with IP addresses.

    a.   Click PC1 and then click the **Desktop** tab.

    b.   Click **IP Configuration**. In the Addressing Table above, you can see that the IP address for PC1 is 192.168.1.1 and the subnet mask is 255.255.255.0. Enter this information for PC1 in the **IP Configuration** window.

    c.   Repeat steps 1a and 1b for PC2.

Step 2.   Test connectivity to switches.

    a.   Click PC1. Close the **IP Configuration** window if it is still open. In the **Desktop** tab, click **Command Prompt**.

    b.   Type the **ping** command and the IP address for S1 and press Enter.

```
Packet Tracer PC Command Line 1.0
PC> ping 192.168.1.253
```

Were you successful? Explain.

_____

_____

Part 3: Configure the Switch Management Interface

Configure S1 and S2 with an IP address.

Step 1.   Configure S1 with an IP address.

Switches can be used as plug-and-play devices. This means that they do not need to be configured for them to work. Switches forward information from one port to another based on MAC addresses. If this is the case, why would we configure it with an IP address?

_____

_____

_____

Use the following commands to configure S1 with an IP address.

```
S1# configure terminal
Enter configuration commands, one per line.  End with CNTL/Z.
S1(config)# interface vlan 1
S1(config-if)# ip address 192.168.1.253 255.255.255.0
S1(config-if)# no shutdown
%LINEPROTO-5-UPDOWN: Line protocol on Interface Vlan1, changed state to up
S1(config-if)#
S1(config-if)# exit
S1#
```

Why do you enter the **no shutdown** command?

_____

Step 2.   Configure S2 with an IP address.

Use the information in the Addressing Table to configure S2 with an IP address.

Step 3.   Verify the IP address configuration on S1 and S2.

Use the **show ip interface brief** command to display the IP address and status of all the switch ports and interfaces. You can also use the **show running-config** command.

Step 4.   Save configurations for S1 and S2 to NVRAM.

Which command is used to save the configuration file in RAM to NVRAM?

_____

Step 5.   Verify network connectivity.

Network connectivity can be verified using the **ping** command. It is very important that connectivity exists throughout the network. Corrective action must be taken if there is a failure. Ping S1 and S2 from PC1 and PC2.

a.   Click PC1 and then click the **Desktop** tab.

b.   Click **Command Prompt**.

c.   Ping the IP address for PC2.

d.   Ping the IP address for S1.

e.   Ping the IP address for S2.

Note: You can also use the **ping** command on the switch CLI and on PC2.

All pings should be successful. If your first ping result is 80%, try again. It should now be 100%. You will learn why a ping may sometimes fail the first time later in your studies. If you are unable to ping any of the devices, recheck your configuration for errors.

Suggested Scoring Rubric

Activity Section	Question Location	Possible Points	Earned Points
Part 1: Perform a Basic Configuration on S1 and S2	Step 3	2	
	Step 5	2	
Part 2: Configure the PCs	Step 2b	2	
Part 3: Configure the Switch Management Interface	Step 1, q1	2	
	Step 1, q2	2	
	Step 4	2	
	Questions	12	
	Packet Tracer Score	88	
	Total Score	100	

2.3.3.3 Lab–Building a Simple Network

Topology

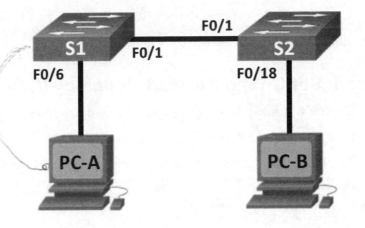

Addressing Table

Device	Interface	IP Address	Subnet Mask
PC-A	NIC	192.168.1.10	255.255.255.0
PC-B	NIC	192.168.1.11	255.255.255.0

Objectives

Part 1: Set Up the Network Topology (Ethernet Only)

Part 2: Configure PC Hosts

Part 3: Configure and Verify Basic Switch Settings

Background/Scenario

Networks are constructed of three major components: hosts, switches, and routers. In this lab, you will build a simple network with two hosts and two switches. You will also configure basic settings including hostname, local passwords, and login banner. Use **show** commands to display the running configuration, IOS version, and interface status. Use the **copy** command to save device configurations.

You will apply IP addressing for this lab to the PCs to enable communication between these two devices. Use the **ping** utility to verify connectivity.

Note: The switches used are Cisco Catalyst 2960s with Cisco IOS Release 15.0(2) (lanbasek9 image). Other switches and Cisco IOS versions can be used. Depending on the model and Cisco IOS version, the commands available and output produced might vary from what is shown in the labs.

Note: Make sure that the switches have been erased and have no startup configurations. Refer to Appendix A for the procedure to initialize and reload a switch.

Required Resources

- 2 Switches (Cisco 2960 with Cisco IOS Release 15.0(2) lanbasek9 image or comparable)
- 2 PCs (Windows 7 or 8 with terminal emulation program, such as Tera Term)
- Console cables to configure the Cisco IOS devices via the console ports
- Ethernet cables as shown in the topology

Part 1: Set Up the Network Topology (Ethernet Only)

In Part 1, you will cable the devices together according to the network topology.

Step 1.   Power on the devices.

Power on all devices in the topology. The switches do not have a power switch; they will power on as soon as you plug in the power cord.

Step 2.   Connect the two switches.

Connect one end of an Ethernet cable to F0/1 on S1 and the other end of the cable to F0/1 on S2. You should see the lights for F0/1 on both switches turn amber and then green. This indicates that the switches have been connected correctly.

Step 3.   Connect the PCs to their respective switches.

    a.   Connect one end of the second Ethernet cable to the NIC port on PC-A. Connect the other end of the cable to F0/6 on S1. After connecting the PC to the switch, you should see the light for F0/6 turn amber and then green, indicating that PC-A has been connected correctly.

    b.   Connect one end of the last Ethernet cable to the NIC port on PC-B. Connect the other end of the cable to F0/18 on S2. After connecting the PC to the switch, you should see the light for F0/18 turn amber and then green, indicating that the PC-B has been connected correctly.

Step 4.   Visually inspect network connections.

After cabling the network devices, take a moment to carefully verify the connections to minimize the time required to troubleshoot network connectivity issues later.

Part 2: Configure PC Hosts

Step 1.   Configure static IP address information on the PCs.

    a.   Click the **Windows Start** icon and then select **Control Panel.**

    b.   In the Network and Internet section, click the **View network status and tasks** link.

Note: If the Control Panel displays a list of icons, click the drop-down option next to the **View by:** and change this option to display by **Category.**

c. In the left pane of the Network and Sharing Center window, click the **Change adapter settings** link.

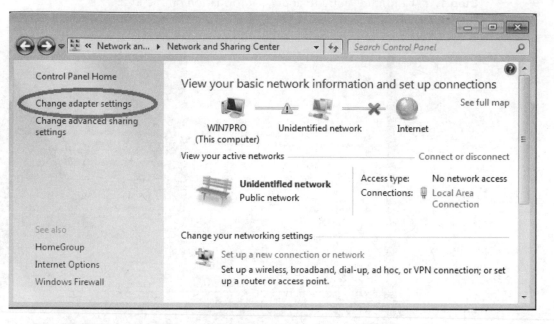

d. The Network Connections window displays the available interfaces on the PC. Right-click the **Local Area Connection** interface and select **Properties**.

e. Select the **Internet Protocol Version 4 (TCP/IPv4)** option and then click **Properties**.

Note: You can also double-click **Internet Protocol Version 4 (TCP/IPv4)** to display the Properties window.

f.   Click the **Use the following IP address** radio button to manually enter an IP address, subnet mask, and default gateway.

Note: In the above example, the IP address and subnet mask have been entered for PC-A. The default gateway has not been entered, because there is no router attached to the network. Refer to the Addressing Table for PC-B's IP address information.

    g. After all the IP information has been entered, click **OK**. Click **OK** on the Local Area Connection Properties window to assign the IP address to the LAN adapter.

    h. Repeat the previous steps to enter the IP address information for PC-B.

Step 2. Verify PC settings and connectivity.

Use the command prompt (**cmd.exe**) window to verify the PC settings and connectivity.

    a. From PC-A, click the **Windows Start** icon, type **cmd** in the **Search programs and files** box, and then press Enter.

    b. The cmd.exe window is where you can enter commands directly to the PC and view the results of those commands. Verify your PC settings by using the **ipconfig /all** command. This command displays the PC hostname and the IPv4 address information.

```
C:\Windows\system32\cmd.exe

C:\Users\NetAcad>ipconfig /all

Windows IP Configuration

   Host Name . . . . . . . . . . . . : PC-A
   Primary Dns Suffix  . . . . . . . :
   Node Type . . . . . . . . . . . . : Hybrid
   IP Routing Enabled. . . . . . . . : No
   WINS Proxy Enabled. . . . . . . . : No

Ethernet adapter Local Area Connection:

   Connection-specific DNS Suffix  . :
   Description . . . . . . . . . . . : Intel(R) PRO/1000 MT Network Connection
   Physical Address. . . . . . . . . : 00-50-56-BE-6C-89
   DHCP Enabled. . . . . . . . . . . : No
   Autoconfiguration Enabled . . . . : Yes
   Link-local IPv6 Address . . . . . : fe80::d428:7de2:997c-b85a%11(Preferred)
   IPv4 Address. . . . . . . . . . . : 192.168.1.10(Preferred)
   Subnet Mask . . . . . . . . . . . : 255.255.255.0
   Default Gateway . . . . . . . . . :
   DHCPv6 IAID . . . . . . . . . . . : 234884137
   DHCPv6 Client DUID. . . . . . . . : 00-01-00-01-17-F6-72-3D-00-0C-29-8D-54-44
```

    c. Type **ping 192.168.1.11** and press Enter.

```
C:\Windows\system32\cmd.exe

Microsoft Windows [Version 6.1.7601]
Copyright (c) 2009 Microsoft Corporation.  All rights reserved.

C:\Users\NetAcad>ping 192.168.1.11

Pinging 192.168.1.11 with 32 bytes of data:
Reply from 192.168.1.11: bytes=32 time=1ms TTL=128
Reply from 192.168.1.11: bytes=32 time<1ms TTL=128
Reply from 192.168.1.11: bytes=32 time<1ms TTL=128
Reply from 192.168.1.11: bytes=32 time<1ms TTL=128

Ping statistics for 192.168.1.11:
    Packets: Sent = 4, Received = 4, Lost = 0 (0% loss),
Approximate round trip times in milli-seconds:
    Minimum = 0ms, Maximum = 1ms, Average = 0ms

C:\Users\NetAcad>
```

Were the ping results successful? _____Yes_____

If not, troubleshoot as necessary.

Note: If you did not get a reply from PC-B, try to ping PC-B again. If you still do not get a reply from PC-B, try to ping PC-A from PC-B. If you are unable to get a reply from the remote PC, then have your instructor help you troubleshoot the problem.

Part 3: Configure and Verify Basic Switch Settings

Step 1.   Console into the switch.

Using Tera Term, establish a console connection to the switch from PC-A.

Step 2.   Enter privileged EXEC mode.

You can access all switch commands in privileged EXEC mode. The privileged EXEC command set includes those commands contained in user EXEC mode, as well as the **configure** command through which access to the remaining command modes are gained. Enter privileged EXEC mode by entering the **enable** command.

```
Switch> enable
Switch#
```

The prompt changed from **Switch>** to **Switch#**, which indicates privileged EXEC mode.

Step 3.   Enter configuration mode.

Use the **configuration terminal** command to enter configuration mode.

```
Switch# configure terminal
Enter configuration commands, one per line. End with CNTL/Z.
Switch(config)#
```

The prompt changed to reflect global configuration mode.

Step 4.   Give the switch a name.

Use the **hostname** command to change the switch name to **S1**.

```
Switch(config)# hostname S1
S1(config)#
```

Step 5.   Prevent unwanted DNS lookups.

To prevent the switch from attempting to translate incorrectly entered commands as though they were hostnames, disable the Domain Name System (DNS) lookup.

```
S1(config)# no ip domain-lookup
S1(config)#
```

Step 6.   Enter local passwords.

To prevent unauthorized access to the switch, passwords must be configured.

```
S1(config)# enable secret class
S1(config)# line con 0
S1(config-line)# password cisco
S1(config-line)# login
S1(config-line)# exit
S1(config)#
```

Step 7.   Enter a login MOTD banner.

A login banner, known as the message of the day (MOTD) banner, should be configured to warn anyone accessing the switch that unauthorized access will not be tolerated.

The **banner motd** command requires the use of delimiters to identify the content of the banner message. The delimiting character can be any character as long as it does not occur in the message. For this reason, symbols, such as the **#**, are often used.

```
S1(config)# banner motd #
Enter TEXT message. End with the character '#'.
Unauthorized access is strictly prohibited and prosecuted to the full extent of the
law. #
S1(config)# exit
S1#
```

Step 8.   Save the configuration.

Use the **copy** command to save the running configuration to the startup file on non-volatile random access memory (NVRAM).

```
S1# copy running-config startup-config
Destination filename [startup-config]? [Enter]
Building configuration...
[OK]
S1#
```

Step 9.   Display the current configuration.

The **show running-config** command displays the entire running configuration, one page at a time. Use the spacebar to advance paging. The commands configured in Steps 1–8 are highlighted below.

```
S1# show running-config
Building configuration...

Current configuration : 1409 bytes
!
! Last configuration change at 03:49:17 UTC Mon Mar 1 1993
!
```

```
version 15.0
no service pad
service timestamps debug datetime msec
service timestamps log datetime msec
no service password-encryption
!
hostname S1
!
boot-start-marker
boot-end-marker
!
enable secret 4 06YFDUHH61wAE/kLkDq9BGho1QM5EnRtoyr8cHAUg.2
!
no aaa new-model
system mtu routing 1500
!
!
no ip domain-lookup
!


<output omitted>


!
banner motd ^C
Unauthorized access is strictly prohibited and prosecuted to the full extent of the
law. ^C
!
line con 0
 password cisco
 login
line vty 0 4
 login
line vty 5 15
 login
!
end

S1#
```

Step 10. Display the IOS version and other useful switch information.

Use the **show version** command to display the IOS version that the switch is running, along with other useful information. Again, you will need to use the spacebar to advance through the displayed information.

```
S1# show version
Cisco IOS Software, C2960 Software (C2960-LANBASEK9-M), Version 15.0(2)SE, RELEASE
SOFTWARE (fc1)
Technical Support: http://www.cisco.com/techsupport
Copyright (c) 1986-2012 by Cisco Systems, Inc.
Compiled Sat 28-Jul-12 00:29 by prod_rel_team
```

```
ROM: Bootstrap program is C2960 boot loader
BOOTLDR: C2960 Boot Loader (C2960-HBOOT-M) Version 12.2(53r)SEY3, RELEASE SOFTWARE
(fc1)


S1 uptime is 1 hour, 38 minutes
System returned to ROM by power-on
System image file is "flash:/c2960-lanbasek9-mz.150-2.SE.bin"


This product contains cryptographic features and is subject to United
States and local country laws governing import, export, transfer and
use. Delivery of Cisco cryptographic products does not imply
third-party authority to import, export, distribute or use encryption.
Importers, exporters, distributors and users are responsible for
compliance with U.S. and local country laws. By using this product you
agree to comply with applicable laws and regulations. If you are unable
to comply with U.S. and local laws, return this product immediately.


A summary of U.S. laws governing Cisco cryptographic products may be found at:
http://www.cisco.com/wwl/export/crypto/tool/stqrg.html


If you require further assistance please contact us by sending email to
export@cisco.com.


cisco WS-C2960-24TT-L (PowerPC405) processor (revision R0) with 65536K bytes of
memory.
Processor board ID FCQ1628Y5LE
Last reset from power-on
1 Virtual Ethernet interface
24 FastEthernet interfaces
2 Gigabit Ethernet interfaces
The password-recovery mechanism is enabled.


64K bytes of flash-simulated non-volatile configuration memory.
Base ethernet MAC Address       : 0C:D9:96:E2:3D:00
Motherboard assembly number     : 73-12600-06
Power supply part number        : 341-0097-03
Motherboard serial number       : FCQ16270N5G
Power supply serial number      : DCA1616884D
Model revision number           : R0
Motherboard revision number     : A0
Model number                    : WS-C2960-24TT-L
System serial number            : FCQ1628Y5LE
Top Assembly Part Number        : 800-32797-02
Top Assembly Revision Number    : A0
Version ID                      : V11
CLEI Code Number                : COM3L00BRF
Hardware Board Revision Number  : 0x0A
```

```
Switch Ports Model              SW Version            SW Image
------ ----- -----              ----------            ----------
*   1 26   WS-C2960-24TT-L      15.0(2)SE             C2960-LANBASEK9-M


Configuration register is 0xF
S1#
```

Step 11. Display the status of the connected interfaces on the switch.

To check the status of the connected interfaces, use the **show ip interface brief** command. Press the spacebar to advance to the end of the list.

```
S1# show ip interface brief
Interface              IP-Address      OK? Method Status              Protocol
Vlan1                  unassigned      YES unset  up                  up
FastEthernet0/1        unassigned      YES unset  up                  up
FastEthernet0/2        unassigned      YES unset  down                down
FastEthernet0/3        unassigned      YES unset  down                down
FastEthernet0/4        unassigned      YES unset  down                down
FastEthernet0/5        unassigned      YES unset  down                down
FastEthernet0/6        unassigned      YES unset  up                  up
FastEthernet0/7        unassigned      YES unset  down                down
FastEthernet0/8        unassigned      YES unset  down                down
FastEthernet0/9        unassigned      YES unset  down                down
FastEthernet0/10       unassigned      YES unset  down                down
FastEthernet0/11       unassigned      YES unset  down                down
FastEthernet0/12       unassigned      YES unset  down                down
FastEthernet0/13       unassigned      YES unset  down                down
FastEthernet0/14       unassigned      YES unset  down                down
FastEthernet0/15       unassigned      YES unset  down                down
FastEthernet0/16       unassigned      YES unset  down                down
FastEthernet0/17       unassigned      YES unset  down                down
FastEthernet0/18       unassigned      YES unset  down                down
FastEthernet0/19       unassigned      YES unset  down                down
FastEthernet0/20       unassigned      YES unset  down                down
FastEthernet0/21       unassigned      YES unset  down                down
FastEthernet0/22       unassigned      YES unset  down                down
FastEthernet0/23       unassigned      YES unset  down                down
FastEthernet0/24       unassigned      YES unset  down                down
GigabitEthernet0/1     unassigned      YES unset  down                down
GigabitEthernet0/2     unassigned      YES unset  down                down
S1#
```

Step 12. Repeat Steps 1 to 11 to configure switch S2.

The only difference for this step is to change the hostname to S2.

Step 13. Record the interface status for the following interfaces.

Interface	S1		S2	
	Status	Protocol	Status	Protocol
F0/1				
F0/6				
F0/18				
VLAN 1				

Why are some FastEthernet ports on the switches up and others are down?

_____

_____

Reflection

What could prevent a ping from being sent between the PCs?

_____

Note: It may be necessary to disable the PC firewall to ping between PCs.

Appendix A: Initializing and Reloading a Switch

Step 1. Connect to the switch.

Console into the switch and enter privileged EXEC mode.

```
Switch> enable
Switch#
```

Step 2. Determine if there have been any virtual local-area networks (VLANs) created.

Use the **show flash** command to determine if any VLANs have been created on the switch.

```
Switch# show flash

Directory of flash:/

    2  -rwx        1919   Mar 1 1993 00:06:33 +00:00  private-config.text
    3  -rwx        1632   Mar 1 1993 00:06:33 +00:00  config.text
    4  -rwx       13336   Mar 1 1993 00:06:33 +00:00  multiple-fs
    5  -rwx    11607161   Mar 1 1993 02:37:06 +00:00  c2960-lanbasek9-mz.150-2.
SE.bin
    6  -rwx         616   Mar 1 1993 00:07:13 +00:00  vlan.dat

32514048 bytes total (20886528 bytes free)
Switch#
```

Step 3.   Delete the VLAN file.

    a.   If the **vlan.dat** file was found in flash, then delete this file.

```
Switch# delete vlan.dat
Delete filename [vlan.dat]?
```

        You will be prompted to verify the filename. At this point, you can change the filename or just press Enter if you have entered the name correctly.

    b.   When you are prompted to delete this file, press Enter to confirm the deletion. (Pressing any other key will abort the deletion.)

```
Delete flash:/vlan.dat? [confirm]
Switch#
```

Step 4.   Erase the startup configuration file.

Use the **erase startup-config** command to erase the startup configuration file from NVRAM. When you are prompted to remove the configuration file, press Enter to confirm the erase. (Pressing any other key will abort the operation.)

```
Switch# erase startup-config
Erasing the nvram filesystem will remove all configuration files! Continue?
[confirm]
[OK]
Erase of nvram: complete
Switch#
```

Step 5.   Reload the switch.

Reload the switch to remove any old configuration information from memory. When you are prompted to reload the switch, press Enter to proceed with the reload. (Pressing any other key will abort the reload.)

```
Switch# reload
Proceed with reload? [confirm]
```

Note: You may receive a prompt to save the running configuration prior to reloading the switch. Type **no** and press Enter.

```
System configuration has been modified. Save? [yes/no]: no
```

Step 6.   Bypass the initial configuration dialog.

After the switch reloads, you should see a prompt to enter the initial configuration dialog. Type **no** at the prompt and press Enter.

```
Would you like to enter the initial configuration dialog? [yes/no]: no
Switch>
```

2.3.3.4 Lab–Configuring a Switch Management Address

Topology

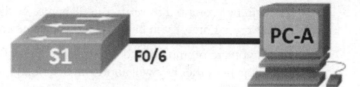

Addressing Table

Device	Interface	IP Address	Subnet Mask
S1	VLAN 1	192.168.1.2	255.255.255.0
PC-A	NIC	192.168.1.10	255.255.255.0

Objectives

Part 1: Configure a Basic Network Device

Part 2: Verify and Test Network Connectivity

Background/Scenario

Cisco switches have a special interface, known as a switch virtual interface (SVI). The SVI can be configured with an IP address, commonly referred to as the management address. The management address is used for remote access to the switch to display or configure settings.

In this lab, you will build a simple network using Ethernet LAN cabling and access a Cisco switch using the console and remote access methods. You will configure basic switch settings and IP addressing, and demonstrate the use of a management IP address for remote switch management. The topology consists of one switch and one host using only Ethernet and console ports.

Note: The switches used are Cisco Catalyst 2960s with Cisco IOS Release 15.0(2) (lanbasek9 image). Other switches and Cisco IOS versions can be used. Depending on the model and Cisco IOS version, the available commands and output produced might vary from what is shown in the labs.

Note: Make sure that the switch has been erased and has no startup configuration. If you are unsure, contact your instructor.

Required Resources

- 1 Switch (Cisco 2960 with Cisco IOS Release 15.0(2) lanbasek9 image or comparable)
- 1 PC (Windows 7 or 8 with terminal emulation program, such as Tera Term)
- Console cables to configure the Cisco IOS devices via the console ports
- Ethernet cables as shown in the topology

Part 1: Configure a Basic Network Device

In Part 1, you will set up the network and configure basic settings, such as hostnames, interface IP addresses, and passwords.

Step 1.   Cable the network.

   a.   Cable the network as shown in the topology.

   b.   Establish a console connection to the switch from PC-A.

Step 2.   Configure basic switch settings.

In this step, you will configure basic switch settings, such as hostname, and configure an IP address for the SVI. Assigning an IP address on the switch is only the first step. As the network administrator, you must specify how the switch will be managed. Telnet and SSH are two of the most common management methods. However, Telnet is a very insecure protocol. All information flowing between the two devices is sent in plaintext. Passwords and other sensitive information can be easily viewed if captured by a packet sniffer.

   a.   Assuming the switch did not have a configuration file stored in NVRAM, you will be at the user EXEC mode prompt on the switch. The prompt will be `Switch>`. Enter privileged EXEC mode.

```
Switch> enable
Switch#
```

   b.   Use the privileged EXEC **show running-config** command to verify a clean configuration file. If a configuration file was previously saved, it will have to be removed. Depending on the switch model and IOS version, your configuration may look slightly different. However, there should not be any configured passwords or IP address set. If your switch does not have a default configuration, ask your instructor for help.

   c.   Enter global configuration mode and assign the switch hostname.

```
Switch# configure terminal
Switch(config)# hostname S1
S1(config)#
```

   d.   Configure the switch password access.

```
S1(config)# enable secret class
S1(config)#
```

   e.   Prevent unwanted DNS lookups.

```
S1(config)# no ip domain-lookup
S1(config)#
```

   f.   Configure a login MOTD banner.

```
S1(config)# banner motd #
Enter Text message.  End with the character '#'.
Unauthorized access is strictly prohibited. #
```

   g.   Verify your access setting by moving between modes.

```
S1(config)# exit
S1#
S1# exit
Unauthorized access is strictly prohibited.
S1>
```

What shortcut keys are used to go directly from global configuration mode to privileged EXEC mode?

_____

h. Return to privileged EXEC mode from user EXEC mode.

```
S1> enable
Password: class
S1#
```

_____

Note: The password will not show up on the screen when entering.

i. Enter global configuration mode to set the SVI IP address to allow remote switch management.

```
S1# config t
S1#(config)# interface vlan 1
S1(config-if)# ip address 192.168.1.2 255.255.255.0
S1(config-if)# no shut
S1(config-if)# exit
S1(config)#
```

j. Restrict console port access. The default configuration is to allow all console connections with no password needed.

```
S1(config)# line con 0
S1(config-line)# password cisco
S1(config-line)# login
S1(config-line)# exit
S1(config)#
```

k. Configure the VTY line for the switch to allow Telnet access. If you do not configure a VTY password, you will not be able to telnet to the switch.

```
S1(config)# line vty 0 4
S1(config-line)# password cisco
S1(config-line)# login
S1(config-line)# end
S1#
*Mar  1 00:06:11.590: %SYS-5-CONFIG_I: Configured from console by console
```

Step 3. Configure an IP address on PC-A.

a. Assign the IP address and subnet mask to the PC, as shown in the Addressing Table. The procedure for assigning an IP address on a PC running Windows 7 is described below:

1) Click the **Windows Start** icon > **Control Panel**.

2) Click **View By:** > **Category**.

3) Choose **View network status and tasks** > **Change adapter settings**.

4) Right-click **Local Area Network Connection** and select **Properties**.

5) Choose **Internet Protocol Version 4 (TCP/IPv4)**, click **Properties** > **OK**.

6) Click the **Use the following IP address** radio button and enter the IP address and subnet mask.

Part 2: Verify and Test Network Connectivity

You will now verify and document the switch configuration, test end-to-end connectivity between PC-A and S1, and test the remote management capability of the switch.

Step 1. Display the S1 device configuration.

    a. Return to your console connection using Tera Term on PC-A. Issue the **show run** command to display and verify your switch configuration. A sample configuration is shown below. The settings you configured are highlighted in gray. The other configuration settings are IOS defaults.

```
S1# show run
Building configuration...

Current configuration : 1508 bytes
!
! Last configuration change at 00:06:11 UTC Mon Mar 1 1993
!
version 15.0
no service pad
service timestamps debug datetime msec
service timestamps log datetime msec
no service password-encryption
!
hostname S1
!
boot-start-marker
boot-end-marker
!
enable secret 4 06YFDUHH61wAE/kLkDq9BGho1QM5EnRtoyr8cHAUg.2
!
no aaa new-model
system mtu routing 1500
!
!
no ip domain-lookup
!
spanning-tree mode pvst
spanning-tree extend system-id
!
vlan internal allocation policy ascending
!
!
interface FastEthernet0/1
!
interface FastEthernet0/2

<output omitted>

interface FastEthernet0/24
!
interface GigabitEthernet0/1
```

```
!
interface GigabitEthernet0/2
!
interface Vlan1
 ip address 192.168.1.2 255.255.255.0
!
ip http server
ip http secure-server
!
banner motd ^C
Unauthorized access is strictly prohibited. ^C
!
line con 0
 password cisco
 login
line vty 0 4
 password cisco
 login
line vty 5 15
 login
!
end
```

b. Verify the status of your SVI management interface. Your VLAN 1 interface should be up/up and have an IP address assigned. Notice that switch port F0/6 is also up because PC-A is connected to it. Because all switch ports are initially in VLAN 1, by default, you can communicate with the switch using the IP address you configured for VLAN 1.

```
S1# show ip interface brief
Interface              IP-Address      OK? Method Status              Protocol
Vlan1                  192.168.1.2     YES manual up                  up
FastEthernet0/1        unassigned      YES unset  down                down
FastEthernet0/2        unassigned      YES unset  down                down
FastEthernet0/3        unassigned      YES unset  down                down
FastEthernet0/4        unassigned      YES unset  down                down
FastEthernet0/5        unassigned      YES unset  down                down
FastEthernet0/6        unassigned      YES unset  up                  up
FastEthernet0/7        unassigned      YES unset  down                down
FastEthernet0/8        unassigned      YES unset  down                down
FastEthernet0/9        unassigned      YES unset  down                down
FastEthernet0/10       unassigned      YES unset  down                down
FastEthernet0/11       unassigned      YES unset  down                down
FastEthernet0/12       unassigned      YES unset  down                down
FastEthernet0/13       unassigned      YES unset  down                down
FastEthernet0/14       unassigned      YES unset  down                down
FastEthernet0/15       unassigned      YES unset  down                down
FastEthernet0/16       unassigned      YES unset  down                down
FastEthernet0/17       unassigned      YES unset  down                down
FastEthernet0/18       unassigned      YES unset  down                down
FastEthernet0/19       unassigned      YES unset  down                down
FastEthernet0/20       unassigned      YES unset  down                down
FastEthernet0/21       unassigned      YES unset  down                down
```

FastEthernet0/22	unassigned	YES unset	down		down
FastEthernet0/23	unassigned	YES unset	down		down
FastEthernet0/24	unassigned	YES unset	down		down
GigabitEthernet0/1	unassigned	YES unset	down		down
GigabitEthernet0/2	unassigned	YES unset	down		down

Step 2.   Test end-to-end connectivity.

Open a command prompt window (cmd.exe) on PC-A by clicking the **Windows Start** icon and entering **cmd** into the **Search for programs and files** field. Verify the IP address of PC-A by using the **ipconfig /all** command. This command displays the PC hostname and the IPv4 address information. Ping PC-A's address and the management address of S1.

   a. Ping the PC-A address first.

       C:\Users\NetAcad> **ping 192.168.1.10**

   Your output should be similar to the following screen:

```
C:\Windows\system32\cmd.exe

Microsoft Windows [Version 6.1.7601]
Copyright (c) 2009 Microsoft Corporation.  All rights reserved.

C:\Users\NetAcad>ping 192.168.1.10

Pinging 192.168.1.10 with 32 bytes of data:
Reply from 192.168.1.10: bytes=32 time<1ms TTL=128
Reply from 192.168.1.10: bytes=32 time<1ms TTL=128
Reply from 192.168.1.10: bytes=32 time<1ms TTL=128
Reply from 192.168.1.10: bytes=32 time<1ms TTL=128

Ping statistics for 192.168.1.10:
    Packets: Sent = 4, Received = 4, Lost = 0 (0% loss),
Approximate round trip times in milli-seconds:
    Minimum = 0ms, Maximum = 0ms, Average = 0ms

C:\Users\NetAcad>
```

   b. Ping the SVI management address of S1.

       C:\Users\NetAcad> **ping 192.168.1.2**

   Your output should be similar to the following screen. If ping results are not successful, troubleshoot the basic device configurations. You should check both the physical cabling and IP addressing if necessary.

```
C:\Users\NetAcad>
C:\Users\NetAcad>ping 192.168.1.2

Pinging 192.168.1.2 with 32 bytes of data:
Request timed out.
Reply from 192.168.1.2: bytes=32 time=2ms TTL=255
Reply from 192.168.1.2: bytes=32 time=2ms TTL=255
Reply from 192.168.1.2: bytes=32 time<1ms TTL=255

Ping statistics for 192.168.1.2:
    Packets: Sent = 4, Received = 3, Lost = 1 (25% loss),
Approximate round trip times in milli-seconds:
    Minimum = 0ms, Maximum = 2ms, Average = 1ms

C:\Users\NetAcad>
```

Step 3.   Test and verify the remote management of S1.

You will now use Telnet to remotely access the switch S1 using the SVI management address. In this lab, PC-A and S1 reside side by side. In a production network, the switch could be in a wiring closet on the top floor while your management PC is located on the ground floor. Telnet is not a secure protocol. However, you will use it in this lab to test remote access. All information sent by Telnet, including passwords and commands, is sent across the session in plaintext. In subsequent labs, you will use SSH to remotely access network devices.

Note: Windows 7 does not natively support Telnet. The administrator must enable this protocol. To install the Telnet client, open a command prompt window and type **pkgmgr /iu:"TelnetClient"**.

```
C:\Users\NetAcad> pkgmgr /iu:"TelnetClient"
```

a.   With the command prompt window still open on PC-A, issue a Telnet command to connect to S1 via the SVI management address. The password is **cisco**.

```
C:\Users\NetAcad> telnet 192.168.1.2
```

Your output should be similar to the following screen:

b.   After entering the **cisco** password, you will be at the user EXEC mode prompt. Type **enable** at the prompt. Enter the **class** password to enter privileged EXEC mode and issue a **show run** command.

Step 4.   Save the configuration file.

a.   From your Telnet session, issue the **copy run start** command at the prompt.

```
S1# copy run start
Destination filename [startup-config]? [Enter]
Building configuration ..
S1#
```

b. Exit the Telnet session by typing **quit**. You will be returned to the Windows 7 command prompt.

Reflection

Why must you use a console connection to initially configure the switch? Why not connect to the switch via Telnet or SSH?

_____

_____

_____

_____

_____

_____

_____

_____

_____

_____

2.4.1.1 Class Activity–Tutor Me!

Objectives

Configure initial settings on a network device using the Cisco IOS Software.

Background/Scenario

(Students will work in pairs. Packet Tracer is required to be used with this activity.)

Assume that a new colleague has asked you for an orientation to the Cisco IOS CLI. This colleague has never worked with Cisco devices before.

You explain the basic CLI commands and structure, because you want your colleague to understand that the CLI is a simple, yet powerful, command language that can be easily understood and navigated.

Use Packet Tracer and one of the activities available in this chapter as a simple network model. Focus on these areas:

- While the commands are technical, do they resemble any statements from plain English?

- How is the set of commands organized into subgroups or modes? How does an administrator know which mode he or she is currently using?

- What are the individual commands to configure the basic settings of a Cisco device? How would you explain this command in laymen's terms? Use parallels to real life whenever appropriate.

Suggest how to group different commands together according to their modes so that a minimum number of moves between modes will be needed.

Required Resources

- Packet Tracer
- Any simple network model activity available from Chapter 2

Reflection

1. After completing Chapter 2, do you feel as though you have a concrete understanding of what the Cisco IOS does and how it operates? What were some of the difficulties you encountered when explaining the basic CLI commands and structure to your colleague? If you were the "new colleague," what would be some of the difficulties that you would have learning the basic CLI commands and structure?

   _____

   _____

   _____

2. Answer the following questions, and discuss your answers with the entire class:

   a. While the commands are technical, do they resemble any statements from plain English?

   _____

   _____

b. How is the set of commands organized into subgroups or modes? How does an administrator know which mode he or she is currently using?

_____

_____

c. What are the individual commands to configure the basic settings of a Cisco device? How would you explain this command in laymen's terms? Use parallels to real life whenever appropriate.

_____

_____

d. With the help of your colleague, try to suggest how to group different commands together according to their modes so that a minimum number of moves between modes will be needed.

_____

_____

Packet Tracer
☐ Activity

2.4.1.2 Packet Tracer–Skills Integration Challenge

Addressing Table

Device	Interface	IP Address	Subnet Mask
[[S1Name]]	VLAN 1	[[S1Add]]	255.255.255.0
[[S2Name]]	VLAN 1	[[S2Add]]	255.255.255.0
[[PC1Name]]	NIC	[[PC1Add]]	255.255.255.0
[[PC2Name]]	NIC	[[PC2Add]]	255.255.255.0

Objectives

- Configure hostnames and IP addresses on two Cisco Internetwork Operating System (IOS) switches using the command-line interface (CLI).
- Use Cisco IOS commands to specify or limit access to the device configurations.
- Use IOS commands to save the running configuration.
- Configure two host devices with IP addresses.
- Verify connectivity between the two PC end devices.

Scenario

As a recently hired LAN technician, your network manager has asked you to demonstrate your ability to configure a small LAN. Your tasks include configuring initial settings on two switches using the Cisco IOS and configuring IP address parameters on host devices to provide end-to-end connectivity. You are to use two switches and two hosts/PCs on a cabled and powered network.

Requirements

- Use a console connection to access each switch.
- Name [[S1Name]] and [[S2Name]] switches.
- Use the [[LinePW]] password for all lines.
- Use the [[SecretPW]] secret password.
- Encrypt all clear text passwords.
- Include the word **warning** in the message-of-the-day (MOTD) Banner.
- Configure addressing for all devices according to the Addressing Table.
- Save your configurations.
- Verify connectivity between all devices.

Note: Click **Check Results** to see your progress. Click **Reset Activity** to generate a new set of requirements. If you click on this before you complete the activity, all configurations will be lost.

CHAPTER 3

Network Protocols and Communications

The Study Guide portion of this chapter uses a combination of matching, fill-in-the-blank, multiple-choice, and open-ended question exercises to test your knowledge and skills of basic router concepts and configuration. The Lab and Activities portion of this chapter includes all the online curriculum labs and Packet Tracer activities to ensure that you have mastered the hands-on skills needed to understand basic IP addressing and router configuration.

As you work through this chapter, use Chapter 3 in *Introduction to Networks v6 Companion Guide* or use the corresponding Chapter 3 in the Introduction to Networks online curriculum for assistance.

Study Guide

The network industry has adopted a framework that provides a common language for understanding current network platforms as well as facilitates the development of new technologies. Central to this framework is the use of generally accepted models that describe network rules and functions.

Rules of Communication

Networks can vary in size, shape, and function. However, simply having the physical connection between end devices is not enough to enable communication. For communication to occur, devices must follow precise rules.

Vocabulary Exercise: Matching

Match the definition on the left with a term on the right. This exercise is a one-to-one matching. Each definition has exactly one matching term.

Definitions

a. Used by source and destination to negotiate correct timing for successful communication.

b. One-to-many delivery of a message.

c. The format each computer message is encapsulated in before it is sent over the network.

d. When this occurs, hosts on the network have rules that specify what action to take if no reply is received.

e. The process of converting information into another, acceptable form, for transmission.

f. The process of converting transmitted information back into an understandable form.

g. One-to-all delivery of a message.

h. Needed by hosts on the network to know when to begin sending messages and how to respond when errors occur.

i. The process of placing one message format inside another message format.

j. One-to-one delivery of a message.

Terms

_____ broadcast

_____ frame

_____ unicast

_____ encoding

_____ multicast

_____ decoding

_____ response timeout

_____ flow control

_____ encapsulation

_____ access method

Network Protocols and Standards

For networked devices to successfully communicate, a network protocol suite must describe precise requirements and interactions. Networking protocols define a common format and set of rules for exchanging messages between devices. A group of interrelated protocols necessary to perform a communication function is called a *protocol suite*. In this section, we review the TCP/IP protocol suite, investigate standards organizations, and compare the OSI and TCP/IP models.

Protocol Definitions: Matching

Match the definition on the left with a protocol acronym on the right. This exercise is a one-to-one matching. Each definition has exactly one matching protocol acronym.

Definitions	Protocol Acronym
a. Dynamically assigns IP addresses to client stations at startup	_____ TCP
b. Translates domain names, such as cisco. com, into IP addresses	_____ ICMP
	_____ FTP
c. Uses composite metric based on bandwidth, delay, load, and reliability	_____ EIGRP
d. Does not confirm successful datagram transmission	_____ ARP
	_____ UDP
e. Enables clients to send email to a mail server	_____ POP
f. Set of rules for exchanging text, graphic images, sound, video, and other multimedia files on the World Wide Web	_____ HTTP
	_____ NAT
	_____ DHCP
g. Enables clients to retrieve email from a mail server	_____ IP
	_____ SMTP
h. Translates IPv4 addresses from a private network into globally unique public IPv4 addresses	_____ DNS
	_____ OSPF
i. Addresses packets for end-to-end delivery over an Internetwork	
j. Provides dynamic address mapping between an IPv4 address and a hardware address	
k. Link-state routing protocol	
l. A reliable, connection-oriented, and acknowledged file delivery protocol	
m. Reliable, acknowledged transmissions that confirm successful delivery	
n. Provides feedback from a destination host to a source host about errors in packet delivery	

Mapping the Protocols of the TCP/IP Suite

In Table 3-1, indicate the layer to which each protocol belongs.

Table 3-1   Protocols of the TCP/IP Suite

Protocol	Application	Transport	Internet	Network Access
POP				
PPP				
FTP				
DHCP				
IMAP				
IP				
TCP				
ICMP				
ARP				
HTTP				
TFTP				
Ethernet				
Interface drivers				
OSPF				
UDP				
DNS				
EIGRP				
SMTP				

Standards Organizations: Matching

Match the responsibility on the left with a standards organization on the right. This exercise is a one-to-one matching. Each responsibility has exactly one matching standards organization.

Responsibility

a. Responsible for overseeing and managing IP address allocation, domain name management, and protocol identifiers.

b. Responsible for promoting the open development and evolution of Internet use throughout the world.

c. Responsible for standards that include radio equipment, cellular towers, Voice over IP (VoIP) devices, satellite communications, and more.

d. Based in the United States, coordinates IP address allocation, the management of domain names, and assignment of other information used in TCP/IP protocols.

e. Defines standards for video compression, Internet Protocol Television (IPTV), and broadband communications, such as a digital subscriber line (DSL).

f. Focused on long-term research related to Internet and TCP/IP protocols such as Anti-Spam Research Group (ASRG), Crypto Forum Research Group (CFRG), and Peer-to-Peer Research Group (P2PRG).

g. Responsible for standards related to electrical wiring, connectors, and the 19-inch racks used to mount networking equipment.

h. Responsible for the overall management and development of Internet standards.

i. Develops, updates, and maintains Internet and TCP/IP technologies. This includes the process and documents for developing new protocols and updating existing protocols known as Requests for Comments (RFC) documents.

j. Responsible for creating standards in a wide area of industries including power and energy, health care, telecommunications, and networking. For networking, this organization manages the 802 working groups and study groups.

Standards Organization

_____ Internet Engineering Task Force (IETF)

_____ Institute of Electrical and Electronics Engineers (IEEE)

_____ Internet Research Task Force (IRTF)

_____ Internet Corporation for Assigned Names and Numbers (ICANN)

_____ Internet Architecture Board (IAB)

_____ International Telecommunications Union-Telecommunication Standardization Sector (ITU-T)

_____ Internet Assigned Numbers Authority (IANA)

_____ Electronic Industries Alliance (EIA)

_____ Telecommunications Industry Association (TIA)

_____ Internet Society (ISOC)

OSI Reference Model Layers: Matching

Match the definition on the left with a layer on the right. This exercise is a one-to-one matching. Each definition has exactly one matching layer.

Definitions

a. Provides services to exchange the individual pieces of data over the network between identified end devices

b. Describes methods for exchanging data frames between devices over a common media

c. Provides for common representation of the data transferred between application layer services

d. Describes the mechanical, electrical, functional, and procedural means to activate, maintain, and deactivate physical connections for bit transmission to and from a network device

e. Provides services to the presentation layer to organize its dialogue and to manage data exchange

f. Defines services to segment, transfer, and reassemble the data for individual communications between the end devices

g. Provides the means for end-to-end connectivity between individuals in the human network using data networks

Layers

_____ presentation

_____ transport

_____ network

_____ application

_____ session

_____ physical

_____ data link

TCP/IP Model Layers: Matching

Match the definition on the left with a layer on the right. This exercise is a one-to-one matching. Each definition has exactly one matching layer.

Definitions

a. Determines the best path through the network

b. Represents data to the user, plus encoding and dialog control

c. Controls the hardware devices and media that make up the network

d. Supports communications between various devices across diverse networks

Layers

_____ transport

_____ network access

_____ application

_____ Internet

Mapping the Layers of the OSI and TCP/IP Models

In Figure 3-1, label the layers for each model.

Figure 3-1   The Layers of the OSI and TCP/IP Model

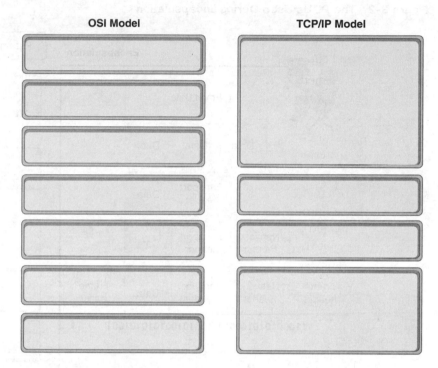

Moving Data in the Network

The data for one transmission—a file, a text, a picture, a video—does not travel from source to destination in one massive, uninterrupted stream of bits. In this section, we review protocol data units (PDUs), encapsulation, and the addressing that makes segmentation of a transmission possible.

Data Encapsulation and the PDUs

In Figure 3-2, label the PDUs at each layer as a message is sent "down the stack" in preparation for transmission.

Figure 3-2   The PDUs Used During Encapsulation

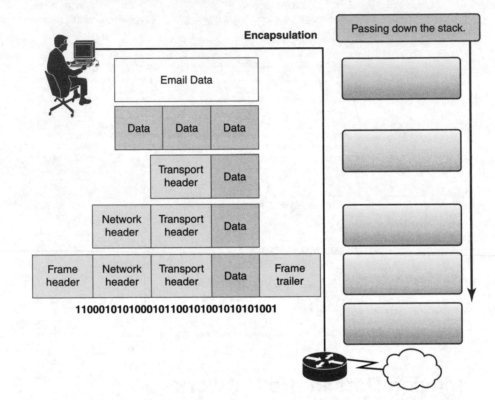

The Role of Addressing in Network Communications

Briefly describe the role of Layer 3 IP addresses.

_____

_____

_____

Briefly describe the purpose of Layer 2 MAC addresses.

_____

_____

_____

_____

Briefly describe the purpose of the default gateway.

_____

_____

_____

Labs and Activities

3.0.1.2 Class Activity–Designing a Communications System

Objectives

Explain the role of protocols and standards organizations in facilitating interoperability in network communications.

Background/Scenario

You have just purchased a new automobile for your personal use. After driving the car for a week or so, you find that it is not working correctly. Discussing the problem with several of your peers, you decide to take it to an automotive repair facility that they highly recommend. It is the only repair facility located in close proximity.

When you arrive at the repair facility, you find that all the mechanics speak another language. You are having difficulty explaining the automobile's performance problems, but the repairs really need to be done. You are not sure you can drive it back home to research other options.

You must find a way to work with the repair facility to ensure your automobile is fixed correctly.

How will you communicate with the mechanics? Design a communications model to ensure that the car is properly repaired.

Reflection

What steps did you identify as important to communicating your repair request? Justify your answer.

_____

_____

_____

_____

_____

_____

_____

_____

_____

3.2.3.4 Lab–Researching Networking Standards

Objectives

Part 1: Research Networking Standards Organizations

Part 2: Reflect on Internet and Computer Networking Experiences

Background/Scenario

Using web search engines like Google, research the non-profit organizations that are responsible for establishing international standards for the Internet and the development of Internet technologies.

Required Resources

Device with Internet access

Part 1: Research Networking Standards Organizations

In Part 1, you will identify some of the major standards organizations and important characteristics, such as the number of years in existence, the size of their membership, the important historical figures, some of the responsibilities and duties, organizational oversight role, and the location of the organization's headquarters.

Use a web browser or websites for various organizations to research information about the following organizations and the people who have been instrumental in maintaining them.

You can find answers to the questions below by searching the following organizational acronyms and terms: ISO, ITU, ICANN, IANA, IEEE, EIA, TIA, ISOC, IAB, IETF, W3C, RFC, and Wi-Fi Alliance.

1. Who is Jonathan B. Postel and what is he known for?

   _____

   _____

   _____

2. Which two related organizations are responsible for managing the top-level domain name space and the root Domain Name System (DNS) name servers on the Internet?

   _____

   _____

3. Vinton Cerf has been called one of main fathers of the Internet. What Internet organizations did he chair or help found? What Internet technologies did he help to develop?

   _____

   _____

4. What organization is responsible for publishing Request for Comments (RFC)?

   _____

5. What do RFC 349 and RFC 1700 have in common?

_____

_____

6. What RFC number is the ARPAWOCKY? What is it?

_____

7. Who founded the World Wide Web Consortium (W3C)?

_____

8. Name 10 World Wide Web (WWW) standards that the W3C develops and maintains?

_____

_____

9. Where is the Institute of Electrical and Electronics Engineers (IEEE) headquarters located and what is the significance of its logo?

_____

_____

10. What is the IEEE standard for the Wi-Fi Protected Access 2 (WPA2) security protocol?

_____

11. Is the Wi-Fi Alliance a non-profit standards organization? What is its goal?

_____

_____

12. Who is Hamadoun Touré?

_____

_____

13. What is the International Telecommunication Union (ITU) and where is it headquartered?

_____

_____

14. Name the three ITU sectors.

_____

15. What does the RS in RS-232 stand for and which organization introduced it?

_____

_____

16. What is SpaceWire?

_____

_____

17. What is the mission of the ISOC and where are its headquarters located?

_____

_____

18. What organizations does the IAB oversee?

_____

_____

19. What organization oversees the IAB?

_____

20. When was the ISO founded and where are its headquarters located?

_____

_____

Part 2: Reflect on Internet and Computer Networking Experiences

Take a moment to think about the Internet today in relation to the organizations and technologies you have just researched. Then answer the following questions.

1. How do the Internet standards allow for greater commerce? What potential problems could we have if we did not have the IEEE?

_____

_____

2. What potential problems could we have if we did not have the W3C?

_____

_____

3. What can we learn from the example of the Wi-Fi Alliance with regard to the necessity of networking standards?

_____

_____

_____

Packet Tracer
☐ Activity

3.2.4.6 Packet Tracer–Investigating the TCP/IP and OSI Models in Action

Topology

Web Server   Web Client

Objectives

Part 1: Examine HTTP Web Traffic

Part 2: Display Elements of the TCP/IP Protocol Suite

Background

This simulation activity is intended to provide a foundation for understanding the TCP/IP protocol suite and the relationship to the OSI model. Simulation mode allows you to view the data contents being sent across the network at each layer.

As data moves through the network, it is broken down into smaller pieces and identified so that the pieces can be put back together when they arrive at the destination. Each piece is assigned a specific name (protocol data unit [PDU]) and associated with a specific layer of the TCP/IP and OSI models. Packet Tracer simulation mode enables you to view each of the layers and the associated PDU. The following steps lead the user through the process of requesting a web page from a web server by using the web browser application available on a client PC.

Even though much of the information displayed will be discussed in more detail later, this is an opportunity to explore the functionality of Packet Tracer and be able to visualize the encapsulation process.

Part 1: Examine HTTP Web Traffic

In Part 1 of this activity, you will use Packet Tracer (PT) Simulation mode to generate web traffic and examine HTTP.

Step 1. Switch from Realtime to Simulation mode.

In the lower right corner of the Packet Tracer interface are tabs to toggle between **Realtime** and **Simulation** mode. PT always starts in **Realtime** mode, in which networking protocols operate with realistic timings. However, a powerful feature of Packet Tracer allows the user to "stop time" by switching to Simulation mode. In Simulation mode, packets are displayed as animated envelopes, time is event driven, and the user can step through networking events.

a. Click the **Simulation** mode icon to switch from **Realtime** mode to **Simulation** mode.

b. Select **HTTP** from the **Event List Filters**.

1) HTTP may already be the only visible event. Click **Edit Filters** to display the available visible events. Toggle the **Show All/None** check box and notice how the check boxes switch from unchecked to checked or checked to unchecked, depending on the current state.

> **2)** Click the **Show All/None** check box until all boxes are cleared and then select **HTTP**. Click anywhere outside of the **Edit Filters** box to hide it. The Visible Events should now only display HTTP.

Step 2. Generate web (HTTP) traffic.

Currently the Simulation Panel is empty. There are six columns listed across the top of the Event List within the Simulation Panel. As traffic is generated and stepped through, events appear in the list. The **Info** column is used to inspect the contents of a particular event.

Note: The Web Server and Web Client are displayed in the left pane. The panels can be adjusted in size by hovering next to the scroll bar and dragging left or right when the double-headed arrow appears.

a. Click **Web Client** in the far left pane.

b. Click the **Desktop** tab and click the **Web Browser** icon to open it.

c. In the URL field, enter **www.osi.local** and click **Go**.

Because time in Simulation mode is event-driven, you must use the **Capture/Forward** button to display network events.

d. Click **Capture/Forward** four times. There should be four events in the Event List.

Look at the Web Client web browser page. Did anything change?

Step 3. Explore the contents of the HTTP packet.

a. Click the first colored square box under the **Event List > Info** column. It may be necessary to expand the **Simulation Panel** or use the scrollbar directly below the **Event List**.

The **PDU Information at Device: Web Client** window displays. In this window, there are only two tabs (**OSI Model** and **Outbound PDU Details**) because this is the start of the transmission. As more events are examined, there will be three tabs displayed, adding a tab for **Inbound PDU Details**. When an event is the last event in the stream of traffic, only the **OSI Model** and **Inbound PDU Details** tabs are displayed.

b. Ensure that the **OSI Model** tab is selected. Under the **Out Layers** column, ensure that the **Layer 7** box is highlighted.

What is the text displayed next to the **Layer 7** label? _____

What information is listed in the numbered steps directly below the **In Layers** and **Out Layers** boxes?

_____

c. Click **Next Layer**. Layer 4 should be highlighted. What is the **Dst Port** value? _____

d. Click **Next Layer**. Layer 3 should be highlighted. What is the **Dest. IP** value?

_____

e. Click **Next Layer**. What information is displayed at this layer?

_____

f. Click the **Outbound PDU Details** tab.

Information listed under the **PDU Details** is reflective of the layers within the TCP/IP model.

Note: The information listed under the **Ethernet II** section provides even more detailed information than is listed under Layer 2 on the **OSI Model** tab. The **Outbound PDU Details** provides more descriptive and detailed information. The values under **DEST MAC** and **SRC MAC** within the **Ethernet II** section of the **PDU Details** appear on the **OSI Model** tab under Layer 2, but are not identified as such.

What is the common information listed under the **IP** section of **PDU Details** as compared to the information listed under the **OSI Model** tab? With which layer is it associated?

What is the common information listed under the **TCP** section of **PDU Details**, as compared to the information listed under the **OSI Model** tab, and with which layer is it associated?

What is the **Host** listed under the **HTTP** section of the **PDU Details**? What layer would this information be associated with under the **OSI Model** tab?

g. Click the next colored square box under the **Event List > Info** column. Only Layer 1 is active (not grayed out). The device is moving the frame from the buffer and placing it on to the network.

h. Advance to the next HTTP **Info** box within the **Event List** and click the colored square box. This window contains both **In Layers** and **Out Layers**. Notice the direction of the arrow directly under the **In Layers** column; it is pointing upward, indicating the direction the information is traveling. Scroll through these layers making note of the items previously viewed. At the top of the column the arrow points to the right. This denotes that the server is now sending the information back to the client.

Comparing the information displayed in the **In Layers** column with that of the **Out Layers** column, what are the major differences?

i. Click the **Outbound PDU Details** tab. Scroll down to the **HTTP** section.

What is the first line in the HTTP message that displays?

j. Click the last colored square box under the **Info** column. How many tabs are displayed with this event and why?

Part 2: Display Elements of the TCP/IP Protocol Suite

In Part 2 of this activity, you will use the Packet Tracer Simulation mode to view and examine some of the other protocols comprising of the TCP/IP suite.

Step 1.   View Additional Events

   a.   Close any open PDU information windows.

   b.   In the Event List Filters > Visible Events section, click **Show All**.

   What additional Event Types are displayed?

   _____

   _____

   _____

   _____

   These extra entries play various roles within the TCP/IP suite. If the Address Resolution Protocol (ARP) is listed, it searches MAC addresses. DNS is responsible for converting a name (for example, **www.osi.local**) to an IP address. The additional TCP events are responsible for connecting, agreeing on communication parameters, and disconnecting the communications sessions between the devices. These protocols have been mentioned previously and will be further discussed as the course progresses. Currently there are over 35 possible protocols (event types) available for capture within Packet Tracer.

   c.   Click the first DNS event in the **Info** column. Explore the **OSI Model** and **PDU Detail** tabs and note the encapsulation process. As you look at the **OSI Model** tab with **Layer 7** highlighted, a description of what is occurring is listed directly below the **In Layers** and **Out Layers** ("1. The DNS client sends a DNS query to the DNS server."). This is very useful information to help understand what is occurring during the communication process.

   d.   Click the **Outbound PDU Details** tab. What information is listed in the **NAME:** in the DNS QUERY section?

   _____

   e.   Click the last DNS **Info** colored square box in the event list. Which device is displayed?

   _____

   What is the value listed next to **ADDRESS:** in the DNS ANSWER section of the **Inbound PDU Details?**

   _____

   f.   Find the first **HTTP** event in the list and click the colored square box of the **TCP** event immediately following this event. Highlight **Layer 4** in the OSI Model tab. In the numbered list directly below the **In Layers** and **Out Layers**, what is the information displayed under items 4 and 5?

   _____

   TCP manages the connecting and disconnecting of the communications channel along with other responsibilities. This particular event shows that the communication channel has been ESTABLISHED.

g. Click the last TCP event. Highlight Layer 4 in the **OSI Model** tab. Examine the steps listed directly below **In Layers** and **Out Layers**. What is the purpose of this event, based on the information provided in the last item in the list (should be item 4)?

Challenge

This simulation provided an example of a web session between a client and a server on a local-area network (LAN). The client makes requests to specific services running on the server. The server must be set up to listen on specific ports for a client request. (Hint: Look at Layer 4 in the **OSI Model** tab for port information.)

Based on the information that was inspected during the Packet Tracer capture, what port number is the **Web Server** listening on for the web request?

What port is the **Web Server** listening on for a DNS request?

Suggested Scoring Rubric

Activity Section	Question Location	Possible Points	Earned Points
Part 1: Examine HTTP Web Traffic	Step 2d	5	
	Step 3b-1	5	
	Step 3b-2	5	
	Step 3c	5	
	Step 3d	5	
	Step 3e	5	
	Step 3f-1	5	
	Step 3f-2	5	
	Step 3f-3	5	
	Step 3h	5	
	Step 3i	5	
	Step 3j	5	
	Part 1 Total	60	
Part 2: Display Elements of the TCP/IP Protocol Suite	Step 1b	5	
	Step 1d	5	
	Step 1e-1	5	
	Step 1e-2	5	
	Step 1f	5	
	Step 1g	5	
	Part 2 Total	30	
Challenge	1	5	
	2	5	
	Part 3 Total	10	
	Total Score	100	

3.4.1.1 Lab–Installing Wireshark

Objectives

Download and Install Wireshark

Background/Scenario

Wireshark is a software protocol analyzer, or "packet sniffer" application, used for network trouble-shooting, analysis, software and protocol development, and education. As data streams travel back and forth over the network, the sniffer "captures" each protocol data unit (PDU) and can decode and analyze its content according to the appropriate RFC or other specifications.

Wireshark is a useful tool for anyone working with networks and can be used with most labs in the CCNA courses for data analysis and troubleshooting. This lab provides instructions for downloading and installing Wireshark.

Required Resources

- 1 PC (Windows 7 or 8 with Internet access)

Download and Install Wireshark

Wireshark has become the industry standard packet-sniffer program used by network engineers. This open source software is available for many different operating systems, including Windows, Mac, and Linux. In this lab, you will download and install the Wireshark software program on your PC.

Note: Before downloading Wireshark, check with your instructor about your academy's software download policy.

Step 1. Download Wireshark.

a. Wireshark can be downloaded from www.wireshark.org.

b. Click **Download Wireshark.**

c. Choose the software version you need based on your PC's architecture and operating system. For instance, if you have a 64-bit PC running Windows, choose **Windows Installer (64-bit).**

After making a selection, the download should start. The location of the downloaded file depends on the browser and operating system that you use. For Windows users, the default location is the **Downloads** folder.

Step 2.   Install Wireshark.

a. The downloaded file is named **Wireshark-win64-x.x.x.exe**, where **x** represents the version number. Double-click the file to start the installation process.

b. Respond to any security messages that may display on your screen. If you already have a copy of Wireshark on your PC, you will be prompted to uninstall the old version before installing the new version. It is recommended that you remove the old version of Wireshark prior to installing another version. Click **Yes** to uninstall the previous version of Wireshark.

c. If this is the first time to install Wireshark, or after you have completed the uninstall process, you will navigate to the Wireshark Setup wizard. Click **Next.**

d. Continue advancing through the installation process. Click **I Agree** when the License Agreement window displays.

e. Keep the default settings on the Choose Components window and click **Next**.

f. Choose your desired shortcut options and click **Next**.

g. You can change the installation location of Wireshark, but unless you have limited disk space, it is recommended that you keep the default location. Click **Next**.

h. To capture live network data, WinPcap must be installed on your PC. If WinPcap is already installed on your PC, the Install check box will be unchecked. If your installed version of WinPcap is older than the version that comes with Wireshark, it is recommended that you allow the newer version to be installed by clicking the **Install WinPcap x.x.x** (version number) check box.

i. Finish the WinPcap Setup Wizard if installing WinPcap.

j. Wireshark starts installing its files and a separate window displays with the status of the installation. Click **Next** when the installation is complete.

Wireshark 1.8.3 (64-bit) Setup

Installation Complete
Setup was completed successfully.

Completed

```
Extract: mergecap.html
Output folder: C:\Program Files\Wireshark
Extract: capinfos.exe
Extract: capinfos.html
Output folder: C:\Program Files\Wireshark
Extract: rawshark.exe
Extract: rawshark.html
Output folder: C:\Program Files\Wireshark
Extract: user-guide.chm
Completed
```

Nullsoft Install System v2.46

< Back   Next >   Cancel

k. Click **Finish** to complete the Wireshark install process.

Wireshark 1.8.3 (64-bit) Setup

Completing the Wireshark 1.8.3 (64-bit) Setup Wizard

Wireshark 1.8.3 (64-bit) has been installed on your computer.

Click Finish to close this wizard.

☐ Run Wireshark 1.8.3 (64-bit)

☐ Show News

< Back   Finish   Cancel

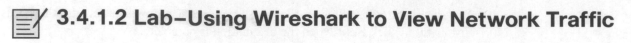 3.4.1.2 Lab–Using Wireshark to View Network Traffic

Topology

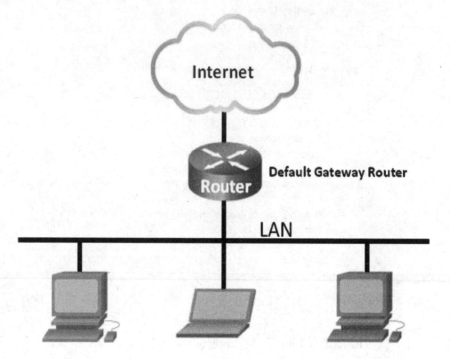

Objectives

Part 1: Capture and Analyze Local ICMP Data in Wireshark

Part 2: Capture and Analyze Remote ICMP Data in Wireshark

Background/Scenario

Wireshark is a software protocol analyzer, or "packet sniffer" application, used for network trouble-shooting, analysis, software and protocol development, and education. As data streams travel back and forth over the network, the sniffer "captures" each protocol data unit (PDU) and can decode and analyze its content according to the appropriate RFC or other specifications.

Wireshark is a useful tool for anyone working with networks and can be used with most labs in the CCNA courses for data analysis and troubleshooting. In this lab, you will use Wireshark to capture ICMP data packet IP addresses and Ethernet frame MAC addresses.

Required Resources

- 1 PC (Windows 7 or 8 with Internet access)
- Additional PC(s) on a local-area network (LAN) will be used to reply to ping requests.

Part 1: Capture and Analyze Local ICMP Data in Wireshark

In Part 1 of this lab, you will ping another PC on the LAN and capture ICMP requests and replies in Wireshark. You will also look inside the frames captured for specific information. This analysis should help to clarify how packet headers are used to transport data to their destination.

Step 1.   Retrieve your PC's interface addresses.

For this lab, you will need to retrieve your PC's IP address and its network interface card (NIC) physical address, also called the MAC address.

a.   Open a command window, type **ipconfig /all**, and then press Enter.

b.   Note your PC interface's IP address and MAC (physical) address.

c.   Ask a team member for her PC's IP address and provide your PC's IP address to her. Do not provide her with your MAC address at this time.

Step 2.   Start Wireshark and begin capturing data.

a.   On your PC, click the Windows **Start** button to see Wireshark listed as one of the programs on the pop-up menu. Double-click **Wireshark**.

b.   After Wireshark starts, click **Interface List**.

Note: Clicking the first interface icon in the row of icons also opens the Interface List.

c.   On the Wireshark: Capture Interfaces window, click the check box next to the interface connected to your LAN.

Note: If multiple interfaces are listed and you are unsure which interface to check, click the **Details** button, and then click the **802.3 (Ethernet)** tab. Verify that the MAC address matches what you noted in Step 1b. Close the Interface Details window after verifying the correct interface.

d. After you have checked the correct interface, click **Start** to start the data capture.

Information will start scrolling down the top section in Wireshark. The data lines will appear in different colors based on protocol.

e. This information can scroll by very quickly depending on what communication is taking place between your PC and the LAN. We can apply a filter to make it easier to view and work with the data that is being captured by Wireshark. For this lab, we are only interested in displaying ICMP (ping) PDUs. Type **icmp** in the Filter box at the top of Wireshark and press Enter or click on the **Apply** button to view only ICMP (ping) PDUs.

f. This filter causes all data in the top window to disappear, but you are still capturing the traffic on the interface. Bring up the command prompt window that you opened earlier and ping the IP address that you received from your team member. Notice that you start seeing data appear in the top window of Wireshark again.

Note: If your team member's PC does not reply to your pings, this may be because their PC firewall is blocking these requests.

g. Stop capturing data by clicking the **Stop Capture** icon.

Step 3.   Examine the captured data.

In Step 3, examine the data that was generated by the ping requests of your team member's PC. Wireshark data is displayed in three sections: 1) The top section displays the list of PDU frames captured with a summary of the IP packet information listed, 2) the middle section lists PDU information for the frame selected in the top part of the screen and separates a captured PDU frame by its protocol layers, and 3) the bottom section displays the raw data of each layer. The raw data is displayed in both hexadecimal and decimal form.

a. Click the first ICMP request PDU frames in the top section of Wireshark. Notice that the Source column has your PC's IP address, and the Destination contains the IP address of the teammate's PC you pinged.

b. With this PDU frame still selected in the top section, navigate to the middle section. Click the plus sign to the left of the Ethernet II row to view the Destination and Source MAC addresses.

Does the Source MAC address match your PC's interface? _____

Does the Destination MAC address in Wireshark match your team member's MAC address? _____

How is the MAC address of the pinged PC obtained by your PC?

_____

Note: In the preceding example of a captured ICMP request, ICMP data is encapsulated inside an IPv4 packet PDU (IPv4 header), which is then encapsulated in an Ethernet II frame PDU (Ethernet II header) for transmission on the LAN.

Part 2: Capture and Analyze Remote ICMP Data in Wireshark

In Part 2, you will ping remote hosts (hosts not on the LAN) and examine the generated data from those pings. You will then determine what is different about this data from the data examined in Part 1.

Step 1.   Start capturing data on the interface.

   a.   Click the **Interface List** icon to bring up the list PC interfaces again.

   b.   Make sure the check box next to the LAN interface is checked, and click **Start**.

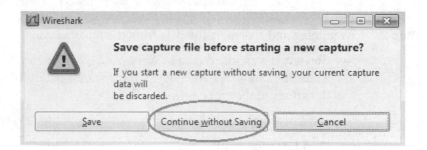

c. A window prompts to save the previously captured data before starting another capture. It is not necessary to save this data. Click **Continue without Saving**.

d. With the capture active, ping the following three website URLs:

1) www.yahoo.com

2) www.cisco.com

3) www.google.com

Note: When you ping the URLs listed, notice that the Domain Name Server (DNS) translates the URL to an IP address. Note the IP address received for each URL.

  e. You can stop capturing data by clicking the **Stop Capture** icon.

Step 2. Examining and analyzing the data from the remote hosts.

  a. Review the captured data in Wireshark, examine the IP and MAC addresses of the three locations that you pinged. List the destination IP and MAC addresses for all three locations in the space provided.

   1st Location: IP: ____.____.____.____ MAC: ___:___:___:___:___:___

   2nd Location: IP: ____.____.____.____ MAC: ___:___:___:___:___:___

   3rd Location: IP: ____.____.____.____ MAC: ___:___:___:___:___:___

  b. What is significant about this information?

   _____

  c. How does this information differ from the local ping information you received in Part 1?

   _____

   _____

Reflection

Why does Wireshark show the actual MAC address of the local hosts, but not the actual MAC address for the remote hosts?

_____

_____

Appendix A: Allowing ICMP Traffic Through a Firewall

If the members of your team are unable to ping your PC, the firewall may be blocking those requests. This appendix describes how to create a rule in the firewall to allow ping requests. It also describes how to disable the new ICMP rule after you have completed the lab.

Step 1. Create a new inbound rule allowing ICMP traffic through the firewall.

  a. From the Control Panel, click the **System and Security** option.

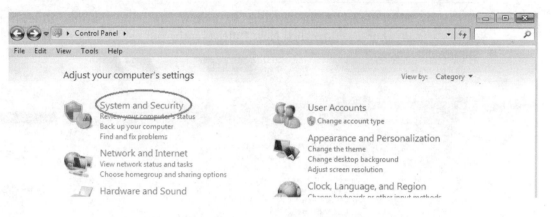

b. From the System and Security window, click **Windows Firewall**.

c. In the left pane of the Windows Firewall window, click **Advanced settings**.

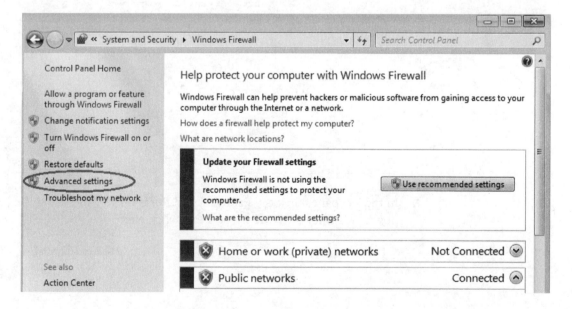

d. On the Advanced Security window, choose the **Inbound Rules** option on the left sidebar and then click **New Rule...** on the right sidebar.

e. This launches the New Inbound Rule Wizard. On the Rule Type screen, click the **Custom** radio button and click **Next**.

f. In the left pane, click the **Protocol and Ports** option and using the Protocol type drop-down menu, select **ICMPv4**, and then click **Next**.

g. In the left pane, click the **Name** option and in the Name field, type **Allow ICMP Requests**. Click **Finish**.

This new rule should allow your team members to receive ping replies from your PC.

Step 2.   Disabling or deleting the new ICMP rule.

After the lab is complete, you may want to disable or even delete the new rule you created in Step 1. Using the **Disable Rule** option allows you to enable the rule again at a later date. Deleting the rule permanently deletes it from the list of Inbound Rules.

a.   On the Advanced Security window, click **Inbound Rules** in the left pane and then locate the rule you created in Step 1.

b.   To disable the rule, click the **Disable Rule** option. When you choose this option, you will see this option change to **Enable Rule**. You can toggle back and forth between Disable Rule and Enable Rule; the status of the rule also shows in the Enabled column of the Inbound Rules list.

c.   To permanently delete the ICMP rule, click **Delete**. If you choose this option, you must re-create the rule again to allow ICMP replies.

It Retr...	All	No	Allow
Cach...	All	No	Allow
iscove...	All	No	Allow
Proje...	Domain	No	Allow
Proje...	Private...	No	Allow
Proje...	Private...	No	Allow
Proje...	Domain	No	Allow
Proje...	Domain	No	Allow
Proje...	Private...	No	Allow

Help

Allow ICMP Requests

Disable Rule

Cut

Copy

Delete

Properties

3.4.1.3 Class Activity–Guaranteed to Work!

Objectives

Explain the role of protocols and standards organizations in facilitating interoperability in network communications.

Background/Scenario

You have just completed the Chapter 3 content regarding network protocols and standards.

Assuming you resolved the beginning of this chapter's modeling activity, how would you compare the following steps taken to design a communications system to the networking models used for communications?

Steps to Communicate	Possible Answers	Associated TCP/IP Model Layer
Establishing a language to communicate		
Dividing the message into small steps, delivered a little at a time, to facilitate understanding of the problem		
Checking to see if the message has been delivered correctly to the mechanic who will be performing the repairs		
Delivery of automobile and wait time for repairs		

Required Resources

- Blank "Steps to Communicate" table (above) for students to record their answers based upon their Chapter 3 content knowledge.

Reflection

How does your network model in developing an automotive repair communications plan compare to a network communications interoperability plan?

_____

CHAPTER 4

Network Access

The Study Guide portion of this chapter uses a combination of matching, fill-in-the-blank, multiple-choice, and open-ended question exercises to test your knowledge and skills of basic router concepts and configuration. The Lab and Activities portion of this chapter includes all the online curriculum labs and Packet Tracer activities to ensure that you have mastered the hands-on skills needed to understand basic IP addressing and router configuration.

As you work through this chapter, use Chapter 4 in *Introduction to Networks v6 Companion Guide* or use the corresponding Chapter 4 in the Introduction to Networks online curriculum for assistance.

Study Guide

Two layers within the OSI model are so closely tied that according to the TCP/IP model they are in essence one layer. In this chapter, we review the general functions of the physical and data link layers.

Physical Layer Protocols

Before any network communications can occur, a physical connection to a local network must be established first. A physical connection can be a wired or a wireless connection. The type of connection depends totally on the setup of the network.

Completion Exercise

_____ (NICs) connect a device to the network. Ethernet NICs are used for a wired connection, whereas _____ (WLAN NICs) are used for wireless.

Explain the difference between wired and wireless access to the media.

_____

_____

_____

_____

_____

_____

The process that data undergoes from source to destination is as follows:

- The user _____ is _____ by the _____ layer, placed into _____ by the _____ layer, and further encapsulated into _____ by the data link layer.

- The _____ layer encodes the _____ and creates the electrical, optical, or radio wave signals that represent the _____ in each frame.

- These signals are then sent on the _____, one at a time.

- The destination node _____ layer retrieves these individual signals from the _____, restores them to their bit representations, and passes the bits up to the _____ layer as a complete _____.

There are three basic forms of network media:

- _____: The signals are patterns of electrical pulses.

- _____: The signals are patterns of light.

- _____: The signals are patterns of microwave transmissions.

List at least four organizations responsible for defining and governing the physical layer hardware, media, encoding, and signaling standards.

- _____
- _____
- _____
- _____
- _____

Different physical media support the transfer of bits at different speeds. Data transfer is usually discussed in terms of _____ and _____.

_____ is the capacity of a medium to carry data and is usually measured in kilobits per second (Kbps) or megabits per second (Mbps). _____ is the measure of the transfer of bits across the media over a given period of time. Due to a number of factors, _____ usually does not match the specified _____ in physical layer implementations. Many factors influence throughput, including the following:

- The amount of _____
- The type of _____
- The _____ created by the number of network devices encountered between source and destination

_____ refers to the amount of time for data to travel from one given point to another.

Network Media

The three major media used in today's networks are copper, fiber, and wireless. Copper media includes UTP, STP, and coaxial cable. Fiber-optic media includes single mode and multimode. Wireless media includes Wi-Fi, Bluetooth, and WiMAX.

Copper Cabling Completion Exercise

Copper cabling is susceptible to what three types of interference?

- _____
- _____
- _____

What three strategies can reduce copper's susceptibility to interference?

- _____
- _____
- _____

What are the three major types of copper media?

- _____

- _____

- _____

_____ cabling is the most common networking media. UTP cabling, terminated with _____ connectors, is used for interconnecting network hosts with intermediate networking devices, such as switches and routers.

_____ provides better noise protection than _____ cabling. However, compared to UTP cable, STP cable is significantly more _____ and difficult to _____. Like _____ cable, _____ uses an _____ connector.

_____ cable design has been adapted for use in the following:

- Wireless installations: Carries radio frequency (RF) energy between the antennas and the radio equipment

- Cable Internet installations: Currently used for the final connection to the customer's location and the wiring inside the customer's premises

Compare UTP, STP, and Coaxial Characteristics

In Table 4-1, indicate the cable type to which each characteristic belongs. Some characteristics may belong to more than one cable type.

Table 4-1   Copper Media Characteristics

Characteristics	UTP	STP	Coaxial
Most common network media.			
Attaches antennas to wireless devices (can be bundled with fiber-optic cabling for two-way data transmission).			
Uses RJ-45 connectors and four pairs of wires to transmit data.			
Terminates with BNC N-type and F-type connectors.			
The new Ethernet 10-GB standard uses this form of copper media.			
Counters EMI and RFI by using shielding techniques and multiple twisted copper wires.			

Limiting the Negative Effect of Crosstalk

Explain the two ways UTP cable can limit the negative effect of crosstalk.

- _____

  _____

- _____

  _____

UTP Cable Categories

In Table 4-2, indicate which category of UTP cabling best fits the description.

Table 4-2   UTP Cable Categories

Description	Cat 3	Cat 5	Cat 5e	Cat 6
Supports 1000 Mbps.				
Most often used for phone lines.				
Supports 100 Mbps and can support 1000 Mbps, but it is not recommended.				
An added separator is between each pair of wires, allowing it to function at higher speeds.				
Supports 1000 Mbps to 10 Gbps, though 10 Gbps is not recommended.				
Used for voice communication.				
Used for data transmission. (Select more than one category.)				

UTP Cable Wiring Standards

Different situations may require UTP cables to be wired according to different wiring conventions. List and describe the three main cable types that use specific wiring conventions.

- _____

- _____

- _____

UTP Cable Pinouts

In Table 4-3, indicate the appropriate pin number for each wire color for the T568A and T568B standards.

Table 4-3   Compare UTP Cable Pinouts

T568A	T568B	Wire Color
		Green
		Green-white
		Brown
		Brown-white
		Orange
		Orange-white
		Blue
		Blue-white

Fiber-Optic Cabling Completion Exercise

Unlike copper wires, fiber-optic cable can transmit signals with less attenuation and is completely immune to _____ and _____ (acronyms).

List and describe the four types of networks that currently use fiber-optic cabling:

- _____

  _____

- _____

  _____

- _____

  _____

- _____

  _____

Although an optical fiber is very thin, it is composed of two kinds of glass and a protective outer shield. Specifically, these are the

- _____: Consists of pure glass and is the part of the fiber where light is carried.

- _____: The glass that surrounds the inner glass and acts as a mirror. This keeps the light pulses contained in the fiber in a phenomenon known as

  _____.

- _____: Typically a PVC covering that protects fiber.

Light pulses representing the transmitted data as bits on the media are generated by either

- _____

- _____

List, describe, and identify the color of the two major types of fiber optic.

- _____

  _____

- _____

  _____

List the three most popular network fiber-optic connectors.

- _____: An older bayonet-style connector with a twist locking mechanism widely used with multimode fiber

- _____: Widely adopted LAN and WAN connector that uses a push-pull mechanism to ensure positive insertion

- _____: Sometimes called a little or local connector, is quickly growing in popularity due to its smaller size

Incorrect termination of fiber-optic media will result in diminished signaling distances or complete transmission failure. Three common types of fiber-optic termination and splicing errors are as follows:

- _____ : The fiber-optic media is not precisely aligned to one another when joined.

- _____ : The media does not completely touch at the splice or connection.

- _____ : The media ends are not well polished, or dirt is present at the termination.

What is a quick and inexpensive field test to find a broken fiber?

_____

_____

Describe three issues with fiber implementations:

- _____

- _____

- _____

Compare Single-Mode and Multimode Fiber

In Table 4-4, indicate whether the description applies to the multimode or single-mode fiber.

Table 4-4   Multimode and Single-Mode Fiber

Fiber Optics Description	Multimode	Single Mode
Can help data travel approximately 1.24 miles or 2km/550 meters		
Used to connect long-distance telephony and cable TV applications		
Can travel approximately 62.5 miles or 100km/100,000 meters		
Uses LEDs as a data light source transmitter		
Uses lasers in a single stream as a data light source transmitter		
Used within a campus network		

Wireless Media Completion Exercise

Wireless media carry electromagnetic signals that represent the binary digits of data communications using radio or microwave frequencies. Wireless media provides the greatest mobility options of all media. However, wireless does have some areas of concern. Briefly describe each.

- Coverage area: _____

_____

- Interference: _____

_____

- Security: _____

_____

_____

- Shared medium: _____

_____

List and describe the three common data communications standards that apply to wireless media:

- Standard IEEE 802.11: _____

_____

_____

- Standard IEEE 802.15: _____

_____

- Standard IEEE 802.16: _____

_____

A common wireless data implementation is enabling devices to wirelessly connect via a LAN. List and describe the two devices required for WLAN connectivity:

- _____

_____

- _____

_____

Data Link Layer Protocols

The data link layer is responsible for the exchange of frames between nodes over a physical network media. It allows the upper layers to access the media and controls how data is placed and received on the media.

Data Link Layer Completion Exercise

List and describe the two sublayers of the data link layer.

- _____

_____

- _____

_____

What four organizations are responsible for defining standards and protocols that apply to the network access layer?

- _____

- _____

- _____

- _____

Media Access Control

Regulating the placement of data frames onto the media is controlled by the media access control sublayer. There are different ways to regulate placing frames onto the media. The protocols at the data link layer define the rules for access to different media.

Topologies and Access Methods Completion Exercise

Among the different implementations of the data link layer protocols, there are different methods of controlling access to the media. These media access control techniques define whether and how the nodes share the media. The actual media access control method used depends on the following:

- _____ : How the connection between the nodes appears to the data link layer.

- _____ : How the nodes share the media. The media sharing can be point to point, such as in WAN connections, or shared, such as in LAN networks.

Describe the two types of topologies:

- Physical topology: _____

   _____

   _____

   _____

- Logical topology: _____

   _____

   _____

   _____

List and describe the main WAN physical topologies:

- _____

- _____

- _____

List and describe the main physical topologies used in shared media LANs.

- _____

- _____

- _____

- _____

Duplex communications refer to the direction of data transmission between two devices. The two types of duplex communications are as follows:

- _____ : Both devices can transmit and receive on the media but cannot do so simultaneously.

- _____ : Both devices can transmit and receive on the media at the same time.

Rules govern how devices share media. List and describe the two basic media access control methods for shared media:

■ _____

_____

■ _____

_____

When using a nondeterministic contention-based method, a network device can attempt to access the medium whenever it has data to send. To prevent complete chaos on the media, these methods use a _____ process to first detect whether the media is carrying a signal.

List and describe the two CSMA methods used for resolving media contention. Include an example of each.

■ _____

_____

_____

_____

■ _____

_____

_____

_____

Label the Generic Frame Fields

There are several frame types, but all of them have some generic features in common. In Figure 4-1, label the generic frame fields.

Figure 4-1   Fields in the Generic Frame

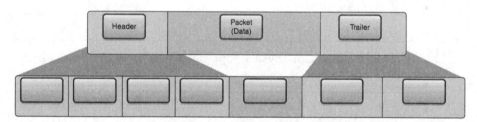

Labs and Activities

 ## 4.0.1.2 Class Activity–Managing the Medium

Objectives

Describe the purpose and function of the data link layer in preparing communication for transmission on specific media.

Background/Scenario

You and your colleague are attending a networking conference. There are many lectures and presentations held during this event, and because they overlap, each of you can attend only a limited set of sessions. Therefore, you decide to split up, each of you attending a separate set of presentations, and after the event ends, you share the slides and the knowledge each of you gained during the event.

Required Resources

- Recording capabilities (paper, tablet, and so on) for reflective comments to be shared with the class.

Reflection

1. How would you personally organize a conference where multiple sessions are held at the same time? Would you put all of them into a single conference room, or would you use multiple rooms? What would be the reason? Explain your answer.

   _____

   _____

2. Assume that the conference room is properly fitted with audiovisual equipment to display large-size video and amplify the speaker's voice. If a person wanted to attend a specific session, does it matter which seat the person takes, or is it sufficient for the person to sit anywhere as long as it is in the appropriate conference room?

   _____

   _____

3. What are the potential consequences or benefits if the speech from one conference room somehow leaked into another?

   _____

   _____

   _____

4. If questions or inquiries arise during a presentation, should an attendee simply shout out his question, or should there be some process of assuring that attendees are given an opportunity to ask questions that everyone can hear? What would happen without this process?

_____

_____

_____

5. Can a session run out of time without going through the entire intended content if an interesting topic elicits a larger discussion where many attendees have questions? If you did not want this to happen, what would be the best way to ensure that it does not occur?

_____

_____

_____

6. Imagine that the session is in a panel format, which allows more free discussion of attendees with the panelists and among themselves. If a person wants to address another person within the same room, can he do it directly? If so, how is this possible? How would a panelist invite another person to join who is not presently in the room?

_____

_____

_____

7. What benefit, if any, was achieved by the isolation of multiple sessions into separate conference rooms if, after the event, people could meet and share the information?

_____

_____

_____

4.1.2.4 Lab–Identifying Network Devices and Cabling

Objectives

Part 1: Identify Network Devices

Part 2: Identify Network Media

Background/Scenario

As a member of the networking support staff, you must be able to identify different networking equipment. You must also understand the function of equipment in the appropriate part of the network. In this lab, you will have access to network devices and media. You will identify the type and characteristics of the network equipment and media.

Part 1: Identify Network Devices

Your instructor will provide various network devices for identification. Each will be tagged with an ID number.

Fill in the table below with the device tag ID number, manufacturer, device model, type (hub, switch, and router), functionality (wireless, router, switch, or combination), and other physical characteristics, such as number of interface types. The first line is filled out as a reference.

ID	Manufacturer	Model	Type	Functionality	Physical Characteristics
1	Cisco	1941	Router	Router	2 Gigabit Ethernet ports
					2 EHWIC slots
					2 CompactFlash slots
					1 ISM slot
					2 Console ports: USB, RJ-45
2					
3					
4					

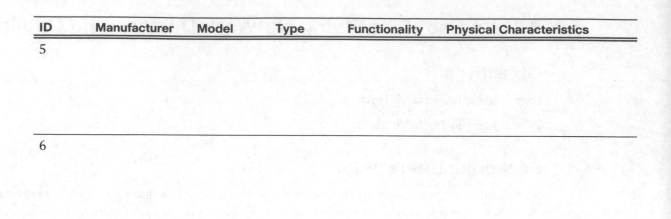

ID	Manufacturer	Model	Type	Functionality	Physical Characteristics
5					
6					

Identify Network Media

Your instructor will provide various network media for identification. You will name the network media, identify the media type (copper, fiber optic, or wireless), and provide a short media description including what device types it connects. Use the table below to record your findings. The first line in the table has been filled out as a reference.

ID	Network Media	Type	Description and to What It Connects
1	UTP	Copper	Connect wired NIC and Ethernet ports on network devices. Cat 5 straight-through wired. Connects PCs and routers to switches and wiring panels.
2			
3			
4			
5			
6			

Reflection

After you have identified the network equipment, where would you find more information about the equipment?

_____

_____

_____

 4.2.2.7 Lab–Building an Ethernet Crossover Cable

Topology

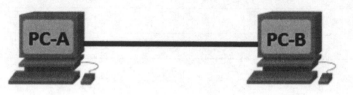

Addressing Table

Device	Interface	IP Address	Subnet Mask	Default Gateway
PC-A	NIC	192.168.10.1	255.255.255.0	N/A
PC-B	NIC	192.168.10.2	255.255.255.0	N/A

Objectives

Part 1: Analyze Ethernet Cabling Standards and Pinouts

Part 2: Build an Ethernet Crossover Cable

Part 3: Test an Ethernet Crossover Cable

Background/Scenario

In this lab, you will build and terminate an Ethernet crossover cable and test it by connecting two PCs together and pinging between them. You will first analyze the Telecommunications Industry Association/Electronic Industries Association (TIA/EIA) 568-A and 568-B standards and how they apply to Ethernet cables. You will then construct an Ethernet crossover cable and test it. Finally, you will use the cable you just constructed to connect two PCs together and test it by pinging between them.

Note: With autosensing capabilities available on many devices, such as the Cisco 1941 Integrated Services Router (ISR) switch, you may see straight-through cables connecting like devices.

Required Resources

- One length of cable, either Category 5 or 5e. Cable length should be 0.6 to 0.9m (2 to 3 ft.)
- 2 RJ-45 connectors
- RJ-45 crimping tool
- Wire cutter
- Wire stripper

- Ethernet cable tester (optional)
- 2 PCs (Windows 7 or 8)

Part 1: Analyze Ethernet Cabling Standards and Pinouts

The TIA/EIA has specified unshielded twisted pair (UTP) cabling standards for use in LAN cabling environments. TIA/EIA 568-A and 568-B stipulates the commercial cabling standards for LAN installations; these are the standards most commonly used in LAN cabling for organizations and they determine which color wire is used on each pin.

With a crossover cable, the second and third pairs on the RJ-45 connector at one end of the cable are reversed at the other end, which reverses the send and receive pairs. The cable pinouts are the 568-A standard on one end and the 568-B standard on the other end. Crossover cables are normally used to connect hubs to hubs or switches to switches, but they can also be used to directly connect two hosts to create a simple network.

Note: With modern networking devices, a straight-through cable can often be used even when connecting like devices because of their autosensing feature. With autosensing, the interfaces detect whether the send and receive circuit pairs are correctly connected. If they are not, the interfaces reverse one end of the connection. Autosensing also alters the speed of the interfaces to match the slowest one. For example, if connecting a Gigabit Ethernet (1000 Mb/s) router interface to a Fast Ethernet (100 Mb/s) switch interface, the connection uses Fast Ethernet.

The Cisco 2960 switch has autosensing turned on, by default; therefore, connecting two 2960 switches together works with either a crossover or a straight-through cable. With some older switches, this is not the case and a crossover cable must be used.

In addition, the Cisco 1941 router Gigabit Ethernet interfaces are autosensing and a straight-through cable may be used to connect a PC directly to the router interface (bypassing the switch). With some older routers, this is not the case and a crossover cable must be used.

When directly connecting two hosts, it is generally advisable to use a crossover cable.

Step 1.   Analyze diagrams and tables for the TIA/EIA 568-A standard Ethernet cable.

The following table and diagrams display the color scheme and pinouts, as well as the function of the four pairs of wires used for the 568-A standard.

Note: In LAN installations using 100Base-T (100 Mb/s), only two pairs out of the four are used.

568-A 10/100/1000Base-TX Ethernet

Pin Number	Pair Number	Wire Color	10Base-T Signal 100Base-TX Signal	1000Base-T Signal
1	2	White/Green	Transmit	BI_DA+
2	2	Green	Transmit	BI_DA-
3	3	White/Orange	Receive	BI_DB+
4	1	Blue	Not Used	BI_DC+
5	1	White/Blue	Not Used	BI_DC-
6	3	Orange	Receive	BI_DB-
7	4	White/Brown	Not Used	BI_DD+
8	4	Brown	Not Used	BI_DD-

The following diagrams display how the wire color and pinouts align with an RJ-45 jack for the 568-A standard.

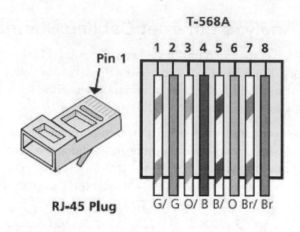

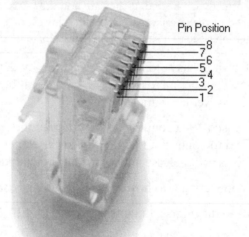

Step 2.   Analyze diagrams and tables for the TIA/EIA 568-B standard Ethernet cable.

The following table and diagram display the color scheme and pinouts for the 568-B standard.

568-B 10/100/1000-BaseTX Ethernet

Pin Number	Pair Number	Wire Color	10Base-T Signal 100Base-TX Signal	1000Base-T Signal
1	2	White/Orange	Transmit	BI_DA+
2	2	Orange	Transmit	BI_DA-
3	3	White/Green	Receive	BI_DB+
4	1	Blue	Not Used	BI_DC+
5	1	White/Blue	Not Used	BI_DC-
6	3	Green	Receive	BI_DB-
7	4	White/Brown	Not Used	BI_DD+
8	4	Brown	Not Used	BI_DD-

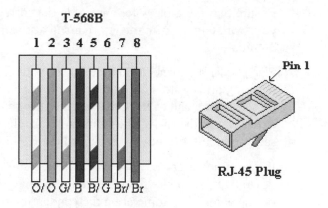

T-568B

Part 2: Build an Ethernet Crossover Cable

A crossover cable has the second and third pairs on the RJ-45 connector at one end, reversed at the other end (refer to the table in Part 1, Step 2). The cable pinouts are the 568-A standard on one end and the 568-B standard on the other end. The following two diagrams illustrate this concept.

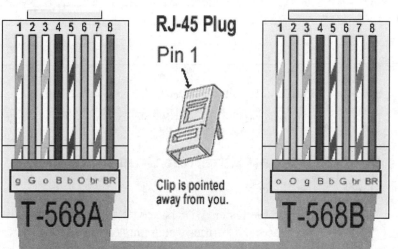

RJ-45 Crossover Ethernet Cable

Step 1.   Build and terminate a TIA/EIA 568-A cable end.

   a.   Determine the cable length required. (Your instructor will let you know the cable length you should make.)

Note: If you were making a cable in a production environment, the general guideline is to add another 12 in. (30.48 cm) to the length.

---

   b.   Cut off a piece of cable to the desired length and using your wire stripper, remove 5.08 cm (2 in.) of the cable jacket from both ends.

   c.   Hold the four pairs of twisted cables tightly where the jacket was cut away. Reorganize the cable pairs into the order of the 568-A wiring standard. Refer to the diagrams, if necessary. Take as much care as possible to maintain the twists in the cable; this provides noise cancellation.

   d.   Flatten, straighten, and line up the wires using your thumb and forefinger.

e. Ensure that the cable wires are still in the correct order for the 568-A standard. Using your wire cutters, trim the four pairs in a straight line to within 1.25 to 1.9 cm (1/2 to 3/4 in.).

f. Place an RJ-45 connector on the end of your cable, with the prong on the underside pointing downward. Firmly insert the wires into the RJ-45 connector. All wires should be seen at the end of the connector in their proper positions. If the wires are not extending to the end of the connector, take the cable out, rearrange the wires as necessary, and reinsert the wires back into the RJ-45 connector.

g. If everything is correct, insert the RJ-45 connector with cable into the crimper. Crimp down hard enough to force the contacts on the RJ-45 connector through the insulation on the wires, thus completing the conducting path. See the following diagram for an example.

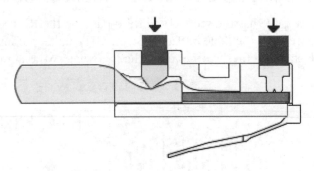

Step 2.   Build and terminate a TIA/EIA 568-B cable end.

Repeat Steps 1a to 1g using the 568-B color wiring scheme for the other end.

Part 3: Test an Ethernet Crossover Cable

Step 1.   Test the cable.

Many cable testers will test for length and mapping of wires. If the cable tester has a wire map feature, it verifies which pins on one end of the cable are connected to which pins on the other end.

If your instructor has a cable tester, test the crossover cable for functionality. If it fails, check with your instructor first as to whether you should re-cable the ends and re-test.

Step 2.   Connect two PCs together via NICs using your Ethernet crossover cable.

a. Working with a lab partner, set your PC to one of the IP addresses shown in the Addressing Table. For example, if your PC is **PC-A**, your IP address should be set to **192.168.10.1** with a **24-bit subnet mask**. You partner's IP address should be **192.168.10.2**. The default gateway address can be left empty.

b. Using the crossover cable you made, connect the two PCs together via their NICs.

c. On the PC-A command prompt, ping the PC-B IP address.

Note: The Windows firewall may have to be temporarily disabled for pings to be successful. If the firewall is disabled, make sure you re-enable it at the conclusion of this lab.

    d.   Repeat the process and ping from PC-B to PC-A.

Assuming IP addressing and firewall are not issues, your pings should be successful if the cables were properly made.

Reflection

1. Which part of making cables did you find the most difficult?

_____

2. Why do you have to learn how to make a cable if you can easily buy pre-made cables?

_____

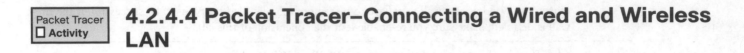

4.2.4.4 Packet Tracer–Connecting a Wired and Wireless LAN

Topology

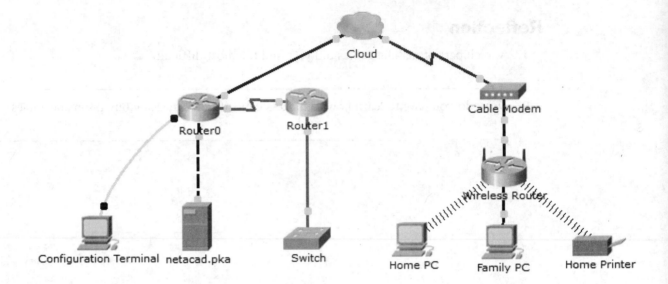

Addressing Table

Device	Interface	IP Address	Connects To
Cloud	Eth6	N/A	F0/0
	Coax7	N/A	Port0
Cable Modem	Port0	N/A	Coax7
	Port1	N/A	Internet
Router0	Console	N/A	RS232
	F0/0	192.168.2.1/24	Eth6
	F0/1	10.0.0.1/24	F0
	Ser0/0/0	172.31.0.1/24	Ser0/0
Router1	Ser0/0	172.31.0.2/24	Ser0/0/0
	F1/0	172.16.0.1/24	F0/1
Wireless Router	Internet	192.168.2.2/24	Port 1
	Eth1	192.168.1.1	F0
Family PC	F0	192.168.1.102	Eth1
Switch	F0/1	172.16.0.2	F1/0
Netacad.pka	F0	10.0.0.254	F0/1
Configuration Terminal	RS232	N/A	Console

Objectives

Part 1: Connect to the Cloud

Part 2: Connect Router0

Part 3: Connect Remaining Devices

Part 4: Verify Connections

Part 5: Examine the Physical Topology

Background

When working in Packet Tracer (a lab environment or a corporate setting), you should know how to select the appropriate cable and how to properly connect devices. This activity will examine device configurations in Packet Tracer, selecting the proper cable based on the configuration, and connecting the devices. This activity will also explore the physical view of the network in Packet Tracer.

Part 1: Connect to the Cloud

Step 1.   Connect the cloud to Router0.

   a.   At the bottom left, click the orange lightning icon to open the available **Connections**.

   b.   Choose the correct cable to connect **Router0 F0/0** to **Cloud Eth6**. **Cloud** is a type of switch, so use a **Copper Straight-Through** connection. If you attached the correct cable, the link lights on the cable turn green.

Step 2.   Connect the cloud to Cable Modem.

   Choose the correct cable to connect **Cloud Coax7** to **Modem Port0**.

   If you attached the correct cable, the link lights on the cable turn green.

Part 2: Connect Router0

Step 1.   Connect Router0 to Router1.

   Choose the correct cable to connect **Router0 Ser0/0/0** to **Router1 Ser0/0**. Use one of the available **Serial** cables.

   If you attached the correct cable, the link lights on the cable turn green.

Step 2.   Connect Router0 to netacad.pka.

   Choose the correct cable to connect **Router0 F0/1** to **netacad.pka F0**. Routers and computers traditionally use the same wires to transmit (1 and 2) and receive (3 and 6). The correct cable to choose consists of these crossed wires. Although many NICs can now autosense which pair is used to transmit and receive, **Router0** and **netacad.pka** do not have autosensing NICs.

   If you attached the correct cable, the link lights on the cable turn green.

Step 3.   Connect Router0 to the Configuration Terminal.

   Choose the correct cable to connect **Router0 Console** to **Configuration Terminal RS232**. This cable does not provide network access to **Configuration Terminal**, but allows you to configure **Router0** through its terminal.

   If you attached the correct cable, the link lights on the cable turn black.

Part 3: Connect Remaining Devices

Step 1.   Connect Router1 to Switch.

Choose the correct cable to connect **Router1 F1/0** to **Switch F0/1**.

If you attached the correct cable, the link lights on the cable turn green. Allow a few seconds for the light to transition from amber to green.

Step 2.   Connect Cable Modem to Wireless Router.

Choose the correct cable to connect **Modem Port1** to **Wireless Router Internet** port.

If you attached the correct cable, the link lights on the cable will turn green.

Step 3.   Connect Wireless Router to Family PC.

Choose the correct cable to connect **Wireless Router Ethernet 1** to **Family PC**.

If you attached the correct cable, the link lights on the cable turn green.

Part 4: Verify Connections

Step 1.   Test the connection from Family PC to netacad.pka.

a.   Open the **Family PC** command prompt and ping **netacad.pka**.

b.   Open the **Web Browser** and the web address **http://netacad.pka**.

Step 2.   Ping the Switch from Home PC.

Open the **Home PC** command prompt and ping the **Switch** IP address of to verify the connection.

Step 3.   Open Router0 from Configuration Terminal.

a.   Open the **Terminal** of **Configuration Terminal** and accept the default settings.

b.   Press **Enter** to view the **Router0** command prompt.

c.   Type **show ip interface brief** to view interface statuses.

Part 5: Examine the Physical Topology

Step 1.   Examine the Cloud.

a.   Click the **Physical Workspace** tab or press **Shift+P** and **Shift+L** to toggle between the logical and physical workspaces.

b.   Click the **Home City** icon.

c.   Click the **Cloud** icon. How many wires are connected to the switch in the blue rack?___

d.   Click **Back** to return to **Home City**.

Step 2.   Examine the Primary Network.

a.   Click the **Primary Network** icon. Hold the mouse pointer over the various cables. What is located on the table to the right of the blue rack? _____

b.   Click **Back** to return to **Home City**.

Step 3.   Examine the Secondary Network.

    a.   Click the **Secondary Network** icon. Hold the mouse pointer over the various cables. Why are there two orange cables connected to each device?

    _____

    b.   Click **Back** to return to **Home City.**

Step 4.   Examine the Home Network.

    a.   Why is there an oval mesh covering the home network?

    _____

    b.   Click the **Home Network** icon. Why is there no rack to hold the equipment?

    _____

    c.   Click the **Logical Workspace** tab to return to the logical topology.

Suggested Scoring Rubric

Activity Section	Question Location	Possible Points	Earned Points
Part 5: Examine the Physical Topology	Step 1c	4	
	Step 2a	4	
	Step 3a	4	
	Step 4a	4	
	Step 4b	4	
	Part 5 Total	20	
	Packet Tracer Score	80	
	Total Score	100	

4.2.4.5 Lab–Viewing Wired and Wireless NIC Information

Objectives

Part 1: Identify and Work with PC NICs

Part 2: Identify and Use the System Tray Network Icons

Background/Scenario

This lab requires you to determine the availability and status of the network interface cards (NICs) on the PC that you use. Windows provides a number of ways to view and work with your NICs.

In this lab, you will access the NIC information of your PC and change the status of these cards.

Required Resources

- 1 PC (Windows 7 or 8 with two NICs, wired and wireless, and a wireless connection)

Note: At the start of this lab, the wired Ethernet NIC in the PC was cabled to one of the integrated switch ports on a wireless router and the Local Area Connection (wired) was enabled. The wireless NIC was disabled initially. If the wired and wireless NICs are both enabled, the PC will receive two different IP addresses and the wireless NIC will take precedence.

Part 1: Identify and Work with PC NICs

In Part 1, you will identify the NIC types in the PC that you are using. You will explore different ways to extract information about these NICs and how to activate and deactivate them.

Note: This lab was performed using a PC running on the Windows 7 operating system. You should be able to perform the lab with one of the other Windows operating systems listed; however, menu selections and screens may vary.

Step 1.   Use the Network and Sharing Center.

    a. Open the **Network and Sharing Center** by clicking the Windows **Start** button > **Control Panel** > **View network status and tasks** under the Network and Internet heading in the Category View.

    b. In the left pane, click the **Change adapter settings** link.

    c. The Network Connections window displays, which provides the list of NICs available on this PC. Look for your Local Area Connection and Wireless Network Connection adapters in this window.

Local Area Connection
TASC
Intel(R) 82577LM Gigabit Network...

Wireless Network Connection
Disabled
Intel(R) Centrino(R) Advanced-N ...

Note: Virtual private network (VPN) adapters and other types of network connections may also be displayed in this window.

Step 2.   Work with your wireless NIC.

    a.   Select the **Wireless Network Connection** option and right-click it to bring up a drop-down list. If your wireless NIC is disabled, you will have an option to **Enable** it. If your NIC was already enabled, then **Disable** would be the first option on this drop-down menu. If your **Wireless Network Connection** is currently disabled, then click **Enable**.

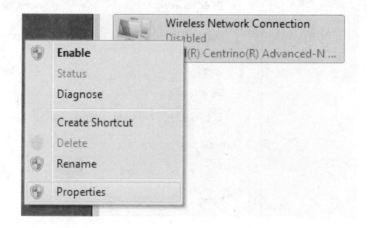

    b.   Right-click the **Wireless Network Connection**, and then click **Status**.

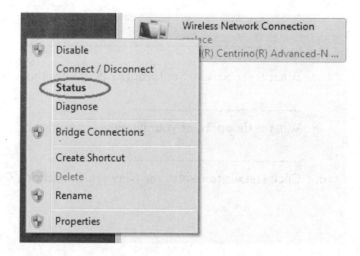

    c.   The Wireless Network Connection Status window displays where you can view information about your wireless connection.

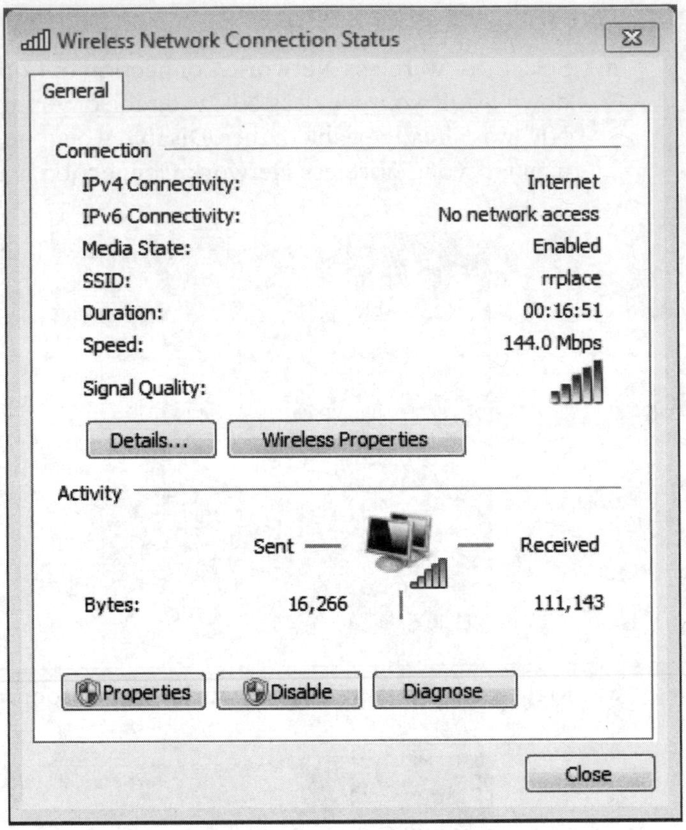

What is the Service Set Identifier (SSID) for the wireless router of your connection?

_____

What is the speed of your wireless connection?

_____

d. Click **Details** to display the Network Connection Details window.

What is the MAC address of your wireless NIC?

_____

Do you have multiple IPv4 DNS servers listed?

_____

Why would multiple DNS servers be listed?

_____

_____

e. When you have reviewed the network connection details, click **Close**.

f. Open a command window prompt and type **ipconfig /all**.

```
Wireless LAN adapter Wireless Network Connection:

   Connection-specific DNS Suffix   . : ph.cox.net
   Description . . . . . . . . . . . : Intel(R) Centrino(R) Advanced-N 6200 AGN
   Physical Address. . . . . . . . . : 58-94-6B-34-92-1C
   DHCP Enabled. . . . . . . . . . . : Yes
   Autoconfiguration Enabled . . . . : Yes
   Link-local IPv6 Address . . . . . : fe80::284c:fc29:c659:f4db%11(Preferred)
   IPv4 Address. . . . . . . . . . . : 192.168.87.118(Preferred)
   Subnet Mask . . . . . . . . . . . : 255.255.255.0
   Lease Obtained. . . . . . . . . . : Thursday, January 17, 2013 8:30:40 AM
   Lease Expires . . . . . . . . . . : Friday, January 18, 2013 8:30:41 AM
   Default Gateway . . . . . . . . . : 192.168.87.1
   DHCP Server . . . . . . . . . . . : 192.168.87.1
   DHCPv6 IAID . . . . . . . . . . . : 307795051
   DHCPv6 Client DUID. . . . . . . . : 00-01-00-01-14-AC-22-0A-5C-26-0A-24-2A-60
   DNS Servers . . . . . . . . . . . : 68.105.28.16
                                       68.105.29.16
                                       192.168.87.1
   NetBIOS over Tcpip. . . . . . . . : Enabled
```

Notice that the information displayed here is the same information that was displayed in the Network Connection Details window in Step d.

g. Close the command window and the Network Connection Details windows. This should bring you back to the Wireless Network Connection Status window. Click **Wireless Properties.**

h. In the **Wireless Network Properties** window, click the **Security** tab.

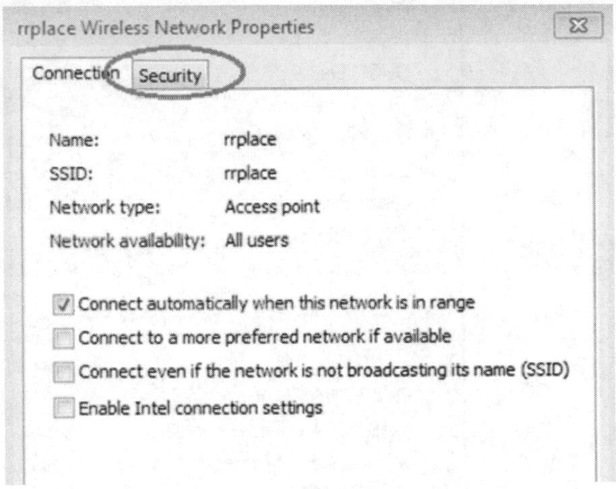

i. The type of security the connected wireless router has implemented displays. Click the **Show characters** check box to display the actual Network security key, instead of the hidden characters, and then click **OK.**

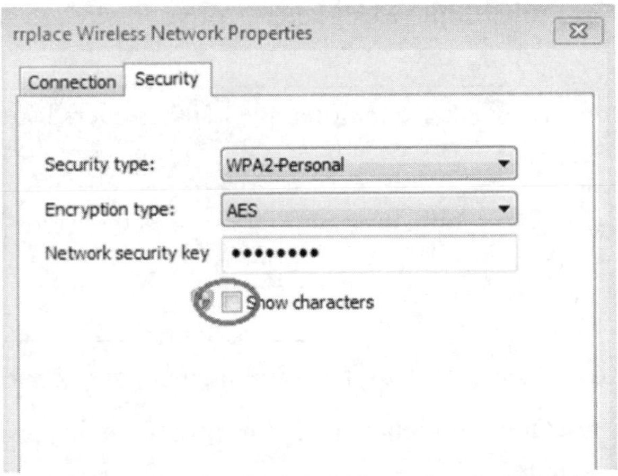

j. Close the Wireless Network Properties and the Network Connection Status windows. Select and right-click the **Wireless Network Connection** option > **Connect/ Disconnect.** A pop-up window should appear at the bottom-right corner of your desktop that displays your current connections, along with a list of SSIDs that are in range of the wireless NIC of your PC. If a scrollbar appears on the right side of this window, you can use it to display additional SSIDs.

k. To join one of the other wireless network SSIDs listed, click the SSID that you want to join, and then click **Connect**.

l. If you have selected a secure SSID, you are prompted to enter the **Security key** for the SSID. Type the security key for that SSID and click **OK**. You can click the **Hide characters** check box to prevent people from seeing what you type in the **Security key** field.

Connect to a Network

Type the network security key

Security key: ●●●●●●●●●●●●

☑ Hide characters

You can also connect by pushing the
button on the router.

OK   Cancel

Step 3.   Work with your wired NIC.

a.   On the Network Connections window, select and right-click the **Local Area Connection** option to display the drop-down list. If the NIC is disabled, enable it, and then click the **Status** option.

Note: You must have an Ethernet cable attaching your PC NIC to a switch or similar device to see the status. Many wireless routers have a small 4-port Ethernet switch built in. You can connect to one of the ports using a straight-through Ethernet patch cable.

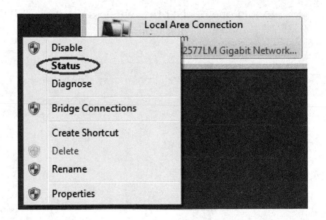

b.   The Local Area Connection Status window will open. This window displays information about your wired connection to the LAN.

```
Local Area Connection Status                    [X]

General

  Connection
    IPv4 Connectivity:                      Internet
    IPv6 Connectivity:            No Internet access
    Media State:                            Enabled
    Duration:                              00:01:00
    Speed:                              100.0 Mbps

    [ Details... ]

  Activity
                     Sent  ———     ———  Received

    Bytes:                      |              16,516

  [ Properties ]  [ Disable ]  [ Diagnose ]

                                          [ Close ]
```

c.   Click **Details...** to view the address information for your LAN connection.

```
Network Connection Details                      [X]

Network Connection Details:

  Property              Value
  Connection-specific DN...  ph.cox.net
  Description           Intel(R) 82577LM Gigabit Network Co
  Physical Address      5C-26-0A-24-2A-60
  DHCP Enabled          Yes
  IPv4 Address          192.168.87.127
  IPv4 Subnet Mask      255.255.255.0
  Lease Obtained        Thursday, January 17, 2013 10:38:14
  Lease Expires         Friday, January 18, 2013 10:38:14 AM
  IPv4 Default Gateway  192.168.87.1
  IPv4 DHCP Server      192.168.87.1
  IPv4 DNS Servers      68.105.28.16
                        68.105.29.16
                        192.168.87.1
  IPv4 WINS Server
  NetBIOS over Tcpip En...  Yes
  Link-local IPv6 Address  fe80::b875:731b:3c7b:c0b1%10

                                          [ Close ]
```

d. Open a command window prompt and type **ipconfig /all**. Find your Local Area Connection information and compare this with the information displayed in the Network Connection Details window.

```
Ethernet adapter Local Area Connection:

   Connection-specific DNS Suffix  . : ph.cox.net
   Description . . . . . . . . . . . : Intel(R) 82577LM Gigabit Network Connection
   Physical Address. . . . . . . . . : 5C-26-0A-24-2A-60
   DHCP Enabled. . . . . . . . . . . : Yes
   Autoconfiguration Enabled . . . . : Yes
   Link-local IPv6 Address . . . . . : fe80::b875:731b:3c7b:c0b1%10(Preferred)
   IPv4 Address. . . . . . . . . . . : 192.168.87.127(Preferred)
   Subnet Mask . . . . . . . . . . . : 255.255.255.0
   Lease Obtained. . . . . . . . . . : Thursday, January 17, 2013 10:38:14 AM
   Lease Expires . . . . . . . . . . : Friday, January 18, 2013 10:38:14 AM
   Default Gateway . . . . . . . . . : 192.168.87.1
   DHCP Server . . . . . . . . . . . : 192.168.87.1
   DHCPv6 IAID . . . . . . . . . . . : 240920074
   DHCPv6 Client DUID. . . . . . . . : 00-01-00-01-14-AC-22-0A-5C-26-0A-24-2A-60
   DNS Servers . . . . . . . . . . . : 68.105.28.16
                                       68.105.29.16
                                       192.168.87.1
   NetBIOS over Tcpip. . . . . . . . : Enabled
```

e. Close all windows on your desktop.

Part 2: Identify and Use the System Tray Network Icons

In Part 2, you will use the network icons in your system tray to determine and control the NICs on your PC.

Step 1.   Use the Wireless Network icon.

a. Click the system tray **Wireless Network** icon to view the pop-up window that displays the SSIDs that are in-range of your wireless NIC. When the system tray displays the Wireless Network icon, the wireless NIC is active.

b. Click the **Open Network and Sharing Center** link. **Note:** This is a shortcut way to bring up this window.

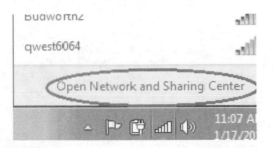

c. In the left pane, click the **Change adapter settings** link to display the Network Connections window.

d. Select and right-click the **Wireless Network Connection**, and then click **Disable** to disable your wireless NIC.

e. Examine your system tray. The **Wireless Network Connection** icon should be replaced by the **Wired Network** icon, which indicates that you are using your wired NIC for network connectivity.

Note: If both NICs are active, the **Wireless Network** icon is the one that is displayed.

Step 2.   Use the Wired Network icon.

a. Click the **Wired Network** icon. Notice that the Wireless SSIDs are no longer displayed in this pop-up window, but you still have the ability to get to the Network and Sharing Center window from here.

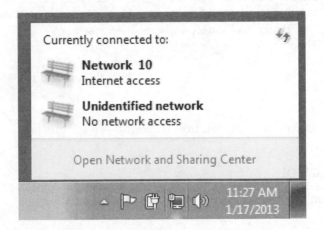

b. Click the **Open Network and Sharing Center** link > **Change adapter settings** and **Enable** your **Wireless Network Connection**. The **Wireless Network** icon should replace the **Wired Network** icon in your system tray.

Step 3.   Identify the Network Problem icon.

   a. On the Network Connections window, disable both the **Wireless Network Connection** and the **Local Area Connection**.

   b. The system tray now displays the **Network Disabled** icon, which indicates that network connectivity has been disabled.

   c. You can click this icon to return to the Network and Sharing Center window. (Examine the network diagram at the top.)

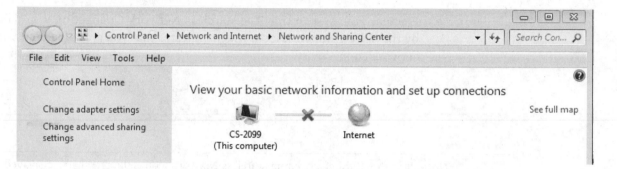

   You can click the red **X** to have the PC troubleshoot the problem with the network connection. Troubleshooting attempts to resolve the network issue for you.

   d. If troubleshooting did not enable one of your NICs, then you should do this manually to restore the network connectivity of your PC.

Note: If a network adapter is enabled and the NIC is unable to establish network connectivity, then the **Network Problem** icon appears in the system tray.

If this icon appears, you can troubleshoot this issue just like you did in Step 3c.

Reflection

Why would you activate more than one NIC on a PC?

_____

4.5.1.1 Class Activity–Linked In!

Objectives

Connect devices using wired and wireless media.

Physical Topology

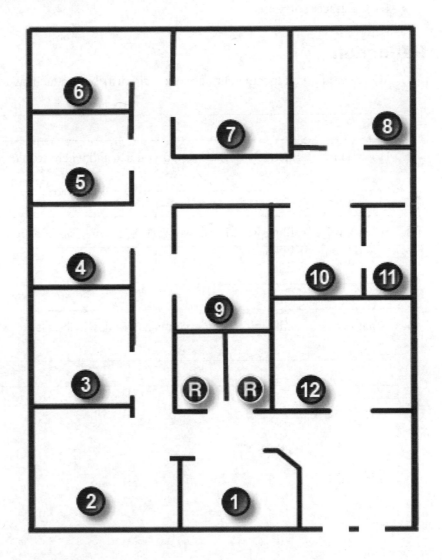

Background/Scenario

Note: This activity is best completed in groups of 2-3 students.

Your small business is moving to a new location! Your building is brand new, and you must come up with a physical topology so that network port installation can begin.

Your instructor will provide you with a blueprint created for this activity. The area on the blueprint, indicated by Number 1, is the reception area and the area numbered RR is the restroom area.

All rooms are within Category 6 UTP specifications (100 meters), so you have no concerns about hard-wiring the building to code. Each room in the diagram must have at least one network connection available for users/intermediary devices.

Do not go into excessive detail on your design. Just use the content from the chapter to be able to justify your decisions to the class.

Required Resources

- Packet Tracer software

Reflection

1. Where would you locate your network main distribution facility, while keeping security in mind?

   _____

   _____

2. How many intermediary devices would you use and where would you place them?

   _____

   _____

3. What kind of cabling would you use (UTP, STP, wireless, fiber optics, and so on) and where would the ports be placed?

   _____

   _____

4. What types of end devices would you use (wired, wireless, laptops, desktops, tablets, and so on)?

   _____

   _____

CHAPTER 5

Ethernet

The Study Guide portion of this chapter uses a combination of matching, fill-in-the-blank, multiple-choice, and open-ended question exercises to test your knowledge and skills of basic router concepts and configuration. The Lab and Activities portion of this chapter includes all the online curriculum labs and Packet Tracer activities to ensure that you have mastered the hands-on skills needed to understand basic IP addressing and router configuration.

As you work through this chapter, use Chapter 5 in *Introduction to Networks v6 Companion Guide* or use the corresponding Chapter 5 in the Introduction to Networks online curriculum for assistance.

Study Guide

Ethernet is now the dominant LAN technology. Ethernet operates in the data link layer and the physical layer. Ethernet standards define both the Layer 2 protocols and the Layer 1 technologies. In this chapter, we review the characteristics and operation of Ethernet.

Ethernet Protocol

In this section, we review the Ethernet protocol, its operation, frame format, and the relationship between the MAC and IP addresses.

Ethernet Operation Completion Exercise

List and briefly describe the two primary responsibilities of the Ethernet MAC sublayer:

- _____

  _____

- _____

  _____

List and briefly describe the three primary functions of data encapsulation:

- _____

  _____

- _____

  _____

- _____

  _____

In your own words, explain the operation of CSMA/CD.

_____

_____

_____

In Table 5-1, indicate which sublayer the characteristic describes.

Table 5-1   MAC and LLC Characteristics

Characteristic	MAC	LLC
Controls the network interface card through software drivers		
Works with hardware to support bandwidth requirements (checks for errors in bits sent and received)		
Remains relatively independent of physical equipment		
Controls access to the media through signaling and physical media standards requirements		
Supports Ethernet technology by using CSMA/CD or CSMA/CA		
Works with the upper layers to add application information for delivery of data to higher-level protocols		

Identify the Ethernet Frame Attributes: Matching

Match the Ethernet frame attribute on the left with a field on the right. This exercise is a one-to-one matching. Each attribute has exactly one matching field.

Frame Attributes

a. Synchronizes sending and receiving devices for frame delivery

b. Detects errors in an Ethernet frame

c. Describes which higher-level protocol has been used

d. Notifies destinations to get ready for a new frame

e. The frame's originating NIC or interface MAC address

f. Uses Pad to increase this frame field to at least 64 bytes

g. Assists a host in determining if the frame received is addressed to them

Fields

_____ Type

_____ Source Address

_____ Start of Frame Delimiter

_____ Frame Check Sequence

_____ Preamble

_____ Destination Address

_____ 802.2 Header and Data

Comparing Decimal, Binary, and Hexadecimal Digits

MAC addresses and IPv6 addresses are both represented in hexadecimal digits. As a networking student, you should become fluent in conversion between decimal, binary, and hexadecimal digits. In Table 5-2, list the equivalent value of each decimal digit in the Binary and Hexadecimal columns.

Table 5-2   Decimal, Binary, and Hexadecimal Digits

Decimal	Binary	Hexadecimal
0	0000	0
1		
2		
3		
4		
5		
6		
7		
8		
9		
10		
11		
12		
13		
14		
15		

Ethernet MAC Address Completion Exercise

What command is used to display the MAC address on a Windows PC?

_____

What command is used to display the MAC address on a MAC or Linux PC?

_____

Describe the structure of a MAC address including the two major parts, the number of bits, the number of bytes, and the number of hexadecimal digits.

_____

_____

_____

_____

MAC addresses can be classified into three categories:

■ _____ MAC addresses are unique addresses used when a frame is sent from a single transmitting device to a single destination device.

■ _____ MAC addresses mean that all hosts on the local network will receive and process the frame.

■ _____ MAC addresses allow a source device to send a packet to a group of devices.

LAN Switches

A Layer 2 LAN switch performs switching and filtering based only on the OSI data link layer (Layer 2) MAC address. A switch is completely transparent to network protocols and user applications. A Layer 2 switch builds a MAC address table that it uses to make forwarding decisions. Layer 2 switches depend on routers to pass data between independent IP subnetworks.

Building the MAC Address Table

In Figure 5-1, PC1 sends an ARP request to PC2. In response, PC2 sends an ARP reply. Circle the correct word in the following steps that explains the process of how a switch builds its MAC address table.

Figure 5-1   Switch and Two PC Topology

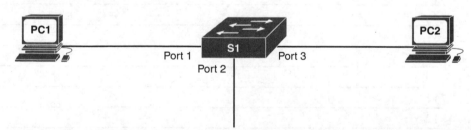

Step 1.   The switch receives a (unicast/broadcast) frame from PC1 on Port 1. _____

Step 2.   The switch enters the (source/destination) (MAC/IP) address of (PC1/PC2) and the switch port that received the frame into the address table. _____

Step 3. Because the destination address is a (unicast/broadcast), the switch floods the frame to all ports, except the port on which it received the frame. _____

Step 4. The destination device replies to the (unicast/broadcast) with a (unicast/broadcast) frame addressed to PC1. _____

Step 5. The switch enters the (source/destination) (MAC/IP) address of (PC1/PC2) and the port number of the switch port that received the frame into the address table. The destination address of the frame and its associated port is found in the MAC address table. _____

True or False: The switch can now forward frames between source and destination devices without flooding because it has entries in the address table that identify the associated ports. _____

Forward the Frame

In the following three scenarios, determine how the switch will forward the frame.

Note: For simplicity, the MAC addresses are simulated using only two hexadecimal digits instead of the full six hexadecimal digits.

Scenario 1

In Figure 5-2, PC 0F is sending a frame to PC 0C. Based on the switch's MAC table entries, answer the questions that follow.

Figure 5-2   Switch Frame Forwarding: Scenario 1

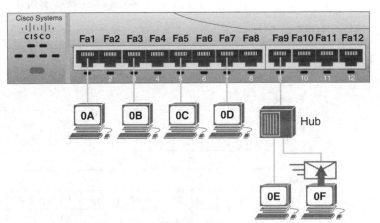

Frame

Preamble	Destination MAC	Source MAC	Length Type	Encapsulated Data	End of Frame
	0C	0F			

MAC Table

Fa1	Fa2	Fa3	Fa4	Fa5	Fa6	Fa7	Fa8	Fa9	Fa10	Fa11	Fa12
								0E 0F			

The switch will forward the frame out which port?

_____

_____

Indicate which of the following statements are true when the switch forwards the frame in Figure 5-2.

Statement	True?
The switch adds the source MAC address to the MAC table.	
The frame is a broadcast frame and will be forwarded to all ports.	
The frame is a unicast frame and will be sent to a specific port only.	
The frame is a unicast frame and will be flooded out all active ports except for the port it was received on.	
The frame is a unicast frame, but it will be dropped by the switch.	

Scenario 2

In Figure 5-3, PC 0E is sending a frame to PC 0F. Based on the switch's MAC table entries, answer the questions that follow.

Figure 5-3   Switch Frame Forwarding: Scenario 2

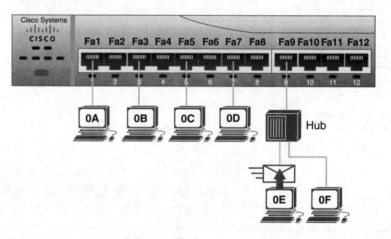

Frame

Preamble	Destination MAC	Source MAC	Length Type	Encapsulated Data	End of Frame
	0F	0E			

MAC Table

Fa1	Fa2	Fa3	Fa4	Fa5	Fa6	Fa7	Fa8	Fa9	Fa10	Fa11	Fa12
						0D		0F			

The switch forwards the frame out which port?

_____

Indicate which of the following statements are true when the switch forwards the frame in Figure 5-3.

Statement	True?
The switch adds the source MAC address to the MAC table.	
The frame is a broadcast frame and will be forwarded to all ports.	
The frame is a unicast frame and will be sent to a specific port only.	
The frame is a unicast frame and will be flooded out all active ports except for the port it was received on.	
The frame is a unicast frame, but it will be dropped by the switch.	

Scenario 3

In Figure 5-4, PC 0A is sending a frame to PC 0E. Based on the switch's MAC table entries, answer the questions that follow.

Figure 5-4   Switch Frame Forwarding: Scenario 3

Frame

Preamble	Destination MAC	Source MAC	Length Type	Encapsulated Data	End of Frame
	0E	0A			

MAC Table

Fa1	Fa2	Fa3	Fa4	Fa5	Fa6	Fa7	Fa8	Fa9	Fa10	Fa11	Fa12
		0B						0E 0F			

The switch forwards the frame out which port? _____

Indicate which of the following statements are true when the switch forwards the frame in Figure 5-4.

Statement	True?
The switch adds the source MAC address to the MAC table.	
The frame is a broadcast frame and will be forwarded to all ports.	
The frame is a unicast frame and will be sent to a specific port only.	
The frame is a unicast frame and will be flooded out all active ports except for the port it was received on.	
The frame is a unicast frame, but it will be dropped by the switch.	

Switching Forwarding Methods Completion Exercise

Describe the two basic switch forwarding methods. Include a description of the two variants of one of the methods.

_____

_____

_____

_____

- _____

    _____

- _____

    _____

    _____

List and explain the difference between the two methods of memory buffering.

_____

_____

_____

Comparing Switch Forwarding Methods

In Table 5-3, indicate which forwarding method applies to the characteristic described.

Table 5-3   Frame Forwarding Methods

Switch Frame Forwarding Methods Descriptions	Store-and-Forward	Cut-Through
No error checking on frames is performed by the switch before releasing the frame out of its ports.		
The destination network interface card (NIC) discards any incomplete frames using this frame forwarding method.		
Buffers frames until the full frame has been received by the switch.		
Checks the frame for errors before releasing it out of its switch ports; if the full frame was not received, the switch discards it.		
The faster switching method, but may produce more errors in data integrity; therefore, more bandwidth may be consumed.		
A great method to use to conserve bandwidth on your network.		

Switching Port Settings Completion Exercise

Explain the difference between half duplex and full duplex.

_____

_____

_____

_____

What are the three duplex settings supported by Cisco switches? What are the default settings for various port speeds?

_____

_____

_____

_____

What is the purpose of the switch interface configuration command **mdix auto**?

_____

_____

_____

Address Resolution Protocol

In Ethernet LAN environments, a device must first know the destination MAC address before it can send data. The Address Resolution Protocol (ARP) provides rules for how a device learns the destination MAC address.

Identify the MAC and IP Addresses

In Figure 5-5, PC1 is sending data to PC2. Fill in the appropriate addresses that will be encapsulated in the frame when PC1 sends the frame out.

Figure 5-5   MAC and IP Addresses in the Frame

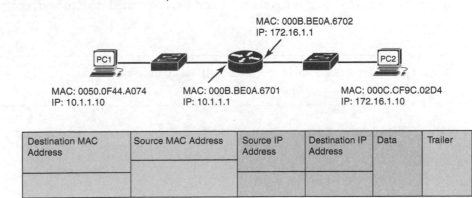

Destination MAC Address	Source MAC Address	Source IP Address	Destination IP Address	Data	Trailer

ARP Completion Exercise

List the two basic functions of ARP:

- _____

- _____

When a packet is sent to the data link layer to be encapsulated into a frame, the device refers a table in its memory to find the _____ address that is mapped to the _____ address. This table is called the _____ table or the _____ cache. It is stored in the _____ of the device.

The sending device will search its ARP table for a destination IPv4 address and a corresponding MAC address.

What will the device do if the packet's destination IPv4 address is on the same network as the source IPv4 address?

_____

What will the device do if the destination IPv4 address is on a different network than the source IPv4 address?

_____

In both cases, the search is for an IPv4 address and a corresponding MAC address for the device. What does the device do if no entry is found?

_____

ARP messages are encapsulated directly within an Ethernet frame. There is no IPv4 header. What two addresses are included in the ARP request?

- _____

- _____

The ARP request is encapsulated in an Ethernet frame using the following header information:

- _____—This is a broadcast address requiring all Ethernet NICs on the LAN to accept and process the ARP request.

- _____—This is the address of the sender of the ARP request.

- _____—ARP message value is 0x806. This informs the receiving NIC that the data portion of the frame needs to be passed to the ARP process.

What does a device do if it has the IPv4 address associated with the target IPv4 address in the ARP request?

_____

What two addresses are included in an ARP reply message?

- _____

- _____

The ARP reply is encapsulated in an Ethernet frame using the following header information:

- _____—This is the MAC address of the sender of the ARP request.

- _____—This is the sender of the ARP reply's MAC address.

- _____—ARP messages have a type field of 0x806. This informs the receiving NIC that the data portion of the frame needs to be passed to the ARP process.

Entries in the ARP table are time stamped. What happens when the time stamp expires?

_____

_____

What command(s) will display the ARP table on a Cisco router?

_____

What command will display the ARP table on a Windows PC?

_____

Labs and Activities

Command Reference

In Table 5-4, record the command, including the correct router or switch prompt, that fits the description. Fill in any blanks with the appropriate missing information.

Table 5-4   Commands for Chapter 5, Ethernet

Command	Description
	Displays the MAC address for a Windows PC.
	Displays the MAC address for MAC or Linux PC.
	Displays the ARP table on a Cisco device.
	Displays the ARP table on a Windows PC.

5.0.1.2 Class Activity–Join My Social Circle

Objectives

Describe the impact of ARP requests on network and host performance.

Background/Scenario

Note: This activity can be completed individually in class or outside of class.

A lot of our network communication is in the form of email, messaging (text or instant), video contact, and social media postings.

For this activity, choose one of the following types of network communications and answer the questions in the Reflection section.

- Text or instant message
- Audio/video conference
- Email
- Online gaming

Required Resources

- Recording capabilities (paper, tablet, and so on) so that reflective comments can be shared with the class.

Reflection

1. Is there a procedure you must follow to register others and yourself so that you can form a communications account? Why do you think that a procedure is needed?

   _____

   _____

2. How do you initiate contact with the person or people with whom you wish to communicate?

   _____

   _____

3. How do you ensure that your conversations are received only by those with whom you wish to communicate?

   _____

   _____

5.1.1.7 Lab–Using Wireshark to Examine Ethernet Frames

Topology

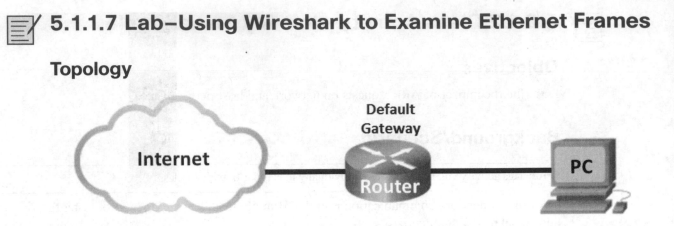

Objectives

Part 1: Examine the Header Fields in an Ethernet II Frame

Part 2: Use Wireshark to Capture and Analyze Ethernet Frames

Background/Scenario

When upper layer protocols communicate with each other, data flows down the Open Systems Interconnection (OSI) layers and is encapsulated into a Layer 2 frame. The frame composition is dependent on the media access type. For example, if the upper layer protocols are TCP and IP and the media access is Ethernet, then the Layer 2 frame encapsulation will be Ethernet II. This is typical for a LAN environment.

When learning about Layer 2 concepts, it is helpful to analyze frame header information. In the first part of this lab, you will review the fields contained in an Ethernet II frame. In Part 2, you will use Wireshark to capture and analyze Ethernet II frame header fields for local and remote traffic.

Required Resources

- 1 PC (Windows 7 or 8 with Internet access with Wireshark installed)

Part 1: Examine the Header Fields in an Ethernet II Frame

In Part 1, you will examine the header fields and content in an Ethernet II Frame. A Wireshark capture will be used to examine the contents in those fields.

Step 1.   Review the Ethernet II header field descriptions and lengths.

Preamble	Destination Address	Source Address	Frame Type	Data	FCS
8 Bytes	6 Bytes	6 Bytes	2 Bytes	46–1,500 Bytes	4 Bytes

Step 2.   Examine the network configuration of the PC.

This PC host IP address is 192.168.1.17 and the default gateway has an IP address of 192.168.1.1.

```
Wireless LAN adapter Wireless Network Connection:

   Connection-specific DNS Suffix  . :
   Description . . . . . . . . . . . : Broadcom 802.11a/b/g WLAN
   Physical Address. . . . . . . . . : 00-1A-73-EA-63-8C
   DHCP Enabled. . . . . . . . . . . : Yes
   Autoconfiguration Enabled . . . . : Yes
   Link-local IPv6 Address . . . . . : fe80::a858:5f3e:35e2:d38f%13(Preferred)
   IPv4 Address. . . . . . . . . . . : 192.168.1.17(Preferred)
   Subnet Mask . . . . . . . . . . . : 255.255.255.0
   Lease Obtained. . . . . . . . . . : Tuesday, June 16, 2015 6:59:54 AM
   Lease Expires . . . . . . . . . . : Wednesday, June 17, 2015 6:59:54 AM
   Default Gateway . . . . . . . . . : 192.168.1.1
   DHCP Server . . . . . . . . . . . : 192.168.1.1
   DHCPv6 IAID . . . . . . . . . . . : 234887795
   DHCPv6 Client DUID. . . . . . . . : 00-01-00-01-1B-07-0A-E1-00-1E-EC-15-74-C2

   DNS Servers . . . . . . . . . . . : 192.168.1.1
   NetBIOS over Tcpip. . . . . . . . : Enabled
```

Step 3.   Examine Ethernet frames in a Wireshark capture.

The Wireshark capture below shows the packets generated by a ping being issued from a PC host to its default gateway. A filter has been applied to Wireshark to view the ARP and ICMP protocols only. The session begins with an ARP query for the MAC address of the gateway router, followed by four ping requests and replies.

```
File  Edit  View  Go  Capture  Analyze  Statistics  Telephony  Tools  Internals  Help

Filter:  arp or icmp                                      ▼  Expression...  Clear  Apply  Save

No.   Time          Source            Destination      Protocol  Length  Info
   9  2.497611000  GemtekTe_ea:63:8 Broadcast          ARP       42  who has 192.168.1.1?  Tell 192.168.1.17
  10  2.502719000  Netgear_ea:b1:7; GemtekTe_ea:63     ARP       42  192.168.1.1 is at 80:37:73:ea:b1:7a
  11  2.502767000  192.168.1.17      192.168.1.1        ICMP      74  Echo (ping) request  id=0x0001, seq=19/4864,
  12  2.503610000  192.168.1.1       192.168.1.17       ICMP      74  Echo (ping) reply    id=0x0001, seq=19/4864,
  14  3.499098000  192.168.1.17      192.168.1.1        ICMP      74  Echo (ping) request  id=0x0001, seq=20/5120,
  15  3.501917000  192.168.1.1       192.168.1.17       ICMP      74  Echo (ping) reply    id=0x0001, seq=20/5120,

⊞ Frame 9: 42 bytes on wire (336 bits), 42 bytes captured (336 bits) on interface 0
⊟ Ethernet II, Src: GemtekTe_ea:63:8c (00:1a:73:ea:63:8c), Dst: Broadcast (ff:ff:ff:ff:ff:ff)
  ⊞ Destination: Broadcast (ff:ff:ff:ff:ff:ff)
  ⊞ Source: GemtekTe_ea:63:8c (00:1a:73:ea:63:8c)
    Type: ARP (0x0806)
⊟ Address Resolution Protocol (request)

0000  ff ff ff ff ff ff 00 1a  73 ea 63 8c 08 06 00 01   ........ s.C.....
0010  08 00 06 04 00 01 00 1a  73 ea 63 8c c0 a8 01 11   ........ s.C.....
0020  00 00 00 00 00 00 c0 a8  01 01                      ........
```

Step 4.   Examine the Ethernet II header contents of an ARP request.

The following table takes the first frame in the Wireshark capture and displays the data in the Ethernet II header fields.

Field	Value	Description
Preamble	Not shown in capture	This field contains synchronizing bits, processed by the NIC hardware.
Destination Address	Broadcast (ff:ff:ff:ff:ff:ff)	Layer 2 addresses for the frame. Each address is 48 bits long, or 6 octets, expressed as 12 hexadecimal digits, `0-9,A-F`.
Source Address	GemtekTe_ea:63:8c (00:1a:73:ea:63:8c)	A common format is `12:34:56:78:9A:BC`. The first six hex numbers indicate the manufacturer of the network interface card (NIC); the last six hex numbers are the serial number of the NIC. The destination address may be a broadcast, which contains all ones, or a unicast. The source address is always unicast.
Frame Type	0x0806	For Ethernet II frames, this field contains a hexadecimal value that is used to indicate the type of upper-layer protocol in the data field. There are numerous upper-layer protocols supported by Ethernet II. Two common frame types are:

Value	Description
`0x0800`	IPv4 Protocol
`0x0806`	Address resolution protocol (ARP)

Field	Value	Description
Data	ARP	Contains the encapsulated upper-level protocol. The data field is between 46–1,500 bytes.
FCS	Not shown in capture	Frame Check Sequence, used by the NIC to identify errors during transmission. The value is computed by the sending machine, encompassing frame addresses, type, and data field. It is verified by the receiver.

What is significant about the contents of the destination address field?

_____

_____

Why does the PC send out a broadcast ARP prior to sending the first ping request?

_____

_____

_____

What is the MAC address of the source in the first frame? _____

What is the Vendor ID (OUI) of the Source's NIC? _____

What portion of the MAC address is the OUI?

_____

What is the Source's NIC serial number? _____

Part 2: Use Wireshark to Capture and Analyze Ethernet Frames

In Part 2, you will use Wireshark to capture local and remote Ethernet frames. You will then examine the information that is contained in the frame header fields.

Step 1. Determine the IP address of the default gateway on your PC.

Open a command prompt window and issue the **ipconfig** command.

What is the IP address of the PC default gateway? _____

Step 2. Start capturing traffic on your PC's NIC.

    a. Open Wireshark.

    b. On the Wireshark Network Analyzer toolbar, click the **Interface List** icon.

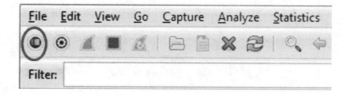

    c. On the Wireshark: Capture Interfaces window, select the interface to start traffic capturing by clicking the appropriate check box, and then click **Start**. If you are uncertain of what interface to check, click **Details** for more information about each interface listed.

Wireshark: Capture Interfaces					
Device	Description	IP	Packets	Packets/s	
☑ Wireless Network Connection	Microsoft	fe80::a858:5f3e:35e2:d38f	1406	3	Details
☐ Local Area Connection	Intel(R) 82566MM Gigabit Network Connection	fe80::705a:a57c:6f90:87eb	1995	2	Details

Help   Start   Stop   Options   Close

    d. Observe the traffic that appears in the Packet List window.

File Edit View Go Capture Analyze Statistics Telephony Tools Internals Help

Filter: Expression... Clear Apply Save

No.	Time	Source	Destination	Protocol	Length	Info
17	3.691404000	192.168.1.17	192.168.1.1	DNS	85	Standard query 0x0c33 A teredo.ipv6.microso
18	3.702954000	192.168.1.1	192.168.1.1	DNS	150	Standard query response 0x0c33 CNAME teredo
19	3.752602000	GemtekTe_ea:63:8	Broadcast	ARP	42	who has 192.168.1.1? Tell 192.168.1.17
20	3.754732000	Netgear_ea:b1:7:	GemtekTe_ea:63	ARP	42	192.168.1.1 is at 80:37:73:ea:b1:7a
21	3.768583000	fe80::a858:5f3e:	ff02::16	ICMPv6	90	Multicast Listener Report Message v2
22	3.768843000	192.168.1.17	224.0.0.22	IGMPv3	54	Membership Report / Leave group 224.0.0.252
23	3.795917000	GemtekTe_ea:63:8	Broadcast	ARP	42	who has 192.168.1.1? Tell 192.168.1.17
24	3.800804000	Netgear_ea:b1:7:	GemtekTe_ea:63	ARP	42	192.168.1.1 is at 80:37:73:ea:b1:7a

Step 3. Filter Wireshark to display only ICMP traffic.

You can use the filter in Wireshark to block visibility of unwanted traffic. The filter does not block the capture of unwanted data; it only filters what to display on the screen. For now, only ICMP traffic is to be displayed.

In the Wireshark **Filter** box, type **icmp**. The box should turn green if you typed the filter correctly. If the box is green, click **Apply** to apply the filter.

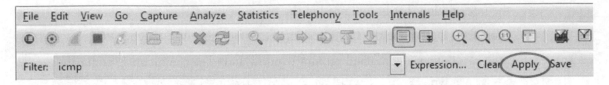

Step 4.   From the command prompt window, ping the default gateway of your PC.

From the command window, ping the default gateway using the IP address that you recorded in Step 1.

Step 5.   Stop capturing traffic on the NIC.

Click the **Stop Capture** icon to stop capturing traffic.

Step 6.   Examine the first Echo (ping) request in Wireshark.

The Wireshark main window is divided into three sections: the Packet List pane (top), the Packet Details pane (middle), and the Packet Bytes pane (bottom). If you selected the correct interface for packet capturing in Step 3, Wireshark should display the ICMP information in the Packet List pane of Wireshark, similar to the following example.

a.   In the Packet List pane (top section), click the first frame listed. You should see **Echo (ping) request** under the **Info** heading. This should highlight the line blue.

b.   Examine the first line in the Packet Details pane (middle section). This line displays the length of the frame; 74 bytes in this example.

c. The second line in the Packet Details pane shows that it is an Ethernet II frame. The source and destination MAC addresses are also displayed.

What is the MAC address of the PC's NIC? _____

What is the default gateway's MAC address? _____

d. You can click the plus (+) sign at the beginning of the second line to obtain more information about the Ethernet II frame. Notice that the plus sign changes to a minus (-) sign.

What type of frame is displayed? _____

e. The last two lines displayed in the middle section provide information about the data field of the frame. Notice that the data contains the source and destination IPv4 address information.

What is the source IP address? _____

What is the destination IP address? _____

f. You can click any line in the middle section to highlight that part of the frame (hex and ASCII) in the Packet Bytes pane (bottom section). Click the **Internet Control Message Protocol** line in the middle section and examine what is highlighted in the Packet Bytes pane.

```
⊞ Frame 11: 74 bytes on wire (592 bits), 74 bytes captured (592 bits) on interface 0
⊟ Ethernet II, Src: GemtekTe_ea:63:8c (00:1a:73:ea:63:8c), Dst: Netgear_ea:b1:7a (80:37:73:ea:b1:7a)
  ⊞ Destination: Netgear_ea:b1:7a (80:37:73:ea:b1:7a)
  ⊞ Source: GemtekTe_ea:63:8c (00:1a:73:ea:63:8c)
    Type: IP (0x0800)
⊞ Internet Protocol Version 4, Src: 192.168.1.17 (192.168.1.17), Dst: 192.168.1.1 (192.168.1.1)
⊟ Internet Control Message Protocol
    Type: 8 (Echo (ping) request)
    Code: 0
    Checksum: 0x4d48 [correct]
◄                                      III

0000  80 37 73 ea b1 7a 00 1a  73 ea 63 8c 08 00 45 00   .7s..z.. s.c...E.
0010  00 3c 0a e6 00 00 80 01  ac 78 c0 a8 01 11 c0 a8   .<...... .x......
0020  01 01 08 00 4d 48 00 01  00 13 61 62 63 64 65 66   ..|.MH.. ..abcdef
0030  67 68 69 6a 6b 6c 6d 6e  6f 70 71 72 73 74 75 76   ghijklmn opqrstuv
0040  77 61 62 63 64 65 66 67  68 69                     wabcdefg hi
```

What do the last two highlighted octets spell? _____

g. Click the next frame in the top section and examine an Echo reply frame. Notice that the source and destination MAC addresses have reversed, because this frame was sent from the default gateway router as a reply to the first ping.

What device and MAC address is displayed as the destination address?

_____

Step 7. Restart packet capture in Wireshark.

Click the **Start Capture** icon to start a new Wireshark capture. You will receive a pop-up window asking if you would like to save the previous captured packets to a file before starting a new capture. Click **Continue without Saving.**

Step 8.   In the command prompt window, ping www.cisco.com.

Step 9.   Stop capturing packets.

Step 10.   Examine the new data in the packet list pane of Wireshark.

In the first echo (ping) request frame, what are the source and destination MAC addresses?

Source: _____

Destination: _____

What are the source and destination IP addresses contained in the data field of the frame?

Source: _____

Destination: _____

Compare these addresses to the addresses you received in Step 6. The only address that changed is the destination IP address. Why has the destination IP address changed, while the destination MAC address remained the same?

_____

_____

_____

_____

Reflection

Wireshark does not display the preamble field of a frame header. What does the preamble contain?

_____

_____

5.1.2.8 Lab–Viewing Network Device MAC Addresses

Topology

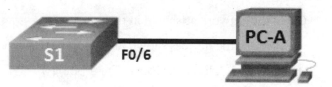

Addressing Table

Device	Interface	IP Address	Subnet Mask	Default Gateway
S1	VLAN 1	192.168.1.1	255.255.255.0	N/A
PC-A	NIC	192.168.1.3	255.255.255.0	192.168.1.1

Objectives

Part 1: Configure Devices and Verify Connectivity

Part 2: Display, Describe, and Analyze Ethernet MAC Addresses

Background/Scenario

Every device on an Ethernet LAN is identified by a Layer 2 MAC address. This address is assigned by the manufacturer and stored in the firmware of the NIC. This lab will explore and analyze the components that make up a MAC address, and how you can find this information on a switch and a PC.

You will cable the equipment as shown in the topology. You will configure the switch and PC to match the addressing table. You will verify your configurations by testing for network connectivity.

After the devices have been configured and network connectivity has been verified, you will use various commands to retrieve information from the devices to answer questions about your network equipment.

Note: The switches used are Cisco Catalyst 2960s with Cisco IOS Release 15.0(2) (lanbasek9 image). Other switches and Cisco IOS versions can be used. Depending on the model and Cisco IOS version, the commands available and the output produced might vary from what is shown in the labs.

Note: Make sure that the switches have been erased and have no startup configurations. If you are unsure, ask your instructor.

Required Resources

- 1 Switch (Cisco 2960 with Cisco IOS Release 15.0(2) lanbasek9 image or comparable)
- 1 PC (Windows 7 or 8 with a terminal emulation program, such as Tera Term)
- Console cable to configure the Cisco switch via the console ports
- Ethernet cables as shown in the topology

Part 1: Configure Devices and Verify Connectivity

In this part, you will set up the network topology and configure basic settings, such as the interface IP addresses and device name. For device name and address information, refer to the Topology and Addressing Table.

Step 1.   Cable the network as shown in the topology.

    a.   Attach the devices shown in the topology and cable as necessary.

    b.   Power on all the devices in the topology.

Step 2.   Configure the IPv4 address for the PC.

    a.   Configure the IPv4 address, subnet mask, and default gateway address for PC-A.

    b.   From the command prompt on PC-A, ping the switch address.

       Were the pings successful? Explain.

_____

Step 3.   Configure basic settings for the switch.

In this step, you will configure the device name and the IP address, and disable DNS lookup on the switch.

    a.   Console into the switch and enter global configuration mode.

```
Switch> enable
Switch# configure terminal
Enter configuration commands, one per line.  End with CNTL/Z.
Switch(config)#
```

    b.   Assign a hostname to the switch based on the Addressing Table.

```
Switch(config)# hostname S1
```

    c.   Disable DNS lookup.

```
S1(config)# no ip domain-lookup
```

    d.   Configure and enable the SVI interface for VLAN 1.

```
S1(config)# interface vlan 1
S1(config-if)# ip address 192.168.1.1 255.255.255.0
S1(config-if)# no shutdown
S1(config-if)# end
*Mar  1 00:07:59.048: %SYS-5-CONFIG_I: Configured from console by console
```

Step 4.   Verify network connectivity.

Ping the switch from PC-A. Were the pings successful? _____

Part 2: Display, Describe, and Analyze Ethernet MAC Addresses

Every device on an Ethernet LAN has a MAC address that is assigned by the manufacturer and stored in the firmware of the NIC. Ethernet MAC addresses are 48-bits long. They are displayed using six sets of hexadecimal digits that are usually separated by dashes, colons, or periods. The following example shows the same MAC address using the three different notation methods:

       00-05-9A-3C-78-00   00:05:9A:3C:78:00   0005.9A3C.7800

Note: MAC addresses are also called physical addresses, hardware addresses, or Ethernet hardware addresses.

You will issue commands to display the MAC addresses on a PC and a switch, and you will analyze the properties of each one.

Step 1.   Analyze the MAC address for the PC-A NIC.

Before you analyze the MAC address on PC-A, look at an example from a different PC NIC. You can issue the **ipconfig /all** command to view the MAC address of your NIC. An example screen output is shown below. When using the **ipconfig /all** command, notice that MAC addresses are referred to as physical addresses. Reading the MAC address from left to right, the first six hex digits refer to the vendor (manufacturer) of this device. These first six hex digits (3 bytes) are also known as the organizationally unique identifier (OUI). This 3-byte code is assigned to the vendor by the IEEE organization. To find the manufacturer, you can use a tool like www.macvendorlookup.com or go to the IEEE web site to find the registered OUI vendor codes. The IEEE web site address for OUI information is http://standards.ieee.org/develop/regauth/oui/public.html. The last six digits are the NIC serial number assigned by the manufacturer.

    a.   Using the output from the **ipconfig /all** command, answer the following questions.

```
Ethernet adapter Local Area Connection:

   Connection-specific DNS Suffix  . :
   Description . . . . . . . . . . . : Intel(R) 82577LM Gigabit Network Connection
   Physical Address. . . . . . . . . : 5C-26-0A-24-2A-60
   DHCP Enabled. . . . . . . . . . . : No
   Autoconfiguration Enabled . . . . : Yes
   Link-local IPv6 Address . . . . . : fe80::b875:731b:3c7b:c0b1%10(Preferred)
   IPv4 Address. . . . . . . . . . . : 192.168.1.3(Preferred)
   Subnet Mask . . . . . . . . . . . : 255.255.255.0
   Default Gateway . . . . . . . . . : 192.168.1.1
   DHCPv6 IAID . . . . . . . . . . . : 240920024
```

What is the OUI portion of the MAC address for this device?

_____

What is the serial number portion of the MAC address for this device?

_____

Using the example above, find the name of the vendor that manufactured this NIC.

_____

    b.   From the command prompt on PC-A, issue the **ipconfig /all** command and identify the OUI portion of the MAC address for the NIC of PC-A.

_____

Identify the serial number portion of the MAC address for the NIC of PC-A.

_____

Identify the name of the vendor that manufactured the NIC of PC-A.

_____

Step 2.   Analyze the MAC address for the S1 F0/6 interface.

You can use a variety of commands to display MAC addresses on the switch.

a.   Console into S1 and use the **show interfaces vlan 1** command to find the MAC address information. A sample is shown below. Use output generated by your switch to answer the questions.

```
S1# show interfaces vlan 1
Vlan1 is up, line protocol is up
  Hardware is EtherSVI, address is 001b.0c6d.8f40 (bia 001b.0c6d.8f40)
  Internet address is 192.168.1.1/24
  MTU 1500 bytes, BW 1000000 Kbit/sec, DLY 10 usec,
     reliability 255/255, txload 1/255, rxload 1/255
  Encapsulation ARPA, loopback not set
  Keepalive not supported
  ARP type: ARPA, ARP Timeout 04:00:00
  Last input never, output 00:14:51, output hang never
  Last clearing of "show interface" counters never
  Input queue: 0/75/0/0 (size/max/drops/flushes); Total output drops: 0
  Queueing strategy: fifo
  Output queue: 0/40 (size/max)
  5 minute input rate 0 bits/sec, 0 packets/sec
  5 minute output rate 0 bits/sec, 0 packets/sec
     0 packets input, 0 bytes, 0 no buffer
     Received 0 broadcasts (0 IP multicasts)
     0 runts, 0 giants, 0 throttles
     0 input errors, 0 CRC, 0 frame, 0 overrun, 0 ignored
     34 packets output, 11119 bytes, 0 underruns
     0 output errors, 2 interface resets
     0 unknown protocol drops
     0 output buffer failures, 0 output buffers swapped out
```

What is the MAC address for VLAN 1 on S1?

_____

What is the MAC serial number for VLAN 1?

_____

What is the OUI for VLAN 1?

_____

Based on this OUI, what is the name of the vendor?

_____

What does bia stand for?

_____

Why does the output show the same MAC address twice?

_____

b. Another way to display the MAC address on the switch is to use the **show arp** command. Use the **show arp** command to display MAC address information. This command maps the Layer 2 address to its corresponding Layer 3 address. A sample is shown below. Use output generated by your switch to answer the questions.

```
S1# show arp
Protocol  Address          Age (min)   Hardware Addr   Type    Interface
Internet  192.168.1.1            -      001b.0c6d.8f40  ARPA    Vlan1
Internet  192.168.1.3            0      5c26.0a24.2a60  ARPA    Vlan1
```

What Layer 2 addresses are displayed on S1?

_____

What Layer 3 addresses are displayed on S1?

_____

Step 3. View the MAC addresses on the switch.

Issue the **show mac address-table** command on S1. A sample is shown below. Use output generated by your switch to answer the questions.

```
S1# show mac address-table
          Mac Address Table
-------------------------------------------


Vlan    Mac Address       Type        Ports
----    -----------       --------    -----
 All    0100.0ccc.cccc    STATIC      CPU
 All    0100.0ccc.cccd    STATIC      CPU
 All    0180.c200.0000    STATIC      CPU
 All    0180.c200.0001    STATIC      CPU
 All    0180.c200.0002    STATIC      CPU
 All    0180.c200.0003    STATIC      CPU
 All    0180.c200.0004    STATIC      CPU
 All    0180.c200.0005    STATIC      CPU
 All    0180.c200.0006    STATIC      CPU
 All    0180.c200.0007    STATIC      CPU
 All    0180.c200.0008    STATIC      CPU
 All    0180.c200.0009    STATIC      CPU
 All    0180.c200.000a    STATIC      CPU
 All    0180.c200.000b    STATIC      CPU
 All    0180.c200.000c    STATIC      CPU
 All    0180.c200.000d    STATIC      CPU
 All    0180.c200.000e    STATIC      CPU
 All    0180.c200.000f    STATIC      CPU
 All    0180.c200.0010    STATIC      CPU
 All    ffff.ffff.ffff    STATIC      CPU
   1    5c26.0a24.2a60    DYNAMIC     Fa0/6
Total Mac Addresses for this criterion: 21
```

Did the switch display the MAC address of PC-A? If you answered yes, what port was it on?

_____

Reflection

1. Can you have broadcasts at the Layer 2 level? If so, what would the MAC address be?

   _____

2. Why would you need to know the MAC address of a device?

   _____

5.2.1.7 Lab–Viewing the Switch MAC Address Table

Topology

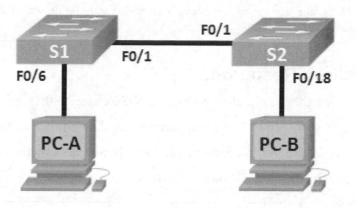

Addressing Table

Device	Interface	IP Address	Subnet Mask	Default Gateway
S1	VLAN 1	192.168.1.11	255.255.255.0	N/A
S2	VLAN 1	192.168.1.12	255.255.255.0	N/A
PC-A	NIC	192.168.1.3	255.255.255.0	N/A
PC-B	NIC	192.168.1.2	255.255.255.0	N/A

Objectives

Part 1: Build and Configure the Network

Part 2: Examine the Switch MAC Address Table

Background/Scenario

The purpose of a Layer 2 LAN switch is to deliver Ethernet frames to host devices on the local network. The switch records host MAC addresses that are visible on the network, and maps those MAC addresses to its own Ethernet switch ports. This process is called building the MAC address table. When a switch receives a frame from a PC, it examines the frame's source and destination MAC addresses. The source MAC address is recorded and mapped to the switch port from which it arrived. Then the destination MAC address is looked up in the MAC address table. If the destination MAC address is a known address, then the frame is forwarded out of the corresponding switch port associated with that MAC address. If the MAC address is unknown, then the frame is broadcasted out of all switch ports, except the one from which it came. It is important to observe and understand the function of a switch and how it delivers data on the network. The way a switch operates has implications for network administrators whose job it is to ensure secure and consistent network communication.

Switches are used to interconnect and deliver information to computers on local-area networks. Switches deliver Ethernet frames to host devices identified by network interface card MAC addresses.

In Part 1, you will build a multi-switch topology with a trunk linking the two switches. In Part 2, you will ping various devices and observe how the two switches build their MAC address tables.

Note: The switches used are Cisco Catalyst 2960s with Cisco IOS Release 15.0(2) (lanbasek9 image). Other switches and Cisco IOS versions can be used. Depending on the model and Cisco IOS version, the commands available and output produced might vary from what is shown in the labs.

Note: Make sure that the switches have been erased and have no startup configurations. If you are unsure, contact your instructor.

Required Resources

- 2 Switches (Cisco 2960 with Cisco IOS Release 15.0(2) lanbasek9 image or comparable)
- 2 PCs (Windows 7 or 8 with terminal emulation program, such as Tera Term)
- Console cables to configure the Cisco IOS devices via the console ports
- Ethernet cables as shown in the topology

Note: The Fast Ethernet interfaces on Cisco 2960 switches are autosensing and an Ethernet straight-through cable may be used between switches S1 and S2. If using another model Cisco switch, it may be necessary to use an Ethernet crossover cable.

Part 1: Build and Configure the Network

Step 1.   Cable the network according to the topology.

Step 2.   Configure PC hosts.

Step 3.   Initialize and reload switches as necessary.

Step 4.   Configure basic settings for each switch.

      a.   Configure device name as shown in the topology.

      b.   Configure IP address as listed in Addressing Table.

      c.   Assign **cisco** as the console and vty passwords.

      d.   Assign **class** as the privileged EXEC password.

Part 2: Examine the Switch MAC Address Table

A switch learns MAC addresses and builds the MAC address table, as network devices initiate communication on the network.

Step 1.   Record network device MAC addresses.

      a.   Open a command prompt on PC-A and PC-B and type **ipconfig /all**. What are the Ethernet adapter physical addresses?

            PC-A MAC Address: _____

            PC-B MAC Address: _____

      b.   Console into switch S1 and S2 and type the **show interface F0/1** command on each switch. On the second line of command output, what are the hardware addresses (or burned-in address [bia])?

            S1 Fast Ethernet 0/1 MAC Address: _____

            S2 Fast Ethernet 0/1 MAC Address: _____

Step 2.   Display the switch MAC address table.

Console into switch S2 and view the MAC address table, both before and after running network communication tests with ping.

   a.   Establish a console connection to S2 and enter privileged EXEC mode.

   b.   In privileged EXEC mode, type the **show mac address-table** command and press Enter.

```
S2# show mac address-table
```

Even though there has been no network communication initiated across the network (i.e., no use of ping), it is possible that the switch has learned MAC addresses from its connection to the PC and the other switch.

Are there any MAC addresses recorded in the MAC address table?

_____

What MAC addresses are recorded in the table? To which switch ports are they mapped and to which devices do they belong? Ignore MAC addresses that are mapped to the CPU.

_____

_____

If you had not previously recorded MAC addresses of network devices in Step 1, how could you tell which devices the MAC addresses belong to, using only the output from the **show mac address-table** command? Does it work in all scenarios?

_____

_____

_____

_____

Step 3.   Clear the S2 MAC address table and display the MAC address table again.

   a.   In privileged EXEC mode, type the **clear mac address-table dynamic** command and press **Enter.**

```
S2# clear mac address-table dynamic
```

   b.   Quickly type the **show mac address-table** command again. Does the MAC address table have any addresses in it for VLAN 1? Are there other MAC addresses listed?

_____

Wait 10 seconds, type the **show mac address-table** command, and press Enter. Are there new addresses in the MAC address table? _____

Step 4.   From PC-B, ping the devices on the network and observe the switch MAC address table.

   a.   From PC-B, open a command prompt and type **arp -a**. Not including multicast or broadcast addresses, how many device IP-to-MAC address pairs have been learned by ARP?

_____

b. From the PC-B command prompt, ping PC-A, S1, and S2. Did all devices have successful replies? If not, check your cabling and IP configurations.

_____

_____

c. From a console connection to S2, enter the **show mac address-table** command. Has the switch added additional MAC addresses to the MAC address table? If so, which addresses and devices?

_____

_____

From PC-B, open a command prompt and retype **arp -a**. Does the PC-B ARP cache have additional entries for all network devices that were sent pings?

_____

Reflection

On Ethernet networks, data is delivered to devices by their MAC addresses. For this to happen, switches and PCs dynamically build ARP caches and MAC address tables. With only a few computers on the network this process seems fairly easy. What might be some of the challenges on larger networks?

_____

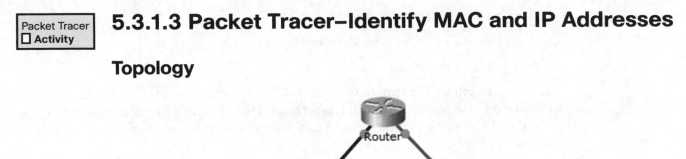

5.3.1.3 Packet Tracer–Identify MAC and IP Addresses

Topology

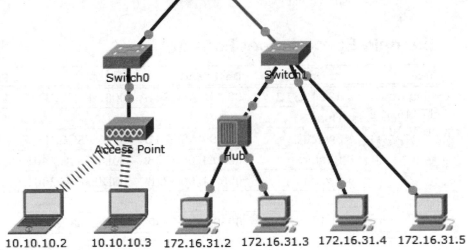

10.10.10.2   10.10.10.3   172.16.31.2   172.16.31.3   172.16.31.4   172.16.31.5

Objectives

Part 1: Gather PDU Information

Part 2: Reflection Questions

Background

This activity is optimized for viewing PDUs. The devices are already configured. You will gather PDU information in simulation mode and answer a series of questions about the data you collect.

Part 1: Gather PDU Information

Note: Review the Reflection Questions in Part 2 before proceeding with Part 1. It will give you an idea of the types of information you will need to gather.

Step 1.   Gather PDU information as a packet travels from 172.16.31.2 to 10.10.10.3.

    a.   Click **172.16.31.2** and open the **Command Prompt**.

    b.   Enter the **ping 10.10.10.3** command.

    c.   Switch to simulation mode and repeat the **ping 10.10.10.3** command. A PDU appears next to **172.16.31.2**.

    d.   Click the PDU and note the following information from the **Outbound PDU Layer** tab:

        ■   Destination MAC Address: 00D0:BA8E:741A

        ■   Source MAC Address: 000C:85CC:1DA7

- Source IP Address: 172.16.31.2
- Destination IP Address: 10.10.10.3
- At Device: Computer

e. Click **Capture / Forward** to move the PDU to the next device. Gather the same information from Step 1d. Repeat this process until the PDU reaches its destination. Record the PDU information you gathered into a spreadsheet using a format like the table shown below:

Example Spreadsheet Format

Test	At Device	Dest. MAC	Src MAC	Src IPv4	Dest IPv4
Ping from 172.16.31.2 to 10.10.10.3	172.16.31.2	00D0:BA8E:741A	000C:85CC:1DA7	172.16.31.2	10.10.10.3
	Hub	--	--	--	--
	Switch1	00D0:BA8E:741A	000C:85CC:1DA7	--	--
	Router	0060:4706:572B	00D0:588C:2401	172.16.31.2	10.10.10.3
	Switch0	0060:4706:572B	00D0:588C:2401	--	--
	Access Point	--	--	--	--
	10.10.10.3	0060:4706:572B	00D0:588C:2401	172.16.31.2	10.10.10.3

Step 2.   Gather additional PDU information from other pings.

Repeat the process in Step 1 and gather the information for the following tests:

- Ping 10.10.10.2 from 10.10.10.3.
- Ping 172.16.31.2 from 172.16.31.3.
- Ping 172.16.31.4 from 172.16.31.5.
- Ping 172.16.31.4 from 10.10.10.2.
- Ping 172.16.31.3 from 10.10.10.2.

Part 2: Reflection Questions

Answer the following questions regarding the captured data:

1. Were there different types of wires used to connect devices? _____

2. Did the wires change the handling of the PDU in any way? _____

3. Did the **Hub** lose any of the information given to it? _____

4. What does the **Hub** do with MAC addresses and IP addresses? _____

5. Did the wireless **Access Point** do anything with the information given to it? _____

6. Was any MAC or IP address lost during the wireless transfer? _____

7. What was the highest OSI layer that the **Hub** and **Access Point** used? _____

8. Did the **Hub** or **Access Point** ever replicate a PDU that was rejected with a red "X"? _____

9. When examining the **PDU Details** tab, which MAC address appeared first, the source or the destination? _____

10. Why would the MAC addresses appear in this order?

_____

11. Was there a pattern to the MAC addressing in the simulation? _____

12. Did the switches ever replicate a PDU that was rejected with a red "X"? _____

13. Every time that the PDU was sent between the 10 network and the 172 network, there was a point where the MAC addresses suddenly changed. Where did that occur? _____

14. Which device uses MAC addresses starting with 00D0? _____

15. To what devices did the other MAC addresses belong? _____

16. Did the sending and receiving IPv4 addresses switch in any of the PDUs? _____

17. If you follow the reply to a ping, sometimes called a *pong*, do the sending and receiving IPv4 addresses switch? _____

18. What is the pattern to the IPv4 addressing in this simulation?

_____

19. Why do different IP networks need to be assigned to different ports of a router?

_____

20. If this simulation was configured with IPv6 instead of IPv4, what would be different?

_____

Suggested Scoring Rubric

There are 20 questions worth 5 points each for a possible score of 100.

5.3.2.8 Packet Tracer–Examine the ARP Table

Topology

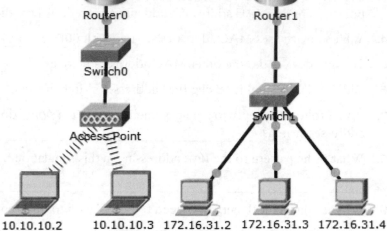

Addressing Table

Device	Interface	MAC Address	Switch Interface
Router0	Gg0/0	0001.6458.2501	G0/1
	S0/0/0	N/A	N/A
Router1	G0/0	00E0.F7B1.8901	G0/1
	S0/0/0	N/A	N/A
10.10.10.2	Wireless	0060.2F84.4AB6	F0/2
10.10.10.3	Wireless	0060.4706.572B	F0/2
172.16.31.2	F0	000C.85CC.1DA7	F0/1
172.16.31.3	F0	0060.7036.2849	F0/2
172.16.31.4	G0	0002.1640.8D75	F0/3

Objectives

Part 1: Examine an ARP Request

Part 2: Examine a Switch MAC Address Table

Part 3: Examine the ARP Process in Remote Communications

Background

This activity is optimized for viewing PDUs. The devices are already configured. You will gather PDU information in simulation mode and answer a series of questions about the data you collect.

Part 1: Examine an ARP Request

Step 1.   Generate ARP requests by pinging 172.16.31.3 from 172.16.31.2.

   a.   Click **172.16.31.2** and open the **Command Prompt**.

   b.   Enter the **arp -d** command to clear the ARP table.

   c.   Enter **Simulation** mode and enter the command **ping 172.16.31.3**. Two PDUs will be generated. The **ping** command cannot complete the ICMP packet without knowing the MAC address of the destination. So the computer sends an ARP broadcast frame to find the MAC address of the destination.

   d.   Click **Capture/Forward** once. The ARP PDU moves **Switch1** while the ICMP PDU disappears, waiting for the ARP reply. Open the PDU and record the destination MAC address. Is this address listed in the table above?_____

   e.   Click **Capture/Forward** to move the PDU to the next device. How many copies of the PDU did **Switch1** make?_____

   f.   What is the IP address of the device that accepted the PDU?_____

   g.   Open the PDU and examine Layer 2. What happened to the source and destination MAC addresses? _____

   _____

   h.   Click **Capture/Forward** until the PDU returns to **172.16.31.2**. How many copies of the PDU did the switch make during the ARP reply?_____

Step 2.   Examine the ARP table.

   a.   Note that the ICMP packet reappears. Open the PDU and examine the MAC addresses. Do the MAC addresses of the source and destination align with their IP addresses?

   _____

   b.   Switch back to **Realtime** and the ping completes.

   c.   Click **172.16.31.2** and enter the **arp –a** command. To what IP address does the MAC address entry correspond?_____

   d.   In general, when does an end device issue an ARP request?

   _____

Part 2: Examine a Switch MAC Address Table

Step 1.   Generate additional traffic to populate the switch MAC address table.

   a.   From **172.16.31.2**, enter the **ping 172.16.31.4** command.

   b.   Click **10.10.10.2** and open the **Command Prompt**.

   c.   Enter the **ping 10.10.10.3** command. How many replies were sent and received?

   _____

Step 2.   Examine the MAC address table on the switches.

   a.   Click **Switch1** and then the **CLI** tab. Enter the **show mac-address-table** command. Do the entries correspond to those in the table above?_____

   b. Click **Switch0**, then the **CLI** tab. Enter the **show mac-address-table** command. Do the entries correspond to those in the table above? _____

   c. Why are two MAC addresses associated with one port?

   _____

Part 3: Examine the ARP Process in Remote Communications

Step 1.   Generate traffic to produce ARP traffic.

   a. Click **172.16.31.2** and open the **Command Prompt**.

   b. Enter the **ping 10.10.10.1** command.

   c. Type **arp –a**. What is the IP address of the new ARP table entry?

   _____

   d. Enter **arp -d** to clear the ARP table and switch to **Simulation** mode.

   e. Repeat the ping to 10.10.10.1. How many PDUs appear? _____

   f. Click **Capture/Forward**. Click the PDU that is now at **Switch1**. What is the target destination IP destination address of the ARP request? _____

   g. The destination IP address is not 10.10.10.1. Why?

   _____

   _____

   _____

Step 2.   Examine the ARP table on Router1.

   a. Switch to **Realtime** mode. Click **Router1** and then the **CLI** tab.

   b. Enter privileged EXEC mode and then the **show mac-address-table** command. How many MAC addresses are in the table? Why?

   _____

   _____

   c. Enter the **show arp** command. Is there an entry for **172.16.31.2**? _____

   d. What happens to the first ping in a situation where the router responds to the ARP request? _____

Suggested Scoring Rubric

Activity Section	Question Location	Possible Points	Earned Points
Part 1: Examine an ARP Request	Step 1	10	
	Step 2	15	
	Part 1 Total	**25**	
Part 2: Examine a Switch MAC Address Table	Step 1	5	
	Step 2	20	
	Part 2 Total	**25**	
Part 3: Examine the ARP Process in Remote Communications	Step 1	25	
	Step 2	25	
	Part 3 Total	**50**	
	Total Score	**100**	

5.4.1.1 Class Activity—MAC and Choose

Objectives

Describe basic switching concepts.

Background/Scenario

Note: This activity is best completed in groups of 2-3 students.

Please view the video titled "The History of Ethernet" and located at the following link:

http://www.netevents.tv/video/bob-metcalfe-the-history-of-ethernet

Topics discussed in the video include not only where we have come from in Ethernet development, but also where we are going with Ethernet technology in the future!

After viewing the video, go to the web and search for information about Ethernet.

Collect three pictures of old, current, and possible future Ethernet physical media and devices. Focus your search on switches if possible. Share these pictures with the class and discuss.

Use the questions in the Reflection section to guide your search.

Required Resources

- Internet access to the video titled "History of Ethernet" and located at http://www.netevents.tv/video/bob-metcalfe-the-history-of-ethernet
- Hard or soft-copy media to record answers to questions and to share in class.

Reflection

1. How was Ethernet used when it was first developed?

   _____

   _____

2. How has Ethernet stayed the same over the past 25 years? What changes are being made to make it more useful/applicable to today's data transmission methods?

   _____

   _____

3. How have Ethernet physical media and intermediary devices changed?

   _____

   _____

4. How have Ethernet physical media and intermediary devices stayed the same?

_____

_____

5. How do you think the Ethernet will change in the future? What factors could influence these changes?

_____

_____

Network Layer

The Study Guide portion of this chapter uses a combination of matching, fill-in-the-blank, multiple-choice, and open-ended question exercises to test your knowledge and skills of basic router concepts and configuration. The Lab and Activities portion of this chapter includes all the online curriculum labs and Packet Tracer activities to ensure that you have mastered the hands-on skills needed to understand basic IP addressing and router configuration.

As you work through this chapter, use Chapter 6 in *Introduction to Networks v6 Companion Guide* or use the corresponding Chapter 6 in the Introduction to Networks online curriculum for assistance.

Study Guide

Network applications and services on one end device can communicate with applications and services running on another end device. The protocols of the OSI model network layer specify addressing and processes that enable transport layer data to be packaged and transported. The network layer encapsulation enables data to be passed to a destination within a network (or on another network) with minimum overhead. In this chapter, we review the role of the network layer including the protocols, basic routing concepts, the role of the router, and configuring a Cisco router.

Network Layer Protocols

The network layer provides services to allow end devices to exchange data across the network. To accomplish this end-to-end transport, the network layer uses a set of protocols.

The Network Layer

Describe the four basic processes of the network layer.

- Addressing end devices: _____

  _____

- Encapsulation: _____

  _____

- Routing: _____

  _____

- De-encapsulation: _____

  _____

  _____

Characteristics of the IP

In Table 6-1, indicate to which category the characteristic of the IP protocol belongs.

Table 6-1   IP Protocol Characteristics

Characteristic	Connectionless	Best-Effort Delivery	Media Independent
No contact is made with the destination host before sending a packet.			
Packet delivery is not guaranteed.			
Will adjust the size of the packet sent depending on what type of network access will be used.			
Fiber-optic cabling, satellites, and wireless can all be used to route the same packet.			
Will send a packet even if the destination host is not able to receive it.			
Does not guarantee that the packet will be delivered.			

Fields of the IPv4 Packet: Matching

Match the IPv4 packet attribute on the left with a field on the right. This exercise is a one-to-one matching. Each attribute has exactly one matching field.

IPv4 Packet Attributes

  a. Maximum value is 65535 bytes.
  b. Identifies the IPv4 address of the recipient host.
  c. Commonly referred to as hop limit.
  d. Always set to 0100 for IPv4.
  e. Identifies the number of 32-bit words in the header.
  f. Error-checks the IPv4 header (if incorrect, discards the packet).
  g. Identifies the priority of each packet.
  h. Identifies the IPv4 address of the sending host.
  i. Identifies the upper-layer protocol.

Fields

____ Differentiated Services
____ Internet Header Length
____ Header Checksum
____ Time-To-Live
____ Version
____ Protocol
____ Destination IPv4 Address
____ Total Length
____ Source IPv4 Address

Fields of the IPv6 Packet: Matching

Match the IPv6 packet attribute on the left with a field on the right. This exercise is a one-to-one matching. Each attribute has exactly one matching field.

IPv6 Packet Attributes

  a. Can be set to use the same pathway flow so that packets are not reordered upon delivery.
  b. Defines the application type to the upper-layer protocol.
  c. Defines the packet size.
  d. When this value reaches 0, the sender is notified that the packet was not delivered.
  e. Classifies packets for congestion control.
  f. Identifies the packet under a field set to 0110.

Fields

____ Version
____ Hop Limit
____ Flow Label
____ Payload Length
____ Next Header
____ Traffic Class

Routing

Routing is the network layer process responsible for forwarding packets from the source to the destination based on the IPv4 or IPv6 address in the packet header. Routers perform this function by looking up the destination network in a routing table. Hosts also have a routing table.

How a Host Routes Packets Completion Exercise

A host can send a packet to itself at IPv4 address _____, to a _____ host if the host is on the same network, or to a _____ host that does not share the same network address. How does a host determine if the packet is local or remote?

_____

_____

_____

When a source device sends a packet to a remote destination device, then the help of routers and routing is needed. The router connected to the local network segment is referred to as the

_____.

List the three primary functions of a default gateway:

- _____

- _____

- _____

IPv4 hosts have a routing table they use to route packets. Example 6-1 shows the routing table for a Windows 7 PC.

Example 6-1   Windows 7 PC Routing Table

```
C:\> netstat -r or route print
<output omitted>
IPv4 Route Table
===========================================================================
Active Routes:
Network Destination        Netmask          Gateway       Interface  Metric
          0.0.0.0          0.0.0.0       10.10.10.1    10.10.10.112     10
       10.10.10.0    255.255.255.0       On-link      10.10.10.112    266
     10.10.10.112  255.255.255.255       On-link      10.10.10.112    266
     10.10.10.255  255.255.255.255       On-link      10.10.10.112    266
        127.0.0.0        255.0.0.0       On-link         127.0.0.1    306
        127.0.0.1  255.255.255.255       On-link         127.0.0.1    306
  127.255.255.255  255.255.255.255       On-link         127.0.0.1    306
        224.0.0.0        240.0.0.0       On-link         127.0.0.1    306
        224.0.0.0        240.0.0.0       On-link      10.10.10.112    266
  255.255.255.255  255.255.255.255       On-link         127.0.0.1    306
  255.255.255.255  255.255.255.255       On-link      10.10.10.112    266
===========================================================================
<output omitted>
```

What Windows 7 commands will display this table?

In Table 6-2, indicate to which column the following descriptions refer.

Table 6-2 The Columns of a Windows PC Routing Table

Column	Description
	Lists the cost of each route and is used to determine the best route to a destination.
	Lists a subnet mask that informs the host how to determine the network and the host portions of the IPv4 address.
	Lists the address used by the local computer to get to a remote network destination. If a destination is directly reachable, it will show as "on-link" in this column.
	Lists the reachable networks.
	Lists the address of the physical interface used to send the packet to the gateway that is used to reach the network destination.

Routing Table Entry: Matching

Refer to the following IPv4 routing table entry:

```
D 10.1.1.0/24 [90/2170112] via 209.165.200.226, 00:00:05, Serial0/0/0
```

Match the description on the left with the entry section on the right. This exercise is a one-to-one matching. Each description has exactly one matching entry section.

Item Description

a. Metric: Identifies the value assigned to reach the remote network. Lower values indicate preferred routes.

b. Destination network: Identifies the address of the remote network.

c. Outgoing interface: Identifies the exit interface to use to forward a packet toward the final destination.

d. Next hop: Identifies the IPv4 address of the next router to forward the packet.

e. Administrative distance: Identifies the trustworthiness of the route source.

f. Route time stamp: Identifies when the route was last heard from.

g. Route source: Identifies how the route was learned.

Item Within Route Entry

_____ 10.1.1.0/24

_____ D

_____ 90

_____ 209.165.200.226

_____ Serial0/0/0

_____ 2170112

_____ 00:00:05

Routers

Regardless of their function, size, or complexity, all router models are essentially computers that require an operating system (OS), a central processing unit (CPU), random access memory (RAM), and a boot process.

Identify Router Components

Match the function/description on the left with the router component on the right. This exercise is a one-to-one matching. Each function/description has exactly one matching router component.

Function/Description

a. A way to remotely access the CLI across a network interface

b. Connects routers to external networks, usually over a large distance

c. A local port that uses USB or low-speed, serial connections to manage network devices

d. A port to manage routers (using telephone lines and modems)

e. Connects computers, switches, and routers for internal networking

Router Component

_____ AUX port

_____ WAN interface

_____ LAN interface

_____ Console port

_____ Telnet or SSH

Router Boot Process Exercise

Figure 6-1 displays an incomplete diagram of the default boot sequence of a router. Provide details where information is missing.

Figure 6-1   Diagram of the Router Boot Sequence

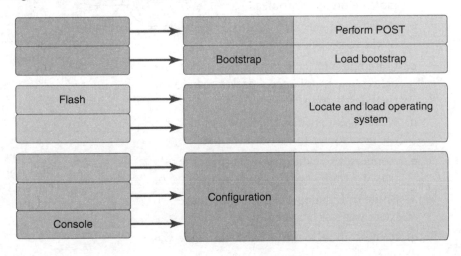

Interpreting the show version Command Exercise

Figure 6-2 displays the output from the **show version** command with parts of the output numbered. Choose the correct label description for each number shown in the figure.

Figure 6-2   The show version Command

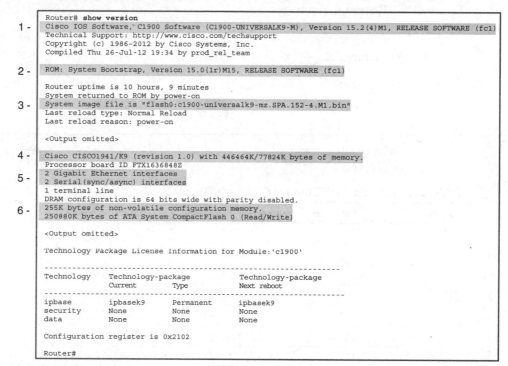

```
      Router# show version
1 -   Cisco IOS Software, C1900 Software (C1900-UNIVERSALK9-M), Version 15.2(4)M1, RELEASE SOFTWARE (fc1)
      Technical Support: http://www.cisco.com/techsupport
      Copyright (c) 1986-2012 by Cisco Systems, Inc.
      Compiled Thu 26-Jul-12 19:34 by prod_rel_team

2 -   ROM: System Bootstrap, Version 15.0(1r)M15, RELEASE SOFTWARE (fc1)

      Router uptime is 10 hours, 9 minutes
      System returned to ROM by power-on
3 -   System image file is "flash0:c1900-universalk9-mz.SPA.152-4.M1.bin"
      Last reload type: Normal Reload
      Last reload reason: power-on

      <Output omitted>

4 -   Cisco CISCO1941/K9 (revision 1.0) with 446464K/77824K bytes of memory.
      Processor board ID FTX1636848Z
5 -   2 Gigabit Ethernet interfaces
      2 Serial(sync/async) interfaces
      1 terminal line
      DRAM configuration is 64 bits wide with parity disabled.
6 -   255K bytes of non-volatile configuration memory.
      250880K bytes of ATA System CompactFlash 0 (Read/Write)

      <Output omitted>

      Technology Package License Information for Module:'c1900'

      ---------------------------------------------------------------
      Technology    Technology-package          Technology-package
                    Current       Type          Next reboot
      ---------------------------------------------------------------
      ipbase        ipbasek9      Permanent     ipbasek9
      security      None          None          None
      data          None          None          None

      Configuration register is 0x2102

      Router#
```

Figure 6-2 label descriptions:

_____   Cisco IOS software currently in RAM

_____   Displays the amount of DRAM

_____   Displays the physical interfaces on the router

_____   Displays where the bootstrap program is located and loaded the Cisco IOS

_____   Displays the amount of NVRAM and flash memory on the router

_____   Software initially used to boot the router

Configuring a Cisco Router

Cisco routers and Cisco switches have many similarities. They support a similar modal operating system, support similar command structures, and support many of the same commands. In addition, both devices have identical initial configuration steps when you're implementing them in a network.

Basic Router Configuration Exercise

When designing a new network or mapping an existing network, it is important to document the network. At a minimum, the documentation should include a topology map of the network and an addressing table that lists the following information:

- Device names
- Interface

- IPv4 address and subnet mask
- Default gateway address for end devices such as PCs

Refer to the topology shown in Figure 6-3 and the addressing scheme in Table 6-3 that follows it to complete this basic configuration exercise.

Figure 6-3   Chapter 6 Topology

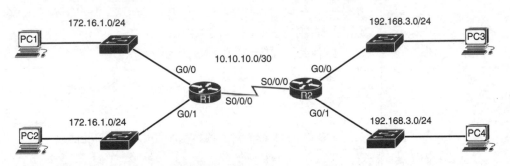

Table 6-3   Addressing Table for Chapter 6 Topology

Device	Interface	IPv4 Address	Subnet Mask	Default Gateway
R1	G0/0	172.16.1.1	255.255.255.0	N/A
	G0/1	172.16.2.1	255.255.255.0	N/A
	S0/0/0	10.10.10.1	255.255.255.252	N/A
R2	G0/0	192.168.3.1	255.255.255.0	N/A
	G0/1	192.168.4.1	255.255.255.0	N/A
	S0/0/0	10.10.10.2	255.255.255.252	N/A
PC1	NIC	172.16.1.10	255.255.255.0	
PC2	NIC	172.16.2.10	255.255.255.0	
PC3	NIC	192.168.3.10	255.255.255.0	
PC4	NIC	192.168.4.10	255.255.255.0	

In Table 6-3, fill in the missing default gateway addresses for the PCs. Recall that the default gateway is the IPv4 address of a router that is on the same network as the PC.

When configuring a router, certain basic tasks are performed, including the following:

- Naming the router
- Setting passwords
- Configuring interfaces
- Configuring a banner
- Saving changes on a router
- Verifying basic configuration and router operations

The first prompt is at user mode and will allow you to view the state of the router. What major limitation does this mode have?

What is the router prompt for this mode?

_____

The **enable** command is used to enter the privileged mode. What is the major difference between this mode and the user mode?

_____

What is the router prompt for this mode?

_____

Applying a Basic Configuration

The following exercise walks you through a basic configuration.

First, enter global configuration mode:

`Router#` _____

Next, apply a unique host name to the router. Use R1 for this example.

`Router(config)#` _____

Now, configure the encrypted password that is to be used to enter privileged EXEC mode. Use **class** as the password.

`Router(config)#` _____

Next, configure the console and Telnet lines with the password **cisco**. The console commands follow:

`R1(config)#` _____

`R1(config-line)#` _____

`R1(config-line)#` _____

The Telnet lines use similar commands:

`R1(config)#` _____

`R1(config-line)#` _____

`R1(config-line)#` _____

From global configuration mode, configure the message-of-the-day banner. Use the following text: Authorized Access Only. A delimiting character such as a $ is used at the beginning and at the end of the message.

`R1(config)#` _____

What is the purpose of the message of the day?

_____

_____

Refer to Figure 6-3 for the correct interface designations. What is the command to enter interface configuration mode for R1's serial interface?

`R1(config)#` _____

Enter the command to configure the IPv4 address using the address in Table 6-3:

`R1(config-if)#` _____

Describe the interface with the following text: Link to R2.

`R1(config-if)#` _____

Activate the interface:

`Router(config-if)#` _____

Now enter the commands to configure and activate the Gigabit Ethernet 0/0 interface on R1. Use the following description text: R1 LAN1.

`R1(config)#` _____

`R1(config-if)#` _____

`R1(config-if)#` _____

`R1(config-if)#` _____

Now enter the commands to configure and activate the Gigabit Ethernet interface on R1. Use the following description text: R1 LAN2.

`R1(config)#` _____

`R1(config-if)#` _____

`R1(config-if)#` _____

`R1(config-if)#` _____

What command will save the current configuration?

`Router#` _____

In the following space, record the script to configure R2. Include the router prompt and the command to save the configuration.

_____

_____

_____

_____

_____

_____

_____

_____

_____

_____

_____

_____

_____

_____

_____

_____

_____

Verifying Basic Router Configuration

Basic configurations can be verified using a few basic **show** commands. In Table 6-4, list the command in the left column that fits the description in the right column.

Table 6-4   Basic Router Configuration Verification Commands

Command	Description
	Displays the current running configuration that is stored in RAM
	Displays the startup configuration file stored in NVRAM
	Displays the IPv4 routing table that the IOS is currently using to choose the best path to its destination networks
	Displays all the interface configuration parameters and statistics
	Displays abbreviated interface configuration information, including IPv4 address and interface status

Packet Tracer Exercise 6-1: Basic Router Configuration

Now you are ready to use Packet Tracer to apply your documented configuration. Download and open the file LSG01-0601.pka found at the companion website for this book. Refer to the Introduction of this book for specifics on accessing files.

Note: The following instructions are also contained within the Packet Tracer Exercise.

In this Packet Tracer activity, you will configure two routers with basic settings and verify connectivity. Use the commands you documented in the section "Apply a Basic Configuration." You will then verify that each PC can ping the other PCs.

Requirements

Configure the routers with the following settings:

- Name the routers **R1** and **R2**.
- The privileged EXEC password is **class**.
- The line password is **cisco**.
- All plaintext passwords should be encrypted
- Users must log in to the console and vty lines.
- The message-of-the-day is **Authorized Access Only**.
- Configure and activate all interfaces according to Table 6-3.
- Save the configurations.
- Verify connectivity between all PCs.

Your completion percentage should be 100%. All the connectivity tests should show a status of "successful." If not, click **Check Results** to see which required components are not yet completed.

Challenge

Although you have not yet learned about dynamic routing protocols, can you determine how R1 and R2 learned about each other's networks? What commands are present in the routers' configurations that enable dynamic routing?

_____

_____

_____

_____

_____

_____

_____

_____

Labs and Activities

Command Reference

In Table 6-5, record the command, including the correct router or switch prompt, that fits the description. Fill in any blanks with the appropriate missing information.

Table 6-5   Commands for Chapter 6, Network Layer

Command	Description
	Enter privileged EXEC mode.
	Exit privileged EXEC mode.
	Enter global configuration mode.
	Configure R1 as the hostname for the router.
	Enter line configuration mode for the console.
	Configure the console password to be "cisco123."
	Require a password for user EXEC mode.
	Encrypt all plaintext passwords.
	Configure "Authorized Access Only!" as the message of the day. Use $ as the delimiting character.
	Enter interface configuration mode for g0/0.
	Configure the IPv4 address 172.16.1.1 255.255.255.0 on interface g0/0.
	Activate the interface.
	Describe the interface as "R1 LAN1."
	View the configuration currently stored in RAM.
	Save the configuration to NVRAM.
	Erase the configuration stored in NVRAM.
	Reboot the switch.
	Test connectivity to another switch at IPv4 address 192.168.2.1.
	Displays the routing table that the IOS is currently using to choose the best path to its destination networks
	Displays all the interface configuration parameters and statistics
	Displays abbreviated interface configuration information, including IPv4 address and interface status

6.0.1.2 Class Activity – The Road Less Traveled...Or Is It?

Objectives

Explain how network devices use routing tables to direct packets to a destination network.

Background/Scenario

During the upcoming weekend, you decide to visit a schoolmate who is currently at home sick. You know his street address but you have never been to his town before.

Instead of looking up the address on the map, you decide to take it easy and to simply ask town residents for directions after you arrive by train.

The citizens you ask for directions are very helpful. However, they all have an interesting habit. Instead of explaining the entire route to your destination, they all tell you, "Take this road and as soon as you arrive at the nearest crossroad, ask somebody there again."

Somewhat bemused at this apparent oddity, you follow these instructions and finally arrive, crossroad by crossroad, and road by road, at your friend's house.

Reflection

1. Would it have made a significant difference if you were told about the whole route or a larger part of the route instead of just being directed to the nearest crossroad?

    _____

    _____

2. Would it have been more helpful to ask about the specific street address or just about the street name?

    _____

    _____

3. What would happen if the person you asked for directions did not know where the destination street was or directed you through an incorrect road?

    _____

    _____

4. Assume that on your way back home, you again choose to ask residents for directions. Is it guaranteed that you will be directed via the same route you took to get to your friend's home? Explain your answer.

    _____

    _____

5. Is it necessary to explain where you depart from when asking directions to an intended destination?

    _____

    _____

6.3.1.8 Packet Tracer–Exploring Internetworking Devices

Topology

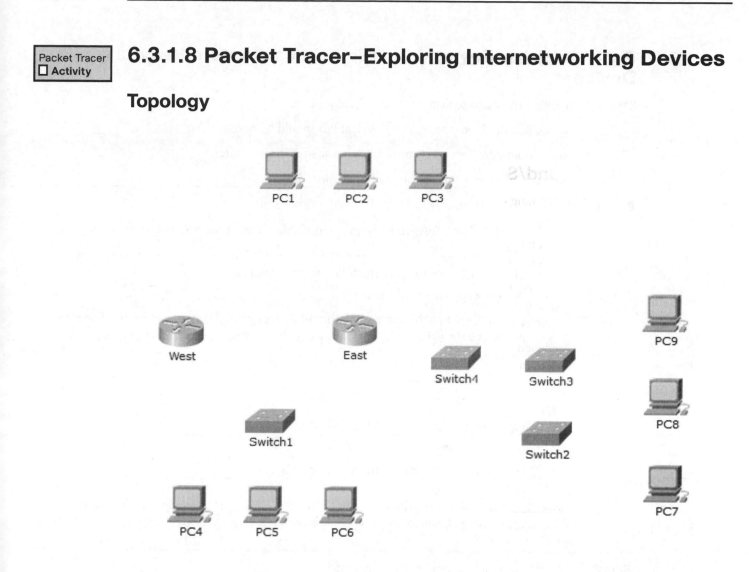

Objectives

Part 1: Identify Physical Characteristics of Internetworking Devices

Part 2: Select Correct Modules for Connectivity

Part 3: Connect Devices

Background

In this activity, you will explore the different options available on internetworking devices. You will also be required to determine which options provide the necessary connectivity when connecting multiple devices. Finally, you will add the correct modules and connect the devices.

Note: Scoring for this activity is a combination of Packet Tracer-automated scoring and your recorded answers to the questions posed in the instructions. See the Suggested Scoring Rubric at the end of this activity, and consult with your instructor to determine your final score.

Part 1: Identify Physical Characteristics of Internetworking Devices

Step 1. Identify the management ports of a Cisco router.

  a. Click the **East** router. The **Physical** tab should be active.

  b. Zoom in and expand the window to see the entire router.

  c. Which management ports are available? _____

Step 2. Identify the LAN and WAN interfaces of a Cisco router

  a. Which LAN and WAN interfaces are available on the **East** router and how many are there? _____

  b. Click the **CLI** tab and enter the following commands:

```
East> show ip interface brief
```

  The output verifies the correct number of interfaces and their designation. The vlan1 interface is a virtual interface that only exists in software. How many physical interfaces are listed? _____

  c. Enter the following commands:

```
East> show interface gigabitethernet 0/0
```

  What is the default bandwidth of this interface? _____

```
East> show interface serial 0/0/0
```

  What is the default bandwidth of this interface? _____

Note: Bandwidth on serial interfaces is used by routing processes to determine the best path to a destination. It does not indicate the actual bandwidth of the interface. Actual bandwidth is negotiated with a service provider.

Step 3. Identify module expansion slots on switches.

  a. How many expansion slots are available to add additional modules to the **East** router? __

  b. Click **Switch2** or **Switch3**. How many expansion slots are available? _____

Part 2: Select Correct Modules for Connectivity

Step 1. Determine which modules provide the required connectivity.

  a. Click **East** and then click the Physical tab. On the left, beneath the Modules label, you see the available options to expand the capabilities of the router. Click each module. A picture and a description displays at the bottom. Familiarize yourself with these options.

  1) You need to connect PCs 1, 2, and 3 to the **East** router, but you do not have the necessary funds to purchase a new switch. Which module can you use to connect the three PCs to the **East** router? _____

  2) How many hosts can you connect to the router using this module? _____

  b. Click **Switch2**. Which module can you insert to provide a Gigabit optical connection to Switch3? _____

Step 2.   Add the correct modules and power up devices.

   a.   Click **East** and attempt to insert the appropriate module from Step 1a.

   b.   The `Cannot add a module when the power is on` message should display. Interfaces for this router model are not hot-swappable. The device must be turned off. Click the power switch located to the right of the Cisco logo to turn off **East**. Insert the appropriate module from Step 1a. When done, click the power switch to power up **East**.

Note: If you insert the wrong module and need to remove it, drag the module down to its picture in the bottom right corner, and release the mouse button.

---

   c.   Using the same procedure, insert the appropriate modules from Step 1b in the empty slot farthest to the right in both **Switch2** and **Switch3**.

   d.   Use the **show ip interface brief** command to identify the slot in which the module was placed.

   Into which slot was it inserted? _____

   e.   Click the **West** router. The **Physical** tab should be active. Install the appropriate module that will add a serial interface to the enhanced high-speed WAN interface card (**eHWIC 0**) slot on the right. You can cover any unused slots to prevent dust from entering the router (optional).

   f.   Use the appropriate command to verify that the new serial interfaces are installed.

Part 3: Connect Devices

This may be the first activity you have done where you are required to connect devices. Although you may not know the purpose of the different cable types, use the table below and follow these guidelines to successfully connect all the devices:

   a.   Select the appropriate cable type.

   b.   Click the first device and select the specified interface.

   c.   Click the second device and select the specified interface.

   d.   If you correctly connected two devices, you will see your score increase.

Example: To connect **East** to **Switch1**, select the **Copper Straight-Through** cable type. Click **East** and choose **GigabitEthernet0/0**. Then, click **Switch1** and choose **GigabitEthernet0/1**. Your score should now be 4/52.

Note: For the purposes of this activity, link lights are disabled. The devices are not configured with any IP addressing, so you are unable to test connectivity.

Device	Interface	Cable Type	Device	Interface
East	GigabitEthernet0/0	Copper Straight-Through	Switch1	GigabitEthernet0/1
East	GigabitEthernet0/1	Copper Straight-Through	Switch4	GigabitEthernet0/1
East	FastEthernet0/1/0	Copper Straight-Through	PC1	FastEthernet0
East	FastEthernet0/1/1	Copper Straight-Through	PC2	FastEthernet0

Device	Interface	Cable Type	Device	Interface
East	FastEthernet0/1/2	Copper Straight-Through	PC3	FastEthernet0
Switch1	FastEthernet0/1	Copper Straight-Through	PC4	FastEthernet0
Switch1	FastEthernet0/2	Copper Straight-Through	PC5	FastEthernet0
Switch1	FastEthernet0/3	Copper Straight-Through	PC6	FastEthernet0
Switch4	GigabitEthernet0/2	Copper Cross-Over	Switch3	GigabitEthernet3/1
Switch3	GigabitEthernet5/1	Fiber	Switch2	GigabitEthernet5/1
Switch2	FastEthernet0/1	Copper Straight-Through	PC7	FastEthernet0
Switch2	FastEthernet1/1	Copper Straight-Through	PC8	FastEthernet0
Switch2	FastEthernet2/1	Copper Straight-Through	PC9	FastEthernet0
East	Serial0/0/0	Serial DCE (connect to East first)	West	Serial0/0/0

Suggested Scoring Rubric

Activity Section	Question Location	Possible Points	Earned Points
Part 1: Identify Physical Characteristics of Internetworking Devices	Step 1c	4	
	Step 2a	4	
	Step 2b	4	
	Step 2c, q1	4	
	Step 2c, q2	4	
	Step 3a	4	
	Step 3b	4	
	Part 1 Total	28	
Part 2: Select Correct Modules for Connectivity	Step 1a, q1	5	
	Step 1a, q2	5	
	Step 1b	5	
	Step 2d	5	
	Part 2 Total	20	
	Packet Tracer Score	52	
	Total Score	100	

6.3.2.7 Lab–Exploring Router Physical Characteristics

Topology

Objectives

Part 1: Examine Router External Characteristics

Part 2: Examine Router Internal Characteristics Using Show Commands

Background/Scenario

In this lab, you will examine the outside of the router to become familiar with its characteristics and components, such as its power switch, management ports, LAN and WAN interfaces, indicator lights, network expansion slots, memory expansion slots, and USB ports.

You will also identify the internal components and characteristics of the IOS by consoling into the router and issuing various commands, such as **show version** and **show interfaces**, from the CLI.

Note: The routers used with CCNA hands-on labs are Cisco 1941 Integrated Services Routers (ISRs) with Cisco IOS Release 15.2(4)M3 (universalk9 image). Other routers and Cisco IOS versions can be used. Depending on the model and Cisco IOS version, the commands available and output produced might vary from what is shown in the labs.

Note: Make sure that the routers have been erased and have no startup configurations. If you are unsure, contact your instructor.

Required Resources

- 1 Router (Cisco 1941 with Cisco IOS Release 15.2(4)M3 universal image or comparable)
- 1 PC (Windows 7 or 8 with terminal emulation program, such as Tera Term)
- Console cables to configure the Cisco IOS devices via the console ports

Part 1: Examine Router External Characteristics

Use the images below, as well as your own direct inspection of the backplane of a Cisco router, to answer the following questions. Feel free to draw arrows and circle the areas of the image that correctly identify the parts.

Note: The router depicted in the images below is a Cisco 1941 router, which may be different from the make and model of the routers in your particular academy. You can find device information and specifications for the Cisco 1941 series routers at the Cisco.com website. Additional information, including answers to many of the questions below, can be found here: http://www.cisco.com/en/US/prod/collateral/routers/ps10538/data_sheet_c78_556319.html

Step 1.   Identify the various parts of a Cisco router.

The image shown in this step is of the backplane of a Cisco 1941 ISR. Use it to answer the questions in this step. In addition, if you are examining a different model router, a space has been provided here for you to draw the backplane and identify components and interfaces as specified in the questions that follow.

a.   Circle and label the router's power switch. Is the power switch on your router in the same area as the router depicted in the image?

b.   Circle and label the management ports. What are the built-in management ports? Are the management ports the same on your router? If not, how are they different?

c.   Circle and label the router's LAN interfaces. How many LAN interfaces does the router in the image have and what is the interface technology type? Are the LAN interfaces the same on your router? If not, how are they different?

d.   Circle and label the router's WAN interfaces. How many WAN interfaces does the router in the image have and what is the interface technology type? Are the WAN interfaces the same on your router? If not, how are they different?

e. The Cisco 1941 ISR is a modular platform and comes with module expansion slots for varied network connectivity requirements. Circle and label the module slots. How many module slots are there? How many are used? What type of module expansion slots are they? Are the module slots the same on your router? If not, how are they different?

_____

f. The Cisco 1941 router comes with CompactFlash memory slots for high speed storage. Circle and label the CompactFlash memory slots. How many memory slots are there? How many are used? How much memory can they hold? Are the memory slots the same on your router? If not, how are they different?

_____

g. The Cisco 1941 router comes with USB 2.0 ports. The built-in USB ports support eToken devices and USB flash memory. The USB eToken device feature provides device authentication and secure configuration of Cisco routers. The USB flash feature provides optional secondary storage capability and an additional boot device. Circle and label the USB ports. How many USB ports are there? Are there USB ports on your router?

_____

h. The Cisco 1941 router also comes with a mini-B USB console port. Circle and label the mini-B USB console port.

_____

Step 2. Examine the router activity and status lights.

The following images highlight the activity and status lights of the front panel and backplane of a powered up and connected Cisco 1941 ISR.

_____

Note: Some of the indicator lights are obscured from view in the image of the backplane of the Cisco 1941 router below.

_____

a. In the top image above, examine the indicator lights on the front panel of the router. The lights are labeled SYS, ACT, and POE. To what do the labels refer? What do the lights in the image indicate about the status of the router? These labels would be readable if they were not lit.

_____

_____

_____

b. In the backplane image, examine the indicator lights on the router. There are three visible activity lights, one for each of the connected interfaces and management ports. Examine the interface lights on your router. How are the lights labeled, and what is their meaning?

_____

_____

_____

c. Aside from the management ports and network interfaces, what other indicator lights are on the backplane of the router and what might their purpose be?

_____

_____

_____

Part 2: Examine Router Internal Characteristics Using Show Commands

Step 1. Establish a console connection to the router and use the **show version** command.

a. Using Tera Term, console into the router and enter privileged EXEC mode using the enable command:

```
Router> enable
Router#
```

b. Display information about the router by using the **show version** command. Use the Spacebar on the keyboard to page through the output.

```
Router# show version
Cisco IOS Software, C1900 Software (C1900-UNIVERSALK9-M), Version 15.2(4)M3,
RELEASE SOFTWARE (fc1)
Technical Support: http://www.cisco.com/techsupport
Copyright (c) 1986-2011 by Cisco Systems, Inc.
Compiled Thu 26-Jul-12 19:34 by prod_rel_team

ROM: System Bootstrap, Version 15.0(1r)M15, RELEASE SOFTWARE (fc1)

Router uptime is 1 day, 14 hours, 46 minutes
System returned to ROM by power-on
System restarted at 07:26:55 UTC Mon Dec 3 2012
System image file is "flash0:c1900-universalk9-mz.SPA.152-4.M3.bin"
Last reload type: Normal Reload
Last reload reason: power-on

<output omitted>

If you require further assistance please contact us by sending email to
export@cisco.com.

Cisco CISCO1941/K9 (revision 1.0) with 487424K/36864K bytes of memory.
Processor board ID FGL16082318
2 Gigabit Ethernet interfaces
2 Serial(sync/async) interfaces
1 terminal line
1 Virtual Private Network (VPN) Module
DRAM configuration is 64 bits wide with parity disabled.
255K bytes of non-volatile configuration memory.
250880K bytes of ATA System CompactFlash 0 (Read/Write)
<output omitted>

Technology Package License Information for Module:'c1900'

-----------------------------------------------------------------
Technology    Technology-package        Technology-package
              Current       Type        Next reboot
-----------------------------------------------------------------
ipbase        ipbasek9      Permanent   ipbasek9
security      securityk9    Permanent   securityk9
data          None          None        None

Configuration register is 0x2102
```

c. Based on the output of the **show version** command, answer the following questions about the router. If you are examining a different model router, include the information about it here.

1) What is the version of the Cisco IOS and what is the system image filename?

_____

2) What is the Bootstrap program version in ROM BIOS?

_____

3) How long has the router been running without a restart (also known as its uptime)?

_____

4) How much dynamic random access memory (DRAM) does the router have?

_____

5) What is the router's processor board ID number?

_____

6) What network interfaces does the router have?

_____

7) How much CompactFlash memory for IOS storage is there?

_____

8) How much nonvolatile random access memory (NVRAM) for configuration file storage is there?

_____

9) What is the setting of the configuration register?

_____

Step 2.　Use the **show interface** command to examine the network interfaces.

a.　Use the **show interface gigabitEthernet 0/0** command to see the status of the Gigabit Ethernet 0/0 interface.

Note　After typing part of the command, for example, **show interface g**, you can use the **Tab** key on your keyboard to complete the gigabitEthernet command parameter.

```
Router# show interface gigabitEthernet 0/0
GigabitEthernet0/0 is administratively down, line protocol is down
  Hardware is CN Gigabit Ethernet, address is 442b.031a.b9a0 (bia 442b.031a.
b9a0)
    MTU 1500 bytes, BW 100000 Kbit/sec, DLY 100 usec,
       reliability 255/255, txload 1/255, rxload 1/255
    Encapsulation ARPA, loopback not set
    Keepalive set (10 sec)
    Full Duplex, 100Mbps, media type is RJ45
    output flow-control is unsupported, input flow-control is unsupported
    ARP type: ARPA, ARP Timeout 04:00:00
    Last input never, output never, output hang never
    Last clearing of "show interface" counters never
```

```
Input queue: 0/75/0/0 (size/max/drops/flushes); Total output drops: 0
Queueing strategy: fifo
Output queue: 0/40 (size/max)
5 minute input rate 0 bits/sec, 0 packets/sec
5 minute output rate 0 bits/sec, 0 packets/sec
   3 packets input, 276 bytes, 0 no buffer
   Received 0 broadcasts (0 IP multicasts)
   0 runts, 0 giants, 0 throttles
   0 input errors, 0 CRC, 0 frame, 0 overrun, 0 ignored
   0 watchdog, 0 multicast, 0 pause input
   0 packets output, 0 bytes, 0 underruns
   0 output errors, 0 collisions, 0 interface resets
   0 unknown protocol drops
   0 babbles, 0 late collision, 0 deferred
   0 lost carrier, 0 no carrier, 0 pause output
   0 output buffer failures, 0 output buffers swapped out
```

b. Given the output of the **show interface gigabitEthernet 0/0** command depicted above, or using the output from your router, answer the following questions:

What is the hardware type and MAC address of the Gigabit Ethernet interface?

What is the interface media type? Is the interface up or down?

c. Use the **show interfaces serial 0/0/0** command to view the status of the Serial 0/0/0 interface.

```
Router# show interface serial 0/0/0

Serial0/0/0 is administratively down, line protocol is down
  Hardware is WIC MBRD Serial
  MTU 1500 bytes, BW 1544 Kbit/sec, DLY 20000 usec,
     reliability 255/255, txload 1/255, rxload 1/255
  Encapsulation HDLC, loopback not set
  Keepalive set (10 sec)
  Last input 07:41:21, output never, output hang never
  Last clearing of "show interface" counters never
  Input queue: 0/75/0/0 (size/max/drops/flushes); Total output drops: 0
  Queueing strategy: fifo
  Output queue: 0/40 (size/max)
  5 minute input rate 0 bits/sec, 0 packets/sec
  5 minute output rate 0 bits/sec, 0 packets/sec
     1 packets input, 24 bytes, 0 no buffer
     Received 1 broadcasts (0 IP multicasts)
     0 runts, 0 giants, 0 throttles
     0 input errors, 0 CRC, 0 frame, 0 overrun, 0 ignored, 0 abort
     0 packets output, 0 bytes, 0 underruns
     0 output errors, 0 collisions, 2 interface resets
     0 unknown protocol drops
     0 output buffer failures, 0 output buffers swapped out
     1 carrier transitions
  DCD=down  DSR=down  DTR=down  RTS=down  CTS=down
```

d. Given the output command depicted above, answer the following questions:

What is the frame encapsulation type?

_____

What is the hardware type? Is the interface up or down?

_____

Reflection

1. Why might you need to use an EHWIC expansion slot?

_____

2. Why might you need to upgrade the Flash memory?

_____

3. What is the purpose of the mini-USB port?

_____

_____

4. What is the purpose of the ISM/WLAN indicator light on the backplane of the router? To what does it refer?

_____

_____

_____

_____

6.4.1.3 Packet Tracer–Configure Initial Router Settings

Topology

PCA   R1

Objectives

Part 1: Verify the Default Router Configuration

Part 2: Configure and Verify the Initial Router Configuration

Part 3: Save the Running Configuration File

Background

In this activity, you will perform basic router configurations. You will secure access to the CLI and console port using encrypted and plain text passwords. You will also configure messages for users logging into the router. These banners also warn unauthorized users that access is prohibited. Finally, you will verify and save your running configuration.

Part 1: Verify the Default Router Configuration

Step 1. Establish a console connection to R1.

    a. Choose a **Console** cable from the available connections.

    b. Click **PCA** and select **RS 232**.

    c. Click **R1** and select **Console**.

    d. Click **PCA > Desktop** tab > **Terminal**.

    e. Click **OK** and press **ENTER**. You are now able to configure **R1**.

Step 2. Enter privileged mode and examine the current configuration.

You can access all the router commands from privileged EXEC mode. However, because many of the privileged commands configure operating parameters, privileged access should be password-protected to prevent unauthorized use.

    a. Enter privileged EXEC mode by entering the **enable** command.

```
Router> enable
Router#
```

Notice that the prompt changed in the configuration to reflect privileged EXEC mode.

    b. Enter the **show running-config** command:

```
Router# show running-config
```

c. Answer the following questions:

What is the router's hostname? _____

How many Fast Ethernet interfaces does the router have? _____

How many Gigabit Ethernet interfaces does the router have? _____

How many Serial interfaces does the router have? _____

What is the range of values shown for the vty lines? _____

d. Display the current contents of NVRAM.

```
Router# show startup-config
startup-config is not present
```

Why does the router respond with the `startup-config is not present` message?

_____

Part 2: Configure and Verify the Initial Router Configuration

To configure parameters on a router, you may be required to move between various configuration modes. Notice how the prompt changes as you navigate through the router.

Step 1.   Configure the initial settings on R1.

Note: If you have difficulty remembering the commands, refer to the content for this topic. The commands are the same as you configured on a switch.

a. **R1** as the hostname.

b. Use the following passwords:

1) Console: **letmein**

2) Privileged EXEC, unencrypted: **cisco**

3) Privileged EXEC, encrypted: **itsasecret**

c. Encrypt all plain text passwords.

d. Message of the day text: `Unauthorized access is strictly prohibited.`

Step 2.   Verify the initial settings on R1.

a. Verify the initial settings by viewing the configuration for R1. What command do you use? _____

b. Exit the current console session until you see the following message:

```
R1 con0 is now available


Press RETURN to get started.
```

c. Press **ENTER**; you should see the following message:

```
Unauthorized access is strictly prohibited.


User Access Verification


Password:
```

Why should every router have a message-of-the-day (MOTD) banner?

_____

_____

_____

If you are not prompted for a password, what console line command did you forget to configure? _____

d. Enter the passwords necessary to return to privileged EXEC mode.

Why would the **enable secret** password allow access to the privileged EXEC mode and the **enable** password no longer be valid? _____

_____

_____

If you configure any more passwords on the router, are they displayed in the configuration file as plain text or in encrypted form? Explain. _____

_____

Part 3: Save the Running Configuration File

Step 1. Save the configuration file to NVRAM.

a. You have configured the initial settings for R1. Now back up the running configuration file to NVRAM to ensure that the changes made are not lost if the system is rebooted or loses power.

What command did you enter to save the configuration to NVRAM? _____

_____

What is the shortest, unambiguous version of this command? _____

Which command displays the contents of the NVRAM? _____

_____

b. Verify that all of the parameters configured are recorded. If not, analyze the output and determine which commands were not done or were entered incorrectly. You can also click **Check Results** in the instruction window.

Step 2. Optional bonus: Save the startup configuration file to flash.

Although you will be learning more about managing the flash storage in a router in later chapters, you may be interested to know now that—as an added backup procedure—you can save your startup configuration file to flash. By default, the router still loads the startup configuration from NVRAM, but if NVRAM becomes corrupt, you can restore the startup configuration by copying it over from flash.

Complete the following steps to save the startup configuration to flash.

a. Examine the contents of flash using the **show flash** command:

```
R1# show flash
```

How many files are currently stored in flash? _____

Which of these files would you guess is the IOS image? _____

_____

Why do you think this file is the IOS image? _____

_____

b. Save the startup configuration file to flash using the following commands:

```
R1# copy startup-config flash
Destination filename [startup-config]
```

The router prompts to store the file in flash using the name in brackets. If the answer is yes, then press **ENTER**; if not, type an appropriate name and press **ENTER**.

c. Use the **show flash** command to verify the startup configuration file is now stored in flash.

Suggested Scoring Rubric

Activity Section	Question Location	Possible Points	Earned Points
Part 1: Verify the Default Router Configuration	Step 2c	10	
	Step 2d	2	
	Part 1 Total	**12**	
Part 2: Configure and Verify the Initial Router Configuration	Step 2a	2	
	Step 2c	5	
	Step 2d	6	
	Part 2 Total	**13**	
Part 3: Save the Running Configuration File	Step 1a	5	
	Step 2a (bonus)	5	
	Part 3 Total	**10**	
	Packet Tracer Score	**80**	
	Total Score (with bonus)	**115**	

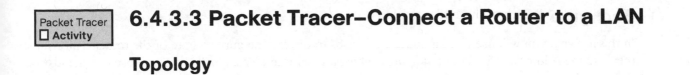

6.4.3.3 Packet Tracer–Connect a Router to a LAN

Topology

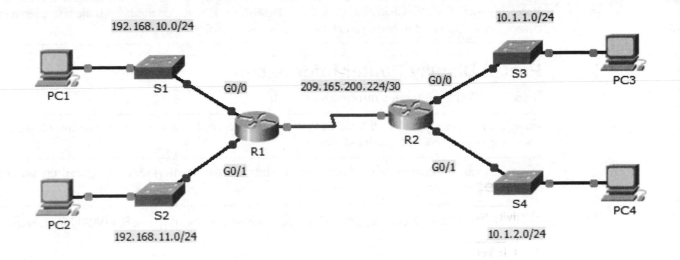

Addressing Table

Device	Interface	IP Address	Subnet Mask	Default Gateway
R1	G0/0	192.168.10.1	255.255.255.0	N/A
	G0/1	192.168.11.1	255.255.255.0	N/A
	S0/0/0 (DCE)	209.165.200.225	255.255.255.252	N/A
R2	G0/0	10.1.1.1	255.255.255.0	N/A
	G0/1	10.1.2.1	255.255.255.0	N/A
	S0/0/0	209.165.200.226	255.255.255.252	N/A
PC1	NIC	192.168.10.10	255.255.255.0	192.168.10.1
PC2	NIC	192.168.11.10	255.255.255.0	192.168.11.1
PC3	NIC	10.1.1.10	255.255.255.0	10.1.1.1
PC4	NIC	10.1.2.10	255.255.255.0	10.1.2.1

Objectives

Part 1: Display Router Information

Part 2: Configure Router Interfaces

Part 3: Verify the Configuration

Background

In this activity, you will use various **show** commands to display the current state of the router. You will then use the Addressing Table to configure router Ethernet interfaces. Finally, you will use commands to verify and test your configurations.

Note: The routers in this activity are partially configured. Some of the configurations are not covered in this course, but are provided to assist you in using verification commands.

Part 1: Display Router Information

Step 1.   Display interface information on R1.

Note: Click a device and then click the **CLI** tab to access the command line directly. The console password is **cisco**. The privileged EXEC password is **class**.

    a.   Which command displays the statistics for all interfaces configured on a router?

    b.   Which command displays the information about the Serial 0/0/0 interface only?

    c.   Enter the command to display the statistics for the Serial 0/0/0 interface on R1 and answer the following questions:

        What is the IP address configured on R1? _____

        What is the bandwidth on the Serial 0/0/0 interface? _____

    d.   Enter the command to display the statistics for the GigabitEthernet 0/0 interface and answer the following questions:

        1)   What is the IP address on R1? _____

        2)   What is the MAC address of the GigabitEthernet 0/0 interface? _____

        3)   What is the bandwidth on the GigabitEthernet 0/0 interface? _____

Step 2.   Display a summary list of the interfaces on R1.

    a.   Which command displays a brief summary of the current interfaces, statuses, and IP addresses assigned to them? _____

    b.   Enter the command on each router and answer the following questions:

        1)   How many serial interfaces are there on R1 and R2? _____

        2)   How many Ethernet interfaces are there on R1 and R2? _____

        3)   Are all the Ethernet interfaces on R1 the same? If no, explain the difference(s).

Step 3.   Display the routing table on R1.

    a.   What command displays the content of the routing table? _____

    b.   Enter the command on R1 and answer the following questions:

      1)   How many connected routes are there (uses the C code)? _____

      2)   Which route is listed? _____

      3)   How does a router handle a packet destined for a network that is not listed in the routing table? _____

Part 2: Configure Router Interfaces

Step 1.   Configure the GigabitEthernet 0/0 interface on R1.

    a.   Enter the following commands to address and activate the GigabitEthernet 0/0 interface on R1:

```
R1(config)# interface gigabitethernet 0/0
R1(config-if)# ip address 192.168.10.1 255.255.255.0
R1(config-if)# no shutdown
%LINK-5-CHANGED: Interface GigabitEthernet0/0, changed state to up
%LINEPROTO-5-UPDOWN: Line protocol on Interface GigabitEthernet0/0, changed
state to up
```

    b.   It is good practice to configure a description for each interface to help document the network information. Configure an interface description indicating to which device it is connected.

```
R1(config-if)# description LAN connection to S1
```

    c.   R1 should now be able to ping PC1.

```
R1(config-if)# end
%SYS-5-CONFIG_I: Configured from console by console
R1# ping 192.168.10.10

Type escape sequence to abort.
Sending 5, 100-byte ICMP Echos to 192.168.10.10, timeout is 2 seconds:
.!!!!
Success rate is 80 percent (4/5), round-trip min/avg/max = 0/2/8 ms
```

Step 2.   Configure the remaining Gigabit Ethernet Interfaces on R1 and R2.

    a.   Use the information in the Addressing Table to finish the interface configurations for R1 and R2. For each interface, do the following:

      1)   Enter the IP address and activate the interface.

      2)   Configure an appropriate description.

    b.   Verify interface configurations.

Step 3.   Back up the configurations to NVRAM.

Save the configuration files on both routers to NVRAM. What command did you use?

Part 3: Verify the Configuration

Step 1. Use verification commands to check your interface configurations.

   a. Use the **show ip interface brief** command on both **R1** and **R2** to quickly verify that the interfaces are configured with the correct IP address and active.

   How many interfaces on **R1** and **R2** are configured with IP addresses and in the "up" and "up" state? _____

   What part of the interface configuration is NOT displayed in the command output?

   _____

   What commands can you use to verify this part of the configuration? _____

   b. Use the **show ip route** command on both **R1** and **R2** to view the current routing tables and answer the following questions:

   1) How many connected routes (uses the **C** code) do you see on each router? _____

   2) How many EIGRP routes (uses the **D** code) do you see on each router?_____

   3) If the router knows all the routes in the network, then the number of connected routes and dynamically learned routes (EIGRP) should equal the total number of LANs and WANs. How many LANs and WANs are in the topology? _____

   4) Does this number match the number of C and D routes shown in the routing table? _____

Note: If your answer is "no," then you are missing a required configuration. Review the steps in Part 2.

Step 2. Test end-to-end connectivity across the network.

You should now be able to ping from any PC to any other PC on the network. In addition, you should be able to ping the active interfaces on the routers. For example, the following should tests should be successful:

- From the command line on PC1, ping PC4.
- From the command line on R2, ping PC2.

Note: For simplicity in this activity, the switches are not configured; you will not be able to ping them.

Suggested Scoring Rubric

Activity Section	Question Location	Possible Points	Earned Points
Part 1: Display Router Information	Step 1a	2	
	Step 1b	2	
	Step 1c	4	
	Step 1d	6	
	Step 2a	2	
	Step 2b	6	
	Step 3a	2	
	Step 3b	6	

Activity Section	Question Location	Possible Points	Earned Points
	Part 1 Total	30	
Part 2: Configure Router Interfaces	Step 3	2	
	Part 2 Total	2	
Part 3: Verify the Configuration	Step 1a	6	
	Step 1b	8	
	Part 3 Total	14	
	Packet Tracer Score	54	
	Total Score	100	

Packet Tracer–Troubleshooting Default Gateway Issues

Topology

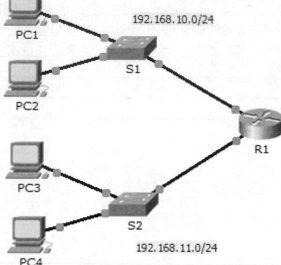

Addressing Table

Device	Interface	IP Address	Subnet Mask	Default Gateway
R1	G0/0	192.168.10.1	255.255.255.0	N/A
	G0/1	192.168.11.1	255.255.255.0	N/A
S1	VLAN 1	192.168.10.2	255.255.255.0	
S2	VLAN 1	192.168.11.2	255.255.255.0	
PC1	NIC	192.168.10.10	255.255.255.0	
PC2	NIC	192.168.10.11	255.255.255.0	
PC3	NIC	192.168.11.10	255.255.255.0	
PC4	NIC	192.168.11.11	255.255.255.0	

Objectives

Part 1: Verify Network Documentation and Isolate Problems

Part 2: Implement, Verify, and Document Solutions

Background

For a device to communicate across multiple networks, it must be configured with an IP address, subnet mask, and a default gateway. The default gateway is used when the host wants to send a packet to a device on another network. The default gateway address is generally the router interface address attached to the local network to which the host is connected. In this activity, you will finish documenting the network. You will then verify the network documentation by testing end-to-end connectivity and troubleshooting issues. The troubleshooting method you will use consists of the following steps:

1. Verify the network documentation and use tests to isolate problems.

2. Determine an appropriate solution for a given problem.

3. Implement the solution.

4. Test to verify the problem is resolved.

5. Document the solution.

Throughout your CCNA studies, you will encounter different descriptions of the troubleshooting method, as well as different ways to test and document issues and solutions. This is intentional. There is no set standard or template for troubleshooting. Each organization develops unique processes and documentation standards (even if that process is "we don't have one"). However, all effective troubleshooting methodologies generally include the above steps.

Note: If you are proficient with default gateway configurations, this activity might seem more involved than it should be. You can, most likely, quickly discover and solve all the connectivity issues faster than following these procedures. However, as you proceed in your studies, the networks and problems you encounter will become increasingly more complex. In such situations, the only effective way to isolate and solve issues is to use a methodical approach such as the one used in this activity.

Part 1: Verify Network Documentation and Isolate Problems

In Part 1 of this activity, complete the documentation and perform connectivity tests to discover issues. In addition, you will determine an appropriate solution for implementation in Part 2.

Step 1.   Verify the network documentation and isolate any problems.

   a.   Before you can effectively test a network, you must have complete documentation. Notice in the **Addressing Table** that some information is missing. Complete the **Addressing Table** by filling in the missing default gateway information for the switches and the PCs.

   b.   Test connectivity to devices on the same network. By isolating and correcting any local access issues, you can better test remote connectivity with the confidence that local connectivity is operational.

   A verification plan can be as simple as a list of connectivity tests. Use the following tests to verify local connectivity and isolate any access issues. The first issue is already documented, but you must implement and verify the solution during Part 2.

Testing and Verification Documentation

Test	Successful?	Issues	Solution	Verified
PC1 to PC2	No	IP address on PC1	Change PC1 IP address	
PC1 to S1				
PC1 to R1				

Note: The table is an example; you must create your own document. You can use paper and pencil to draw a table, or you can use a text editor or spreadsheet. Consult your instructor if you need further guidance.

    c. Test connectivity to remote devices (such as from PC1 to PC4) and document any problems. This is frequently referred to as *end-to-end connectivity*. This means that all devices in a network have the full connectivity allowed by the network policy.

Note: Remote connectivity testing may not be possible yet, because you must first resolve local connectivity issues. After you have solved those issues, return to this step and test connectivity between networks.

Step 2. Determine an appropriate solution for the problem.

    a. Using your knowledge of the way networks operate and your device configuration skills, search for the cause of the problem. For example, S1 is not the cause of the connectivity issue between PC1 and PC2. The link lights are green and no configuration on S1 would cause traffic to not pass between PC1 and PC2. So the problem must be with PC1, PC2, or both.

    b. Verify the device addressing to ensure it matches the network documentation. For example, the IP address for PC1 is incorrect as verified with the **ipconfig** command.

    c. Suggest a solution that you think will resolve the problem and document it. For example, change the IP address for PC1 to match the documentation.

Note: Often there is more than one solution. However, it is a troubleshooting best practice to implement one solution at a time. Implementing more than one solution could introduce additional issues in a more complex scenario.

Part 2: Implement, Verify, and Document Solutions

In Part 2 of this activity, you will implement the solutions you identified in Part 1. You will then verify the solution worked. You may need to return to Part 1 to finish isolating all the problems.

Step 1. Implement solutions to connectivity problems.

Refer to your documentation in Part 1. Choose the first issue and implement your suggested solution. For example, correct the IP address on PC1.

Step 2. Verify that the problem is now resolved.

    a. Verify your solution has solved the problem by performing the test you used to identify the problem. For example, can PC1 now ping PC2?

    b. If the problem is resolved, indicate so in your documentation. For example, in the table above, a simple checkmark would suffice in the "Verified" column.

Step 3. Verify that all issues are resolved.

    a. If you still have an outstanding issue with a solution that has not yet been implemented, return to Part 2, Step 1.

    b. If all your current issues are resolved, have you also resolved any remote connectivity issues (such as can PC1 ping PC4)? If the answer is no, return to Part 1, Step 1c to test remote connectivity.

Suggested Scoring Rubric

Task	Possible Points	Earned Points
Complete Network Documentation	20	
Document Issues and Solutions	45	
Packet Tracer Score (Issues Resolved)	35	
Total Score	100	

6.5.1.1 Class Activity–Can You Read This Map?

Objectives

Explain how network devices use routing tables to direct packets to a destination network.

Background/Scenario

Note: It is suggested that students work in pairs; however, if preferred, students can complete this activity individually.

Your instructor will provide you with output generated by a router's **show ip route** command. Use Packet Tracer to build a topology model using this routing information.

At a minimum, the following should be used in your topology model:

- 1 Catalyst 2960 switch
- 1 Cisco Series 1941 Router with one HWIC-4ESW switching port modular card and IOS version 15.1 or higher
- 3 PCs (can be servers, generic PCs, laptops, and so on)

Use the note tool in Packet Tracer to indicate the addresses of the router interfaces and possible addresses for the end devices you chose for your model.

Label all end devices, ports, and addresses ascertained from the **show ip route** output/routing table information in your Packet Tracer file. Save your work in hard or soft copy to share with the class.

Required Resources

- Packet Tracer software program.
- Routing **Table 1** – Students can use the table to assist each other as they read the information provided and then construct the model using Packet Tracer.

Table 1

```
R1# show ip route
Codes: L - local, C - connected, S - static, R - RIP, M - mobile, B -
BGP
D - EIGRP, EX - EIGRP external, O - OSPF, IA - OSPF inter area
N1 - OSPF NSSA external type 1, N2 - OSPF NSSA external type 2
E1 - OSPF external type 1, E2 - OSPF external type 2
i - IS-IS, su - IS-IS summary, L1 - IS-IS level-1, L2 - IS-IS level-2
ia - IS-IS inter area, * - candidate default, U - per-user static
route
o - ODR, P - periodic downloaded static route, H - NHRP, l - LISP
+ - replicated route, % - next hop override

Gateway of last resort is not set

      192.168.0.0/24 is variably subnetted, 2 subnets, 2 masks
C     192.168.0.0/24 is directly connected, GigabitEthernet0/0
L     192.168.0.1/32 is directly connected, GigabitEthernet0/0
      192.168.1.0/24 is variably subnetted, 2 subnets, 2 masks
C     192.168.1.0/24 is directly connected, GigabitEthernet0/1
L     192.168.1.1/32 is directly connected, GigabitEthernet0/1
```

Reflection

What was the hardest part of designing this network model? Explain your answer.

_____

_____

6.5.1.2 Lab – Building a Switch and Router Network

Topology

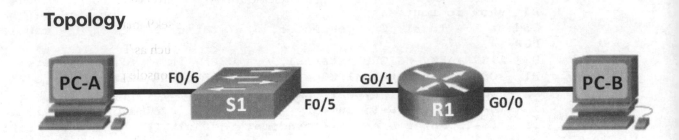

Addressing Table

Device	Interface	IP Address	Subnet Mask	Default Gateway
R1	G0/0	192.168.0.1	255.255.255.0	N/A
	G0/1	192.168.1.1	255.255.255.0	N/A
PC-A	NIC	192.168.1.3	255.255.255.0	192.168.1.1
PC-B	NIC	192.168.0.3	255.255.255.0	192.168.0.1

Objectives

Part 1: Set Up the Topology and Initialize Devices

Part 2: Configure Devices and Verify Connectivity

Part 3: Display Device Information

Background/Scenario

This is a comprehensive lab to review previously covered IOS commands. In this lab, you will cable the equipment as shown in the topology diagram. You will then configure the devices to match the addressing table. After the configurations have been saved, you will verify your configurations by testing for network connectivity.

After the devices have been configured and network connectivity has been verified, you will use IOS commands to retrieve information from the devices to answer questions about your network equipment.

This lab provides minimal assistance with the actual commands necessary to configure the router. Test your knowledge by trying to configure the devices without referring to the appendix.

Note: The routers used with CCNA hands-on labs are Cisco 1941 Integrated Services Routers (ISRs) with Cisco IOS Release 15.2(4)M3 (universalk9 image). The switches used are Cisco Catalyst 2960s with Cisco IOS Release 15.0(2) (lanbasek9 image). Other routers, switches, and Cisco IOS versions can be used. Depending on the model and Cisco IOS version, the commands available and output produced might vary from what is shown in the labs. Refer to the Router Interface Summary Table at the end of this lab for the correct interface identifiers.

Note: Ensure that the routers and switches have been erased and have no startup configurations. Refer to Appendix B for the procedure to initialize and reload a router and switch.

Required Resources

- 1 Router (Cisco 1941 with Cisco IOS Release 15.2(4)M3 universal image or comparable)
- 1 Switch (Cisco 2960 with Cisco IOS Release 15.0(2) lanbasek9 image or comparable)
- 2 PCs (Windows 7 or 8 with terminal emulation program, such as Tera Term)
- Console cables to configure the Cisco IOS devices via the console ports
- Ethernet cables as shown in the topology

Note: The Gigabit Ethernet interfaces on Cisco 1941 routers are autosensing and an Ethernet straight-through cable may be used between the router and PC-B. If using another model Cisco router, it may be necessary to use an Ethernet crossover cable.

Part 1: Set Up Topology and Initialize Devices

Step 1.   Cable the network as shown in the topology.

    a.   Attach the devices shown in the topology diagram, and cable, as necessary.

    b.   Power on all the devices in the topology.

Step 2.   Initialize and reload the router and switch.

    If configuration files were previously saved on the router and switch, initialize and reload these devices back to their basic configurations. For information on how to initialize and reload these devices, refer to Appendix B.

Part 2: Configure Devices and Verify Connectivity

In Part 2, you will set up the network topology and configure basic settings, such as the interface IP addresses, device access, and passwords. Refer to the Topology and Addressing Table at the beginning of this lab for device names and address information.

Note: Appendix A provides configuration details for the steps in Part 2. You should attempt to complete Part 2 prior to reviewing this appendix.

Step 1.   Assign static IP information to the PC interfaces.

    a.   Configure the IP address, subnet mask, and default gateway settings on PC-A.

    b.   Configure the IP address, subnet mask, and default gateway settings on PC-B.

    c.   Ping PC-B from a command prompt window on PC-A.

    Why were the pings not successful?

Step 2.   Configure the router.

    a.   Console into the router and enable privileged EXEC mode.

    b.   Enter configuration mode.

    c.   Assign a device name to the router.

    d. Disable DNS lookup to prevent the router from attempting to translate incorrectly entered commands as though they were hostnames.

    e. Assign **class** as the privileged EXEC encrypted password.

    f. Assign **cisco** as the console password and enable login.

    g. Assign **cisco** as the VTY password and enable login.

    h. Encrypt the clear text passwords.

    i. Create a banner that warns anyone accessing the device that unauthorized access is prohibited.

    j. Configure and activate both interfaces on the router.

    k. Configure an interface description for each interface indicating which device is connected to it.

    l. Save the running configuration to the startup configuration file.

    m. Set the clock on the router.

Note: Use the question mark (?) to help with the correct sequence of parameters needed to execute this command.

    n. Ping PC-B from a command prompt window on PC-A.

        Were the pings successful? Why or why not?

_____

_____

_____

Part 3: Display Device Information

In Part 3, you will use **show** commands to retrieve information from the router and switch.

Step 1.   Retrieve hardware and software information from the network devices.

    a. Use the **show version** command to answer the following questions about the router.

        What is the name of the IOS image that the router is running?

_____

        How much DRAM memory does the router have?

_____

_____

        How much NVRAM memory does the router have?

_____

        How much Flash memory does the router have?

_____

b. Use the **show version** command to answer the following questions about the switch.

What is the name of the IOS image that the switch is running?

_____

How much dynamic random access memory (DRAM) does the switch have?

_____

How much nonvolatile random access memory (NVRAM) does the switch have?

_____

What is the model number of the switch?

_____

Step 2. Display the routing table on the router.

Use the **show ip route** command on the router to answer the following questions.

What code is used in the routing table to indicate a directly connected network? _____

How many route entries are coded with a C code in the routing table? _____

What interface types are associated to the C coded routes?

_____

Step 3. Display interface information on the router.

Use the **show interfaces g0/1** command to answer the following questions.

What is the operational status of the G0/1 interface?

_____

What is the Media Access Control (MAC) address of the G0/1 interface?

_____

How is the Internet address displayed in this command?

_____

Step 4. Display a summary list of the interfaces on the router and switch.

There are several commands that can be used to verify an interface configuration. One of the most useful of these is the **show ip interface brief** command. The command output displays a summary list of the interfaces on the device and provides immediate feedback to the status of each interface.

a. Enter the **show ip interface brief** command on the router.

```
R1# show ip interface brief
Interface                  IP-Address      OK? Method Status                Protocol
Embedded-Service-Engine0/0 unassigned      YES unset  administratively down down
GigabitEthernet0/0         192.168.0.1     YES manual up                    up
GigabitEthernet0/1         192.168.1.1     YES manual up                    up
Serial0/0/0                unassigned      YES unset  administratively down down
Serial0/0/1                unassigned      YES unset  administratively down down
R1#
```

b. Enter the **show ip interface brief** command on the switch.

```
Switch# show ip interface brief
Interface           IP-Address      OK? Method Status
Protocol
Vlan1               unassigned      YES manual up                      up
FastEthernet0/1     unassigned      YES unset  down                    down
FastEthernet0/2     unassigned      YES unset  down                    down
FastEthernet0/3     unassigned      YES unset  down                    down
FastEthernet0/4     unassigned      YES unset  down                    down
FastEthernet0/5     unassigned      YES unset  up                      up
FastEthernet0/6     unassigned      YES unset  up                      up
FastEthernet0/7     unassigned      YES unset  down                    down
FastEthernet0/8     unassigned      YES unset  down                    down
FastEthernet0/9     unassigned      YES unset  down                    down
FastEthernet0/10    unassigned      YES unset  down                    down
FastEthernet0/11    unassigned      YES unset  down                    down
FastEthernet0/12    unassigned      YES unset  down                    down
FastEthernet0/13    unassigned      YES unset  down                    down
FastEthernet0/14    unassigned      YES unset  down                    down
FastEthernet0/15    unassigned      YES unset  down                    down
FastEthernet0/16    unassigned      YES unset  down                    down
FastEthernet0/17    unassigned      YES unset  down                    down
FastEthernet0/18    unassigned      YES unset  down                    down
FastEthernet0/19    unassigned      YES unset  down                    down
FastEthernet0/20    unassigned      YES unset  down                    down
FastEthernet0/21    unassigned      YES unset  down                    down
FastEthernet0/22    unassigned      YES unset  down                    down
FastEthernet0/23    unassigned      YES unset  down                    down
FastEthernet0/24    unassigned      YES unset  down                    down
GigabitEthernet0/1  unassigned      YES unset  down                    down
GigabitEthernet0/2  unassigned      YES unset  down                    down
Switch#
```

Reflection

1. If the G0/1 interface showed administratively down, what interface configuration command would you use to turn the interface up?

   _____

2. What would happen if you had incorrectly configured interface G0/1 on the router with an IP address of 192.168.1.2?

   _____

   _____

Router Interface Summary Table

Router Interface Summary

Router Model	Ethernet Interface #1	Ethernet Interface #2	Serial Interface #1	Serial Interface #2
1800	Fast Ethernet 0/0 (F0/0)	Fast Ethernet 0/1 (F0/1)	Serial 0/0/0 (S0/0/0)	Serial 0/0/1 (S0/0/1)
1900	Gigabit Ethernet 0/0 (G0/0)	Gigabit Ethernet 0/1 (G0/1)	Serial 0/0/0 (S0/0/0)	Serial 0/0/1 (S0/0/1)
2801	Fast Ethernet 0/0 (F0/0)	Fast Ethernet 0/1 (F0/1)	Serial 0/1/0 (S0/1/0)	Serial 0/1/1 (S0/1/1)
2811	Fast Ethernet 0/0 (F0/0)	Fast Ethernet 0/1 (F0/1)	Serial 0/0/0 (S0/0/0)	Serial 0/0/1 (S0/0/1)
2900	Gigabit Ethernet 0/0 (G0/0)	Gigabit Ethernet 0/1 (G0/1)	Serial 0/0/0 (S0/0/0)	Serial 0/0/1 (S0/0/1)

Note: To find out how the router is configured, look at the interfaces to identify the router type and how many interfaces the router has. There is no way to effectively list all the combinations of configurations for each router class. This table includes identifiers for the possible combinations of Ethernet and Serial interfaces in the device. The table does not include any other type of interface, even though a specific router may contain one. An example of this might be an ISDN BRI interface. The string in parentheses is the legal abbreviation that can be used in Cisco IOS commands to represent the interface.

Packet Tracer
☐ Activity

6.5.1.3 Packet Tracer—Skills Integration Challenge

Topology

You will receive one of three possible topologies.

Addressing Table

Device	Interface	IP Address	Subnet Mask	Default Gateway
[[R1Name]]	G0/0	[[R1G0Add]]	255.255.255.0	N/A
	G0/1	[[R1G1Add]]	255.255.255.0	N/A
[[S1Name]]	VLAN 1	[[S1Add]]	255.255.255.0	
[[S2Name]]	VLAN 1	[[S2Add]]	255.255.255.0	
[[PC1Name]]	NIC	[[PC1Add]]	255.255.255.0	
[[PC2Name]]	NIC	[[PC2Add]]	255.255.255.0	
[[PC3Name]]	NIC	[[PC3Add]]	255.255.255.0	
[[PC4Name]]	NIC	[[PC4Add]]	255.255.255.0	

Objectives

- Finish the network documentation.
- Perform basic device configurations on a router and a switch.
- Verify connectivity and troubleshoot any issues.

Scenario

Your network manager is impressed with your performance in your job as a LAN technician. She would like you to now demonstrate your ability to configure a router connecting two LANs. Your tasks include configuring basic settings on a router and a switch using the Cisco IOS. You will then verify your configurations, as well as configurations on existing devices by testing end-to-end connectivity.

Note: After completing this activity, you can choose to click the **Reset Activity** button to generate a new set of requirements. Variable aspects include device names, IP addressing schemes, and the topology.

Requirements

- Provide the missing information in the Addressing Table.
- Name the router **[[R1Name]]** and the second switch **[[S2Name]]**. You will not be able to access **[[S1Name]]**.
- Use **cisco** as the user EXEC password for all lines.
- Use **class** as the privileged EXEC password.
- Encrypt all plain text passwords.
- Configure an appropriate banner.

- Configure addressing for all devices according to the Addressing Table.

- Document interfaces with descriptions, including the **[[S2Name]]** VLAN 1 interface.

- Save your configurations.

- Verify connectivity between all devices. All devices should be able to ping any other device.

- Troubleshoot and document any issues.

- Implement the solutions necessary to enable and verify full end-to-end connectivity.

Note: Click the **Check Results** button to see your progress. Click the **Reset Activity** button to generate a new set of requirements.

CHAPTER 7

IP Addressing

The Study Guide portion of this chapter uses a combination of matching, fill-in-the-blank, multiple-choice, and open-ended question exercises to test your knowledge and skills of basic router concepts and configuration. The Lab and Activities portion of this chapter includes all the online curriculum labs and Packet Tracer activities to ensure that you have mastered the hands-on skills needed to understand basic IP addressing and router configuration.

As you work through this chapter, use Chapter 7 in *Introduction to Networks v6 Companion Guide* or use the corresponding Chapter 7 in the Introduction to Networks online curriculum for assistance.

Study Guide

Designing, implementing, and managing an effective IP addressing plan ensures that networks can operate effectively and efficiently. Addressing is a key function of network layer protocols that enable data communication between hosts. Both Internet Protocol Version 4 (IPv4) and Internet Protocol Version 6 (IPv6) provide hierarchical addressing for packets that carry data. In this chapter, we review the structure of IP addresses and their application to the construction and testing of IP networks and subnetworks.

IPv4 Network Addresses

At the most basic level, all data is represented in <u>binary</u> <u>digits</u> or bits. Therefore, both IPv4 and IPv6 addresses are simply a series of 1s and 0s that, when grouped logically, can be used to represent the location of a specific device or a grouping of devices—a network. Because numbering systems are foundational to computer and networking code, your ability to convert between binary, hexadecimal, and decimal numbering systems is an essential skill.

IPv4 Address Structure

In IPv4, addresses are _____ -bit binary numbers. However, for ease of use by people, binary patterns representing IPv4 addresses are expressed as _____ . This is first accomplished by separating each _____ (8 bits) of the _____ -bit binary pattern, called an _____ , with a dot. It is called an _____ because each decimal number represents 1 _____ or 8 bits.

In Table 7-1, convert the binary addresses into their dotted-decimal equivalent.

Table 7-1   Binary to Decimal IPv4 Address Conversion

IPv4 Binary Representation	IPv4 Dotted-Decimal Representation
11000000 10101000 00001010 00110010	
10101100 00010000 00100011 00010111	
00001010 01100100 11001000 00110010	
01000000 01100110 00010110 10000010	
11010001 10100101 11001111 11110101	

In Table 7-2, convert the dotted-decimal addresses into their binary equivalent.

Table 7-2   Decimal to Binary IPv4 Address Conversion

IPv4 Binary Representation	IPv4 Dotted-Decimal Representation
	198.133.219.15
	192.127.7.63
	128.107.25.100
	172.31.32.64
	10.86.175.27

With your Cisco user login, you have access to the Binary Game at The Cisco Learning Network in either PC format

https://learningnetwork.cisco.com/docs/DOC-1803

or for mobile devices (shown in Figure 7-1):

https://learningnetwork.cisco.com/docs/DOC-11119

This game is a fun and effective way to learn to convert 8-bit binary numbers.

Figure 7-1   Binary Game for Mobile Devices

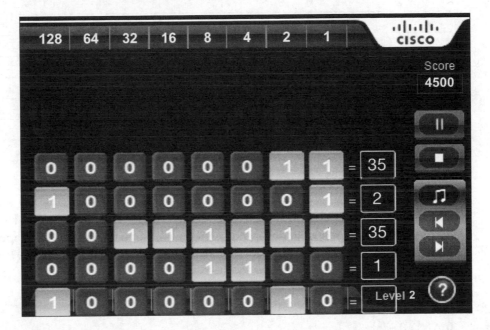

IPv4 Subnet Mask

Understanding binary notation is important when determining whether two hosts are in the same network. Within the 32-bit IPv4 address, a portion of the far-left bits makes up the network and the remainder of the far-right bits makes up the host. The subnet mask is used to mark this network|host bit boundary. Starting from the far-left bits, the subnet mask is represented by a series of 1s. A 1 indicates a network bit. Where the series of 1s ends and the series of 0s begins marks the bit boundary, as shown in Example 7-1.

Example 7-1   Bit Boundaries for IPv4 Address 10.32.48.240/11

IPv4 Address:	00001010.00100000.00110000.11110000
Subnet Mask:	11111111.11100000.00000000.00000000
Network Address:	00001010.00100000.00000000.00000000

The dotted-decimal format for a /11 subnet mask is 255.224.0.0 because /11 means that the first 11 far-left bits are 1s. Converted to dotted decimal, /11 is 255.224.0.0. The 224 is called the last nonzero octet in the subnet mask. You should know by now how to convert all the possible nonzero octets in a subnet mask from binary to decimal.

The Last Nonzero Octet

Fill in Table 7-3 with the correct decimal value for each bit position and for the last nonzero octet in a subnet mask.

Table 7-3   The Last Nonzero Octet in a Subnet Mask

Decimal Value	128							
				Bit Value				
255	1	1	1	1	1	1	1	1
	1	1	1	1	1	1	1	0
	1	1	1	1	1	1	0	0
	1	1	1	1	1	0	0	0
	1	1	1	1	0	0	0	0
	1	1	1	0	0	0	0	0
	1	1	0	0	0	0	0	0
	1	0	0	0	0	0	0	0

ANDing to Determine the Network Address

The bitwise AND operation is used by computers and networking devices to determine the network address from a given host address and subnet mask comparison. An AND operation is the comparison of two bits. Fill in the correct results for each of the following bitwise AND operations.

1 AND 1 = _____

0 AND 1 = _____

0 AND 0 = _____

1 AND 0 = _____

In Table 7-4, convert the prefix notion for a subnet mask to the dotted-decimal format. Then use the AND operation to determine the network address. For now, leave the Broadcast Address column empty.

Table 7-4   Determine the Network Address

Host Address/Prefix	Subnet Mask in Dotted Decimal	Network Address	Broadcast Address
192.168.1.10/24	255.255.255.0	192.168.1.0	192.168.1.255
192.168.25.130/27			
192.168.35.162/30			
192.168.1.137/23			
172.16.23.76/20			
172.31.254.172/15			
10.50.160.63/18			
10.220.100.9/17			
10.152.112.66/12			

The broadcast address for a given network address is the last available address in the range of addresses. For example, the broadcast address for 192.168.1.0/24 is 192.168.1.255. Now complete Table 7-4, filling in the broadcast address for each network.

Note: Plenty of calculators are available on the Internet that you can use to check your answers (for example, http://www.subnetmask.info). However, you will not be able to use a calculator while taking any Cisco exam. So, you should practice these problems without a calculator. Make these conversions on your own, and then use a calculator to check your answers.

IPv4 Unicast, Broadcast, and Multicast

In an IPv4 network, the hosts can communicate one of three ways:

- _____ : The process of sending a packet from one host to another individual host

- _____ : The process of sending a packet from one host to all hosts in the network

- _____ : The process of sending a packet from one host to a selected group of hosts, possibly in different networks

In an IPv4 network, the _____ addresses applied to an end device are referred to as the host addresses. A _____ broadcast is sent to all hosts on a nonlocal network. The _____ broadcast is used for communication with hosts on the same local network. These packets always use a destination IPv4 address _____ .

Explain why broadcast traffic should be limited.

_____

_____

_____

IPv4 has a block of addresses reserved for addressing multicast groups: _____ to _____ . The IPv4 multicast addresses _____ to _____ are reserved for multicasting on the local network only.

Types of IPv4 Addresses

IPv4 addresses that are not routed on the Internet can be classified into several types.

Private Addresses

Private addresses are defined in RFC _____ , *Address Allocation for Private Internets*. The private address blocks are as follows:

- __.0.0.0 to __.255.255.255 (__.0.0.0/__)

- ___.__.0.0 to ___.__.255.255 (___.__.0.0/__)

- ___.___.___.0 to ___.___.___.255 (___.___.___.0/__)

What distinguishes a private address from a public address?

_____

Loopback Addresses

Explain the purpose of the loopback address ____.____.____.____.

_____

_____

Link-Local Addresses

IPv4 addresses in the address block ____.____.____.____ to ____.____.____.____
(____.____.____.____) are designated as link-local addresses.

When would an IPv4 link-local address be used by a host?

_____

_____

What is the major limitation to link-local addresses?

_____

Test-Net Addresses

The address block ____.____.____.____ to ____.____.____.____ (____.____.____.____) is set
aside for teaching and learning purposes. These addresses can be used in documentation and network
examples.

What is a router's default behavior toward test-net and link-local addresses?

_____

Note: Although the test-net addresses are set aside for teaching and learning purposes, we also make use of the
private address space (in addition to the Cisco-owned public addresses) for examples in this book.

IPv6 Network Addresses

As you surely know by now, IPv6 was designed to be the successor to IPv4 with its much larger 128-bit
address space, providing for 340 undecillion addresses. The sensor-equipped, Internet-ready devices of
tomorrow will include everything from automobiles and biomedical devices, to household appliances
and natural ecosystems—the Internet of Things. With an increasing Internet population, limited IPv4
address space, issues with NAT, and the Internet of Things, the transition is well underway to convert
networks to IPv6 addressing.

There are basically three migration techniques to move from IPv4 to IPv6:

- _____ : Allows IPv4 and IPv6 to coexist on the same network

- _____ : Transporting an IPv6 packet over an IPv4 network

- _____ : Allows IPv6-enabled devices to communicate with IPv4-enabled devices
  using a technique similar to NAT for IPv4

Representing IPv6 Addresses

IPv6 addresses are 128 bits in length and written as a string of hexadecimal values. Every 4 bits is represented by a single hexadecimal digit, for a total of 32 hexadecimal values.

The preferred format for writing an IPv6 address is x:x:x:x:x:x:x:x, with each x consisting of four hexadecimal values. A *hextet* is the unofficial term used to refer to a segment of 16 bits or four hexadecimal values. Each x is a single hextet, 16 bits or four hexadecimal digits.

Preferred format means the IPv6 address is written using all 32 hexadecimal digits. It does not necessarily mean it is the ideal method for representing the IPv6 address.

What are the two rules used to reduce the number of digits required to represent an IPv6 address?

_____

_____

Table 7-5 provides a listing of ten fictitious IPv6 addresses. Use the two rules to practice compressing the IPv6 addresses into a shorter form.

Table 7-5   IPv6 Address Representations

Full IPv6 Address	Compressed IPv6 Address
2001:0DB8:0123:4567:89AB:CDEF:0020:0001	
2001:0DB8:0000:1234:5678:9101:1112:1113	
2001:0DB8:BFF3:9125:1111:0101:1111:0101	
2001:0DB8:0DB8:1111:0000:0000:0000:0200	
2001:0DB8:0000:1234:6678:9101:0000:34AB	
FE80:1984:2233:4455:6677:0000:0000:0101	
FE80:1976:0001:0002:0003:0004:0000:0101	
0000:0000:0000:0000:0000:0000:0000:0001	
FEED:0000:0000:0000:0000:0000:0101:1111	
FEED:ABCD:EF01:2345:0678:0910:AAAA:BBBB	

Identify IPv6 Address Types

Match the description on the left with the type of IPv6 address on the right. This exercise is a one-to-one matching.

Descriptions

a. Typical IPv6 prefix used to indicate the network portion of the address

b. IPv6 address represented as ::/128 (compressed format) (cannot be assigned to an interface)

c. Unique, Internet-routable IPv6 address (dynamic or static)

d. Used to communicate with other devices only on the same IPv6 subnet

e. IPv6 address represented as ::1/128 (compressed format)

f. IPv6 address in the range of FC00::/7 to FDFF::/7

IPv6 Address Types

_____ unspecified

_____ /64

_____ unique local

_____ loopback

_____ link local

_____ global unicast

Match the IPv6 address type on the left with the IPv6 address on the right. Some answers may be used more than once.

IPv6 Address Type	IPv6 Address
a. loopback address	_____ 2001:0DB8:1:ACAD::FE55:6789:B210
b. global unicast address	_____ ::1
c. link-local address	_____ FC00:22:A:2::CD4:23E4:76FA
d. unique-local address	_____ FF00::
e. multicast address	_____ FF02::2
	_____ 2001:DB8:1:1:22:A33D:259A:21FE
	_____ FE80::3201:CC01:65B1
	_____ FF00::DB7:4322:A231:67C

IPv6 Unicast Addresses

IPv6 global unicast addresses are globally unique and routable on the IPv6 Internet. Currently, only global unicast addresses with the first 3 bits of 001 or 2000::/3 are being assigned.

Note: The 2001:0DB8::/32 address has been reserved for documentation purposes, including use in examples. So, it will be used throughout this book.

Figure 7-2 shows the structure and range of a global unicast address. Fill in the blanks to indicate how many bits are used by each of the three parts.

Figure 7-2   IPv6 Global Unicast Address Structure

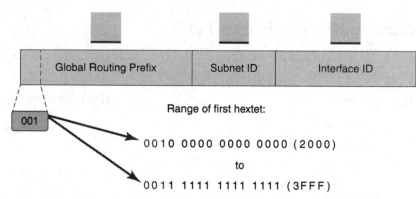

Currently, regional Internet registries (RIRs) assign a /48 global routing prefix to customers. This includes everyone from enterprise business networks to individual households. This is more than enough address space for most customers.

The 3-1-4 Rule

The IPv6 global unicast address can look complicated. Rick Graziani, in his book *IPv6 Fundamentals*, explains his 3-1-4 rule for breaking down a global unicast address into its three parts. Each number in the 3-1-4 rule refers to the number of hextets, as follows:

- 3: Indicates the three hextets, or 48 bits, of the global routing prefix.

- 1: Indicates the one hextet, or 16 bits, of the subnet ID.

- 4: Indicates the four hextets, or 64 bits, of the interface ID.

Using the 3-1-4 rule, complete Table 7-6, indicating which portion of the IPv6 global unicast address is the global routing prefix, the subnet ID, and the interface ID.

Table 7-6   Examples of /48 Global Unicast Addresses

Global Unicast Address	Global Routing Prefix (3)	Subnet ID (1)	Interface ID (4)
2001:0DB8:AAAA:1234:1111:2222:3333:4444			
2001:0DB8:BBBB:4321:AAAA:BBBB:CCCC:DDDD			
2001:0DB8:AAAA:0001:0000:0000:0000:0100			
2001:0DB8:AAAA:9:0:0:0:A			
2001:0DB8:AAAA:0001::0200			
2001:DB8:AAAA::200			
2001:DB8::ABC:0			
2001:DB8:ABC::			
2001:DB8:ABC::FFFF:FFFF:FFFF:FFFF			
2001:DB8::FFFF:FFFF:FFFF:FFFF:FFFF			

Static Configuration of Global Unicast Addressing

To configure a router interface with an IPv6 global unicast address, use the command **ipv6 address** *ipv6-address/prefix-length*. Given the topology shown in Figure 7-3, finish the router script for configuring the R1 interfaces with IPv6 addressing.

Figure 7-3   IPv6 Addressing Topology

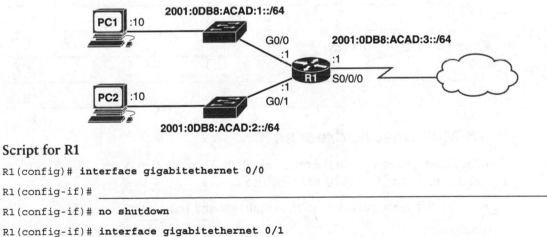

Script for R1

```
R1(config)# interface gigabitethernet 0/0
R1(config-if)# _____
R1(config-if)# no shutdown
R1(config-if)# interface gigabitethernet 0/1
R1(config-if)# _____
R1(config-if)# no shutdown
R1(config-if)# interface serial 0/0/0
R1(config-if)# _____
R1(config-if)# no shutdown
```

Dynamic Configuration of Global Unicast Addressing

Define and briefly explain SLAAC.

_____

_____

_____

IPv6 routers periodically send out ICMPv6 _____ (RA) messages to all IPv6-enabled devices on the network. By default, Cisco routers send out RA messages every _____ seconds. An IPv6 device on the network does not have to wait for these periodic RA messages. A device can send a _____ (RS) message to the router, to which the router will respond with an RA.

However, before a router can send RA messages, it must first be enabled as an IPv6 router with the _____ command.

RA messages contain the prefix, prefix length, and other information for the device. In addition, the RA message can contain one of three options for the device to use to obtain its addressing information. Explain each option.

- Option 1, SLAAC Only: _____

_____

_____

- Option 2, SLAAC and DHCPv6: _____

_____

_____

- Option 3, DHCPv6 Only: _____

_____

_____

IPv6 Multicast Addresses

IPv6 multicast addresses have the prefix FF00::/8. There are two types of IPv6 multicast addresses: assigned multicast and solicited node multicast.

Explain the difference between assigned multicast and solicited node multicast.

_____

_____

_____

_____

_____

_____

_____

_____

Connectivity Verification

Verifying end-to-end connectivity is important when first implementing a network. But it is also an important troubleshooting tool. Using connectivity tools, the network administrator can track the source of a connectivity issue.

ICMP Message Types

Internet Control Message Protocol (ICMP) messages common to both ICMPv4 and ICMPv6 include the following:

- Host Confirmation: The local host sends an ICMP _____ to a destination host. If available, the destination host responds with an _____ . The _____ command can be used by an administrator to generate this verification test.

- Destination or Service Unreachable: This message is used when a host or gateway receives a packet that it cannot deliver. The message will include a code that indicates why the packet could not be delivered. What is the meaning of each of the following Destination Unreachable codes for ICMPv4?

    - 0— _____

    - 1— _____

    - 2— _____

    - 3— _____

- Time Exceeded: If a router receives a packet and decrements the _____ field in the IPv4 packet to _____ , it discards the packet and sends a Time Exceeded message to the source host. Instead of the _____ field, ICMPv6 uses the _____ field.

- Route Redirection: Explain this message type. _____

    _____

    _____

    _____

Testing the Path

To test the path from end to end and locate the place in the path where connectivity fails, use the _____ utility. The command for this test is _____ in Cisco IOS and _____ in Windows.

Explain how this testing utility works.

_____

_____

_____

_____

_____

_____

Labs and Activities

Command Reference

In Table 7-7, record the command, including the correct router or switch prompt, that fits the description. Fill in any blanks with the appropriate missing information.

Table 7-7   Commands for Chapter 7, IP Addressing

Command	Description
	Enable IPv6 routing
	Configure the IPv6 address 2001:DB8:1:1/64
	Configure the IPv6 link-local address as FE80::1
	Use the "brief" command to verify IPv6 addresses configured on the switch
	Displays the IPv6 routing table that the IOS is currently using to choose the best path to its destination networks

7.0.1.2 Class Activity–Modeling the Internet of Everything (IoE)

Objectives

Explain how network devices use routing tables to direct packets to a destination network.

Background/Scenario

Today, more than 99% of our world remains unconnected. Tomorrow, we will be connected to almost everything. 37 billion devices will be connected to the Internet by 2020. From trees to water to cars, the organic and the digital will work together for a more intelligent and connected world. This tomorrow of networking is known as "The Internet of Everything" or "IoE."

If traffic, transportation, networking, and space exploration depend on digital information sharing, how will that information be identified from its source to its destination?

In this activity, you will begin to think about not only what will be identified in the IoE world, but also how everything will be addressed in the same world!

Activity directions for class or individual students:

1) Navigate to the IoE main page located at http://www.cisco.com/c/r/en/us/internet-of-everything-ioe.

2) Next, watch some videos or read through some content from the IoE main page that interests you.

3) Write five comments or questions about what you saw or read. Be prepared to share with the class.

Required Resources

- Internet connectivity for research on the cisco.com site. Headphones may also be useful if students are individually completing this activity within a group setting.

- Recording capabilities (paper, tablet, and so on) for comments or questions regarding the videos, blogs and/or .pdfs read or viewed for Step 3.

Reflection

Why do you think there is a need to address trees? Windmills? Cars? Refrigerators? Why will just about anything be able to use an IP address?

7.1.2.8 Lab–Using the Windows Calculator with Network Addresses

Objectives

Part 1: Access the Windows Calculator

Part 2: Convert between Numbering Systems

Part 3: Convert Host IPv4 Addresses and Subnet Masks into Binary

Part 4: Determine the Number of Hosts in a Network Using Powers of 2

Part 5: Convert MAC Addresses and IPv6 Addresses to Binary

Background/Scenario

Network technicians use binary, decimal, and hexadecimal numbers when working with computers and networking devices. Microsoft provides a built-in Calculator application as part of the operating system. The Windows 7 version of Calculator includes a Standard view that can be used to perform basic arithmetic tasks such as addition, subtraction, multiplication, and division. The Calculator application also has advanced programming, scientific, and statistical capabilities.

In this lab, you will use the Windows 7 Calculator application Programmer view to convert between the binary, decimal, and hexadecimal number systems. You will also use the Scientific view powers function to determine the number of hosts that can be addressed based on the number of host bits available.

Required Resources

- 1 PC (Windows 7 or 8)

Note: If using an operating system other than Windows 7, the Calculator application views and functions available may vary from those shown in this lab. However, you should be able to perform the calculations.

Part 1: Access the Windows Calculator

In Part 1, you will become familiar with the Microsoft Windows built-in calculator application and view the available modes.

Step 1:   Click the Windows Start button and select All Programs.

Step 2:   Click the Accessories folder and select Calculator.

Step 3:   After Calculator opens, click the View menu.

What are the four available modes?

_____

Note: The Programmer and Scientific modes are used in this lab.

Part 2: Convert Between Numbering Systems

In the Windows Calculator Programmer view, several number system modes are available: Hex (Hexadecimal or base 16), Dec (Decimal or base 10), Oct (Octal or base 8), and Bin (Binary or base 2).

We are accustomed to using the decimal numbering system that uses the digits 0 to 9. The decimal numbering system is used in everyday life for all counting, money, and financial transactions. Computers and other electronic devices use the binary numbering system with only the digits 0 and 1 for data storage, data transmission, and numerical calculations. All computer calculations are ultimately performed internally in binary (digital) form, regardless of how they are displayed.

One disadvantage of binary numbers is that the binary number equivalent of a large decimal number can be quite long. This makes them difficult to read and write. One way to overcome this problem is to arrange binary numbers into groups of four as hexadecimal numbers. Hexadecimal numbers are base 16, and a combination of numbers from 0 to 9 and the letters A to F are used to represent the binary or decimal equivalent. Hexadecimal characters are used when writing or displaying IPv6 and MAC addresses.

The octal numbering system is very similar in principle to hexadecimal. Octal numbers represent binary numbers in groups of three. This numbering system uses digits 0 to 7. Octal numbers are also a convenient way to represent a large binary number in smaller groups, but this numbering system is not commonly used.

In this lab, the Windows 7 Calculator is used to convert between different numbering systems in the Programmer mode.

a.   Click the **View** menu and select **Programmer** to switch to Programmer mode.

Note: For Windows XP and Vista, only two modes, Standard and Scientific, are available. If you are using one of these operating systems, you can use the Scientific mode to perform this lab.

Which number system is currently active? _____

Which numbers on the number pad are active in decimal mode? _____

b. Click the **Bin** (Binary) radio button. Which numbers are active on the number pad now?

_____

Why do you think the other numbers are grayed out?

_____

c. Click the **Hex** (Hexadecimal) radio button. Which characters are activated on the number pad now?

_____

d. Click the **Dec** radio button. Using your mouse, click the number **1** followed by the number **5** on the number pad. The decimal number **15** is now entered.

Note: The numbers and letters on the keyboard can also be used to enter the values. If using the numerical keypad, type the number **15**. If the number does not enter into the calculator, press the **Num Lock** key to enable the numeric keypad.

Click the **Bin** radio button. What happened to the number 15?

_____

e. Numbers are converted from one numbering system to another by selecting the desired number mode. Click the **Dec** radio button again. The number converts back to decimal.

f. Click the **Hex** radio button to change to Hexadecimal mode. Which hexadecimal character (0 through 9 or A to F) represents decimal 15? _____

g. As you were switching between the numbering systems, you may have noticed the binary number 1111 is displayed during the conversion. This assists you in relating the binary digits to other numbering system values. Each set of 4 bits represents a hexadecimal character or potentially multiple decimal characters.

```
                                                              15

 0000   0000   0000   0000   0000   0000   0000   0000
 63                          47                     32
 0000   0000   0000   0000   0000   0000   0000   1111
 31                          15                      0
```

h. Clear the values in the window by clicking C above the 9 on the calculator keypad. Convert the following numbers between the binary, decimal, and hexadecimal numbering systems.

Decimal	Binary	Hexadecimal
86		
175		
204		
	0001 0011	
	0100 1101	

Decimal	Binary	Hexadecimal
	0010 1010	
		38
		93
		E4

As you record the values in the table above, do you see a pattern between the binary and hexadecimal numbers?

_____

_____

Part 3: Convert Host IPv4 Addresses and Subnet Masks into Binary

Internet Protocol version 4 (IPv4) addresses and subnet masks are represented in a dotted decimal format (four octets), such as 192.168.1.10 and 255.255.255.0, respectively. This makes these addresses more readable to humans. Each of the decimal octets in the address or a mask can be converted to 8 binary bits. An octet is always 8 binary bits. If all 4 octets were converted to binary, how many bits would there be? _____

a. Use the Windows Calculator application to convert the IP address 192.168.1.10 into binary and record the binary numbers in the following table:

Decimal	Binary
192	
168	
1	
10	

Subnet masks, such as 255.255.255.0, are also represented in a dotted decimal format. A subnet mask will always consist of four 8-bit octets, each represented as a decimal number. Using the Windows Calculator, convert the 8 possible decimal subnet mask octet values to binary numbers and record the binary numbers in the following table:

Decimal	Binary
0	
128	
192	
224	
240	
248	
252	
254	
255	

With the combination of IPv4 address and the subnet mask, the network portion can be determined and the number of hosts available in a given IPv4 subnet can also be calculated. The process is examined in Part 4.

Part 4: Determine the Number of Hosts in a Network Using Powers of 2

Given an IPv4 network address and a subnet mask, the network portion can be determined along with the number of hosts available in the network.

a. To calculate the number of hosts on a network, you must determine the network and host portion of the address.

Using the example of 192.168.1.10 with a subnet of 255.255.248.0, the address and subnet mask are converted to binary numbers. Align the bits as you record your conversions to binary numbers.

Decimal IP Address and Subnet Mask	Binary IP Address and Subnet Mask
192.168.1.10	
255.255.248.0	

Because the first 21 bits in the subnet mask are consecutive numeral ones, the corresponding first 21 bits in the IP address in binary is 110000001010100000000; these represent the network portion of the address. The remaining 11 bits are 00100001010 and represent the host portion of the address.

What is the decimal and binary network number for this address?

_____

What is the decimal and binary host portion for this address?

_____

Because the network number and the broadcast address use two addresses out of the subnet, the formula to determine the number of hosts available in an IPv4 subnet is the number 2 to the power of the number of host bits available, minus 2:

Number of available hosts = $2^{\text{(number of host bits)}} - 2$

b. Using the Windows Calculator application, switch to the Scientific mode by clicking the **View** menu, and then select **Scientific**.

c. Input 2. Click the x^y key. This key raises a number to a power.

d. Input **11**. Click **=**, or press **Enter** on the keyboard for the answer.

e. Subtract **2** from the answer by using the calculator if desired.

f. In this example, 2046 hosts are available on this network (2^{11}-2).

g. If given the number of host bits, determine the number of hosts available and record the number in the following table.

Number of Available Host Bits	Number of Available Hosts
5	
14	
24	
10	

For a given subnet mask, determine the number of hosts available and record the answer in the following table.

Subnet Mask	Binary Subnet Mask	Number of Available Host Bits	Number of Available Hosts
255.255.255.0			
255.255.240.0			
255.255.255.128			
255.255.255.252			
255.255.0.0			

Part 5: Convert MAC Addresses and IPv6 Addresses to Binary

Both Media Access Control (MAC) and Internet Protocol version 6 (IPv6) addresses are represented as hexadecimal digits for readability. However, computers understand only binary digits and use these binary digits for computations. In this part, you will convert these hexadecimal addresses to binary addresses.

Step 1:   Convert MAC addresses to binary digits.

   a. The MAC or physical address is normally represented as 12 hexadecimal characters, grouped in pairs and separated by hyphens (-). Physical addresses on a Windows-based computer are displayed in a format of xx-xx-xx-xx-xx-xx, where each x is a number from 0 to 9 or a letter from A to F. Each of the hex characters in the address can be converted to 4 binary bits, which is what the computer understands. If all 12 hex characters were converted to binary, how many bits would there be?

   b. Record the MAC address for your PC.

   c. Convert the MAC address into binary digits using the Windows Calculator application.

Step 2:   Convert an IPv6 address into binary digits.

   IPv6 addresses are also written in hexadecimal characters for human convenience. These IPv6 addresses can be converted to binary numbers for computer use.

   a. IPv6 addresses are binary numbers represented in human-readable notations: 2001:0DB8:ACAD:0001:0000:0000:0000:0001 or in a shorter format: 2001:DB8:ACAD:1::1.

b. An IPv6 address is 128 bits long. Using the Windows Calculator application, convert the sample IPv6 address into binary numbers and record it in the table below.

Hexadecimal	Binary
2001	
0DB8	
ACAD	
0001	
0000	
0000	
0000	
0001	

Reflection

1. Can you perform all the conversions without the assistance of the calculator? What can you do to make it happen?

_____

2. For most IPv6 addresses, the network portion of the address is usually 64 bits. How many hosts are available on a subnet where the first 64 bits represent the network? Hint: All host addresses are available in the subnet for hosts.

_____

7.1.2.9 Lab–Converting IPv4 Addresses to Binary

Objectives

Part 1: Convert IPv4 Addresses from Dotted Decimal to Binary

Part 2: Use Bitwise ANDing Operation to Determine Network Addresses

Part 3: Apply Network Address Calculations

Background/Scenario

Every IPv4 address is composed of two parts: a network portion and a host portion. The network portion of an address is the same for all devices that reside in the same network. The host portion identifies a specific host within a given network. The subnet mask is used to determine the network portion of an IP address. Devices on the same network can communicate directly; devices on different networks require an intermediary Layer 3 device, such as a router, to communicate.

To understand the operation of devices on a network, we need to look at addresses the way devices do—in binary notation. To do this, we must convert the dotted decimal form of an IP address and its subnet mask to binary notation. After this has been done, we can use the bitwise ANDing operation to determine the network address.

This lab provides instructions on how to determine the network and host portion of IP addresses by converting addresses and subnet masks from dotted decimal to binary, and then using the bitwise ANDing operation. You will then apply this information to identify addresses in the network.

Part 1: Convert IPv4 Addresses from Dotted Decimal to Binary

In Part 1, you will convert decimal numbers to their binary equivalent. After you have mastered this activity, you will convert IPv4 addresses and subnet masks from dotted decimal to their binary form.

Step 1:   Convert decimal numbers to their binary equivalent.

Fill in the following table by converting the decimal number to an 8-bit binary number. The first number has been completed for your reference. Recall that the eight binary bit values in an octet are based on the powers of 2, and from left to right are 128, 64, 32, 16, 8, 4, 2, and 1.

Decimal	Binary
192	11000000
168	
10	
255	
2	

Step 2:   Convert the IPv4 addresses to their binary equivalent.

An IPv4 address can be converted using the same technique you used above. Fill in the table below with the binary equivalent of the addresses provided. To make your answers easier to read, separate the binary octets with a period.

Decimal	Binary
192.168.10.10	11000000.10101000.00001010.00001010
209.165.200.229	
172.16.18.183	
10.86.252.17	
255.255.255.128	
255.255.192.0	

Part 2: Use Bitwise ANDing Operation to Determine Network Addresses

In Part 2, you will use the bitwise ANDing operation to calculate the network address for the provided host addresses. You will first need to convert an IPv4 decimal address and subnet mask to their binary equivalent. Once you have the binary form of the network address, convert it to its decimal form.

Note: The ANDing process compares the binary value in each bit position of the 32-bit host IP with the corresponding position in the 32-bit subnet mask. If there are two 0s or a 0 and a 1, the ANDing result is 0. If there are two 1s, the result is a 1, as shown in the example here.

Step 1:   Determine the number of bits to use to calculate the network address.

Description	Decimal	Binary
IP Address	192.168.10.131	11000000.10101000.00001010.10000011
Subnet Mask	255.255.255.192	11111111.11111111.11111111.11000000
Network Address	192.168.10.128	11000000.10101000.00001010.10000000

How do you determine what bits to use to calculate the network address?

In the example above, how many bits are used to calculate the network address?

Step 2:   Use the ANDing operation to determine the network address.

a.   Enter the missing information into the table below:

Description	Decimal	Binary
IP Address	172.16.145.29	
Subnet Mask	255.255.0.0	
Network Address		

b. Enter the missing information into the table below:

Description	Decimal	Binary
IP Address	192.168.10.10	
Subnet Mask	255.255.255.0	
Network Address		

c. Enter the missing information into the table below:

Description	Decimal	Binary
IP Address	192.168.68.210	
Subnet Mask	255.255.255.128	
Network Address		

d. Enter the missing information into the table below:

Description	Decimal	Binary
IP Address	172.16.188.15	
Subnet Mask	255.255.240.0	
Network Address		

e. Enter the missing information into the table below:

Description	Decimal	Binary
IP Address	10.172.2.8	
Subnet Mask	255.224.0.0	
Network Address		

Part 3: Apply Network Address Calculations

In Part 3, you must calculate the network address for the given IP addresses and subnet masks. After you have the network address, you should be able to determine the responses needed to complete the lab.

Step 1: Determine whether IP addresses are on same network.

a. You are configuring two PCs for your network. PC-A is given an IP address of 192.168.1.18, and PC-B is given an IP address of 192.168.1.33. Both PCs receive a subnet mask of 255.255.255.240.

What is the network address for PC-A? _____

What is the network address for PC-B? _____

Will these PCs be able to communicate directly with each other? _____

What is the highest address that can be given to PC-B that allows it to be on the same network as PC-A?

_____

b. You are configuring two PCs for your network. PC-A is given an IP address of 10.0.0.16, and PC-B is given an IP address of 10.1.14.68. Both PCs receive a subnet mask of 255.254.0.0.

What is the network address for PC-A? _____

What is the network address for PC-B? _____

Will these PCs be able to communicate directly with each other? _____

What is the lowest address that can be given to PC-B that allows it to be on the same network as PC-A?

_____

Step 2:   Identify the default gateway address.

a. Your company has a policy to use the first IP address in a network as the default gateway address. A host on the local-area network (LAN) has an IP address of 172.16.140.24 and a subnet mask of 255.255.192.0.

What is the network address for this network?

_____

What is the default gateway address for this host?

_____

b. Your company has a policy to use the first IP address in a network as the default gateway address. You have been instructed to configure a new server with an IP address of 192.168.184.227 and a subnet mask of 255.255.255.248.

What is the network address for this network?

_____

What is the default gateway for this server?

_____

Reflection

Why is the subnet mask important in determining the network address?

_____

_____

7.1.3.8 Packet Tracer–Investigate Unicast, Broadcast, and Multicast Traffic

Topology

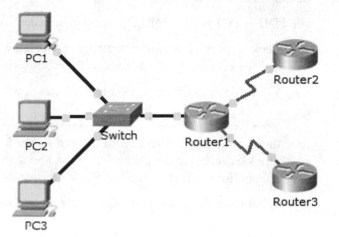

Objectives

Part 1: Generate Unicast Traffic

Part 2: Generate Broadcast Traffic

Part 3: Investigate Multicast Traffic

Background/Scenario

This activity will examine unicast, broadcast, and multicast behavior. Most traffic in a network is unicast. When a PC sends an ICMP echo request to a remote router, the source address in the IP packet header is the IP address of the sending PC. The destination address in the IP packet header is the IP address of the interface on the remote router. The packet is sent only to the intended destination.

Using the **ping** command or the Add Complex PDU feature of Packet Tracer, you can directly ping broadcast addresses to view broadcast traffic.

For multicast traffic, you will view EIGRP traffic. EIGRP is used by Cisco routers to exchange routing information between routers. Routers using EIGRP send packets to multicast address 224.0.0.10, which represents the group of EIGRP routers. Although these packets are received by other devices, they are dropped at Layer 3 by all devices except EIGRP routers, with no other processing required.

Part 1: Generate Unicast Traffic

Step 1:   Use ping to generate traffic.

    a.   Click **PC1** and click the **Desktop** tab > **Command Prompt**.

    b.   Enter the **ping 10.0.3.2** command. The ping should succeed.

Step 2:   Enter Simulation mode.

    a.   Click the **Simulation** tab to enter Simulation mode.

    b.   Click **Edit Filters** and verify that only ICMP and EIGRP events are selected.

    c.   Click **PC1** and enter the **ping 10.0.3.2** command.

Step 3:   Examine unicast traffic.

The PDU at **PC1** is an ICMP echo request intended for the serial interface on **Router3**.

    a.   Click **Capture/Forward** repeatedly and watch while the echo request is sent to **Router3** and the echo reply is sent back to **PC1**. Stop when the first echo reply reaches PC1.

    Which devices did the packet travel through with the unicast transmission?

_____

    b.   In the Simulation Panel Event List section, the last column contains a colored box that provides access to detailed information about an event. Click the colored box in the last column for the first event. The PDU Information window opens.

    What layer does this transmission start at and why?

_____

    c.   Examine the Layer 3 information for all of the events. Notice that both the source and destination IP addresses are unicast addresses that refer to PC1 and the serial interface on Router3.

    What two changes take place at Layer 3 when the packet arrives at Router3?

_____

    d.   Click **Reset Simulation**.

Part 2: Generate Broadcast Traffic

Step 1:   Add a complex PDU.

    a.   Click **Add Complex PDU**. The icon for this is in the right toolbar and shows an open envelope.

    b.   Float the mouse cursor over the topology and the pointer changes to an envelope with a plus (+) sign.

    c.   Click **PC1** to serve as the source for this test message and the **Create Complex PDU** dialog window opens. Enter the following values:

        ■   Destination IP Address: **255.255.255.255** (broadcast address)

        ■   Sequence Number: 1

        ■   One Shot Time: **0**

    Within the PDU settings, the default for **Select Application:** is PING. What are at least 3 other applications available for use?

_____

_____

d. Click **Create PDU**. This test broadcast packet now appears in the **Simulation Panel Event List**. It also appears in the PDU List window. It is the first PDU for Scenario 0.

e. Click **Capture/Forward** twice. This packet is sent to the switch and then broadcasted to **PC2**, **PC3**, and **Router1**. Examine the Layer 3 information for all of the events. Notice that the destination IP address is 255.255.255.255, which is the IP broadcast address you configured when you created the complex PDU.

Analyzing the OSI Model information, what changes occur in the Layer 3 information of the Out Layers column at Router1, PC2, and PC3?

_____

f. Click **Capture/Forward** again. Does the broadcast PDU ever forward on to Router2 or Router3? Why?

_____

_____

g. After you are done examining the broadcast behavior, delete the test packet by clicking **Delete** below **Scenario 0**.

Part 3: Investigate Multicast Traffic

Step 1:   Examine the traffic generated by routing protocols.

a. Click **Capture/Forward**. EIGRP packets are at Router1 waiting to be multicast out of each interface.

b. Examine the contents of these packets by opening the PDU Information window and click **Capture/Forward** again. The packets are sent to the two other routers and the switch. The routers accept and process the packets, because they are part of the multicast group. The switch will forward the packets to the PCs.

c. Click **Capture/Forward** until you see the EIGRP packet arrive at the PCs.

What do the hosts do with the packets?

_____

Examine the Layer 3 and Layer 4 information for all of the EIGRP events.

What is the destination address of each of the packets?

_____

d. Click one of the packets delivered to one of the PCs. What happens to those packets?

_____

Based on the traffic generated by the three types of IP packets, what are the major differences in delivery?

_____

_____

Suggested Scoring Rubric

Activity Section	Question Location	Possible Points	Earned Points
Part 1: Unicast Traffic	Step 3a	10	
	Step 3b	10	
	Step 3c	10	
	Part 1 Total	**30**	
Part 2: Broadcast Traffic	Step 1c	10	
	Step 1e	10	
	Step 1f	10	
	Part 2 Total	**30**	
Part 3: Multicast Traffic	Step 1c, q1	10	
	Step 1c, q2	10	
	Step 1d, q1	10	
	Step 1d, q2	10	
	Part 3 Total	**40**	
	Total Score	**100**	

7.1.4.9 Lab–Identifying IPv4 Addresses

Objectives

Part 1: Identify IPv4 Addresses

Part 2: Classify IPv4 Addresses

Background/Scenario

In this lab, you will examine the structure of Internet Protocol version 4 (IPv4) addresses. You will identify the various types of IPv4 addresses and the components that help comprise the address, such as network portion, host portion, and subnet mask. Types of addresses covered include public, private, unicast, and multicast.

Required Resources

- Device with Internet access
- Optional: IPv4 address calculator

Part 1: Identify IPv4 Addresses

In Part 1, you will be given several examples of IPv4 addresses and will complete tables with appropriate information.

Step 1:   Analyze the table shown below and identify the network portion and host portion of the given IPv4 addresses.

The first two rows show examples of how the table should be completed.

Key for table:

N = All 8 bits for an octet are in the network portion of the address

n = A bit in the network portion of the address

H = All 8 bits for an octet are in the host portion of the address

h = A bit in the host portion of the address

IP Address/Prefix	Network/Host N,n = Network, H,h = Host	Subnet Mask	Network Address
192.168.10.10/24	N.N.N.H	255.255.255.0	192.168.10.0
10.101.99.17/23	N.N.nnnnnnnh.H	255.255.254.0	10.101.98.0
209.165.200.227/27			
172.31.45.252/24			
10.1.8.200/26			
172.16.117.77/20			
10.1.1.101/25			
209.165.202.140/27			
192.168.28.45/28			

Step 2:   Analyze the table below and list the range of host and broadcast addresses given a network/ prefix mask pair.

The first row shows an example of how the table should be completed.

IP Address/Prefix	First Host Address	Last Host Address	Broadcast Address
192.168.10.10/24	192.168.10.1	192.168.10.254	192.168.10.255
10.101.99.17/23			
209.165.200.227/27			
172.31.45.252/24			
10.1.8.200/26			
172.16.117.77/20			
10.1.1.101/25			
209.165.202.140/27			
192.168.28.45/28			

Part 2: Classify IPv4 Addresses

In Part 2, you will identify and classify several examples of IPv4 addresses.

Step 1:   Analyze the table shown below and identify the type of address (network, host, multicast, or broadcast address).

The first row shows an example of how the table should be completed.

IP Address	Subnet Mask	Address Type
10.1.1.1	255.255.255.252	host
192.168.33.63		
239.192.1.100		
172.25.12.52		
10.255.0.0		
172.16.128.48		
209.165.202.159		
172.16.0.255		
224.10.1.11		

Step 2:   Analyze the table shown below and identify the address as public or private.

IP Address/Prefix	Public or Private
209.165.201.30/27	
192.168.255.253/24	
10.100.11.103/16	
172.30.1.100/28	
192.31.7.11/24	
172.20.18.150/22	

IP Address/Prefix	Public or Private
128.107.10.1/16	
192.135.250.10/24	
64.104.0.11/16	

Step 3:   Analyze the table shown below and identify whether the address/prefix pair is a valid host address.

IP Address/Prefix	Valid Host Address?	Reason
127.1.0.10/24		
172.16.255.0/16		
241.19.10.100/24		
192.168.0.254/24		
192.31.7.255/24		
64.102.255.255/14		
224.0.0.5/16		
10.0.255.255/8		
198.133.219.8/24		

Reflection

Why should we continue to study and learn about IPv4 addressing if the available IPv4 address space is depleted?

_____

_____

7.2.4.9 Packet Tracer–Configuring IPv6 Addressing

Topology

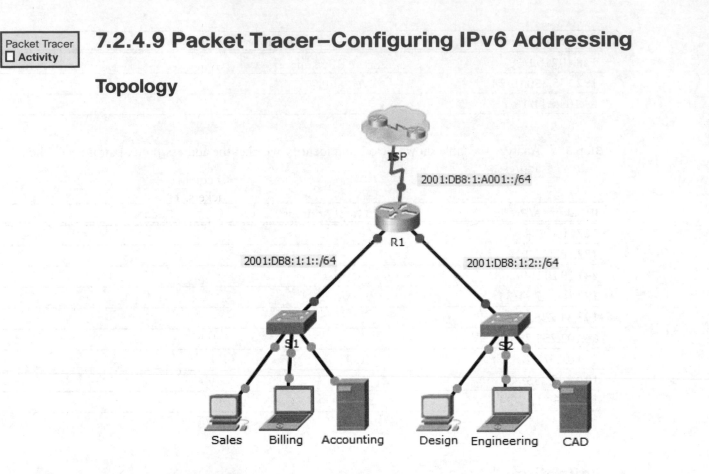

Addressing Table

Device	Interface	IPv6 Address/Prefix	Default Gateway
R1	G0/0	2001:DB8:1:1::1/64	N/A
	G0/1	2001:DB8:1:2::1/64	N/A
	S0/0/0	2001:DB8:1:A001::2/64	N/A
	Link-local	FE80::1	N/A
Sales	NIC	2001:DB8:1:1::2/64	FE80::1
Billing	NIC	2001:DB8:1:1::3/64	FE80::1
Accounting	NIC	2001:DB8:1:1::4/64	FE80::1
Design	NIC	2001:DB8:1:2::2/64	FE80::1
Engineering	NIC	2001:DB8:1:2::3/64	FE80::1
CAD	NIC	2001:DB8:1:2::4/64	FE80::1

Objectives

Part 1: Configure IPv6 Addressing on the Router

Part 2: Configure IPv6 Addressing on Servers

Part 3: Configure IPv6 Addressing on Clients

Part 4: Test and Verify Network Connectivity

Background

In this activity, you will practice configuring IPv6 addresses on a router, servers, and clients. You will also practice verifying your IPv6 addressing implementation.

Part 1: Configure IPv6 Addressing on the Router

Step 1:   Enable the router to forward IPv6 packets.

a. Enter the ipv6 unicast-routing global configuration command. This command must be configured to enable the router to forward IPv6 packets. This command will be discussed in a later semester.

```
R1(config)# ipv6 unicast-routing
```

Step 2:   Configure IPv6 addressing on GigabitEthernet0/0.

a. Click **R1** and then the **CLI** tab. Press **Enter**.

b. Enter privileged EXEC mode.

c. Enter the commands necessary to transition to interface configuration mode for GigabitEthernet0/0.

d. Configure the IPv6 address with the following command:

```
R1(config-if)# ipv6 address 2001:DB8:1:1::1/64
```

e. Configure the link-local IPv6 address with the following command:

```
R1(config-if)# ipv6 address FE80::1 link-local
```

f. Activate the interface.

Step 3:   Configure IPv6 addressing on GigabitEthernet0/1.

a. Enter the commands necessary to transition to interface configuration mode for GigabitEthernet0/1.

b. Refer to the **Addressing Table** to obtain the correct IPv6 address.

c. Configure the IPv6 address, the link-local address, and activate the interface.

Step 4:   Configure IPv6 addressing on Serial0/0/0.

a. Enter the commands necessary to transition to interface configuration mode for Serial0/0/0.

b. Refer to the **Addressing Table** to obtain the correct IPv6 address.

c. Configure the IPv6 address, the link-local address, and activate the interface.

Part 2: Configure IPv6 Addressing on the Servers

Step 1:   Configure IPv6 addressing on the Accounting Server.

a. Click **Accounting** and click the **Desktop** tab > **IP Configuration**.

b. Set the **IPv6 Address** to **2001:DB8:1:1::4** with a prefix of **/64**.

c. Set the **IPv6 Gateway** to the link-local address, **FE80::1**.

Step 2:   Configure IPv6 addressing on the CAD Server.

Repeat Steps 1a to 1c for the **CAD** server. Refer to the **Addressing Table** for the IPv6 address.

Part 3: Configure IPv6 Addressing on the Clients

Step 1:   Configure IPv6 addressing on the Sales and Billing Clients.

    a.   Click **Billing** and then select the **Desktop** tab followed by **IP Configuration**.

    b.   Set the **IPv6 Address** to **2001:DB8:1:1::3** with a prefix of **/64**.

    c.   Set the **IPv6 Gateway** to the link-local address, **FE80::1**.

    d.   Repeat Steps 1a through 1c for **Sales**. Refer to the **Addressing Table** for the IPv6 address.

Step 2:   Configure IPv6 Addressing on the Engineering and Design Clients.

    a.   Click **Engineering** and then select the **Desktop** tab followed by **IP Configuration**.

    b.   Set the **IPv6 Address** to **2001:DB8:1:2::3** with a prefix of **/64**.

    c.   Set the **IPv6 Gateway** to the link-local address, **FE80::1**.

    d.   Repeat Steps 1a through 1c for **Design**. Refer to the **Addressing Table** for the IPv6 address.

Part 4: Test and Verify Network Connectivity

Step 1:   Open the server web pages from the clients.

    a.   Click **Sales** and click the **Desktop** tab. Close the **IP Configuration** window, if necessary.

    b.   Click **Web Browser**. Enter **2001:DB8:1:1::4** in the URL box and click **Go**. The **Accounting** website should appear.

    c.   Enter **2001:DB8:1:2::4** in the URL box and click **Go**. The **CAD** website should appear.

    d.   Repeat steps 1a through 1d for the rest of the clients.

Step 2:   Ping the ISP.

    a.   Open any client computer configuration window by clicking the icon.

    b.   Click the **Desktop** tab > **Command Prompt**.

    c.   Test connectivity to the ISP by entering the following command:

```
PC> ping 2001:DB8:1:A001::1
```

    d.   Repeat the **ping** command with other clients until full connectivity is verified.

7.2.5.3 Lab–Identifying IPv6 Addresses

Topology

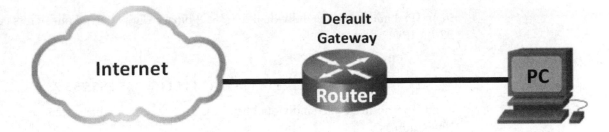

Objectives

Part 1: Identify the Different Types of IPv6 Addresses

Part 2: Examine a Host IPv6 Network Interface and Address

Part 3: Practice IPv6 Address Abbreviation

Background/Scenario

With the depletion of the Internet Protocol version 4 (IPv4) network address space and the adoption and transition to IPv6, networking professionals must understand how both IPv4 and IPv6 networks function. Many devices and applications already support IPv6. This includes extensive Cisco device Internetwork Operating System (IOS) support and workstation/server operating system support, such as that found in Windows and Linux.

This lab focuses on IPv6 addresses and the components of the address. In Part 1, you will identify the IPv6 address types, and in Part 2, you will view the IPv6 settings on a PC. In Part 3, you will practice IPv6 address abbreviation.

Required Resources

- 1 PC (Windows 7 or 8 with Internet access)

Part 1: Identify the Different Types of IPv6 Addresses

In Part 1, you will review the characteristics of IPv6 addresses to identify the different types of IPv6 addresses.

Step 1:   Review the different types of IPv6 addresses.

An IPv6 address is 128 bits long. It is most often presented as 32 hexadecimal characters. Each hexadecimal character is the equivalent of 4 bits (4 x 32 = 128). A non-abbreviated IPv6 host address is shown here:

2001:0DB8:0001:0000:0000:0000:0000:0001

A hextet is the hexadecimal, IPv6 version of an IPv4 octet. An IPv4 address is 4 octets long, separated by dots. An IPv6 address is 8 hextets long, separated by colons.

An IPv4 address is 4 octets and is commonly written or displayed in decimal notation.

255.255.255.255

An IPv6 address is 8 hextets and is commonly written or displayed in hexadecimal notation.

FFFF:FFFF:FFFF:FFFF:FFFF:FFFF:FFFF:FFFF

In an IPv4 address, each individual octet is 8 binary digits (bits). Four octets equals one 32-bit IPv4 address.

11111111 = 255

11111111.11111111.11111111.11111111 = 255.255.255.255

In an IPv6 address, each individual hextet is 16 bits long. Eight hextets equals one 128-bit IPv6 address.

1111111111111111 = FFFF

1111111111111111.1111111111111111.1111111111111111.1111111111111 111. 1111111111111111.1111111111111111.1111111111111111.111111111 1111111 = FFFF:FFFF:FFFF:FFFF:FFFF:FFFF:FFFF:FFFF

If we read an IPv6 address starting from the left, the first (or far left) hextet identifies the IPv6 address type. For example, if the IPv6 address has all zeros in the far left hextet, then the address is possibly a loopback address.

0000:0000:0000:0000:0000:0000:0000:0001 = loopback address

::1 = loopback address abbreviated

As another example, if the IPv6 address has FE80 in the first hextet, then the address is a link-local address.

FE80:0000:0000:0000:C5B7:CB51:3C00:D6CE = link-local address

FE80::C5B7:CB51:3C00:D6CE = link-local address abbreviated

Study the chart below to help you identify the different types of IPv6 address based on the numbers in the first hextet.

First Hextet (Far Left)	Type of IPv6 Address
0000 to 00FF	Loopback address, any address, unspecified address, or IPv4-compatible
2000 to 3FFF	Global unicast address (a routable address in a range of addresses that is currently being handed out by the Internet Assigned Numbers Authority [IANA])
FE80 to FEBF	Link-local (a unicast address that identifies the host computer on the local network)
FC00 to FCFF	Unique-local (a unicast address that can be assigned to a host to identify it as being part of a specific subnet on the local network)
FF00 to FFFF	Multicast address

There are other IPv6 address types that are either not yet widely implemented, or have already become deprecated, and are no longer supported. For instance, an **anycast address** is new to IPv6 and can be used by routers to facilitate load sharing and provide alternative path flexibility if a router becomes unavailable. Only routers should respond to an anycast address. Alternatively, **site-local addresses** have been deprecated and replaced by unique-local addresses. Site-local addresses were identified by the numbers FEC0 in the initial hextet.

In IPv6 networks, there are no network (wire) addresses or broadcast addresses as there are in IPv4 networks.

Step 2:   Match the IPv6 address to its type.

Match the IPv6 addresses to their corresponding address type. Notice that the addresses have been compressed to their abbreviated notation and that the slash network prefix number is not shown. Some answer choices must be used more than once.

IPv6 Address	Answer	Answer Choices
2001:0DB8:1:ACAD::FE55:6789:B210	1. b	a. Loopback address
::1	2. a	b. Global unicast address
FC00:22:A:2::CD4:23E4:76FA	3. d	c. Link-local address
2033:DB8:1:1:22:A33D:259A:21FE	4. b	d. Unique-local address
FE80::3201:CC01:65B1	5. c	e. Multicast address
FF00::	6. e	
FF00::DB7:4322:A231:67C	7. e	
FF02::2	8. e	

Part 2: Examine a Host IPv6 Network Interface and Address

In Part 2, you will check the IPv6 network settings of your PC to identify your network interface IPv6 address.

Step 1:   Check your PC IPv6 network address settings.

a.   Verify that the IPv6 protocol is installed and active on your PC-A. (Check your Local Area Connection settings.)

b.   Click the Windows **Start** button and then **Control Panel** and change **View by: Category** to **View by: Small icons.**

c.   Click the **Network and Sharing Center** icon.

d.   On the left side of the window, click **Change adapter settings.** You should now see icons representing your installed network adapters. Right-click your active network interface (it may be a **Local Area Connection** or a **Wireless Network Connection**), and then click **Properties.**

e.   You should now see your Network Connection Properties window. Scroll through the list of items to determine whether IPv6 is present, which indicates that it is installed, and if it is also check marked, which indicates that it is active.

f. Select the item **Internet Protocol Version 6 (TCP/IPv6)** and click **Properties.** You should see the IPv6 settings for your network interface. Your IPv6 properties window is likely set to **Obtain an IPv6 address automatically.** This does not mean that IPv6 relies on the Dynamic Host Configuration Protocol (DHCP). Instead of using DHCP, IPv6 looks to the local router for IPv6 network information and then auto-configures its own IPv6 addresses. To manually configure IPv6, you must provide the IPv6 address, the subnet prefix length, and the default gateway.

Note: The local router can refer host requests for IPv6 information, especially Domain Name System (DNS) information, to a DHCPv6 server on the network.

```
Internet Protocol Version 6 (TCP/IPv6) Properties                    [?] [x]

 General

 You can get IPv6 settings assigned automatically if your network supports this capability.
 Otherwise, you need to ask your network administrator for the appropriate IPv6 settings.

   ⦿ Obtain an IPv6 address automatically
   ◯ Use the following IPv6 address:
     IPv6 address:                [                          ]
     Subnet prefix length:        [     ]
     Default gateway:             [                          ]

   ⦿ Obtain DNS server address automatically
   ◯ Use the following DNS server addresses:
     Preferred DNS server:        [                          ]
     Alternate DNS server:        [                          ]

   ☐ Validate settings upon exit                     [ Advanced... ]

                                        [  OK  ]  [  Cancel  ]
```

g. After you have verified that IPv6 is installed and active on your PC, you should check your IPv6 address information. To do this, click the **Start** button, type **cmd** in the *Search programs and files* form box, and press Enter. This opens a Windows command prompt window.

h. Type **ipconfig /all** and press Enter. Your output should look similar to this:

```
C:\Users\user> ipconfig /all


Windows IP Configuration


<output omitted>


Wireless LAN adapter Wireless Network Connection:


   Connection-specific DNS Suffix  . :
   Description . . . . . . . . . . . : Intel(R) Centrino(R) Advanced-N 6200 AGN
   Physical Address. . . . . . . . . : 02-37-10-41-FB-48
   DHCP Enabled. . . . . . . . . . . : Yes
   Autoconfiguration Enabled . . . . : Yes
   Link-local IPv6 Address . . . . . : fe80::8d4f:4f4d:3237:95e2%14(Preferred)
   IPv4 Address. . . . . . . . . . . : 192.168.2.106(Preferred)
   Subnet Mask . . . . . . . . . . . : 255.255.255.0
   Lease Obtained. . . . . . . . . . : Sunday, January 06, 2013 9:47:36 AM
   Lease Expires . . . . . . . . . . : Monday, January 07, 2013 9:47:38 AM
   Default Gateway . . . . . . . . . : 192.168.2.1
   DHCP Server . . . . . . . . . . . : 192.168.2.1
   DHCPv6 IAID . . . . . . . . . . . : 335554320
   DHCPv6 Client DUID. . . . . . . . : 00-01-00-01-14-57-84-B1-1C-C1-DE-91-C3-
5D
```

```
DNS Servers . . . . . . . . . . . : 192.168.1.1
                                    8.8.4.4
<output omitted>
```

i. You can see from the output that the client PC has an IPv6 link-local address with a randomly generated interface ID. What does it indicate about the network regarding IPv6 global unicast address, IPv6 unique-local address, or IPv6 gateway address?

_____

_____

j. What kind of IPv6 addresses did you find when using **ipconfig /all**?

_____

_____

Part 3: Practice IPv6 Address Abbreviation

In Part 3, you will study and review rules for IPv6 address abbreviation to correctly compress and decompress IPv6 addresses.

Step 1:   Study and review the rules for IPv6 address abbreviation.

Rule 1: In an IPv6 address, a string of four zeros (0s) in a hextet can be abbreviated as a single zero.

2001:0404:0001:1000:**0000:0000**:0EF0:BC00

2001:0404:0001:1000:**0:0**:0EF0:BC00 (abbreviated with single zeros)

Rule 2: In an IPv6 address, the leading zeros in each hextet can be omitted; trailing zeros cannot be omitted.

2001:0404:**0001**:1000:0000:0000:**0**EF0:BC00

2001:404:1:1000:0:0:EF0:BC00 (abbreviated with leading zeros omitted)

Rule 3: In an IPv6 address, a single continuous string of four or more zeros can be abbreviated as a double colon (::). The double colon abbreviation can only be used one time in an IP address.

2001:0404:0001:1000:**0000:0000**:0EF0:BC00

2001:404:1:1000::EF0:BC00 (abbreviated with leading zeroes omitted and continuous zeros replaced with a double colon)

The image below illustrates these rules of IPv6 address abbreviation:

```
    FF01:0000:0000:0000:0000:0000:0000:1
=   FF01:0:0:0:0:0:0:1
=   FF01::1
```

```
    E3D7:0000:0000:0000:51F4:00C8:C0A8:6420
=   E3D7::51F4:C8:C0A8:6420
```

```
    3FFE:0501:0008:0000:0260:97FF:FE40:EFAB
=   3FFE:501:8:0:260:97FF:FE40:EFAB
=   3FFE:501:8::260:97FF:FE40:EFAB
```

Step 2:   Practice compressing and decompressing IPv6 addresses.

Using the rules of IPv6 address abbreviation, either compress or decompress the following addresses:

1) 2002:0EC0:0200:0001:0000:04EB:44CE:08A2

_____

2) FE80:0000:0000:0001:0000:60BB:008E:7402

_____

3) FE80::7042:B3D7:3DEC:84B8

_____

4) FF00::

_____

5) 2001:0030:0001:ACAD:0000:330E:10C2:32BF

_____

Reflection

1. How do you think you must support IPv6 in the future?

_____

_____

2. Do you think IPv4 networks will continue on, or will everyone eventually switch over to IPv6? How long do you think it will take?

_____

_____

7.2.5.4 Lab–Configuring IPv6 Addresses on Network Devices

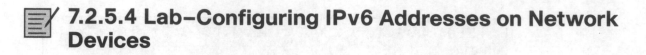

Topology

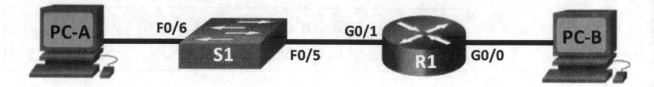

Addressing Table

Device	Interface	IPv6 Address	Prefix Length	Default Gateway
R1	G0/0	2001:DB8:ACAD:A::1	64	N/A
	G0/1	2001:DB8:ACAD:1::1	64	N/A
S1	VLAN 1	2001:DB8:ACAD:1::B	64	N/A
PC-A	NIC	2001:DB8:ACAD:1::3	64	FE80::1
PC-B	NIC	2001:DB8:ACAD:A::3	64	FE80::1

Objectives

Part 1: Set Up Topology and Configure Basic Router and Switch Settings

Part 2: Configure IPv6 Addresses Manually

Part 3: Verify End-to-End Connectivity

Background/Scenario

Knowledge of the Internet Protocol version 6 (IPv6) multicast groups can be helpful when assigning IPv6 addresses manually. Understanding how the all-router multicast group is assigned and how to control address assignments for the Solicited Nodes multicast group can prevent IPv6 routing issues and help ensure best practices are implemented.

In this lab, you will configure hosts and device interfaces with IPv6 addresses and explore how the all-router multicast group is assigned to a router. You will use **show** commands to view IPv6 unicast and multicast addresses. You will also verify end-to-end connectivity using the **ping** and **traceroute** commands.

Note: The routers used with CCNA hands-on labs are Cisco 1941 ISRs with Cisco IOS Release 15.2(4)M3 (universalk9 image). The switches used are Cisco Catalyst 2960s with Cisco IOS Release 15.0(2) (lanbasek9 image). Other routers, switches, and Cisco IOS versions can be used. Depending on the model and Cisco IOS version, the commands available and output produced might vary from what is shown in the labs. Refer to the Router Interface Summary table at the end of the lab for the correct interface identifiers.

Note: Make sure that the routers and switches have been erased and have no startup configurations. If you are unsure, contact your instructor.

Required Resources

- 1 Router (Cisco 1941 with Cisco IOS Software, Release 15.2(4)M3 universal image or comparable)

- 1 Switch (Cisco 2960 with Cisco IOS Release 15.0(2) lanbasek9 image or comparable)

- 2 PCs (Windows 7 or 8 with terminal emulation program, such as Tera Term)

- Console cables to configure the Cisco IOS devices via the console ports

- Ethernet cables as shown in the topology

Note: The Gigabit Ethernet interfaces on Cisco 1941 routers are autosensing and an Ethernet straight-through cable may be used between the router and PC-B. If using another model Cisco router, it may be necessary to use an Ethernet crossover cable.

Part 1: Set Up Topology and Configure Basic Router and Switch Settings

Step 1: Cable the network as shown in the topology.

Step 2: Initialize and reload the router and switch.

Step 3: Verify that the PC interfaces are configured to use the IPv6 protocol.

Verify that the IPv6 protocol is active on both PCs by ensuring that the **Internet Protocol Version 6 (TCP/IPv6)** check box is selected in the Local Area Connection Properties window.

Step 4:   Configure the router.

   a.   Console into the router and enable privileged EXEC mode.

   b.   Assign the device name to the router.

   c.   Disable DNS lookup to prevent the router from attempting to translate incorrectly entered commands as though they were hostnames.

   d.   Assign **class** as the privileged EXEC encrypted password.

   e.   Assign **cisco** as the console password and enable login.

   f.   Assign **cisco** as the VTY password and enable login.

   g.   Encrypt the clear text passwords.

   h.   Create a banner that warns anyone accessing the device that unauthorized access is prohibited.

   i.   Save the running configuration to the startup configuration file.

Step 5:   Configure the switch.

   a.   Console into the switch and enable privileged EXEC mode.

   b.   Assign the device name to the switch.

   c.   Disable DNS lookup to prevent the router from attempting to translate incorrectly entered commands as though they were hostnames.

   d.   Assign **class** as the privileged EXEC encrypted password.

   e.   Assign **cisco** as the console password and enable login.

   f.   Assign **cisco** as the VTY password and enable login.

   g.   Encrypt the clear text passwords.

   h.   Create a banner that warns anyone accessing the device that unauthorized access is prohibited.

   i.   Save the running configuration to the startup configuration file.

Part 2: Configure IPv6 Addresses Manually

Step 1:   Assign the IPv6 addresses to Ethernet interfaces on R1.

   a.   Assign the IPv6 global unicast addresses, listed in the Addressing Table, to both Ethernet interfaces on R1.

```
R1(config)# interface g0/0
R1(config-if)# ipv6 address 2001:db8:acad:a::1/64
R1(config-if)# no shutdown
R1(config-if)# interface g0/1
R1(config-if)# ipv6 address 2001:db8:acad:1::1/64
R1(config-if)# no shutdown
R1(config-if)# end
R1#
```

b.   Issue the **show ipv6 interface brief** command to verify that the correct IPv6 unicast address is assigned to each interface.

```
R1# show ipv6 interface brief
Em0/0                        [administratively down/down]
    unassigned
GigabitEthernet0/0           [up/up]
    FE80::D68C:B5FF:FECE:A0C0
    2001:DB8:ACAD:A::1
GigabitEthernet0/1           [up/up]
    FE80::D68C:B5FF:FECE:A0C1
    2001:DB8:ACAD:1::1
<output omitted>
```

c.   Issue the **show ipv6 interface g0/0** command. Notice that the interface is listing two Solicited Nodes multicast groups, because the IPv6 link-local (FE80) Interface ID was not manually configured to match the IPv6 unicast Interface ID.

Note: The link-local address displayed is based on EUI-64 addressing, which automatically uses the interface Media Access Control (MAC) address to create a 128-bit IPv6 link-local address.

```
R1# show ipv6 interface g0/0
GigabitEthernet0/0 is up, line protocol is up
  IPv6 is enabled, link-local address is FE80::D68C:B5FF:FECE:A0C0
  No Virtual link-local address(es):
  Global unicast address(es):
    2001:DB8:ACAD:A::1, subnet is 2001:DB8:ACAD:A::/64
  Joined group address(es):
    FF02::1
    FF02::1:FF00:1
    FF02::1:FFCE:A0C0
  MTU is 1500 bytes
<output omitted>
```

d.   To get the link-local address to match the unicast address on the interface, manually enter the link-local addresses on each of the Ethernet interfaces on R1.

```
R1# config t
Enter configuration commands, one per line.  End with CNTL/Z.
R1(config)# interface g0/0
R1(config-if)# ipv6 address fe80::1 link-local
R1(config-if)# interface g0/1
R1(config-if)# ipv6 address fe80::1 link-local
R1(config-if)# end
R1#
```

Note: Each router interface belongs to a separate network. Packets with a link-local address never leave the local network; therefore, you can use the same link-local address on both interfaces.

e.   Re-issue the **show ipv6 interface g0/0** command. Notice that the link-local address has been changed to **FE80::1** and that there is only one Solicited Nodes multicast group listed.

```
R1# show ipv6 interface g0/0
GigabitEthernet0/0 is up, line protocol is up
```

```
      IPv6 is enabled, link-local address is FE80::1
      No Virtual link-local address(es):
      Global unicast address(es):
        2001:DB8:ACAD:A::1, subnet is 2001:DB8:ACAD:A::/64
      Joined group address(es):
        FF02::1
        FF02::1:FF00:1
      MTU is 1500 bytes
    <output omitted>
```

What multicast groups have been assigned to interface G0/0?

_____

Step 2:   Enable IPv6 routing on R1.

   a. On a PC-B command prompt, enter the **ipconfig** command to examine IPv6 address information assigned to the PC interface.

   Has an IPv6 unicast address been assigned to the network interface card (NIC) on PC-B? _____

   b. Enable IPv6 routing on R1 using the **IPv6 unicast-routing** command.

```
    R1 # configure terminal
    R1(config)# ipv6 unicast-routing
    R1(config)# exit
    R1#
    *Dec 17 18:29:07.415: %SYS-5-CONFIG_I: Configured from console by console
```

   c. Use the **show ipv6 interface g0/0** command to see what multicast groups are assigned to interface G0/0. Notice that the all-router multicast group (FF02::2) now appears in the group list for interface G0/0.

_____

Note: This will allow the PCs to obtain their IP address and default gateway information automatically using Stateless Address Autoconfiguration (SLAAC).

_____

```
    R1# show ipv6 interface g0/0
    GigabitEthernet0/0 is up, line protocol is up
      IPv6 is enabled, link-local address is FE80::1
      No Virtual link-local address(es):
      Global unicast address(es):
        2001:DB8:ACAD:A::1, subnet is 2001:DB8:ACAD:A::/64 [EUI]
      Joined group address(es):
        FF02::1
        FF02::2
        FF02::1:FF00:1
      MTU is 1500 bytes
    <output omitted>
```

    d. Now that R1 is part of the all-router multicast group, re-issue the **ipconfig** command on PC-B. Examine the IPv6 address information.

    Why did PC-B receive the Global Routing Prefix and Subnet ID that you configured on R1?

    _____

    _____

Step 3: Assign IPv6 addresses to the management interface (SVI) on S1.

    a. Assign the IPv6 address listed in the Addressing Table to the management interface (VLAN 1) on S1. Also assign a link-local address for this interface. IPv6 command syntax is the same as on the router.

    _____

    _____

    _____

    _____

    b. Verify that the IPv6 addresses are properly assigned to the management interface using the **show ipv6 interface vlan1** command.

    _____

    _____

    _____

    _____

    _____

    _____

    _____

    _____

    _____

Note: The default 2960 Switch Database Manager (SDM) template does not support IPv6. It may be necessary to issue the command **sdm prefer dual-ipv4-and-ipv6 default** to enable IPv6 addressing before applying an IPv6 address to the VLAN 1 SVI.

Step 4: Assign static IPv6 addresses to the PCs.

    a. Open the Local Area Connection Properties window on PC-A. Select **Internet Protocol Version 6 (TCP/IPv6)** and click **Properties.**

b. Click the **Use the following IPv6 address** radio button. Refer to the Addressing Table and enter the **IPv6 address, Subnet prefix length**, and **Default gateway** information. Click **OK**.

c. Click **Close** to close the Local Area Connection Properties window.

d. Repeat Steps 4a to c to enter the static IPv6 information on PC-B. For the correct IPv6 address information, refer to the Addressing Table.

e. Issue the **ipconfig** command from the command line on PC-B to verify the IPv6 address information.

Part 3: Verify End-to-End Connectivity

a. From PC-A, ping **FE80::1**. This is the link-local address assigned to G0/1 on R1.

```
C:\>ping fe80::1

Pinging fe80::1 with 32 bytes of data:
Reply from fe80::1: time<1ms
Reply from fe80::1: time<1ms
Reply from fe80::1: time<1ms
Reply from fe80::1: time<1ms

Ping statistics for fe80::1:
    Packets: Sent = 4, Received = 4, Lost = 0 (0% loss),
Approximate round trip times in milli-seconds:
    Minimum = 0ms, Maximum = 0ms, Average = 0ms

C:\>
```

Note: You can also test connectivity by using the global unicast address, instead of the link-local address.

b. Ping the S1 management interface from PC-A.

```
C:\>ping 2001:db8:acad:1::b

Pinging 2001:db8:acad:1::b with 32 bytes of data:
Reply from 2001:db8:acad:1::b: time=14ms
Reply from 2001:db8:acad:1::b: time=2ms
Reply from 2001:db8:acad:1::b: time=2ms
Reply from 2001:db8:acad:1::b: time=3ms

Ping statistics for 2001:db8:acad:1::b:
    Packets: Sent = 4, Received = 4, Lost = 0 (0% loss),
Approximate round trip times in milli-seconds:
    Minimum = 2ms, Maximum = 14ms, Average = 5ms

C:\>
```

c. Use the **tracert** command on PC-A to verify that you have end-to-end connectivity to PC-B.

```
C:\>tracert 2001:db8:acad:a::3

Tracing route to 2001:db8:acad:a::3 over a maximum of 30 hops

  1    <1 ms    <1 ms    <1 ms  2001:db8:acad:1::1
  2     5 ms    <1 ms    <1 ms  2001:db8:acad:a::3

Trace complete.

C:\>
```

d. From PC-B, ping PC-A.

```
C:\>ping 2001:db8:acad:1::3

Pinging 2001:db8:acad:1::3 with 32 bytes of data:
Reply from 2001:db8:acad:1::3: time<1ms
Reply from 2001:db8:acad:1::3: time<1ms
Reply from 2001:db8:acad:1::3: time<1ms
Reply from 2001:db8:acad:1::3: time<1ms

Ping statistics for 2001:db8:acad:1::3:
    Packets: Sent = 4, Received = 4, Lost = 0 (0% loss),
Approximate round trip times in milli-seconds:
    Minimum = 0ms, Maximum = 0ms, Average = 0ms

C:\>
```

e. From PC-B, ping the link-local address for G0/0 on R1.

```
C:\>ping fe80::1

Pinging fe80::1 with 32 bytes of data:
Reply from fe80::1: time<1ms
Reply from fe80::1: time<1ms
Reply from fe80::1: time<1ms
Reply from fe80::1: time<1ms

Ping statistics for fe80::1:
    Packets: Sent = 4, Received = 4, Lost = 0 (0% loss),
Approximate round trip times in milli-seconds:
    Minimum = 0ms, Maximum = 0ms, Average = 0ms

C:\>
```

Note: If end-to-end connectivity is not established, troubleshoot your IPv6 address assignments to verify that you entered the addresses correctly on all devices.

Reflection

1. Why can the same link-local address, FE80::1, be assigned to both Ethernet interfaces on R1?

_____

_____

2. What is the Subnet ID of the IPv6 unicast address 2001:db8:acad::aaaa:1234/64?

_____

Router Interface Summary Table

| | Router Interface Summary | | | |
Router Model	Ethernet Interface #1	Ethernet Interface #2	Serial Interface #1	Serial Interface #2
1800	Fast Ethernet 0/0 (F0/0)	Fast Ethernet 0/1 (F0/1)	Serial 0/0/0 (S0/0/0)	Serial 0/0/1 (S0/0/1)
1900	Gigabit Ethernet 0/0 (G0/0)	Gigabit Ethernet 0/1 (G0/1)	Serial 0/0/0 (S0/0/0)	Serial 0/0/1 (S0/0/1)
2801	Fast Ethernet 0/0 (F0/0)	Fast Ethernet 0/1 (F0/1)	Serial 0/1/0 (S0/0/0)	Serial 0/1/1 (S0/0/1)
2811	Fast Ethernet 0/0 (F0/0)	Fast Ethernet 0/1 (F0/1)	Serial 0/0/0 (S0/0/0)	Serial 0/0/1 (S0/0/1)
2900	Gigabit Ethernet 0/0 (G0/0)	Gigabit Ethernet 0/1 (G0/1)	Serial 0/0/0 (S0/0/0)	Serial 0/0/1 (S0/0/1)

Note: To find out how the router is configured, look at the interfaces to identify the type of router and how many interfaces the router has. There is no way to effectively list all the combinations of configurations for each router class. This table includes identifiers for the possible combinations of Ethernet and Serial interfaces in the device. The table does not include any other type of interface, even though a specific router may contain one. An example of this might be an ISDN BRI interface. The string in parentheses is the legal abbreviation that can be used in Cisco IOS commands to represent the interface.

7.3.2.5 Packet Tracer–Verifying IPv4 and IPv6 Addressing

Topology

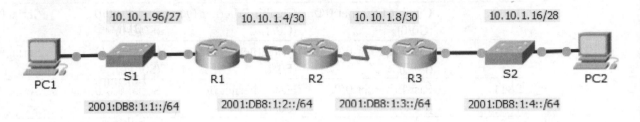

Addressing Table

Device	Interface	IPv4 Address	Subnet Mask	Default Gateway
		IPv6 Address/Prefix		
R1	G0/0	10.10.1.97	255.255.255.224	N/A
		2001:DB8:1:1::1/64		N/A
	S0/0/1	10.10.1.6	255.255.255.252	N/A
		2001:DB8:1:2::2/64		N/A
	Link-local	FE80::1		N/A
R2	S0/0/0	10.10.1.5	255.255.255.252	N/A
		2001:DB8:1:2::1/64		N/A
	S0/0/1	10.10.1.9	255.255.255.252	N/A
		2001:DB8:1:3::1/64		N/A
	Link-local	FE80::2		N/A
R3	G0/0	10.10.1.17	255.255.255.240	N/A
		2001:DB8:1:4::1/64		N/A
	S0/0/1	10.10.1.10	255.255.255.252	N/A
		2001:DB8:1:3::2/64		N/A
	Link-local	FE80::3		N/A
PC1	NIC			
PC2	NIC			

Objectives

Part 1: Complete the Addressing Table Documentation

Part 2: Test Connectivity Using Ping

Part 3: Discover the Path by Tracing the Route

Background

Dual-stack allows IPv4 and IPv6 to coexist on the same network. In this activity, you will investigate a dual-stack implementation including documenting the IPv4 and IPv6 configuration for end devices, testing connectivity for both IPv4 and IPv6 using **ping**, and tracing the path from end to end for IPv4 and IPv6.

Part 1: Complete the Addressing Table Documentation

Step 1: Use ipconfig to verify IPv4 addressing.

    a. Click **PC1** and click the **Desktop** tab > **Command Prompt**.

    b. Enter the **ipconfig /all** command to collect the IPv4 information. Fill in the **Addressing Table** with the IPv4 address, subnet mask, and default gateway.

    c. Click **PC2** and click the **Desktop** tab > **Command Prompt**.

    d. Enter the **ipconfig /all** command to collect the IPv4 information. Fill in the **Addressing Table** with the IPv4 address, subnet mask, and default gateway.

Step 2: Use ipv6config to verify IPv6 addressing.

    a. On **PC1**, enter the **ipv6config /all** command to collect the IPv6 information. Fill in the **Addressing Table** with the IPv6 address, subnet prefix, and default gateway.

    b. On **PC2**, enter the **ipv6config /all** command to collect the IPv6 information. Fill in the **Addressing Table** with the IPv6 address, subnet prefix, and default gateway.

Part 2: Test Connectivity Using Ping

Step 1: Use ping to verify IPv4 connectivity.

    a. From PC1, ping the IPv4 address for PC2. Was the result successful? _____

    b. From PC2, ping the IPv4 address for PC1. Was the result successful? _____

Step 2: Use ping to verify IPv6 connectivity.

    a. From PC1, ping the IPv6 address for PC2. Was the result successful? _____

    b. From PC2, ping the IPv6 address of PC1. Was the result successful? _____

Part 3: Discover the Path by Tracing the Route

Step 1: Use tracert to discover the IPv4 path.

    a. From PC1, trace the route to **PC2**.

```
PC> tracert 10.10.1.20
```

What addresses were encountered along the path? _____

_____

With which interfaces are the four addresses associated? _____

_____

b. From **PC2**, trace the route to **PC1**.

What addresses were encountered along the path? _____

_____

With which interfaces are the four addresses associated? _____

_____

Step 2: Use tracert to discover the IPv6 path.

a. From **PC1**, trace the route to the IPv6 address for **PC2**.

`PC> tracert 2001:DB8:1:4::A`

What addresses were encountered along the path? _____

_____

With which interfaces are the four addresses associated? _____

_____

b. From **PC2**, trace the route to the IPv6 address for **PC1**.

What addresses were encountered along the path? _____

_____

With which interfaces are the four addresses associated? _____

_____

Suggested Scoring Rubric

Activity Section	Question Location	Possible Points	Earned Points
Part 1: Complete the Addressing Table Documentation	Step 1b	10	
	Step 1d	10	
	Step 2a	10	
	Step 2b	10	
	Part 1 Total	40	
Part 2: Test Connectivity Using Ping	Step 1a	7	
	Step 1b	7	
	Step 2a	7	
	Step 2b	7	
	Part 2 Total	28	
Part 3: Discover the Path by Tracing the Route	Step 1a	8	
	Step 1b	8	
	Step 2a	8	
	Step 2b	8	
	Part 3 Total	32	
	Total Score	100	

Packet Tracer–Pinging and Tracing to Test the Path

Topology

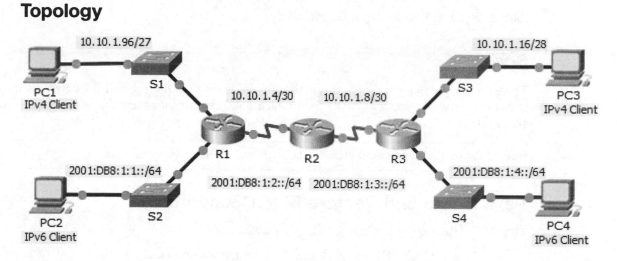

Addressing Table

Device	Interface	IPv4 Address	Subnet Mask	Default Gateway
		IPv6 Address/Prefix		
R1	G0/0	2001:DB8:1:1::1/64		N/A
	G0/1	10.10.1.97	255.255.255.224	N/A
	S0/0/1	10.10.1.6	255.255.255.252	N/A
		2001:DB8:1:2::2/64		N/A
	Link-local	FE80::1		N/A
R2	S0/0/0	10.10.1.5	255.255.255.252	N/A
		2001:DB8:1:2::1/64		N/A
	S0/0/1	10.10.1.9	255.255.255.252	N/A
		2001:DB8:1:3::1/64		N/A
	Link-local	FE80::2		N/A
R3	G0/0	2001:DB8:1:4::1/64		N/A
	G0/1	10.10.1.17	255.255.255.240	N/A
	S0/0/1	10.10.1.10	255.255.255.252	N/A
		2001:DB8:1:3::2/64		N/A
	Link-local	FE80::3		N/A
PC1	NIC			
PC2	NIC			
PC3	NIC			
PC4	NIC			

Objectives

Part 1: Test and Restore IPv4 Connectivity

Part 2: Test and Restore IPv6 Connectivity

Scenario

There are connectivity issues in this activity. In addition to gathering and documenting information about the network, you will locate the problems and implement acceptable solutions to restore connectivity.

Note: The user EXEC password is **cisco**. The privileged EXEC password is **class**.

Part 1: Test and Restore IPv4 Connectivity

Step 1:   Use ipconfig and ping to verify connectivity.

    a.   Click **PC1** and click the **Desktop** tab > **Command Prompt**.

    b.   Enter the **ipconfig /all** command to collect the IPv4 information. Complete the **Addressing Table** with the IPv4 address, subnet mask, and default gateway.

    c.   Click **PC3** and click the **Desktop** tab > **Command Prompt**.

    d.   Enter the **ipconfig /all** command to collect the IPv4 information. Complete the **Addressing Table** with the IPv4 address, subnet mask, and default gateway.

    e.   Test connectivity between **PC1** and **PC3**. The ping should fail.

Step 2:   Locate the source of connectivity failure.

    a.   From **PC1**, enter the necessary command to trace the route to **PC3**. What is the last successful IPv4 address that was reached? _____

    b.   The trace will eventually end after 30 attempts. Enter **Ctrl+C** to stop the trace before 30 attempts.

    c.   From **PC3**, enter the necessary command to trace the route to **PC1**. What is the last successful IPv4 address that was reached? _____

    d.   Enter **Ctrl+C** to stop the trace.

    e.   Click **R1** and then the **CLI** tab. Press **ENTER** and log in to the router.

    f.   Enter the **show ip interface brief** command to list the interfaces and their status. There are two IPv4 addresses on the router. One should have been recorded in Step 2a. What is the other? _____

    g.   Enter the **show ip route** command to list the networks to which the router is connected. Note that there are two networks connected to the **Serial0/0/1** interface. What are they? _____

    h.   Repeat step 2e to 2g with **R3** and the answers here. _____

    Notice how the serial interface for R3 changes.

    i.   Run more tests if it helps visualize the problem. Simulation mode is available.

Step 3:   Propose a solution to solve the problem.

    a.   Compare your answers in Step 2 to the documentation you have available for the network. What is the error? _____

_____

    b.   What solution would you propose to correct the problem? _____

_____

Step 4:   Implement the plan.

Implement the solution you proposed in Step 3b.

Step 5:   Verify that connectivity is restored.

    a.   From **PC1** test connectivity to **PC3**.

    b.   From **PC3** test connectivity to **PC1**. Is the problem resolved? _____

Step 6:   Document the solution.

Part 2: Test and Restore IPv6 Connectivity

Step 1:   Use ipv6config and ping to verify connectivity.

    a.   Click **PC2** and click the **Desktop** tab > **Command Prompt**.

    b.   Enter the **ipv6config /all** command to collect the IPv6 information. Complete the **Addressing Table** with the IPv6 address, subnet prefix, and default gateway.

    c.   Click **PC4** and click the **Desktop** tab > **Command Prompt**.

    d.   Enter the **ipv6config /all** command to collect the IPv6 information. Complete the **Addressing Table** with the IPv6 address, subnet prefix, and default gateway.

    e.   Test connectivity between **PC2** and **PC4**. The ping should fail.

Step 2:   Locate the source of connectivity failure.

    a.   From **PC2**, enter the necessary command to trace the route to **PC4**. What is the last successful IPv6 address that was reached? _____

    b.   The trace will eventually end after 30 attempts. Enter **Ctrl+C** to stop the trace before 30 attempts.

    c.   From **PC4**, enter the necessary command to trace the route to **PC2**. What is the last successful IPv6 address that was reached? _____

    d.   Enter **Ctrl+C** to stop the trace.

    e.   Click **R3** and then the **CLI** tab. Press **ENTER** and log in to the router.

    f.   Enter the **show ipv6 interface brief** command to list the interfaces and their status. There are two IPv6 addresses on the router. One should match the gateway address recorded in Step 1d. Is there a discrepancy? _____

    g.   Run more tests if it helps visualize the problem. Simulation mode is available.

Step 3:   Propose a solution to solve the problem.

   a.   Compare your answers in Step 2 to the documentation you have available for the network. What is the error? _____

   b.   What solution would you propose to correct the problem? _____

_____

Step 4:   Implement the plan.

Implement the solution you proposed in Step 3b.

Step 5:   Verify that connectivity is restored.

   a.   From **PC2** test connectivity to **PC4**.

   b.   From **PC4** test connectivity to **PC2**. Is the problem resolved? _____

Step 6:   Document the solution.

Suggested Scoring Rubric

Activity Section	Question Location	Possible Points	Earned Points
Part 1: Test and Restore Connectivity Between PC1 and PC3	Step 1b	5	
	Step 1d	5	
	Step 2a	5	
	Step 2c	5	
	Step 2f	5	
	Step 2g	5	
	Step 2h	5	
	Step 3a	5	
	Step 3b	5	
	Part 1 Total	45	
Part 2: Test and Restore Connectivity Between PC2 and PC4	Step 1b	5	
	Step 1d	5	
	Step 2a	5	
	Step 2c	5	
	Step 2f	5	
	Step 3a	5	
	Step 3b	5	
	Part 2 Total	35	
	Packet Tracer Score	20	
	Total Score	100	

7.3.2.7 Lab–Testing Network Connectivity with Ping and Traceroute

Topology

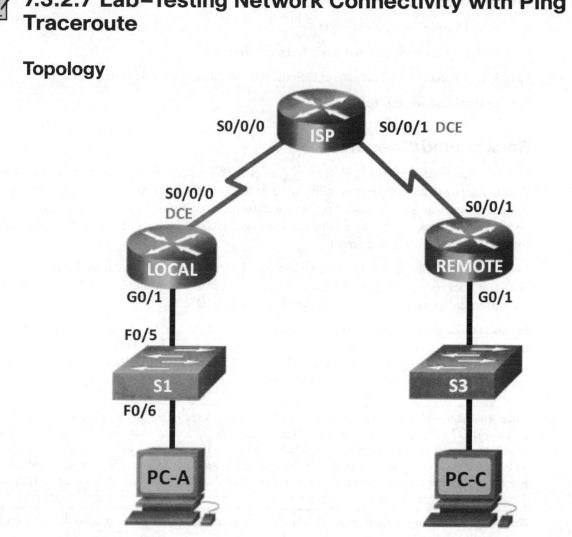

Addressing Table

Device	Interface	IP Address	Subnet Mask	Default Gateway
LOCAL	G0/1	192.168.1.1	255.255.255.0	N/A
	S0/0/0 (DCE)	10.1.1.1	255.255.255.252	N/A
ISP	S0/0/0	10.1.1.2	255.255.255.252	N/A
	S0/0/1 (DCE)	10.2.2.2	255.255.255.252	N/A
REMOTE	G0/1	192.168.3.1	255.255.255.0	N/A
	S0/0/1	10.2.2.1	255.255.255.252	N/A
S1	VLAN 1	192.168.1.11	255.255.255.0	192.168.1.1
S3	VLAN 1	192.168.3.11	255.255.255.0	192.168.3.1
PC-A	NIC	192.168.1.3	255.255.255.0	192.168.1.1
PC-C	NIC	192.168.3.3	255.255.255.0	192.168.3.1

Objectives

Part 1: Build and Configure the Network

Part 2: Use Ping Command for Basic Network Testing

Part 3: Use Tracert and Traceroute Commands for Basic Network Testing

Part 4: Troubleshoot the Topology

Background/Scenario

Ping and traceroute are two tools that are indispensable when testing TCP/IP network connectivity. Ping is a network administration utility used to test the reachability of a device on an IP network. This utility also measures the round-trip time for messages sent from the originating host to a destination computer. The ping utility is available on Windows, UNIX-like operating systems (OS), and the Cisco Internetwork Operating System (IOS).

The traceroute utility is a network diagnostic tool for displaying the route and measuring the transit delays of packets traveling an IP network. The tracert utility is available on Windows, and a similar utility, traceroute, is available on UNIX-like OS and Cisco IOS.

In this lab, the **ping** and **traceroute** commands are examined and command options are explored to modify the command behavior. Cisco devices and PCs are used in this lab for command exploration. Cisco routers will use Enhanced Interior Gateway Routing Protocol (EIGRP) to route packets between networks. The necessary Cisco device configurations are provided in this lab.

Note: The routers used with CCNA hands-on labs are Cisco 1941 Integrated Services Routers (ISRs) with Cisco IOS Release 15.2(4)M3 (universalk9 image). The switches used are Cisco Catalyst 2960s with Cisco IOS Release 15.0(2) (lanbasek9 image). Other routers, switches and Cisco IOS versions can be used. Depending on the model and Cisco IOS version, the commands available and output produced might vary from what is shown in the labs. Refer to the Router Interface Summary Table at the end of this lab for the correct interface identifiers.

Note: Make sure that the routers and switches have been erased and have no startup configurations. If you are unsure, contact your instructor.

Required Resources

- 3 Routers (Cisco 1941 with Cisco IOS Release 15.2(4)M3 universal image or comparable)
- 2 Switches (Cisco 2960 with Cisco IOS Release 15.0(2) lanbasek9 image or comparable)
- 2 PCs (Windows 7 or 8 with terminal emulation program, such as Tera Term)
- Console cables to configure the Cisco IOS devices via the console ports
- Ethernet and serial cables as shown in the topology

Part 1: Build and Configure the Network

In Part 1, you will set up the network in the topology and configure the PCs and Cisco devices. The initial configurations for the routers and switches are provided for your reference. In this topology, EIGRP is used to route packets between networks.

Step 1: Cable the network as shown in the topology.

Step 2: Erase the configurations on the routers and switches, and reload the devices.

Step 3: Configure PC IP addresses and default gateways according to the Addressing Table.

Step 4: Configure the LOCAL, ISP, and REMOTE routers using the initial configurations provided below.

At the switch or router global config mode prompt, copy and paste the configuration for each device. Save the configuration to startup-config.

Initial configurations for the LOCAL router:

```
hostname LOCAL
no ip domain-lookup
interface s0/0/0
 ip address 10.1.1.1 255.255.255.252
 clock rate 56000
 no shutdown
interface g0/1
 ip add 192.168.1.1 255.255.255.0
 no shutdown
router eigrp 1
 network 10.1.1.0 0.0.0.3
 network 192.168.1.0 0.0.0.255
 no auto-summary
```

Initial configurations for ISP:

```
hostname ISP
no ip domain-lookup
interface s0/0/0
 ip address 10.1.1.2 255.255.255.252
 no shutdown
interface s0/0/1
 ip add 10.2.2.2 255.255.255.252
 clock rate 56000
 no shutdown
router eigrp 1
 network 10.1.1.0 0.0.0.3
 network 10.2.2.0 0.0.0.3
 no auto-summary
end
```

Initial configurations for REMOTE:

```
hostname REMOTE
no ip domain-lookup
interface s0/0/1
 ip address 10.2.2.1 255.255.255.252
 no shutdown
interface g0/1
 ip add 192.168.3.1 255.255.255.0
 no shutdown
```

```
router eigrp 1
 network 10.2.2.0 0.0.0.3
 network 192.168.3.0 0.0.0.255
 no auto-summary
end
```

Step 5: Configure the S1 and S3 switches with the initial configurations.

Initial configurations for S1:

```
hostname S1
no ip domain-lookup
interface vlan 1
 ip add 192.168.1.11 255.255.255.0
 no shutdown
 exit
ip default-gateway 192.168.1.1
end
```

Initial configurations for S3:

```
hostname S3
no ip domain-lookup
interface vlan 1
 ip add 192.168.3.11 255.255.255.0
 no shutdown
 exit
ip default-gateway 192.168.3.1
end
```

Step 6: Configure an IP host table on the LOCAL router.

The IP host table allows you to use a hostname to connect to a remote device rather than an IP address. The host table provides name resolution for the device with the following configurations. Copy and paste the following configurations for the LOCAL router. The configurations will allow you to use the hostnames for **ping** and **traceroute** commands on the LOCAL router.

```
ip host REMOTE 10.2.2.1 192.168.3.1
ip host ISP 10.1.1.2 10.2.2.2
ip host LOCAL 192.168.1.1 10.1.1.1
ip host PC-C 192.168.3.3
ip host PC-A 192.168.1.3
ip host S1 192.168.1.11
ip host S3 192.168.3.11
end
```

Part 2: Use Ping Command for Basic Network Testing

In Part 2 of this lab, use the **ping** command to verify end-to-end connectivity. Ping operates by sending Internet Control Message Protocol (ICMP) echo request packets to the target host and then waiting for an ICMP response. It can record the round trip time and any packet loss.

You will examine the results with the **ping** command and the additional ping options that are available on Windows-based PCs and Cisco devices.

Step 1:   Test network connectivity from the LOCAL network using PC-A.

All the pings from PC-A to other devices in the topology should be successful. If they are not, check the topology and the cabling, as well as the configuration of the Cisco devices and the PCs.

a.   Ping from PC-A to its default gateway (LOCAL's GigabitEthernet 0/1 interface).

```
C:\Users\User1> ping 192.168.1.1
Pinging 192.168.1.1 with 32 bytes of data:
Reply from 192.168.1.1: bytes=32 time<1ms TTL=255
Reply from 192.168.1.1: bytes=32 time<1ms TTL=255
Reply from 192.168.1.1: bytes=32 time<1ms TTL=255
Reply from 192.168.1.1: bytes=32 time<1ms TTL=255

Ping statistics for 192.168.1.1:
    Packets: Sent = 4, Received = 4, Lost = 0 (0% loss),
Approximate round trip times in milli-seconds:
    Minimum = 0ms, Maximum = 0ms, Average = 0ms
```

In this example, four (4) ICMP requests, 32 bytes each, were sent and the responses were received in less than one millisecond with no packet loss. The transmission and reply time increases as the ICMP requests and responses are processed by more devices during the journey to and from the final destination.

b.   From PC-A, ping the addresses listed in the following table and record the average round trip time and Time To Live (TTL).

Destination	Average Round Trip Time (ms)	TTL
192.168.1.1 (LOCAL)		
192.168.1.11 (S1)		
10.1.1.1 (LOCAL)		
10.1.1.2 (ISP)		
10.2.2.2 (ISP)		
10.2.2.1 (REMOTE)		
192.168.3.1 (REMOTE)		
192.168.3.11 (S3)		
192.168.3.3 (PC-C)		

Notice the average round trip time to 192.168.3.3 (PC-C). The time increased because the ICMP requests were processed by three routers before PC-A received the reply from PC-C.

```
C:\Users\User1> ping 192.168.3.3
Pinging 192.168.3.3 with 32 bytes of data:
Reply from 192.168.3.3: bytes=32 time=41ms TTL=125
Reply from 192.168.3.3: bytes=32 time=41ms TTL=125
Reply from 192.168.3.3: bytes=32 time=40ms TTL=125
Reply from 192.168.3.3: bytes=32 time=41ms TTL=125
```

```
Ping statistics for 192.168.3.3:
    Packets: Sent = 4, Received = 4, Lost = 0 (0% loss),
Approximate round trip times in milli-seconds:
    Minimum = 40ms, Maximum = 41ms, Average = 40ms
```

Step 2:   Use extended ping commands on a PC.

The default **ping** command sends four requests at 32 bytes each. It waits 4,000 milliseconds (4 seconds) for each response to be returned before displaying the "Request timed out" message. The **ping** command can be fine-tuned for troubleshooting a network.

a.   At the command prompt, type **ping** and press Enter.

```
C:\Users\User1> ping
Usage: ping [-t] [-a] [-n count] [-l size] [-f] [-i TTL] [-v TOS]
            [-r count] [-s count] [[-j host-list] | [-k host-list]]
            [-w timeout] [-R] [-S srcaddr] [-4] [-6] target_name

Options:
    -t              Ping the specified host until stopped.
                    To see statistics and continue - type Control-Break;
                    To stop - type Control-C.
    -a              Resolve addresses to hostnames.
    -n count        Number of echo requests to send.
    -l size         Send buffer size.
    -f              Set Don't Fragment flag in packet (IPv4-only).
    -i TTL          Time To Live.
    -v TOS          Type Of Service (IPv4-only. This setting has been deprecated
                    and has no effect on the type of service field in the IP
                    Header).
    -r count        Record route for count hops (IPv4-only).
    -s count        Timestamp for count hops (IPv4-only).
    -j host-list    Loose source route along host-list (IPv4-only).
    -k host-list    Strict source route along host-list (IPv4-only).
    -w timeout      Timeout in milliseconds to wait for each reply.
    -R              Use routing header to test reverse route also (IPv6-only).
    -S srcaddr      Source address to use.
    -4              Force using IPv4.
    -6              Force using IPv6.
```

b.   Using the **−t** option, ping PC-C to verify that PC-C is reachable.

```
C:\Users\User1> ping -t 192.168.3.3
Reply from 192.168.3.3: bytes=32 time=41ms TTL=125
Reply from 192.168.3.3: bytes=32 time=40ms TTL=125
```

To illustrate the results when a host is unreachable, disconnect the cable between the REMOTE router and the S3 switch, or shut down the GigabitEthernet 0/1 interface on the REMOTE router.

```
Reply from 192.168.3.3: bytes=32 time=41ms TTL=125
Reply from 192.168.1.3: Destination host unreachable.
Reply from 192.168.1.3: Destination host unreachable.
```

While the network is functioning correctly, the **ping** command can determine whether the destination responded and how long it took to receive a reply from the destination. If a network connectivity problem exists, the **ping** command displays an error message.

c. Reconnect the Ethernet cable or enable the GigabitEthernet interface on the REMOTE router (using the **no shutdown** command) before moving onto the next step. After about 30 seconds, the ping should be successful again.

```
Request timed out.
Request timed out.
Request timed out.
Request timed out.
Reply from 192.168.3.3: bytes=32 time=41ms TTL=125
Reply from 192.168.3.3: bytes=32 time=40ms TTL=125
```

d. Press **Ctrl+C** to stop the ping command.

Step 3: Test network connectivity from the LOCAL network using Cisco devices.

The **ping** command is also available on Cisco devices. In this step, the **ping** command is examined using the LOCAL router and the S1 switch.

a. Ping PC-C on the REMOTE network using the IP address of 192.168.3.3 from the LOCAL router.

```
LOCAL# ping 192.168.3.3
Type escape sequence to abort.
Sending 5, 100-byte ICMP Echos to 192.168.3.3, timeout is 2 seconds:
!!!!!
Success rate is 100 percent (5/5), round-trip min/avg/max = 60/64/68 ms
```

The exclamation point (!) indicates that the ping was successful from the LOCAL router to PC-C. The round trip takes an average of 64 ms with no packet loss, as indicated by a 100% success rate.

b. Because a local host table was configured on the LOCAL router, you can ping PC-C on the REMOTE network using the hostname configured from the LOCAL router.

```
LOCAL# ping PC-C
Type escape sequence to abort.
Sending 5, 100-byte ICMP Echos to 192.168.3.3, timeout is 2 seconds:
!!!!!
Success rate is 100 percent (5/5), round-trip min/avg/max = 60/63/64 ms
```

c. There are more options available for the **ping** command. At the CLI, type **ping** and press Enter. Input **192.168.3.3** or **PC-C** for the Target IP address. Press Enter to accept the default value for other options.

```
LOCAL# ping
Protocol [ip]:
Target IP address: PC-C
Repeat count [5]:
Datagram size [100]:
Timeout in seconds [2]:
Extended commands [n]:
Sweep range of sizes [n]:
Type escape sequence to abort.
Sending 5, 100-byte ICMP Echos to 192.168.3.3, timeout is 2 seconds:
!!!!!
Success rate is 100 percent (5/5), round-trip min/avg/max = 60/63/64 ms
```

d. You can use an extended ping to observe when there is a network issue. Start the **ping** command to 192.168.3.3 with a repeat count of 500. Then, disconnect the cable between the REMOTE router and the S3 switch or shut down the GigabitEthernet 0/1 interface on the REMOTE router.

Reconnect the Ethernet cable or enable the GigabitEthernet interface on the REMOTE router after the exclamation points (!) have been replaced by the letter U and periods (.). After about 30 seconds, the ping should be successful again. Press **Ctrl+Shift+6** to stop the **ping** command if desired.

```
LOCAL# ping
Protocol [ip]:
Target IP address: 192.168.3.3
Repeat count [5]: 500
Datagram size [100]:
Timeout in seconds [2]:
Extended commands [n]:
Sweep range of sizes [n]:
Type escape sequence to abort.
Sending 500, 100-byte ICMP Echos to 192.168.3.3, timeout is 2 seconds:
!!!!!!!!!!!!!!!!!!!!!!!!!!!!!!!!!!!!!!!!!!!!!!!!!!!!!!!!!!!!!!!!!!!!!!!!!!
!!!!!!!!!!!!!!!!!!!!!!!!!!!!!!!!!!!!!!!!!!!!!!!!!!!!!!!!!!!!!!!!!!!!!!!!!!
!!!!!!!!!!!!!!!!!!!!!!!!!!!!!!!!!!!!!!!!!!!!!!!!!!!!!!!!!!!!!!!U...............
....!!!!!!!!!!!!!!!!!!!!!!!!!!!!!!!!!!!!!!!!!!!!!!!!!!!!!!!!!!!!!!!!!!!!!!!
!!!!!!!!!!!!!!!!!!!!!!!!!!!!!!!!!!!!!!!!!!!!!!!!!!!!!!!!!!!!!!!!!!!!!!!!!!
!!!!!!!!!!!!!!!!!!!!!!!!!!!!!!!!!!!!!!!!!!!!!!!!!!!!!!!!!!!!!!!!!!!!!!!!!!
!!!!!!!!!!!!!!!!!!!!!!!!!!!!!!!!!!!!!!!!!!!!!!!!!!!!!!!!!!!!!!!!!!!!!!!!!!
!!!!!!!!!!!
Success rate is 95 percent (479/500), round-trip min/avg/max = 60/63/72 ms
```

The letter U in the results indicates that a destination is unreachable. An error protocol data unit (PDU) was received by the LOCAL router. Each period (.) in the output indicates that the ping timed out while waiting for a reply from PC-C. In this example, 5% of the packets were lost during the simulated network outage.

Note: You can also use the following command for the same results:
```
LOCAL# ping 192.168.3.3 repeat 500
```
or
```
LOCAL# ping PC-C repeat 500
```

e. You can also test network connectivity with a switch. In this example, the S1 switch pings the S3 switch on the REMOTE network.

```
S1# ping 192.168.3.11
Type escape sequence to abort.
Sending 5, 100-byte ICMP Echos to 192.168.3.11, timeout is 2 seconds:
!!!!!
Success rate is 100 percent (5/5), round-trip min/avg/max = 67/67/68 ms
```

The **ping** command is extremely useful when troubleshooting network connectivity. However, ping cannot indicate the location of a problem when a ping is not successful. The **tracert** (or **traceroute**) command can display network latency and path information.

Part 3: Use Tracert and Traceroute Commands for Basic Network Testing

The commands for tracing routes can be found on PCs and network devices. For a Windows-based PC, the **tracert** command uses ICMP messages to trace the path to the final destination. The **traceroute** command utilizes the User Datagram Protocol (UDP) datagrams for tracing routes to the final destination for Cisco devices and other UNIX-like PCs.

In Part 3, you will examine the traceroute commands and determine the path that a packet travels to its final destination. You will use the **tracert** command from the Windows PCs and the **traceroute** command from the Cisco devices. You will also examine the options that are available for fine-tuning the traceroute results.

Step 1: Use the tracert command from PC-A to PC-C.

a. At the command prompt, type **tracert 192.168.3.3**.

```
C:\Users\User1> tracert 192.168.3.3
Tracing route to PC-C [192.168.3.3]
Over a maximum of 30 hops:

  1    <1 ms    <1 ms    <1 ms    192.168.1.1
  2    24 ms    24 ms    24 ms    10.1.1.2
  3    48 ms    48 ms    48 ms    10.2.2.1
  4    59 ms    59 ms    59 ms    PC-C [192.168.3.3]

Trace complete.
```

The tracert results indicate the path from PC-A to PC-C is from PC-A to LOCAL to ISP to REMOTE to PC-C. The path to PC-C traveled through three router hops to the final destination of PC-C.

Step 2: Explore additional options for the tracert command.

a. At the command prompt, type **tracert** and press Enter.

```
C:\Users\User1> tracert

Usage: tracert [-d] [-h maximum_hops] [-j host-list] [-w timeout]
               [-R] [-S srcaddr] [-4] [-6] target_name

Options:
    -d                 Do not resolve addresses to hostnames.
    -h maximum_hops    Maximum number of hops to search for target.
    -j host-list       Loose source route along host-list (IPv4-only).
    -w timeout         Wait timeout milliseconds for each reply.
    -R                 Trace round-trip path (IPv6-only).
    -S srcaddr         Source address to use (IPv6-only).
    -4                 Force using IPv4.
    -6                 Force using IPv6.
```

b. Use the **-d** option. Notice that the IP address of 192.168.3.3 is not resolved as PC-C.

```
C:\Users\User1> tracert -d 192.168.3.3
Tracing route to 192.168.3.3 over a maximum of 30 hops:

  1    <1 ms    <1 ms    <1 ms    192.168.1.1
  2    24 ms    24 ms    24 ms    10.1.1.2
```

```
3    48 ms    48 ms    48 ms    10.2.2.1
4    59 ms    59 ms    59 ms    192.168.3.3
```

Trace complete.

Step 3: Use the traceroute command from the LOCAL router to PC-C.

a. At the command prompt, type **traceroute 192.168.3.3** or **traceroute PC-C** on the LOCAL router. The hostnames are resolved because a local IP host table was configured on the LOCAL router.

```
LOCAL# traceroute 192.168.3.3
Type escape sequence to abort.
Tracing the route to PC-C (192.168.3.3)
VRF info: (vrf in name/id, vrf out name/id)
  1 ISP (10.1.1.2) 16 msec 16 msec 16 msec
  2 REMOTE (10.2.2.1) 28 msec 32 msec 28 msec
  3 PC-C (192.168.3.3) 32 msec 28 msec 32 msec


LOCAL# traceroute PC-C
Type escape sequence to abort.
Tracing the route to PC-C (192.168.3.3)
VRF info: (vrf in name/id, vrf out name/id)
  1 ISP (10.1.1.2) 16 msec 16 msec 16 msec
  2 REMOTE (10.2.2.1) 28 msec 32 msec 28 msec
  3 PC-C (192.168.3.3) 32 msec 32 msec 28 msec
```

Step 4: Use the traceroute command from the S1 switch to PC-C.

a. On the S1 switch, type **traceroute 192.168.3.3**. The hostnames are not displayed in the traceroute results because a local IP host table was not configured on this switch.

```
S1# traceroute 192.168.3.3
Type escape sequence to abort.
Tracing the route to 192.168.3.3
VRF info: (vrf in name/id, vrf out name/id)
  1 192.168.1.1 1007 msec 0 msec 0 msec
  2 10.1.1.2 17 msec 17 msec 16 msec
  3 10.2.2.1 34 msec 33 msec 26 msec
  4 192.168.3.3 33 msec 34 msec 33 msec
```

The **traceroute** command has additional options. You can use the ? or just press Enter after typing **traceroute** at the prompt to explore these options.

The following link provides more information regarding the **ping** and **traceroute** commands for a Cisco device:

http://www.cisco.com/en/US/products/sw/iosswrel/ps1831/products_tech_note-09186a00800a6057.shtml

Part 4: Troubleshoot the Topology

Step 1:   Erase the configurations on the REMOTE router.

Step 2:   Reload the REMOTE router.

Step 3:   Copy and paste the following configuration into the REMOTE router.

```
hostname REMOTE
no ip domain-lookup
interface s0/0/1
 ip address 10.2.2.1 255.255.255.252
 no shutdown
interface g0/1
 ip add 192.168.8.1 255.255.255.0
 no shutdown
router eigrp 1
 network 10.2.2.0 0.0.0.3
 network 192.168.3.0 0.0.0.255
 no auto-summary
end
```

Step 4:   From the LOCAL network, use ping and tracert or traceroute commands to troubleshoot and correct the problem on the REMOTE network.

    a.   Use the **ping** and **tracert** commands from PC-A.

        You can use the **tracert** command to determine end-to-end network connectivity. This tracert result indicates that PC-A can reach its default gateway of 192.168.1.1, but PC-A does not have network connectivity with PC-C.

```
C:\Users\User1> tracert 192.168.3.3


Tracing route to 192.168.3.3 over a maximum of 30 hops
  1    <1 ms     <1 ms     <1 ms   192.168.1.1
  2  192.168.1.1  reports: Destination host unreachable.


Trace complete.
```

        One way to locate the network issue is to ping each hop in the network to PC-C. First determine if PC-A can reach the ISP router Serial 0/0/1 interface with an IP address of 10.2.2.2.

```
C:\Users\Utraser1> ping 10.2.2.2


Pinging 10.2.2.2 with 32 bytes of data:
Reply from 10.2.2.2: bytes=32 time=41ms TTL=254
Reply from 10.2.2.2: bytes=32 time=41ms TTL=254
Reply from 10.2.2.2: bytes=32 time=41ms TTL=254
Reply from 10.2.2.2: bytes=32 time=41ms TTL=254


Ping statistics for 10.2.2.2:
    Packets: Sent = 4, Received = 4, Lost = 0 (0% loss),
Approximate round trip times in milli-seconds:
    Minimum = 20ms, Maximum = 21ms, Average = 20ms
```

The ping was successful to the ISP router. The next hop in the network is the REMOTE router. Ping the REMOTE router Serial 0/0/1 interface with an IP address of 10.2.2.1.

```
C:\Users\User1> ping 10.2.2.1

Pinging 10.2.2.1 with 32 bytes of data:
Reply from 10.2.2.1: bytes=32 time=41ms TTL=253
Reply from 10.2.2.1: bytes=32 time=41ms TTL=253
Reply from 10.2.2.1: bytes=32 time=41ms TTL=253
Reply from 10.2.2.1: bytes=32 time=41ms TTL=253

Ping statistics for 10.2.2.1:
    Packets: Sent = 4, Received = 4, Lost = 0 (0% loss),
Approximate round trip times in milli-seconds:
    Minimum = 40ms, Maximum = 41ms, Average = 40ms
```

PC-A can reach the REMOTE router. Based on the successful ping results from PC-A to the REMOTE router, the network connectivity issue is with 192.168.3.0/24 network. Ping the default gateway to PC-C, which is the GigabitEthernet 0/1 interface of the REMOTE router.

```
C:\Users\User1> ping 192.168.3.1

Pinging 192.168.3.1 with 32 bytes of data:
Reply from 192.168.1.1: Destination host unreachable.
Reply from 192.168.1.1: Destination host unreachable.
Reply from 192.168.1.1: Destination host unreachable.
Reply from 192.168.1.1: Destination host unreachable.

Ping statistics for 192.168.3.1:
    Packets: Sent = 4, Received = 4, Lost = 0 (0% loss),
```

PC-A cannot reach the GigabitEthernet 0/1 interface of the REMOTE router, as displayed by the results from the **ping** command.

The S3 switch can also be pinged from PC-A to verify the location of the networking connectivity issue by typing **ping 192.168.3.11** at the command prompt. Because PC-A cannot reach GigabitEthernet 0/1 of the REMOTE router, PC-A probably cannot ping the S3 switch successfully, as indicated by the results below.

```
C:\Users\User1> ping 192.168.3.11

Pinging 192.168.3.11 with 32 bytes of data:
Reply from 192.168.1.1: Destination host unreachable.
Reply from 192.168.1.1: Destination host unreachable.
Reply from 192.168.1.1: Destination host unreachable.
Reply from 192.168.1.1: Destination host unreachable.

Ping statistics for 192.168.3.11:
    Packets: Sent = 4, Received = 4, Lost = 0 (0% loss),
```

The tracert and ping results conclude that PC-A can reach the LOCAL, ISP, and REMOTE routers, but not PC-C or the S3 switch, nor the default gateway for PC-C.

b. Use the **show** commands to examine the running configurations for the REMOTE router.

```
REMOTE# show ip interface brief
Interface                   IP-Address     OK? Method Status                Protocol
Embedded-Service-Engine0/0  unassigned     YES unset  administratively down down
GigabitEthernet0/0          unassigned     YES unset  administratively down down
GigabitEthernet0/1          192.168.8.1    YES manual up                    up
Serial0/0/0                 unassigned     YES unset  administratively down down
Serial0/0/1                 10.2.2.1       YES manual up                    up


REMOTE# show run
<output omitted>
interface GigabitEthernet0/0
 no ip address
 shutdown
 duplex auto
 speed auto
!
interface GigabitEthernet0/1
 ip address 192.168.0.1 255.255.255.0
 duplex auto
 speed auto
!
interface Serial0/0/0
 no ip address
 shutdown
 clock rate 2000000
!
interface Serial0/0/1
 ip address 10.2.2.1 255.255.255.252
<output omitted>
```

The outputs of the **show run** and **show ip interface brief** commands indicate that the GigabitEthernet 0/1 interface is up/up, but was configured with an incorrect IP address.

c. Correct the IP address for GigabitEthernet 0/1.

```
REMOTE# configure terminal
Enter configuration commands, one per line.  End with CNTL/Z.
REMOTE(config)# interface GigabitEthernet 0/1
REMOTE(config-if)# ip address 192.168.3.1 255.255.255.0
```

d. Verify that PC-A can ping and tracert to PC-C.

```
C:\Users\User1> ping 192.168.3.3
Pinging 192.168.3.3 with 32 bytes of data:
Reply from 192.168.3.3: bytes=32 time=44ms TTL=125
Reply from 192.168.3.3: bytes=32 time=41ms TTL=125
Reply from 192.168.3.3: bytes=32 time=40ms TTL=125
Reply from 192.168.3.3: bytes=32 time=41ms TTL=125

Ping statistics for 192.168.3.3:
    Packets: Sent = 4, Received = 4, Lost = 0 (0% loss),
```

```
Approximate round trip times in milli-seconds:
    Minimum = 40ms, Maximum = 44ms, Average = 41ms


C:\Users\User1> tracert 192.168.3.3

Tracing route to PC-C [192.168.3.3]
Over a maximum of 30 hops:

    1    <1 ms    <1 ms    <1 ms    192.168.1.1
    2    24 ms    24 ms    24 ms    10.1.1.2
    3    48 ms    48 ms    48 ms    10.2.2.1
    4    59 ms    59 ms    59 ms    PC-C [192.168.3.3]


Trace complete.
```

Note: This can also be accomplished using **ping** and **traceroute** commands from the CLI on the LOCAL router and the S1 switch after verifying that there are no network connectivity issues on the 192.168.1.0/24 network.

Reflection

1. What could prevent ping or traceroute responses from reaching the originating device beside network connectivity issues?

_____

_____

2. If you ping a non-existent address on the remote network, such as 192.168.3.4, what is the message displayed by the **ping** command? What does this mean? If you ping a valid host address and receive this response, what should you check?

_____

_____

3. If you ping an address that does not exist in any network in your topology, such as 192.168.5.3, from a Windows-based PC, what is the message displayed by the **ping** command? What does this message indicate?

_____

_____

Router Interface Summary Table

Router Interface Summary				
Router Model	Ethernet Interface #1	Ethernet Interface #2	Serial Interface #1	Serial Interface #2
1800	Fast Ethernet 0/0 (F0/0)	Fast Ethernet 0/1 (F0/1)	Serial 0/0/0 (S0/0/0)	Serial 0/0/1 (S0/0/1)
1900	Gigabit Ethernet 0/0 (G0/0)	Gigabit Ethernet 0/1 (G0/1)	Serial 0/0/0 (S0/0/0)	Serial 0/0/1 (S0/0/1)
2801	Fast Ethernet 0/0 (F0/0)	Fast Ethernet 0/1 (F0/1)	Serial 0/1/0 (S0/1/0)	Serial 0/1/1 (S0/1/1)
2811	Fast Ethernet 0/0 (F0/0)	Fast Ethernet 0/1 (F0/1)	Serial 0/0/0 (S0/0/0)	Serial 0/0/1 (S0/0/1)
2900	Gigabit Ethernet 0/0 (G0/0)	Gigabit Ethernet 0/1 (G0/1)	Serial 0/0/0 (S0/0/0)	Serial 0/0/1 (S0/0/1)

Note: To find out how the router is configured, look at the interfaces to identify the type of router and how many interfaces the router has. There is no way to effectively list all the combinations of configurations for each router class. This table includes identifiers for the possible combinations of Ethernet and Serial interfaces in the device. The table does not include any other type of interface, even though a specific router may contain one. An example of this might be an ISDN BRI interface. The string in parentheses is the legal abbreviation that can be used in Cisco IOS commands to represent the interface.

7.3.2.8 Lab–Mapping the Internet

Objectives

Part 1: Test Network Connectivity Using Ping

Part 2: Trace a Route to a Remote Server Using Windows Tracert

Background

Route tracing computer software is a utility that lists the networks data has to traverse from the user's originating end device to a distant destination network.

This network tool is typically executed at the command line as:

```
tracert <destination network name or end device address>
```
(Microsoft Windows systems)

or

```
traceroute <destination network name or end device address>
```
(UNIX and similar systems)

Route tracing utilities allow a user to determine the path or routes as well as the delay across an IP network. Several tools exist to perform this function.

The **traceroute** (or **tracert**) tool is often used for network troubleshooting. By showing a list of routers traversed, it allows the user to identify the path taken to reach a particular destination on the network or across internetworks. Each router represents a point where one network connects to another network and through which the data packet was forwarded. The number of routers is known as the number of "hops" the data traveled from source to destination.

The displayed list can help identify data flow problems when trying to access a service such as a website. It can also be useful when performing tasks such as downloading data. If there are multiple websites (mirrors) available for the same data file, one can trace each mirror to get a good idea of which mirror would be the fastest to use.

Two trace routes between the same source and destination conducted some time apart may produce different results. This is due to the "meshed" nature of the interconnected networks that comprise the Internet and the Internet Protocols' ability to select different pathways over which to send packets.

Command-line-based route tracing tools are usually embedded with the operating system of the end device.

Scenario

Using an Internet connection, you will use three route tracing utilities to examine the Internet pathway to destination networks. This activity should be performed on a computer that has Internet access and access to the command line. First, you will use the Windows embedded tracert utility.

Required Resources

1 PC (Windows 7 or 8 with Internet access)

Part 1: Test Network Connectivity Using Ping

Step 1:   Determine whether the remote server is reachable.

To trace the route to a distant network, the PC used must have a working connection to the Internet.

a.   The first tool we will use is ping. Ping is a tool used to test whether a host is reachable. Packets of information are sent to the remote host with instructions to reply. Your local PC measures whether a response is received to each packet, and how long it takes for those packets to cross the network. The name ping comes from active sonar technology in which a pulse of sound is sent underwater and bounced off of terrain or other ships.

b.   From your PC, click the **Windows Start** icon, type **cmd** in the **Search programs and files** box, and then press Enter.

c.   At the command-line prompt, type **ping www.cisco.com**.

```
C:\>ping www.cisco.com

Pinging e144.dscb.akamaiedge.net [23.1.48.170] with 32 bytes of data:
Reply from 23.1.48.170: bytes=32 time=56ms TTL=57
Reply from 23.1.48.170: bytes=32 time=55ms TTL=57
Reply from 23.1.48.170: bytes=32 time=54ms TTL=57
Reply from 23.1.48.170: bytes=32 time=54ms TTL=57

Ping statistics for 23.1.48.170:
    Packets: Sent = 4, Received = 4, Lost = 0 (0% loss),
Approximate round trip times in milli-seconds:
    Minimum = 54ms, Maximum = 56ms, Average = 54ms
```

d.   The first output line displays the Fully Qualified Domain Name (FQDN) e144.dscb. akamaiedge.net. This is followed by the IP address 23.1.48.170. Cisco hosts the same web content on different servers throughout the world (known as mirrors). Therefore, depending upon where you are geographically, the FQDN and the IP address will be different.

e.   From this portion of the output:

```
Ping statistics for 23.1.48.170:
    Packets: Sent = 4, Received = 4, Lost = 0 (0% loss),
Approximate round trip times in milli-seconds:
    Minimum = 54ms, Maximum = 56ms, Average = 54ms
```

Four pings were sent and a reply was received from each ping. Because each ping was responded to, there was 0% packet loss. On average, it took 54 ms (54 milliseconds) for the packets to cross the network. A millisecond is 1/1,000th of a second.

Streaming video and online games are two applications that suffer when there is packet loss, or a slow network connection. A more accurate determination of an Internet connection speed can be determined by sending 100 pings, instead of the default 4. Here is how to do that:

```
C:\>ping -n 100 www.cisco.com
```

And here is what the output from that looks like:

```
Ping statistics for 23.45.0.170:
    Packets: Sent = 100, Received = 100, Lost = 0 (0% loss),
Approximate round trip times in milli-seconds:
    Minimum = 46ms, Maximum = 53ms, Average = 49ms
```

f. Now ping Regional Internet Registry (RIR) websites located in different parts of the world:

For Africa:

```
C:\> ping www.afrinic.net
```

```
C:\>ping www.afrinic.net

Pinging www.afrinic.net [196.216.2.136] with 32 bytes of data:
Reply from 196.216.2.136: bytes=32 time=314ms TTL=111
Reply from 196.216.2.136: bytes=32 time=312ms TTL=111
Reply from 196.216.2.136: bytes=32 time=313ms TTL=111
Reply from 196.216.2.136: bytes=32 time=313ms TTL=111

Ping statistics for 196.216.2.136:
    Packets: Sent = 4, Received = 4, Lost = 0 (0% loss),
Approximate round trip times in milli-seconds:
    Minimum = 312ms, Maximum = 314ms, Average = 313ms
```

For Australia:

```
C:\> ping www.apnic.net
```

```
C:\>ping www.apnic.net

Pinging www.apnic.net [202.12.29.194] with 32 bytes of data:
Reply from 202.12.29.194: bytes=32 time=286ms TTL=49
Reply from 202.12.29.194: bytes=32 time=287ms TTL=49
Reply from 202.12.29.194: bytes=32 time=286ms TTL=49
Reply from 202.12.29.194: bytes=32 time=286ms TTL=49

Ping statistics for 202.12.29.194:
    Packets: Sent = 4, Received = 4, Lost = 0 (0% loss),
Approximate round trip times in milli-seconds:
    Minimum = 286ms, Maximum = 287ms, Average = 286ms
```

For Europe:

```
C:\> ping www.ripe.net
```

```
C:\>ping www.ripe.net

Pinging www.ripe.net [193.0.6.139] with 32 bytes of data:
Request timed out.
Request timed out.
Request timed out.
Request timed out.

Ping statistics for 193.0.6.139:
    Packets: Sent = 4, Received = 0, Lost = 4 (100% loss),
```

For South America:

```
C:\> ping www.lacnic.net
```

```
C:\>ping www.lacnic.net

Pinging www.lacnic.net [200.3.14.147] with 32 bytes of data:
Reply from 200.3.14.147: bytes=32 time=158ms TTL=51
Reply from 200.3.14.147: bytes=32 time=158ms TTL=51
Reply from 200.3.14.147: bytes=32 time=158ms TTL=51
Reply from 200.3.14.147: bytes=32 time=157ms TTL=51

Ping statistics for 200.3.14.147:
    Packets: Sent = 4, Received = 4, Lost = 0 (0% loss),
Approximate round trip times in milli-seconds:
    Minimum = 157ms, Maximum = 158ms, Average = 157ms
```

All these pings were run from a computer located in the United States. What happens to the average ping time in milliseconds when data is traveling within the same continent (North America) as compared to data from North America traveling to different continents?

What is interesting about the pings that were sent to the European website?

_____

_____

Part 2: Trace a Route to a Remote Server Using Tracert

Step 1:   Determine what route across the Internet traffic takes to the remote server.

Now that basic reachability has been verified by using the ping tool, it is helpful to look more closely at each network segment that is crossed. To do this, the **tracert** tool will be used.

a.   At the command-line prompt, type **tracert www.cisco.com**.

```
C:\>tracert www.cisco.com

Tracing route to e144.dscb.akamaiedge.net [23.1.144.170]
over a maximum of 30 hops:

  1    <1 ms    <1 ms    <1 ms    dslrouter.westell.com [192.168.1.1]
  2    38 ms    38 ms    37 ms    10.18.20.1
  3    37 ms    37 ms    37 ms    G3-0-9-2204.ALBYNY-LCR-02.verizon-gni.net [130.8
1.196.190]
  4    43 ms    43 ms    42 ms    so-5-1-1-0.NY325-BB-RTR2.verizon-gni.net [130.81
.22.46]
  5    43 ms    43 ms    65 ms    0.so-4-0-2.XT2.NYC4.ALTER.NET [152.63.1.57]
  6    45 ms    45 ms    45 ms    0.so-3-2-0.XL4.EWR6.ALTER.NET [152.63.17.109]
  7    46 ms    48 ms    46 ms    TenGigE0-5-0-0.GW8.EWR6.ALTER.NET [152.63.21.14]

  8    45 ms    45 ms    45 ms    a23-1-144-170.deploy.akamaitechnologies.com [23.
1.144.170]

Trace complete.
```

b.   Save the tracert output in a text file as follows:

1)   Right-click the title bar of the Command Prompt window and choose **Edit > Select All.**

2)   Right-click the title bar of the Command Prompt window again and choose **Edit > Copy.**

3)   Open the **Windows Notepad** program: **Windows Start** icon > **All Programs** > **Accessories** > **Notepad.**

4)   To paste the output into Notepad, choose **Edit > Paste.**

5)   Choose **File > Save As** and save the Notepad file to your desktop as **tracert1.txt.**

c.   Run **tracert** for each destination website and save the output in sequentially numbered files.

```
C:\> tracert www.afrinic.net
C:\> tracert www.lacnic.net
```

d. Interpreting **tracert** outputs.

Routes traced can go through many hops and a number of different Internet Service Providers (ISPs), depending on the size of your ISP, and the location of the source and destination hosts. Each "hop" represents a router. A router is a specialized type of computer used to direct traffic across the Internet. Imagine taking an automobile trip across several countries using many highways. At different points in the trip, you come to a fork in the road in which you have the option to select from several different highways. Now further imagine that there is a device at each fork in the road that directs you to take the correct highway to your final destination. That is what a router does for packets on a network.

Because computers talk in numbers, rather than words, routers are uniquely identified using IP addresses (numbers with the format x.x.x.x). The **tracert** tool shows you what path through the network a packet of information takes to reach its final destination. The **tracert** tool also gives you an idea of how fast traffic is going on each segment of the network. Three packets are sent to each router in the path, and the return time is measured in milliseconds. Now use this information to analyze the **tracert** results to www.cisco.com. Below is the entire traceroute:

```
C:\>tracert www.cisco.com

Tracing route to e144.dscb.akamaiedge.net [23.1.144.170]
over a maximum of 30 hops:

  1    <1 ms    <1 ms    <1 ms   dslrouter.westell.com [192.168.1.1]
  2    38 ms    38 ms    37 ms   10.18.20.1
  3    37 ms    37 ms    37 ms   G3-0-9-2204.ALBYNY-LCR-02.verizon-gni.net [130.8
1.196.190]
  4    43 ms    43 ms    42 ms   so-5-1-1-0.NY325-BB-RTR2.verizon-gni.net [130.81
.22.46]
  5    43 ms    43 ms    65 ms   0.so-4-0-2.XT2.NYC4.ALTER.NET [152.63.1.57]
  6    45 ms    45 ms    45 ms   0.so-3-2-0.XL4.EWR6.ALTER.NET [152.63.17.109]
  7    46 ms    48 ms    46 ms   TenGigE0-5-0-0.GW8.EWR6.ALTER.NET [152.63.21.14]

  8    45 ms    45 ms    45 ms   a23-1-144-170.deploy.akamaitechnologies.com [23.
1.144.170]

Trace complete.
```

Below is the breakdown:

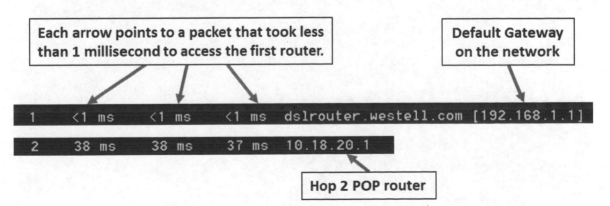

Each arrow points to a packet that took less than 1 millisecond to access the first router.

Default Gateway on the network

```
1    <1 ms    <1 ms    <1 ms   dslrouter.westell.com [192.168.1.1]
2    38 ms    38 ms    37 ms   10.18.20.1
```

Hop 2 POP router

In the example output shown above, the tracert packets travel from the source PC to the local router default gateway (hop 1: 192.168.1.1) to the ISPs Point of Presence (POP) router (hop 2: 10.18.20.1). Every ISP has numerous POP routers. These POP routers are at the edge of the ISP's network and are the means by which customers connect to the Internet. The packets travel along the Verizon network for two hops and then jump to a router that belongs to alter.net. This could mean that the packets have traveled to another ISP. This is significant because sometimes there is packet loss in the transition between ISPs, or sometimes one ISP is slower than another. How could we determine if alter.net is another ISP or the same ISP?

e. There is an Internet tool known as whois. The whois tool allows us to determine who owns a domain name. A web-based whois tool is found at http://whois.domaintools.com/. This domain is also owned by Verizon according to the web-based whois tool.

```
Registrant:
        Verizon Business Global LLC
        Verizon Business Global LLC
        One Verizon Way
         Basking Ridge NJ 07920
        US
           domainlegalcontact@verizon.com  +1.7033513164 Fax: +1.7033513669

   Domain Name: alter.net
```

To summarize, Internet traffic starts at a home PC and travels through the home router (hop 1). It then connects to the ISP and travels through its network (hops 2-7) until it arrives at the remote server (hop 8). This is a relatively unusual example in which there is only one ISP involved from start to finish. It is typical to have two or more ISPs involved as displayed in the following examples.

f. Now examine an example that involves Internet traffic crossing multiple ISPs. Below is the tracert for www.afrinic.net:

```
C:\>tracert www.afrinic.net

Tracing route to www.afrinic.net [196.216.2.136]
over a maximum of 30 hops:

  1     1 ms    <1 ms    <1 ms  dslrouter.westell.com [192.168.1.1]
  2    39 ms    38 ms    37 ms  10.18.20.1
  3    40 ms    38 ms    39 ms  G4-0-0-2204.ALBYNY-LCR-02.verizon-gni.net [130.8
1.197.182]
  4    44 ms    43 ms    43 ms  so-5-1-1-0.NY325-BB-RTR2.verizon-gni.net [130.81
.22.46]
  5    43 ms    43 ms    42 ms  0.so-4-0-0.XT2.NYC4.ALTER.NET [152.63.9.249]
  6    43 ms    71 ms    43 ms  0.ae4.BR3.NYC4.ALTER.NET [152.63.16.185]
  7    47 ms    47 ms    47 ms  te-7-3-0.edge2.NewYork2.level3.net [4.68.111.137
]
  8    43 ms    55 ms    43 ms  vlan51.ebr1.NewYork2.Level3.net [4.69.138.222]
  9    52 ms    51 ms    51 ms  ae-3-3.ebr2.Washington1.Level3.net [4.69.132.89]

 10   130 ms   132 ms   132 ms  ae-42-42.ebr2.Paris1.Level3.net [4.69.137.53]
 11   139 ms   145 ms   140 ms  ae-46-46.ebr1.Frankfurt1.Level3.net [4.69.143.13
7]
 12   148 ms   140 ms   152 ms  ae-91-91.csw4.Frankfurt1.Level3.net [4.69.140.14
]
 13   144 ms   144 ms   146 ms  ae-92-92.ebr2.Frankfurt1.Level3.net [4.69.140.29
]
 14   151 ms   150 ms   150 ms  ae-23-23.ebr2.London1.Level3.net [4.69.148.193]

 15   150 ms   150 ms   150 ms  ae-58-223.csw2.London1.Level3.net [4.69.153.138]

 16   156 ms   156 ms   156 ms  ae-227-3603.edge3.London1.Level3.net [4.69.166.1
54]
 17   157 ms   159 ms   160 ms  195.50.124.34
 18   353 ms   340 ms   341 ms  168.209.201.74
 19   333 ms   333 ms   332 ms  csw4-pk1-gi1-1.ip.isnet.net [196.26.0.101]
 20   331 ms   331 ms   331 ms  196.37.155.180
 21   318 ms   316 ms   318 ms  fa1-0-1.ar02.jnb.afrinic.net [196.216.3.132]
 22   332 ms   334 ms   332 ms  196.216.2.136

Trace complete.
```

What happens at hop 7? Is level3.net the same ISP as hops 2-6, or a different ISP? Use the whois tool to answer this question.

What happens in hop 10 to the amount of time it takes for a packet to travel between Washington D.C. and Paris, as compared with the earlier hops 1-9?

What happens in hop 18? Do a whois lookup on 168.209.201.74 using the whois tool. Who owns this network?

g. Type tracert www.lacnic.net.

```
C:\>tracert www.lacnic.net

Tracing route to www.lacnic.net [200.3.14.147]
over a maximum of 30 hops:

  1    <1 ms    <1 ms    <1 ms  dslrouter.westell.com [192.168.1.1]
  2    38 ms    38 ms    37 ms  10.18.20.1
  3    38 ms    38 ms    39 ms  G3-0-9-2204.ALBYNY-LCR-02.verizon-gni.net [130.8
1.196.190]
  4    42 ms    43 ms    42 ms  so-5-1-1-0.NY325-BB-RTR2.verizon-gni.net [130.81
.22.46]
  5    82 ms    47 ms    47 ms  0.ae2.BR3.NYC4.ALTER.NET [152.63.16.49]
  6    46 ms    47 ms    56 ms  204.255.168.194
  7   157 ms   158 ms   157 ms  ge-1-1-0.100.gw1.gc.registro.br [159.63.48.38]
  8   156 ms   157 ms   157 ms  xe-5-0-1-0.core1.gc.registro.br [200.160.0.174]

  9   161 ms   161 ms   161 ms  xe-4-0-0-0.core2.nu.registro.br [200.160.0.164]

 10   158 ms   157 ms   157 ms  ae0-0.ar3.nu.registro.br [200.160.0.249]
 11   176 ms   176 ms   170 ms  gw02.lacnic.registro.br [200.160.0.213]
 12   158 ms   158 ms   158 ms  200.3.12.36
 13   157 ms   158 ms   157 ms  200.3.14.147

Trace complete.
```

What happens in hop 7?

_____

_____

_____

Reflection

What are the functional differences between the commands **ping** and **tracert**?

_____

_____

7.3.2.9 Packet Tracer–Troubleshooting IPv4 and IPv6 Addressing

Topology

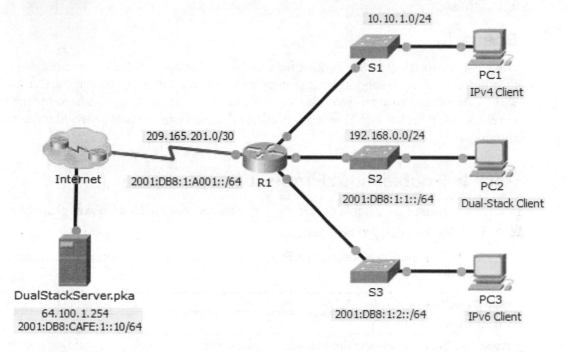

Addressing Table

Device	Interface	IPv4 Address	Subnet Mask	Default Gateway
		IPv6 Address/Prefix		
R1	G0/0	10.10.1.1	255.255.255.0	N/A
	G0/1	192.168.0.1	255.255.255.0	N/A
		2001:DB8:1:1::1/64		N/A
	G0/2	2001:DB8:1:2::1/64		N/A
	S0/0/0	209.165.201.2	255.255.255.252	N/A
		2001:DB8:1:A001::2/64		N/A
	Link-local	FE80::1		N/A
Dual Stack Server	NIC	64.100.1.254	255.255.255.0	64.100.1.1
		2001:DB8:CAFE:1::10/64		FE80::A
DNS Server	NIC	64.100.1.254	255.255.255.0	64.100.1.1
		2001:DB8:CAFE:1::10/64		FE80::A
PC1	NIC	10.10.1.2	255.255.255.0	10.10.1.1
PC2	NIC	192.168.0.2	255.255.255.0	192.168.0.1
		2001:DB8:1:1::2/64		FE80::1
PC3	NIC	2001:DB8:1:2::2/64		FE80::1

Objectives

Part 1: Troubleshoot First Issue

Part 2: Troubleshoot Second Issue

Part 3: Troubleshoot Third Issue

Scenario

You are a network technician working for a company that has decided to migrate from IPv4 to IPv6. In the interim, they must support both protocols (dual-stack). Three co-workers have called the help desk with problems and have received limited assistance. The help desk has escalated the matter to you, a Level 2 support technician. Your job is to locate the source of the problems and implement appropriate solutions.

Part 1: Troubleshoot First Issue

A customer using **PC1** complains that she cannot access the **dualstackserver.pka** web page.

Step 1: Verify a detailed help desk ticket.

The help desk collected the following information from the customer, over the phone. Verify that it is correct.

Help Desk Ticket	
Client Identifier: PC1	
Issue: Unable to access the dualstackserver.pka web page.	
Detailed information about the issue	
Test: Does the computer have an IP address using **ipconfig**?	Yes
Test: Can the computer contact its gateway using **ping**?	Yes
Test: Can the computer contact the server using **tracert**?	Yes
Test: Can the computer contact the server using **nslookup**?	No
Resolution: Escalate to Level 2 support.	

Step 2: Consider probable causes for the failure.

   a. Note the tests that have been conducted. If possible, discuss possible scenarios that would create this situation with your fellow network technicians (classmates).

   b. Run more tests if it helps visualize the problem. Simulation mode is available.

Step 3: Propose a solution to solve the problem.

Make a list of things that could be changed to solve this problem. Start with the solution that is most likely to work.

Step 4: Implement the plan.

Try the most likely solution from the list. If it has already been tried, move on to the next solution.

Step 5:   Verify the solution resolved the problem.

    a.   Repeat the tests from the help desk ticket. Did it solve the problem?

    b.   If the problem still exists, reverse the change if you are not sure it is correct and return to Step 4.

Step 6:   Document the solution.

Record the solution to the problem. If you ever encounter the same problem again, your notes will be very valuable. _____

Part 2: Troubleshoot Second Issue

A customer using **PC2** complains that he cannot access files on the **DualStackServer.pka** at 2001:DB8:CAFE:1::10.

Step 1:   Verify a detailed help desk ticket.

The help desk collected the following information from the customer, over the phone. Verify that it is correct.

Help Desk Ticket	
Client Identifier: PC2	
Issue: Unable to access the FTP service of 2001:DB8:CAFE:1:10.	
Detailed information about the issue	
Test: Does the computer have an IPv6 address using **ipv6config**?	Yes
Test: Can the computer contact its gateway using **ping**?	Yes
Test: Can the computer contact the server using **tracert**?	No
Resolution: Escalate to Level 2 support.	

Step 2:   Complete Steps 2 to 5 from Part 1 for this problem.

Step 3:   Document the solution.

Record the solution to the problem. If you ever encounter the same problem again, your notes will be very valuable. _____

Part 3: Troubleshoot Third Issue

A customer using **PC3** complains that he cannot communicate with **PC2**.

Step 1:   Verify a detailed help desk ticket.

The help desk collected the following information from the user over the phone. Verify that it is correct.

Help Desk Ticket

Client Identifier: PC3	
Issue: Unable to communicate with PC2.	
Detailed information about the issue	
Test: Does the computer have an IP address using **ipconfig**?	Yes
Test: Does the computer have an IPv6 address using **ipv6config**?	Yes
Test: Can the computer contact its IPv4 gateway using **ping**?	No
Test: Can the computer contact its IPv6 gateway using **ping**?	Yes
Test: Can the computer contact the IPv4 client using **tracert**?	No
Test: Can the computer contact the IPv6 client using **tracert**?	Yes
Resolution: Escalate to Level 2 support.	

Step 2:   Complete Steps 2 to 5 from Part 1 for this problem.

Step 3:   Document the solution.

Record the solution to the problem. If you ever encounter the same problem again, your notes will be very valuable.

7.4.1.1 Class Activity–The Internet of Everything... Naturally

Objectives

Explain the need for IPv6 network addresses.

Background /Scenario

Note: This activity may be completed individually or in small/large groups.

This chapter discussed the ways that small- to medium-sized businesses are connected to networks in groups. The IoE was introduced in the Modeling Activity at the beginning of this chapter.

For this activity, choose one of the following:

- Online banking
- World news
- Weather forecasting/climate
- Traffic conditions

Devise an IPv6 addressing scheme for the area you have chosen. Your addressing scheme should include how you would plan for:

- Subnetting
- Unicasts
- Multicasts

Keep a copy of your scheme to share with the class or learning community. Be prepared to explain:

- How subnetting, unicasts, and multicasts could be incorporated
- Where your addressing scheme could be used
- How small- to medium-size businesses would be affected by using your plan

Required Resources

- Paper, pens or pencils, or tablets
- Packet Tracer (if you would like to display how your network would look physically)
- Hard or soft copy of the final network topology with IPv6 addressing indicated for sharing with the class.

Reflection

What was the hardest part of designing this network model? Explain your answer.

_____

_____

_____

_____

7.4.1.2 Packet Tracer–Skills Integration Challenge

Packet Tracer
☐ Activity

Topology

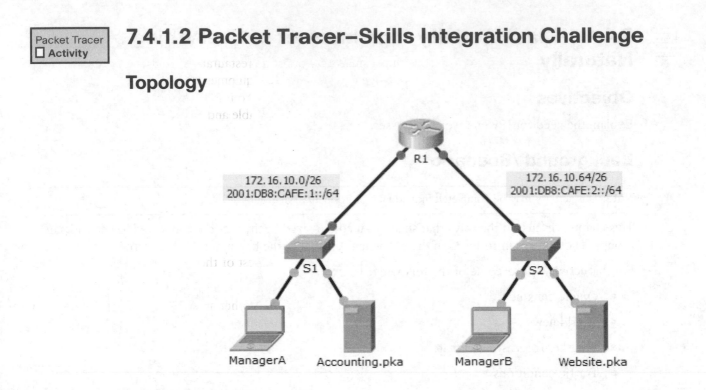

Addressing Table

Device	Interface	IPv4 Address	Subnet Mask	Default Gateway
		IPv6 Address/Prefix		
R1	G0/0	172.16.10.1	255.255.255.192	N/A
		2001:DB8:CAFE:1::1/64		N/A
	G0/1	172.16.10.65	255.255.255.192	N/A
		2001:DB8:CAFE:2::1/64		N/A
	Link-local	FE80::1		N/A
S1	VLAN1	172.16.10.62	255.255.255.192	172.16.10.1
S2	VLAN1	172.16.10.126	255.255.255.192	172.16.10.65
ManagerA	NIC	172.16.10.3	255.255.255.192	
		2001:DB8:CAFE:1::3/64		
Accounting.pka	NIC	172.16.10.2	255.255.255.192	
		2001:DB8:CAFE:1::2/64		
ManagerB	NIC	172.16.10.67	255.255.255.192	
		2001:DB8:CAFE:2::3/64		
Website.pka	NIC	172.16.10.66	255.255.255.192	
		2001:DB8:CAFE:2::2/64		

Scenario

Your company has won a contract to set up a small network for a restaurant owner. There are two restaurants near each other, and they all share one connection. The equipment and cabling is installed and the network administrator has designed the implementation plan. Your job is to implement the rest of the addressing scheme according to the abbreviated Addressing Table and verify connectivity.

Requirements

- Complete the **Addressing Table** documentation.
- Configure **R1** with IPv4 and IPv6 addressing.
- Configure **S1** with IPv4 addressing. **S2** is already configured.
- Configure **ManagerA** with IPv4 and IPv6 addressing. The rest of the clients are already configured.
- Verify connectivity. All clients should be able to ping each other and access the websites on **Accounting.pka** and **Website.pka**.

Suggested Scoring Rubric

Packet Tracer scores 80 points. Completing the **Addressing Table** is worth 20 points.

CHAPTER 8

Subnetting IP Networks

The Study Guide portion of this chapter uses a combination of matching, fill-in-the-blank, multiple-choice, and open-ended question exercises to test your knowledge and skills of basic router concepts and configuration. The Lab and Activities portion of this chapter includes all the online curriculum labs and Packet Tracer activities to ensure that you have mastered the hands-on skills needed to understand basic IP addressing and router configuration.

As you work through this chapter, use Chapter 8 in *Introduction to Networks v6 Companion Guide* or use the corresponding Chapter 8 in the Introduction to Networks online curriculum for assistance.

Study Guide

Understanding the hierarchical structure of the IP address and how to modify that hierarchy in order to more efficiently meet routing requirements is an important part of planning an IP addressing scheme. This chapter reviews the process of subnetting IP networks. First, we review a process for subnetting IPv4 networks. Then, you practice subnetting skills, including several scenarios. Then, we briefly review subnetting IPv6 networks.

Subnetting an IPv4 Network

The process of segmenting a network, by dividing it into multiple smaller network spaces, is called *subnetting*. These subnetworks are called *subnets*. Although subnetting calculators are plentiful and freely accessible on the Internet, you must know how to subnet without using a calculator when you sit for any certification exam. Furthermore, subnetting skills will serve you well when troubleshooting common IP addressing issues.

Note: I use the following method for subnetting in classrooms and lectures. If you are already comfortable with subnetting, you can skip to Subnetting Scenario 1.

Subnetting in Four Steps

Everyone has a preferred method of subnetting. Each teacher will use a slightly different strategy to help students master this crucial skill. The method I prefer can be broken down into four steps:

Step 1.   Determine how many bits to borrow based on the network requirements.

Step 2.   Determine the new subnet mask.

Step 3.   Determine the subnet multiplier.

Step 4.   List the subnets, including subnetwork address, host range, and broadcast address.

Subnetting Example

The best way to demonstrate the four steps of subnetting is to use an example. Let's assume that you are given the network address 192.168.1.0/24, you need 30 hosts per network, and you want to create as many subnets as possible.

Determine How Many Bits to Borrow

Because our requirement specifies 30 host addresses per subnet, we need to first determine the minimum number of host bits to leave. The remaining bits can be borrowed:

Host Bits = Bits Borrowed + Bits Left

To provide enough address space for 30 hosts, we need to leave 5 bits. Use the following formula:

$2^{BL} - 2$ = number of host addresses

where the exponent BL is bits left in the host portion.

Remember, the "minus 2" is to account for the network and broadcast addresses that cannot be assigned to hosts.

In this example, leaving 5 bits in the host portion will provide the right number of host addresses:

$2^5 - 2 = 30$

Because we have 3 bits remaining in the original host portion, we borrow all these bits to satisfy the requirement to "create as many subnets as possible." To determine how many subnets we can create, use the following formula:

2^{BB} = Number of subnets

where the exponent *BB* is bits borrowed from the host portion.

In this example, borrowing 3 bits from the host portion will create 8 subnets: $2^3 = 8$.

As shown in Table 8-1, the 3 bits are borrowed from the far-left bits in the host portion. The highlighted bits in the table show all possible combinations of manipulating the 8 bits borrowed to create the subnets.

Table 8-1   Binary and Decimal Value of the Subnetted Octet

Subnet Number	Last Octet Binary Value	Last Octet Decimal Value
0	00000000	.0
1	00100000	.32
2	01000000	.64
3	01100000	.96
4	10000000	.128
5	10100000	.160
6	11000000	.192
7	11100000	.224

Determine the New Subnet Mask

Notice in Table 8-1 that the network bits now include the 3 borrowed host bits in the last octet. Add these 3 bits to the 24 bits in the original subnet mask and you have a new subnet mask, /27. In decimal format, you turn on the 128, 64, and 32 bits in the last octet for a value of 224. So, the new subnet mask is 255.255.255.224.

Determine the Subnet Multiplier

Notice in Table 8-1 that the last octet decimal value increments by 32 with each subnet number. The number 32 is the subnet multiplier. You can quickly find the subnet multiplier using one of two methods:

- **Method 1:** Subtract the last nonzero octet of the subnet mask from 256. In this example, the last nonzero octet is 224. So, the subnet multiplier is 256 − 224 = 32.

- **Method 2:** The decimal value of the last bit borrowed is the subnet multiplier. In this example, we borrowed the 128 bit, the 64 bit, and the 32 bit. The 32 bit is the last bit we borrowed and is, therefore, the subnet multiplier.

By using the subnet multiplier, you no longer have to convert binary subnet bits to decimal.

List the Subnets, Host Ranges, and Broadcast Addresses

Listing the subnets, host ranges, and broadcast addresses helps you see the flow of addresses within one address space. Table 8-2 documents our subnet addressing scheme for the 192.168.1.0/24 address space. Fill in any missing information.

Table 8-2   Subnet Addressing Scheme for 192.168.1.0/24: 30 Hosts Per Subnet

Subnet Number	Subnet Address	Host Range	Broadcast Address
0	192.168.1.0	192.168.1.1–192.168.1.30	192.168.1.31
1	192.168.1.32	192.168.1.33–192.168.1.62	
2		192.168.1.65–192.168.1.94	192.168.1.95
3	192.168.1.96		
4	192.168.1.128	192.168.1.129–192.168.1.158	192.168.1.159
5		192.168.1.161–192.168.1.190	192.168.1.191
6	192.168.1.192		
7			

Use the four subnetting steps to complete the following scenarios.

Subnetting Scenario 1

Subnet the address space 10.10.0.0/16 to provide at least 100 host addresses per subnet while creating as many subnets as possible.

1. How many bits should you borrow? _____

2. What is the new subnet mask in dotted-decimal and prefix notation? _____

3. What is the subnet multiplier? _____

In Table 8-3, list the first three subnets, host ranges, and broadcast addresses.

Table 8-3   Subnet Addressing Scheme for Scenario 1

Subnet Number	Subnet Address	Host Range	Broadcast Address
0			
1			
2			

Subnetting Scenario 2

Subnet the address space 10.10.0.0/16 to provide at least 500 subnet addresses.

1. How many bits should you borrow? _____

2. What is the new subnet mask in dotted-decimal and prefix notation? _____

3. What is the subnet multiplier? _____

In Table 8-4, list the first three subnets, host ranges, and broadcast addresses.

Table 8-4   Subnet Addressing Scheme for Scenario 2

Subnet Number	Subnet Address	Host Range	Broadcast Address
0			
1			
2			

Subnetting Scenario 3

Subnet the address space 10.10.10.0/23 to provide at least 60 host addresses per subnet while creating as many subnets as possible.

1. How many bits should you borrow? _____

2. What is the new subnet mask in dotted-decimal and prefix notation? _____

3. What is the subnet multiplier? _____

In Table 8-5, list the first three subnets, host ranges, and broadcast addresses.

Table 8-5   Subnet Addressing Scheme for Example 3

Subnet Number	Subnet Address	Host Range	Broadcast Address
0			
1			
2			

VLSM Addressing Schemes

Variable-length subnet masking (VLSM) subnetting is similar to traditional subnetting in that bits are borrowed to create subnets. The formulas to calculate the number of hosts per subnet, and the number of subnets created still apply. The difference is that subnetting is not a single-pass activity.

VLSM Review

You probably noticed that the starting address space in Subnetting Scenario 3 is not an entire classful address. In fact, it is subnet 5 from Subnetting Scenario 2. So in Subnetting Scenario 3, you "subnetted a subnet." That is what VLSM is in a nutshell: subnetting a subnet.

Let's use a small example. Given the address space 172.30.4.0/22 and the network requirements shown in Figure 8-1, apply an addressing scheme that conserves the most amount of addresses for future growth.

Figure 8-1 VLSM Example Topology

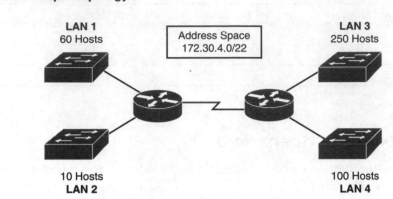

We need five subnets: four LAN subnets and one WAN subnet. Starting with the largest host requirement on LAN 3, begin subnetting the address space.

To satisfy the 250 hosts requirement, we leave 8 hosts bits ($2^8 - 2 = 254$ hosts per subnet). Because we have 10 host bits total, we borrow 2 bits to create the first round of subnets ($2^2 = 4$ subnets). The starting subnet mask is /22 or 255.255.252.0. We turn on the next two bits in the subnet mask to get /24 or 255.255.255.0. The multiplier is 1. The four subnets are as follows:

- Subnet 0: 172.30.4.0/24

- Subnet 1: 172.30.5.0/24

- Subnet 2: 172.30.6.0/24

- Subnet 3: 172.30.7.0/24

Assigning Subnet 0 to LAN 3, we are left with three /24 subnets. Continuing on to the next largest host requirement on LAN 4, we take Subnet 1, 172.30.5.0/24, and subnet it further.

To satisfy the 100 hosts requirement, we leave 7 bits ($2^7 - 2 = 128$ hosts per subnet). Because we have 8 host bits total, we can borrow only 1 bit to create the subnets ($2^1 = 2$ subnets). The starting subnet mask is /24 or 255.255.255.0. We turn on the next bit in the subnet mask to get /25 or 255.255.255.128. The multiplier is 128. The two subnets are as follows:

- Subnet 0: 172.30.5.0/25

- Subnet 1: 172.30.5.128/25

Assigning Subnet 0 to LAN 4, we are left with one /25 subnet and two /24 subnets. Continuing on to the next largest host requirement on LAN 1, we take Subnet 1, 172.30.5.128/25, and subnet it further.

To satisfy the 60 hosts requirement, we leave 6 bits ($2^6 - 2 = 62$ hosts per subnet). Because we have 7 host bits total, we borrow 1 bit to create the subnets ($2^1 = 2$ subnets). The starting subnet mask is /25 or 255.255.255.128. We turn on the next bit in the subnet mask to get /26 or 255.255.255.192. The multiplier is 64. The two subnets are as follows:

- Subnet 0: 172.30.5.128/26

- Subnet 1: 172.30.5.192/26

Assigning Subnet 0 to LAN 1, we are left with one /26 subnet and two /24 subnets. Finishing our LAN subnetting with LAN 2, we take Subnet 1, 172.30.5.192/26, and subnet it further.

To satisfy the 10 hosts requirement, we leave 4 bits ($2^4 - 2 = 14$ hosts per subnet). Because we have 6 host bits total, we borrow 2 bits to create the subnets ($2^2 = 4$ subnets). The starting subnet mask is /26 or 255.255.255.192. We turn on the next two bits in the subnet mask to get /28 or 255.255.255.240.

The multiplier is 16. The four subnets are as follows:

- Subnet 0: 172.30.5.192/28

- Subnet 1: 172.30.5.208/28

- Subnet 2: 172.30.5.224/28

- Subnet 3: 172.30.5.240/28

Assigning Subnet 0 to LAN 2, we are left with three /28 subnets and two /24 subnets. To finalize our addressing scheme, we need to create a subnet only for the WAN link, which needs only two host addresses. We take Subnet 1, 172.30.5.208/28, and subnet it further.

To satisfy the two hosts requirement, we leave 2 bits ($2^2 - 2 = 2$ hosts per subnet). Because we have 4 host bits total, we borrow 2 bits to create the subnets ($2^2 = 4$ subnets). The starting subnet mask is /28 or 255.255.255.240. We turn on the next 2 bits in the subnet mask to get /30 or 255.255.255.252. The multiplier is 4. The four subnets are as follows:

- Subnet 0: 172.30.5.208/30

- Subnet 1: 172.30.5.212/30

- Subnet 2: 172.30.5.216/30

- Subnet 3: 172.30.5.220/30

We assign Subnet 0 to the WAN link. We are left with three /30 subnets, two /28 subnets, and two /24 subnets.

VLSM Addressing Design Exercises

In the following VLSM addressing design exercises, you apply your VLSM addressing skills to a three router topology. Each exercise is progressively more difficult than the last. There may be more than one correct answer in some situations. However, you should always practice good addressing design by assigning your subnets contiguously.

Exercise 1

Assume that 4 bits were borrowed from the host portion of 192.168.1.0/24. You are *not* using VLSM. Starting with Subnet 0, label Figure 8-2 contiguously with subnets. Start with the LAN on RTA and proceed clockwise.

Figure 8-2   Addressing Design Exercise 1 Topology: Subnets

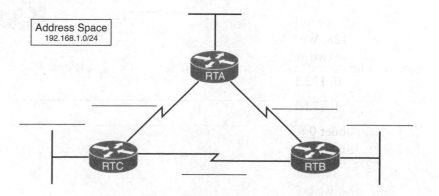

How many *total* valid host addresses will be wasted on the WAN links?

_____

_____

Now come up with a better addressing scheme using VLSM. Start with the same 4 bits borrowed from the host portion of 192.168.1.0/24. Label each of the LANs with a subnet. Then subnet the next available subnet to provide WAN subnets without wasting any host addresses. Label Figure 8-3 with the subnets.

Figure 8-3   Addressing Design Exercise 1 Topology: VLSM Subnets

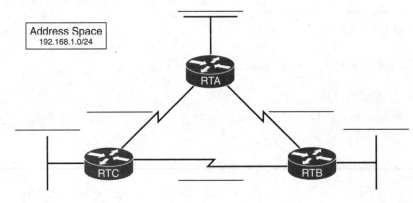

List the address space that is still available for future expansion.

_____

The topology shown in Figure 8-4 has LAN subnets already assigned out of the 192.168.1.0/24 address space. Using VLSM, create and label the WANs with subnets from the remaining address space.

Figure 8-4   Addressing Design Exercise 1 Topology: WAN Subnets

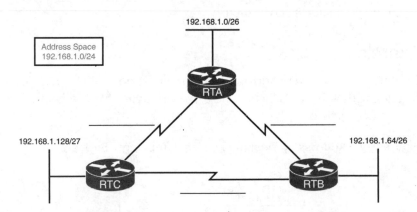

List the address space that is still available for future expansion.

_____

_____

Exercise 2

Your address space is 192.168.1.192/26. Each LAN needs to support ten hosts. Use VLSM to create a contiguous IP addressing scheme. Label Figure 8-5 with your addressing scheme. Don't forget the WAN links.

Figure 8-5   Addressing Design Exercise 2 Topology

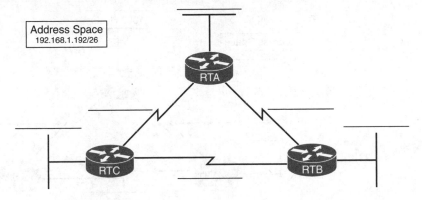

List the address space that is still available for future expansion.

Exercise 3

Your address space is 192.168.6.0/23. The number of hosts needed for each LAN is shown in Figure 8-6. Use VLSM to create a contiguous IPv4 addressing scheme. Label Figure 8-6 with your addressing scheme. Don't forget the WAN links.

Figure 8-6   Addressing Design Exercise 3 Topology

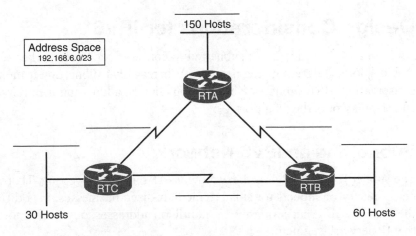

List the address space that is still available for future expansion.

Exercise 4

Your address space is 10.10.96.0/21. The number of hosts needed for each LAN is shown in Figure 8-7. Use VLSM to create a contiguous IP addressing scheme. Label Figure 8-7 with your addressing scheme. Don't forget the WAN links.

Figure 8-7   Addressing Design Exercise 4 Topology

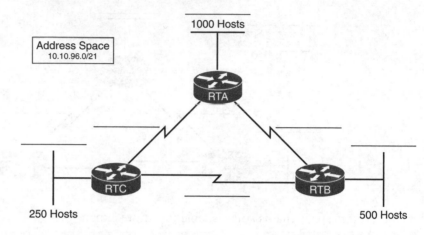

List the address space that is still available for future expansion.

_____

_____

_____

Design Considerations for IPv6

An IPv6 address space is not subnetted to conserve addresses; rather, it is subnetted to support hierarchical, logical design of the network. Whereas IPv4 subnetting is mostly about managing address conservation, IPv6 subnetting is about building an addressing hierarchy based on the number of routers and the networks they support.

Subnetting an IPv6 Network

The subnet ID of an IPv6 address provides 16 bits for subnetting. That's a total of 2^{16} or 65,536 subnets—plenty of subnets for small to medium-sized businesses. In addition, each subnet has 64 bits for the interface ID. That's roughly 18 quintillion addresses, obviously more than will ever be needed in one IP network segment.

Subnets created from the subnet ID are easy to represent because there is no conversion to binary required. To determine the next available subnet, just count up in hexadecimal, as shown in Figure 8-8.

Figure 8-8   Subnetting an IPv6 Address by Incrementing the Subnet ID

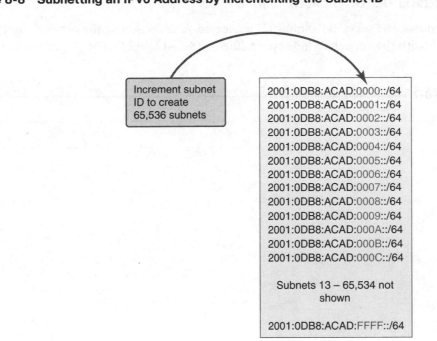

IPv6 Subnetting Practice

In practice, subnetting IPv6 is straightforward. The only possible difficulty is counting in hexadecimal as you increment the subnet ID.

IPv6 Subnetting Scenario 1

Assume that the network administrator allotted your section of the network four /64 IPv6 subnets starting with the subnet address space 2001:DB8:CAFE:F00D::/64. What would be the next three /64 subnets?

_____

_____

_____

IPv6 Subnetting Scenario 2

Assume that the network administrator allotted your section of the network four /64 IPv6 subnets starting with the subnet address space 2001:DB8:CAFE:AA9F::/64. What would be the next three /64 subnets?

_____

_____

_____

IPv6 Subnetting Scenario 3

Assume that the network administrator allotted your section of the network four /64 IPv6 subnets starting with the subnet address space 2001:DB8:CAFE:9EFD::/64. What would be the next three /64 subnets?

Labs and Activities

8.0.1.2 Class Activity–Call Me!

Objectives

Explain why routing is necessary for hosts on different subnets to communicate.

Background/Scenario

In this chapter, you will be learning how devices can be grouped into subnets, or smaller network groups, from a large network.

In this Modeling Activity, you are asked to think about a number you probably use every day, a number such as your telephone number. As you complete the activity, think about how your telephone number compares to strategies that network administrators might use to identify hosts for efficient data communication.

Complete the two sections listed below and record your answers. Save the two sections in either hard- or soft-copy format to use later for class discussion purposes.

- Explain how your smartphone or landline telephone number is divided into identifying groups of numbers. Does your telephone number use an area code? An ISP identifier? A city, state, or country code?

- In what ways does separating your telephone number into managed parts assist in contacting or communicating with others?

Required Resources

- Recording capabilities (paper, tablet, and so on) for reflective comments to be shared with the class.

Reflection

Why do you think ISPs need your telephone number when setting up your account parameters?

_____

_____

_____

_____

8.1.4.6 Lab–Calculating IPv4 Subnets

Objectives

Part 1: Determine IPv4 Address Subnetting

Part 2: Calculate IPv4 Address Subnetting

Background/Scenario

The ability to work with IPv4 subnets and determine network and host information based on a given IP address and subnet mask is critical to understanding how IPv4 networks operate. The first part is designed to reinforce how to compute network IP address information from a given IP address and subnet mask. When given an IP address and subnet mask, you will be able to determine other information about the subnet.

Required Resources

- 1 PC (Windows 7 or 8 with Internet access)
- Optional: IPv4 address calculator

Part 1: Determine IPv4 Address Subnetting

In Part 1, you will determine the network and broadcast addresses, as well as the number of hosts, given an IPv4 address and subnet mask.

REVIEW: To determine the network address, perform binary ANDing on the IPv4 address using the subnet mask provided. The result will be the network address. Hint: If the subnet mask has decimal value 255 in an octet, the result will ALWAYS be the original value of that octet. If the subnet mask has decimal value 0 in an octet, the result will ALWAYS be 0 for that octet.

Example:

IP Address	192.168.10.10
Subnet Mask	255.255.255.0
	==========
Result (Network)	192.168.10.0

Knowing this, you may only have to perform binary ANDing on an octet that does not have 255 or 0 in its subnet mask portion.

Example:

IP Address	172.30.239.145
Subnet Mask	255.255.192.0

Analyzing this example, you can see that you only have to perform binary ANDing on the third octet. The first two octets will result in 172.30 due to the subnet mask. The fourth octet will result in 0 due to the subnet mask.

IP Address	172.30.239.145
Subnet Mask	255.255.192.0
	==========
Result (Network)	172.30.?.0

Perform binary ANDing on the third octet.

	Decimal	Binary
	239	11101111
	192	11000000
		=======
Result	**192**	11000000

Analyzing this example again produces the following result:

IP Address	172.30.239.145
Subnet Mask	255.255.192.0
	==========
Result (Network)	172.30.192.0

Continuing with this example, determining the number of hosts per network can be calculated by analyzing the subnet mask. The subnet mask will be represented in dotted decimal format, such as 255.255.192.0, or in network prefix format, such as /18. An IPv4 address always has 32 bits. Subtracting the number of bits used for the network portion (as represented by the subnet mask) gives you the number of bits used for hosts.

Using our example above, the subnet mask 255.255.192.0 is equivalent to /18 in prefix notation. Subtracting 18 network bits from 32 bits results in 14 bits left for the host portion. From there, it is a simple calculation:

$$2^{(number\ of\ host\ bits)} - 2 = Number\ of\ hosts$$

$$2^{14} = 16{,}384 - 2 = 16{,}382\ hosts$$

Determine the network and broadcast addresses and number of host bits and hosts for the given IPv4 addresses and prefixes in the following table.

IPv4 Address/Prefix	Network Address	Broadcast Address	Total Number of Host Bits	Total Number of Hosts
192.168.100.25/28				
172.30.10.130/30				
10.1.113.75/19				
198.133.219.250/24				
128.107.14.191/22				
172.16.104.99/27				

Part 2: Calculate IPv4 Address Subnetting

When given an IPv4 address, the original subnet mask, and the new subnet mask, you will be able to determine:

- Network address of this subnet

- Broadcast address of this subnet

- Range of host addresses of this subnet

- Number of subnets created

- Number of hosts per subnet

The following example shows a sample problem along with the solution for solving this problem:

Given:	
Host IP Address:	172.16.77.120
Original Subnet Mask	255.255.0.0
New Subnet Mask:	255.255.240.0
Find:	
Number of Subnet Bits	4
Number of Subnets Created	16
Number of Host Bits per Subnet	
Number of Hosts per Subnet	
Network Address of This Subnet	
IPv4 Address of First Host on This Subnet	
IPv4 Address of Last Host on This Subnet	
IPv4 Broadcast Address on This Subnet	

Let's analyze how this table was completed.

The original subnet mask was 255.255.0.0 or /16. The new subnet mask is 255.255.240.0 or /20. The resulting difference is 4 bits. Because 4 bits were borrowed, we can determine that 16 subnets were created because $2^4 = 16$.

The new mask of 255.255.240.0 or /20 leaves 12 bits for hosts. With 12 bits left for hosts, we use the following formula: $2^{12} = 4,096 - 2 = 4,094$ hosts per subnet.

Binary ANDing will help you determine the subnet for this problem, which results in the network 172.16.64.0.

Finally, you need to determine the first host, last host, and broadcast address for each subnet. One method to determine the host range is to use binary math for the host portion of the address. In our example, the last 12 bits of the address is the host portion. The first host would have all significant bits set to zero and the least significant bit set to 1. The last host would have all significant bits set to 1 and the least significant bit set to 0. In this example, the host portion of the address resides in the 3rd and 4th octets.

Description	1st Octet	2nd Octet	3rd Octet	4th Octet	Description
Network/Host	nnnnnnnn	nnnnnnnn	nnnnhhhh	hhhhhhhh	Subnet Mask
Binary	10101100	00010000	01000000	00000001	First Host
Decimal	172	16	64	1	First Host
Binary	10101100	00010000	01001111	11111110	Last Host
Decimal	172	16	79	254	Last Host
Binary	10101100	00010000	01001111	11111111	Broadcast
Decimal	172	16	79	255	Broadcast

Step 1. Fill out the tables below with appropriate answers given the IPv4 address, original subnet mask, and new subnet mask.

a. Problem 1:

Given:	
Host IP Address:	192.168.200.139
Original Subnet Mask	255.255.255.0
New Subnet Mask:	255.255.255.224

Find:	
Number of Subnet Bits	
Number of Subnets Created	
Number of Host Bits per Subnet	
Number of Hosts per Subnet	
Network Address of This Subnet	
IPv4 Address of First Host on This Subnet	
IPv4 Address of Last Host on This Subnet	
IPv4 Broadcast Address on This Subnet	

b. Problem 2:

Given:	
Host IP Address:	10.101.99.228
Original Subnet Mask	255.0.0.0
New Subnet Mask:	255.255.128.0

Find:	
Number of Subnet Bits	
Number of Subnets Created	
Number of Host Bits per Subnet	
Number of Hosts per Subnet	
Network Address of This Subnet	
IPv4 Address of First Host on This Subnet	
IPv4 Address of Last Host on This Subnet	
IPv4 Broadcast Address on This Subnet	

c.   Problem 3:

Given:	
Host IP Address:	172.22.32.12
Original Subnet Mask	255.255.0.0
New Subnet Mask:	255.255.224.0
Find:	
Number of Subnet Bits	
Number of Subnets Created	
Number of Host Bits per Subnet	
Number of Hosts per Subnet	
Network Address of This Subnet	
IPv4 Address of First Host on This Subnet	
IPv4 Address of Last Host on This Subnet	
IPv4 Broadcast Address on This Subnet	

d.   Problem 4:

Given:	
Host IP Address:	192.168.1.245
Original Subnet Mask	255.255.255.0
New Subnet Mask:	255.255.255.252
Find:	
Number of Subnet Bits	
Number of Subnets Created	
Number of Host Bits per Subnet	
Number of Hosts per Subnet	
Network Address of This Subnet	
IPv4 Address of First Host on This Subnet	
IPv4 Address of Last Host on This Subnet	
IPv4 Broadcast Address on This Subnet	

e.   Problem 5:

Given:	
Host IP Address:	128.107.0.55
Original Subnet Mask	255.255.0.0
New Subnet Mask:	255.255.255.0
Find:	
Number of Subnet Bits	
Number of Subnets Created	
Number of Host Bits per Subnet	
Number of Hosts per Subnet	

Find:	
Network Address of this Subnet	
IPv4 Address of First Host on This Subnet	
IPv4 Address of Last Host on This Subnet	
IPv4 Broadcast Address on This Subnet	

     f.   Problem 6:

Given:	
Host IP Address:	192.135.250.180
Original Subnet Mask	255.255.255.0
New Subnet Mask:	255.255.255.248

Find:	
Number of Subnet Bits	
Number of Subnets Created	
Number of Host Bits per Subnet	
Number of Hosts per Subnet	
Network Address of This Subnet	
IPv4 Address of First Host on This Subnet	
IPv4 Address of Last Host on This Subnet	
IPv4 Broadcast Address on This Subnet	

Reflection

Why is the subnet mask so important when analyzing an IPv4 address?

_____

_____

_____

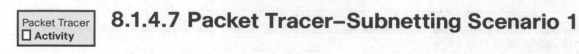

8.1.4.7 Packet Tracer–Subnetting Scenario 1

Topology

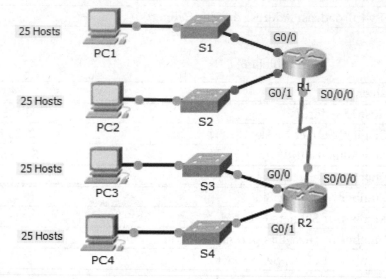

Addressing Table

Device	Interface	IP Address	Subnet Mask	Default Gateway
R1	G0/0			
	G0/1			
	S0/0/0			
R2	G0/0			
	G0/1			
	S0/0/0			
S1	VLAN 1			
S2	VLAN 1			
S3	VLAN 1			
S4	VLAN 1			
PC1	NIC			
PC2	NIC			
PC3	NIC			
PC4	NIC			

Objectives

Part 1: Design an IP Addressing Scheme

Part 2: Assign IP Addresses to Network Devices and Verify Connectivity

Scenario

In this activity, you are given the network address of 192.168.100.0/24 to subnet and provide the IP addressing for the network shown in the topology. Each LAN in the network requires enough space for, at least, 25 addresses for end devices, the switch, and the router. The connection between R1 to R2 will require an IP address for each end of the link.

Part 1: Design an IP Addressing Scheme

Step 1.   Subnet the 192.168.100.0/24 network into the appropriate number of subnets.

    a.   Based on the topology, how many subnets are needed? _____

    b.   How many bits must be borrowed to support the number of subnets in the topology table? _____

    c.   How many subnets does this create? _____

    d.   How many usable hosts does this create per subnet? _____

Note: If your answer is less than the 25 hosts required, then you borrowed too many bits.

---

    e.   Calculate the binary value for the first five subnets. The first subnet is already shown.

```
Net 0: 192 . 168 . 100 . 0   0   0   0   0   0   0   0

Net 1: 192 . 168 . 100 . ___ ___ ___ ___ ___ ___ ___ ___

Net 2: 192 . 168 . 100 . ___ ___ ___ ___ ___ ___ ___ ___

Net 3: 192 . 168 . 100 . ___ ___ ___ ___ ___ ___ ___ ___

Net 4: 192 . 168 . 100 . ___ ___ ___ ___ ___ ___ ___ ___
```

    f.   Calculate the binary and decimal value of the new subnet mask.

```
11111111.11111111.11111111. ___ ___ ___ ___ ___ ___ ___ ___

     255 .   255 .   255 . _____
```

    g.   Fill in the **Subnet Table**, listing the decimal value of all available subnets, the first and last usable host address, and the broadcast address. Repeat until all addresses are listed.

Note: You may not need to use all rows.

Subnet Table

Subnet Number	Subnet Address	First Usable Host Address	Last Usable Host Address	Broadcast Address
0				
1				
2				
3				
4				
5				
6				
7				
8				
9				
10				

Step 2.   Assign the subnets to the network shown in the topology.

    a.   Assign Subnet 0 to the LAN connected to the GigabitEthernet 0/0 interface of R1:

    b.   Assign Subnet 1 to the LAN connected to the GigabitEthernet 0/1 interface of R1:

    c.   Assign Subnet 2 to the LAN connected to the GigabitEthernet 0/0 interface of R2:

    d.   Assign Subnet 3 to the LAN connected to the GigabitEthernet 0/1 interface of R2:

    e.   Assign Subnet 4 to the WAN link between R1 to R2:

Step 3.   Document the addressing scheme.

Fill in the **Subnet Table** using the following guidelines:

    a.   Assign the first usable IP addresses to R1 for the two LAN links and the WAN link.

    b.   Assign the first usable IP addresses to R2 for the LANs links. Assign the last usable IP address for the WAN link.

    c.   Assign the second usable IP addresses to the switches.

    d.   Assign the last usable IP addresses to the hosts.

Part 2: Assign IP Addresses to Network Devices and Verify Connectivity

Most of the IP addressing is already configured on this network. Implement the following steps to complete the addressing configuration.

Step 1.   Configure IP addressing on R1 LAN interfaces.

Step 2.   Configure IP addressing on S3, including the default gateway.

Step 3.   Configure IP addressing on PC4, including the default gateway.

Step 4.   Verify connectivity.

You can only verify connectivity from R1, S3, and PC4. However, you should be able to ping every IP address listed in the **Addressing Table**.

Suggested Scoring Rubric

Note: The majority of points are allocated to designing and documenting the addressing scheme. Implementation of the addresses in Packet Tracer is of minimal consideration.

Activity Section	Question Location	Possible Points	Earned Points
Part 1: Design an IP Addressing Scheme	Step 1a	1	
	Step 1b	1	
	Step 1c	1	
	Step 1d	1	
	Step 1e	4	
	Step 1f	2	
Complete Subnet Table	Step 1g	10	
Assign Subnets	Step 2	10	
Document Addressing	Step 3	40	
	Part 1 Total	70	
	Packet Tracer Score	30	
	Total Score	100	

8.1.4.8 Lab–Designing and Implementing a Subnetted IPv4 Addressing Scheme

Topology

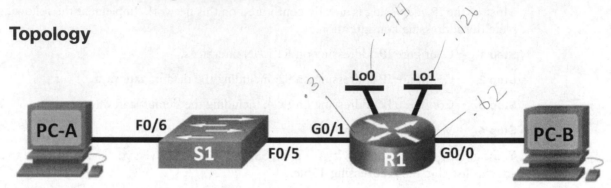

Addressing Table

Device	Interface	IP Address	Subnet Mask	Default Gateway
R1	G0/0	192.168.0.36		N/A
	G0/1	192.168.0.62		N/A
	Lo0	.94		N/A
	Lo1	.126		N/A
S1	VLAN 1	N/A	N/A	N/A
PC-A	NIC	192.168.0.1		.30
PC-B	NIC	192.168.0.33		.62

Objectives

Part 1: Design a Network Subnetting Scheme

Part 2: Configure the Devices

Part 3: Test and Troubleshoot the Network

Background/Scenario

In this lab, starting from a single network address and network mask, you will subnet the network into multiple subnets. The subnet scheme should be based on the number of host computers required in each subnet, as well as other network considerations, like future network host expansion.

After you have created a subnetting scheme and completed the network diagram by filling in the host and interface IP addresses, you will configure the host PCs and router interfaces, including loopback interfaces. The loopback interfaces are created to simulate additional LANs attached to router R1.

After the network devices and host PCs have been configured, you will use the **ping** command to test for network connectivity.

This lab provides minimal assistance with the actual commands necessary to configure the router. However, the required commands are provided in Appendix A. Test your knowledge by trying to configure the devices without referring to the appendix.

Note: The routers used with CCNA hands-on labs are Cisco 1941 Integrated Services Routers (ISRs) with Cisco IOS Release 15.2(4)M3 (universalk9 image). The switches used are Cisco Catalyst 2960s with Cisco IOS Release 15.0(2) (lanbasek9 image). Other routers, switches and Cisco IOS versions can be used. Depending on the model and Cisco IOS version, the commands available and output produced might vary from what is shown in the labs. Refer to the Router Interface Summary Table at the end of this lab for the correct interface identifiers.

Note: Make sure that the routers and switches have been erased and have no startup configurations. If you are unsure, contact your instructor.

Required Resources

- 1 Router (Cisco 1941 with Cisco IOS Release 15.2(4)M3 universal image or comparable)

- 1 Switch (Cisco 2960 with Cisco IOS Release 15.0(2) lanbasek9 image or comparable)

- 2 PCs (Windows 7 or 8 with terminal emulation program, such as Tera Term)

- Console cables to configure the Cisco IOS devices via the console ports

- Ethernet cables as shown in the topology

Note: The Gigabit Ethernet interfaces on Cisco 1941 routers are autosensing. An Ethernet straight-through cable may be used between the router and PC-B. If using another Cisco router model, it may be necessary to use an Ethernet crossover cable.

Part 1: Design a Network Subnetting Scheme

Step 1. Create a subnetting scheme that meets the required number of subnets and required number of host addresses.

In this scenario, you are a network administrator for a small subdivision within a larger company. You must create multiple subnets out of the 192.168.0.0/24 network address space to meet the following requirements:

- The first subnet is the employee network. You need a minimum of 25 host IP addresses.

- The second subnet is the administration network. You need a minimum of 10 IP addresses.

- The third and fourth subnets are reserved as virtual networks on virtual router interfaces, loopback 0 and loopback 1. These virtual router interfaces simulate LANs attached to R1.

- You also need two additional unused subnets for future network expansion.

Note: Variable length subnet masks will not be used. All of the device subnet masks will be the same length.

Answer the following questions to help create a subnetting scheme that meets the stated network requirements:

1) How many host addresses are needed in the largest required subnet? _____

2) What is the minimum number of subnets required? _____

3) The network that you are tasked to subnet is 192.168.0.0/24. What is the /24 subnet mask in binary?

192.168.255.0

4) The subnet mask is made up of two portions, the network portion, and the host portion. This is represented in the binary by the ones and the zeros in the subnet mask.

In the network mask, what do the ones represent? _____

In the network mask, what do the zeros represent? _____

5) To subnet a network, bits from the host portion of the original network mask are changed into subnet bits. The number of subnet bits defines the number of subnets. Given each of the possible subnet masks depicted in the following binary format, how many subnets and how many hosts are created in each example?

Hint: Remember that the number of host bits (to the power of 2) defines the number of hosts per subnet (minus 2), and the number of subnet bits (to the power of 2) defines the number of subnets. The subnet bits (depicted in bold typeface) are the bits that have been borrowed beyond the original network mask of /24. The /24 is the slash prefix notation and corresponds to a dotted decimal mask of 255.255.255.0.

(/25) 11111111.11111111.11111111.**1**0000000

Dotted decimal subnet mask equivalent: _____

Number of subnets? _____   Number of hosts? _____

(/26) 11111111.11111111.11111111.**11**000000

Dotted decimal subnet mask equivalent: _____

Number of subnets? _____   Number of hosts? _____

(/27) 11111111.11111111.11111111.**111**00000

Dotted decimal subnet mask equivalent: _____

Number of subnets? _____   Number of hosts? _____

(/28) 11111111.11111111.11111111.**1111**0000

Dotted decimal subnet mask equivalent: _____

Number of subnets? _____   Number of hosts? _____

(/29) 11111111.11111111.11111111.**11111**000

Dotted decimal subnet mask equivalent: _____

Number of subnets? _____   Number of hosts? _____

(/30) 11111111.11111111.11111111.**111111**00

Dotted decimal subnet mask equivalent: _____

Number of subnets? _____   Number of hosts? _____

6) Considering your answers, which subnet masks meet the required number of minimum host addresses?

_____

7) Considering your answers, which subnet masks meet the minimum number of subnets required?

_____

8) Considering your answers, which subnet mask meets both the required minimum number of hosts and the minimum number of subnets required?

_____

9) When you have determined which subnet mask meets all of the stated network requirements, you will derive each of the subnets starting from the original network address. List the subnets from first to last below. Remember that the first subnet is 192.168.0.0 with the newly acquired subnet mask.

Subnet Address	/	Prefix	Subnet Mask (dotted decimal)
_____	/	___	255.255.255.224
_____	/	___	_____
_____	/	___	_____
_____	/	___	_____
_____	/	___	_____
_____	/	___	_____
_____	/	___	_____
_____	/	___	_____
_____	/	___	_____
_____	/		

Step 2.   Complete the diagram showing where the host IP addresses will be applied.

On the following lines provided, fill in the IP addresses and subnet masks in slash prefix notation. On the router, use the first usable address in each subnet for each of the interfaces, Gigabit Ethernet 0/0, Gigabit Ethernet 0/1, loopback 0, and loopback 1. Fill in an IP address for both PC-A and PC-B. Also enter this information into the Addressing Table.

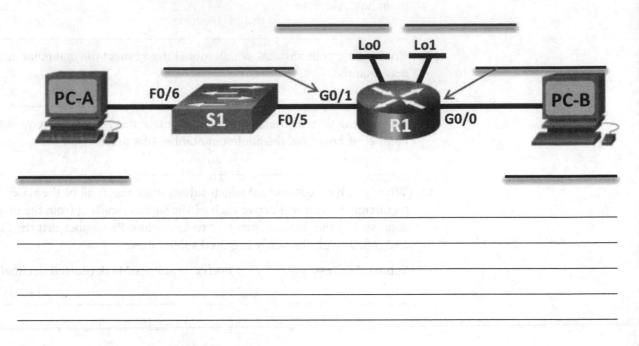

_____

_____

_____

_____

_____

_____

Part 2: Configure the Devices

In Part 2, set up the network topology and configure basic settings on the PCs and router, such as the router Gigabit Ethernet interface IP addresses, and the PC's IP addresses, subnet masks, and default gateways. Refer to the Addressing Table for device names and address information.

Note: Appendix A provides configuration details for the steps in Part 2. You should attempt to complete Part 2 prior to reviewing Appendix A.

Step 1.   Configure the router.

    a.   Enter into privileged EXEC mode and then global config mode.

    b.   Assign **R1** as the hostname for the router.

    c.   Configure both the **G0/0** and **G0/1** interfaces with IP addresses and subnet masks, and then enable them.

    d.   Loopback interfaces are created to simulate additional LANs on R1 router. Configure the loopback interfaces with IP addresses and subnet masks. After they are created, loopback interfaces are enabled, by default. (To create the loopback addresses, enter the command **interface loopback 0** at the global config mode.)

    Note: You can create additional loopbacks for testing with different addressing schemes, if desired.

    e.   Save the running configuration to the startup configuration file.

Step 2.   Configure the PC interfaces.

    a.   Configure the IP address, subnet mask, and default gateway settings on PC-A.

    b.   Configure the IP address, subnet mask, and default gateway settings on PC-B.

Part 3: Test and Troubleshoot the Network

In Part 3, you will use the **ping** command to test network connectivity.

    a. Test to see if PC-A can communicate with its default gateway. From PC-A, open a command prompt and ping the IP address of the router Gigabit Ethernet 0/1 interface. Do you get a reply? _____

    b. Test to see if PC-B can communicate with its default gateway. From PC-B, open a command prompt and ping the IP address of the router Gigabit Ethernet 0/0 interface. Do you get a reply? _____

    c. Test to see if PC-A can communicate with PC-B. From PC-A, open a command prompt and ping the IP address of PC-B. Do you get a reply? _____

    d. If you answered "no" to any of the preceding questions, then you should go back and check all of your IP address and subnet mask configurations, and ensure that the default gateways have been correctly configured on PC-A and PC-B.

    e. If you verify that all of the settings are correct, and you can still not ping successfully, then there are a few additional factors that can block ICMP pings. On PC-A and PC-B within Windows, make sure that the Windows Firewall is turned off for the Work, Home, and Public networks.

    f. Experiment by purposely misconfiguring the gateway address on PC-A to 10.0.0.1. What happens when you try and ping from PC-B to PC-A? Do you receive a reply?

_____

_____

Reflection

1. Subnetting one larger network into multiple smaller subnetworks allows for greater flexibility and security in network design. However, what do you think some of the drawbacks are when the subnets are limited to being the same size?

_____

_____

2. Why do you think the gateway/router IP address is usually the first usable IP address in the network?

_____

_____

Router Interface Summary Table

	Router Interface Summary			
Router Model	Ethernet Interface #1	Ethernet Interface #2	Serial Interface #1	Serial Interface #2
1800	Fast Ethernet 0/0 (F0/0)	Fast Ethernet 0/1 (F0/1)	Serial 0/0/0 (S0/0/0)	Serial 0/0/1 (S0/0/1)
1900	Gigabit Ethernet 0/0 (G0/0)	Gigabit Ethernet 0/1 (G0/1)	Serial 0/0/0 (S0/0/0)	Serial 0/0/1 (S0/0/1)
2801	Fast Ethernet 0/0 (F0/0)	Fast Ethernet 0/1 (F0/1)	Serial 0/1/0 (S0/1/0)	Serial 0/1/1 (S0/1/1)
2811	Fast Ethernet 0/0 (F0/0)	Fast Ethernet 0/1 (F0/1)	Serial 0/0/0 (S0/0/0)	Serial 0/0/1 (S0/0/1)
2900	Gigabit Ethernet 0/0 (G0/0)	Gigabit Ethernet 0/1 (G0/1)	Serial 0/0/0 (S0/0/0)	Serial 0/0/1 (S0/0/1)

Note: To find out how the router is configured, look at the interfaces to identify the type of router and how many interfaces the router has. There is no way to effectively list all the combinations of configurations for each router class. This table includes identifiers for the possible combinations of Ethernet and Serial interfaces in the device. The table does not include any other type of interface, even though a specific router may contain one. An example of this might be an ISDN BRI interface. The string in parentheses is the legal abbreviation that can be used in Cisco IOS commands to represent the interface.

Appendix A: Configuration Details for Steps in Part 2

Step 1.   Configure the router.

a. Console into the router and enable privileged EXEC mode.

```
Router> enable
Router#
```

b. Enter into configuration mode.

```
Router# conf t
Enter configuration commands, one per line.  End with CNTL/Z.
Router(config)#
```

c. Assign a device name to the router.

```
Router(config)# hostname R1
R1(config)#
```

d. Configure both the **G0/0** and **G0/1** interfaces with IP addresses and subnet masks, and enable them.

```
R1(config)# interface g0/0
R1(config-if)# ip address <ip address> <subnet mask>
R1(config-if)# no shutdown
R1(config-if)# interface g0/1
R1(config-if)# ip address <ip address> <subnet mask>
R1(config-if)# no shutdown
```

e. Loopback interfaces are created to simulate additional LANs off of router R1. Configure the loopback interfaces with IP addresses and subnet masks. When they are created, loopback interfaces are enabled, by default.

```
R1(config)# interface loopback 0
R1(config-if)# ip address <ip address> <subnet mask>
R1(config-if)# interface loopback 1
R1(config-if)# ip address <ip address> <subnet mask>
R1(config-if)# end
```

f. Save the running configuration to the startup configuration file.

```
R1# copy running-config startup-config
```

Step 2. Configure the PC interfaces.

a. Configure the IP address, subnet mask, and default gateway settings on PC-A.

Internet Protocol Version 4 (TCP/IPv4) Properties

General

You can get IP settings assigned automatically if your network supports this capability. Otherwise, you need to ask your network administrator for the appropriate IP settings.

○ Obtain an IP address automatically
● Use the following IP address:

IP address: 192 . 168 . 0 . 34
Subnet mask: 255 . 255 . 255 . 224
Default gateway: 192 . 168 . 0 . 33

b. Configure the IP address, subnet mask, and default gateway settings on PC-B.

Internet Protocol Version 4 (TCP/IPv4) Properties

General

You can get IP settings assigned automatically if your network supports this capability. Otherwise, you need to ask your network administrator for the appropriate IP settings.

○ Obtain an IP address automatically
● Use the following IP address:

IP address: 192 . 168 . 0 . 2
Subnet mask: 255 . 255 . 255 . 224
Default gateway: 192 . 168 . 0 . 1

8.2.1.4 Packet Tracer–Designing and Implementing a VLSM Addressing Scheme

Topology

You will receive one of three possible topologies.

Addressing Table

Device	Interface	IP Address	Subnet Mask	Default Gateway
[[R1Name]]	G0/0			N/A
	G0/1			N/A
	S0/0/0			N/A
[[R2Name]]	G0/0			N/A
	G0/1			N/A
	S0/0/0			N/A
[[S1Name]]	VLAN 1			
[[S2Name]]	VLAN 1			
[[S3Name]]	VLAN 1			
[[S4Name]]	VLAN 1			
[[PC1Name]]	NIC			
[[PC2Name]]	NIC			
[[PC3Name]]	NIC			
[[PC4Name]]	NIC			

Objectives

Part 1: Examine the Network Requirements

Part 2: Design the VLSM Addressing Scheme

Part 3: Assign IP Addresses to Devices and Verify Connectivity

Background

In this activity, you are given a /24 network address to use to design a VLSM addressing scheme. Based on a set of requirements, you will assign subnets and addressing, configure devices, and verify connectivity.

Part 1: Examine the Network Requirements

Step 1.   Determine the number of subnets needed.

You will subnet the network address [[DisplayNet]]. The network has the following requirements:

- [[S1Name]] LAN will require [[HostReg1]] host IP addresses
- [[S2Name]] LAN will require [[HostReg2]] host IP addresses

  - [[S3Name]] LAN will require [[HostReg3]] host IP addresses
  - [[S4Name]] LAN will require [[HostReg4]] host IP addresses

How many subnets are needed in the network topology? 5

Step 2.   Determine the subnet mask information for each subnet.

  a.   Which subnet mask will accommodate the number of IP addresses required for [[S1Name]]?

  How many usable host addresses will this subnet support?

  b.   Which subnet mask will accommodate the number of IP addresses required for [[S2Name]]?

  How many usable host addresses will this subnet support?

  c.   Which subnet mask will accommodate the number of IP addresses required for [[S3Name]]?

  How many usable host addresses will this subnet support?

  d.   Which subnet mask will accommodate the number of IP addresses required for [[S4Name]]?

  How many usable host addresses will this subnet support?

  e.   Which subnet mask will accommodate the number of IP addresses required for the connection between [[R1Name]] and [[R2Name]]?

Part 2: Design the VLSM Addressing Scheme

Step 1.   Divide the [[DisplayNet]] network based on the number of hosts per subnet.

  a.   Use the first subnet to accommodate the largest LAN.

  b.   Use the second subnet to accommodate the second largest LAN.

  c.   Use the third subnet to accommodate the third largest LAN.

  d.   Use the fourth subnet to accommodate the fourth largest LAN.

  e.   Use the fifth subnet to accommodate the connection between [[R1Name]] and [[R2Name]].

Step 2.   Document the VLSM subnets.

  Complete the **Subnet Table**, listing the subnet descriptions (e.g. [[S1Name]] LAN), number of hosts needed, then network address for the subnet, the first usable host address, and the broadcast address. Repeat until all addresses are listed.

Subnet Table

Subnet Description	Number of Hosts Needed	Network Address/ CIDR	First Usable Host Address	Broadcast Address

Step 3. Document the addressing scheme.

    a. Assign the first usable IP addresses to **[[R1Name]]** for the two LAN links and the WAN link.

    b. Assign the first usable IP addresses to **[[R2Name]]** for the two LANs links. Assign the last usable IP address for the WAN link.

    c. Assign the second usable IP addresses to the switches.

    d. Assign the last usable IP addresses to the hosts.

Part 3: Assign IP Addresses to Devices and Verify Connectivity

Most of the IP addressing is already configured on this network. Implement the following steps to complete the addressing configuration.

Step 1. Configure IP addressing on [[R1Name]] LAN interfaces.

Step 2. Configure IP addressing on [[S3Name]], including the default gateway.

Step 3. Configure IP addressing on [[PC4Name]], including the default gateway.

Step 4. Verify connectivity.

You can only verify connectivity from [[R1Name]], [[S3Name]], and [[PC4Name]]. However, you should be able to ping every IP address listed in the **Addressing Table**.

Suggested Scoring Rubric

Activity Section	Question Location	Possible Points	Earned Points
Part 1: Examine the Network Requirements	Step 1	1	
	Step 2	4	
	Part 1 Total	5	
Part 2: Design the VLSM Addressing Scheme			
	Complete Subnet Table	25	
	Document Addressing	40	
	Part 2 Total	65	
	Packet Tracer Score	30	
	Total Score	100	

8.2.1.5 Lab–Designing and Implementing a VLSM Addressing Scheme

Topology

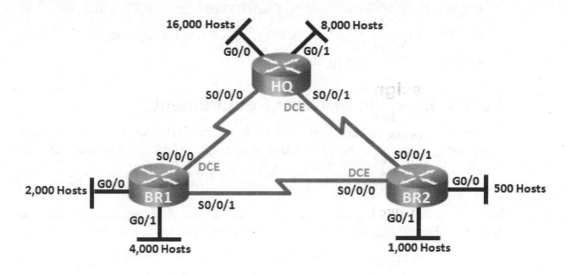

Objectives

Part 1: Examine Network Requirements

Part 2: Design the VLSM Address Scheme

Part 3: Cable and Configure the IPv4 Network

Background/Scenario

Variable Length Subnet Mask (VLSM) was designed to avoid wasting IP addresses. With VLSM, a network is subnetted and then re-subnetted. This process can be repeated multiple times to create subnets of various sizes based on the number of hosts required in each subnet. Effective use of VLSM requires address planning.

In this lab, use the 172.16.128.0/17 network address to develop an address scheme for the network displayed in the topology diagram. VLSM is used to meet the IPv4 addressing requirements. After you have designed the VLSM address scheme, you will configure the interfaces on the routers with the appropriate IP address information.

Note: The routers used with CCNA hands-on labs are Cisco 1941 Integrated Services Routers (ISRs) with Cisco IOS Release 15.2(4)M3 (universalk9 image). Other routers and Cisco IOS versions can be used. Depending on the model and Cisco IOS version, the commands available and output produced might vary from what is shown in the labs. Refer to the Router Interface Summary Table at the end of this lab for the correct interface identifiers.

Note: Make sure that the routers have been erased and have no startup configurations. If you are unsure, contact your instructor.

Required Resources

- 3 routers (Cisco 1941 with Cisco IOS software, Release 15.2(4)M3 universal image or comparable)

- 1 PC (with terminal emulation program, such as Tera Term, to configure routers)

- Console cable to configure the Cisco IOS devices via the console ports

- Ethernet (optional) and serial cables, as shown in the topology

- Windows Calculator (optional)

Part 1: Examine Network Requirements

In Part 1, you will examine the network requirements to develop a VLSM address scheme for the network displayed in the topology diagram using the 172.16.128.0/17 network address.

Note: You can use the Windows Calculator application and the www.ipcalc.org IP subnet calculator to help with your calculations.

Step 1.   Determine how many host addresses and subnets are available.

How many host addresses are available in a /17 network? _____

What is the total number of host addresses needed in the topology diagram? _____

How many subnets are needed in the network topology? _____

Step 2.   Determine the largest subnet.

What is the subnet description (e.g. BR1 G0/1 LAN or BR1-HQ WAN link)?

_____

How many IP addresses are required in the largest subnet? _____

What subnet mask can support that many host addresses?

_____

How many total host addresses can that subnet mask support? _____

Can you subnet the 172.16.128.0/17 network address to support this subnet? _____

What are the two network addresses that would result from this subnetting?

_____

_____

Use the first network address for this subnet.

Step 3.   Determine the second largest subnet.

What is the subnet description? _____

How many IP addresses are required for the second largest subnet? _____

What subnet mask can support that many host addresses?_____

How many total host addresses can that subnet mask support? _____

Can you subnet the remaining subnet again and still support this subnet? _____

What are the two network addresses that would result from this subnetting?

_____

_____

Use the first network address for this subnet.

Step 4.   Determine the next largest subnet.

What is the subnet description? _____

How many IP addresses are required for the next largest subnet? _____

What subnet mask can support that many host addresses?

_____

How many total host addresses can that subnet mask support? _____

Can you subnet the remaining subnet again and still support this subnet? _____

What are the two network addresses that would result from this subnetting?

_____

_____

Use the first network address for this subnet.

Step 5.   Determine the next largest subnet.

What is the subnet description? _____

How many IP addresses are required for the next largest subnet? _____

What subnet mask can support that many host addresses?

_____

How many total host addresses can that subnet mask support? _____

Can you subnet the remaining subnet again and still support this subnet? _____

What are the two network addresses that would result from this subnetting?

_____

_____

Use the first network address for this subnet.

Step 6.   Determine the next largest subnet.

What is the subnet description? _____

How many IP addresses are required for the next largest subnet? _____

What subnet mask can support that many host addresses?

_____

How many total host addresses can that subnet mask support? _____

Can you subnet the remaining subnet again and still support this subnet? _____

What are the two network addresses that would result from this subnetting?

_____

_____

Use the first network address for this subnet.

Step 7.   Determine the next largest subnet.

What is the subnet description? _____

How many IP addresses are required for the next largest subnet? _____

What subnet mask can support that many host addresses?

_____

How many total host addresses can that subnet mask support? _____

Can you subnet the remaining subnet again and still support this subnet? _____

What are the two network addresses that would result from this subnetting?

_____

_____

Use the first network address for this subnet.

Step 8.   Determine the subnets needed to support the serial links.

How many host addresses are required for each serial subnet link? _____

What subnet mask can support that many host addresses?

_____

a.   Continue subnetting the first subnet of each new subnet until you have four /30 subnets. Write the first three network addresses of these /30 subnets below.

_____

_____

_____

b.   Enter the subnet descriptions for these three subnets below.

_____

_____

_____

Part 2: Design the VLSM Address Scheme

Step 1.   Calculate the subnet information.

Use the information that you obtained in Part 1 to fill in the following table.

Subnet Description	Number of Hosts Needed	Network Address/ CIDR	First Host Address	Broadcast Address
HQ G0/0	16,000			
HQ G0/1	8,000			
BR1 G0/1	4,000			
BR1 G0/0	2,000			
BR2 G0/1	1,000			
BR2 G0/0	500			
HQ S0/0/0–BR1 S0/0/0	2			
HQ S0/0/1–BR2 S0/0/1	2			
BR1 S0/0/1–BR2 S0/0/0	2			

Step 2.   Complete the device interface address table.

Assign the first host address in the subnet to the Ethernet interfaces. HQ should be given the first host address on the Serial links to BR1 and BR2. BR1 should be given the first host address for the serial link to BR2.

Device	Interface	IP Address	Subnet Mask	Device Interface
HQ	G0/0			16,000 Host LAN
	G0/1			8,000 Host LAN
	S0/0/0			BR1 S0/0/0
	S0/0/1			BR2 S0/0/1
BR1	G0/0			2,000 Host LAN
	G0/1			4,000 Host LAN
	S0/0/0			HQ S0/0/0
	S0/0/1			BR2 S0/0/0
BR2	G0/0			500 Host LAN
	G0/1			1,000 Host LAN
	S0/0/0			BR1 S0/0/1
	S0/0/1			HQ S0/0/1

Part 3: Cable and Configure the IPv4 Network

In Part 3, you will cable the network topology and configure the three routers using the VLSM address scheme that you developed in Part 2.

Step 1. Cable the network as shown in the topology.

Step 2. Configure basic settings on each router.

    a. Assign the device name to the router.

    b. Disable DNS lookup to prevent the router from attempting to translate incorrectly entered commands as though they were hostnames.

    c. Assign **class** as the privileged EXEC encrypted password.

    d. Assign **cisco** as the console password and enable login.

    e. Assign **cisco** as the VTY password and enable login.

    f. Encrypt the clear text passwords.

    g. Create a banner that will warn anyone accessing the device that unauthorized access is prohibited.

Step 3. Configure the interfaces on each router.

    a. Assign an IP address and subnet mask to each interface using the table that you completed in Part 2.

    b. Configure an interface description for each interface.

    c. Set the clocking rate on all DCE serial interfaces to 128000.

```
HQ(config-if)# clock rate 128000
```

    d. Activate the interfaces.

Step 4. Save the configuration on all devices.

Step 5. Test Connectivity.

    a. From HQ, ping BR1's S0/0/0 interface address.

    b. From HQ, ping BR2's S0/0/1 interface address.

    c. From BR1, ping BR2's S0/0/0 interface address.

    d. Troubleshoot connectivity issues if pings were not successful.

Note: Pings to the GigabitEthernet interfaces on other routers will not be successful. The LANs defined for the GigabitEthernet interfaces are simulated. Because no devices are attached to these LANs they will be in down/down state. A routing protocol needs to be in place for other devices to be aware of those subnets. The GigabitEthernet interfaces also need to be in an up/up state before a routing protocol can add the subnets to the routing table. These interfaces will remain in a down/down state until a device is connected to the other end of the Ethernet interface cable. The focus of this lab is on VLSM and configuring the interfaces.

Reflection

Can you think of a shortcut for calculating the network addresses of consecutive /30 subnets?

_____

_____

_____

_____

Router Interface Summary Table

Router Interface Summary				
Router Model	Ethernet Interface #1	Ethernet Interface #2	Serial Interface #1	Serial Interface #2
1800	Fast Ethernet 0/0 (F0/0)	Fast Ethernet 0/1 (F0/1)	Serial 0/0/0 (S0/0/0)	Serial 0/0/1 (S0/0/1)
1900	Gigabit Ethernet 0/0 (G0/0)	Gigabit Ethernet 0/1 (G0/1)	Serial 0/0/0 (S0/0/0)	Serial 0/0/1 (S0/0/1)
2801	Fast Ethernet 0/0 (F0/0)	Fast Ethernet 0/1 (F0/1)	Serial 0/1/0 (S0/1/0)	Serial 0/1/1 (S0/1/1)
2811	Fast Ethernet 0/0 (F0/0)	Fast Ethernet 0/1 (F0/1)	Serial 0/0/0 (S0/0/0)	Serial 0/0/1 (S0/0/1)
2900	Gigabit Ethernet 0/0 (G0/0)	Gigabit Ethernet 0/1 (G0/1)	Serial 0/0/0 (S0/0/0)	Serial 0/0/1 (S0/0/1)

Note: To find out how the router is configured, look at the interfaces to identify the type of router and how many interfaces the router has. There is no way to effectively list all the combinations of configurations for each router class. This table includes identifiers for the possible combinations of Ethernet and Serial interfaces in the device. The table does not include any other type of interface, even though a specific router may contain one. An example of this might be an ISDN BRI interface. The string in parentheses is the legal abbreviation that can be used in Cisco IOS commands to represent the interface.

8.3.1.4 Packet Tracer–Implementing a Subnetted IPv6 Addressing Scheme

Topology

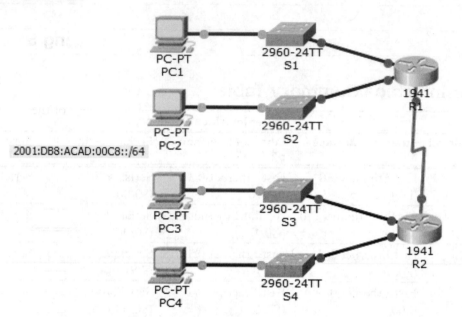

PC-PT
PC1

2960-24TT
S1

PC-PT
PC2

2960-24TT
S2

1941
R1

2001:DB8:ACAD:00C8::/64

PC-PT
PC3

2960-24TT
S3

PC-PT
PC4

2960-24TT
S4

1941
R2

Addressing Table

Device	Interface	IPv6 Address	Link-Local
R1	G0/0		FE80::1
	G0/1		FE80::1
	S0/0/0		FE80::1
R2	G0/0		FE80::2
	G0/1		FE80::2
	S0/0/0		FE80::2
PC1	NIC	Auto Config	
PC2	NIC	Auto Config	
PC3	NIC	Auto Config	
PC4	NIC	Auto Config	

Objectives

Part 1: Determine the IPv6 Subnets and Addressing Scheme

Part 2: Configure the IPv6 Addressing on Routers and PCs and Verify Connectivity

Scenario

Your network administrator wants you to assign five /64 IPv6 subnets to the network shown in the topology. Your job is to determine the IPv6 subnets, assign IPv6 addresses to the routers, and set the PCs to automatically receive IPv6 addressing. Your final step is to verify connectivity between IPv6 hosts.

Part 1: Determine the IPv6 Subnets and Addressing Scheme

Step 1.   Determine the number of subnets needed.

Start with the IPv6 subnet 2001:DB8:ACAD:00C8::/64 and assign it to the R1 LAN attached to GigabitEthernet 0/0, as shown in the **Subnet Table**. For the rest of the IPv6 subnets, increment the 2001:DB8:ACAD:00C8::/64 subnet address by 1 and complete the **Subnet Table** with the IPv6 subnet addresses.

Subnet Table

Subnet Description	Subnet Address
R1 G0/0 LAN	2001:DB8:ACAD:00C8::0/64
R1 G0/1 LAN	
R2 G0/0 LAN	
R2 G0/1 LAN	
WAN Link	

Step 2:   Assign IPv6 addressing to the routers.

  a.   Assign the first IPv6 addresses to R1 for the two LAN links and the WAN link.

  b.   Assign the first IPv6 addresses to R2 for the two LANs. Assign the second IPv6 address for the WAN link.

  c.   Document the IPv6 addressing scheme in the **Addressing Table**.

Part 2: Configure the IPv6 Addressing on Routers and PCs and Verify Connectivity

Step 1.   Configure the routers with IPv6 addressing.

> **Note:** This network is already configured with some IPv6 commands that are covered in a later course. At this point in your studies, you only need to know how to configure IPv6 address on an interface.

Configure R1 and R2 with the IPv6 addresses you specified in the **Addressing Table** and activate the interfaces.

```
Router(config-if)# ipv6 address ipv6-address/prefix
Router(config-if)# ipv6 address ipv6-link-local link-local
```

Step 2.   Configure the PCs to automatically receive IPv6 addressing.

Configure the four PCs for autoconfiguration. Each should then automatically receive full IPv6 addresses from the routers.

Step 3.   Verify connectivity between the PCs.

Each PC should be able to ping the other PCs and the routers.

Suggested Scoring Rubric

Activity Section	Question Location	Possible Points	Earned Points
Part 1: Determine IPv6 Subnets and Addressing Scheme	Subnet Table	30	
	Addressing Table	30	
	Part 1 Total	60	
	Packet Tracer Score	40	
	Total Score	100	

8.4.1.1 Class Activity–Can You Call Me Now

Objectives

Calculate the necessary subnet mask in order to accommodate a given number of hosts.

Background/Scenario

Note: This activity may be completed individually or in small/large groups using Packet Tracer software.

- You are setting up a dedicated, computer addressing scheme for patient rooms in a hospital. The switch will be centrally located in the nurses' station, as each of the five rooms will be wired so that patients can just connect to an RJ45 port built into the wall of their room. Devise a physical and logical topology for only one of the six floors using the following addressing scheme requirements: There are six floors with five patient rooms on each floor for a total of 30 connections. Each room needs a network connection.

- Subnetting must be incorporated into your scheme.

- Use one router, one switch, and five host stations for addressing purposes.

- Validate that all PCs can connect to the hospital's in-house services.

Keep a copy of your scheme to share later with the class or learning community. Be prepared to explain how subnetting, unicasts, multicasts, and broadcasts would be incorporated, and where your addressing scheme could be used.

Required Resources

- Packet Tracer software

Reflection

How would you change your addressing scheme if you were going to add an additional network connection to the hospital rooms with a total of 10 connections per floor or 2 ports per room?

_____

_____

_____

_____

<table>
<tr><td>Packet Tracer
☐ Activity</td></tr>
</table>

8.4.1.2 Packet Tracer–Skills Integration Challenge

Topology

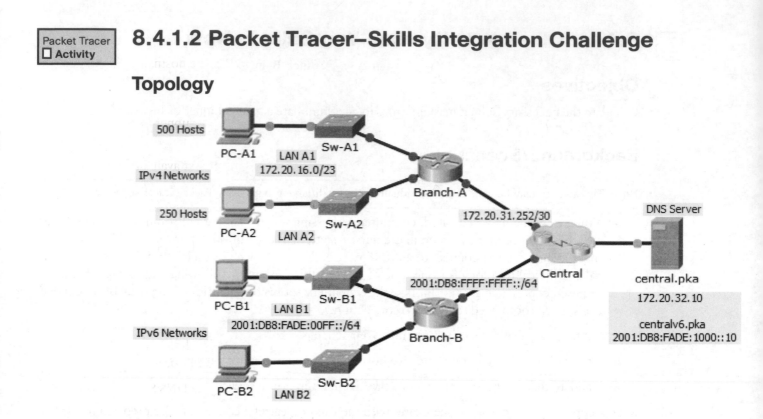

Addressing Table

Device	Interface	IPv4 Address	Subnet Mask	Default Gateway
		IPv6 Address/Prefix		
Branch-A	G0/0			N/A
	G0/1			N/A
	G0/2	172.20.31.254	255.255.255.252	N/A
Branch-B	G0/0			N/A
	G0/1			N/A
	G0/2	2001:DB8:FFFF:FFFF::2/64		N/A
PC-A1	NIC			
PC-A2	NIC			
PC-B1	NIC			
PC-B2	NIC			

Scenario

As a network technician familiar with IPv4 and IPv6 addressing implementations, you are now ready to take an existing network infrastructure and apply your knowledge and skills to finalize the configuration. In this activity, the network administrator has already configured some commands on the routers. **Do not erase or modify those configurations.** Your task is to complete the IPv4 and IPv6 addressing scheme, implement IPv4 and IPv6 addressing, and verify connectivity.

Requirements

- Configure the initial settings on **Branch-A** and **Branch-B**, including the hostname, banner, lines, and passwords. Use **cisco** as the user EXEC password and **class** as the privileged EXEC password. Encrypt all passwords.

- LAN A1 is using the subnet 172.20.16.0/23. Assign the next available subnet to LAN A2 for a maximum of 250 hosts.

- LAN B1 is using the subnet 2001:DB8:FADE:00FF::/64. Assign the next available subnet to LAN B2.

- Finish documenting the addressing scheme in the **Addressing Table** using the following guidelines:

    - Assign the first IP address for LAN A1, LAN A2, LAN B1, and LAN B2 to the router interface.

    - For the IPv4 networks, assign the last IPv4 address to the PCs.

    - For the IPv6 networks, assign the 16th IPv6 address to the PCs.

- Configure the router addressing according to your documentation. Include an appropriate description for each router interface. Branch-B uses FE80::B as the link-local address.

- Configure PCs with addressing according to your documentation. The DNS Server addresses for IPv4 and IPv6 are shown in the topology.

- Verify connectivity between the IPv4 PCs and between the IPv6 PCs.

- Verify the IPv4 PCs can access the web page at **central.pka**.

- Verify the IPv6 PCs can access the web page at **centralv6.pka**.

Suggested Scoring Rubric

Activity Section	Possible Points	Earned Points
Addressing Table Documentation	25	
Packet Tracer Score	75	
Total Score	100	

CHAPTER 9

Transport Layer

The Study Guide portion of this chapter uses a combination of matching, fill-in-the-blank, multiple-choice, and open-ended question exercises to test your knowledge and skills of basic router concepts and configuration. The Lab and Activities portion of this chapter includes all the online curriculum labs and Packet Tracer activities to ensure that you have mastered the hands-on skills needed to understand basic IP addressing and router configuration.

As you work through this chapter, use Chapter 9 in *Introduction to Networks v6 Companion Guide* or use the corresponding Chapter 9 in the Introduction to Networks online curriculum for assistance.

Study Guide

On a single device, people can use multiple applications and services such as email, the Web, and instant messaging to send messages or retrieve information. The transport layer enables these multiple applications to send data over the network at the same time and ensures that, if necessary, all the data is received by the destination. In this chapter, we review the role of the transport layer in encapsulating application data for use by the network layer.

Transport Layer Protocols

The transport layer is responsible for establishing a temporary communication session between two applications and delivering data between them. In TCP/IP, this process is handled by two very different transport layer protocols: Transmission Control Protocol (TCP) and User Datagram Protocol (UDP).

Transportation of Data Completion Exercise

List and briefly describe the three primary transport layer responsibilities

- _____

- _____

- _____

Briefly explain how the transport layer can handle delivery of a video stream while you are also sending an email and chatting with your friends.

_____

_____

TCP/IP provides two transport layer protocols. _____ is considered a _____, full-featured transport layer protocol, which ensures that all the data arrives at the destination. In contrast, _____ is a very simple transport layer protocol that does not provide for any _____.

What are the three basic TCP operations that ensure reliability?

- _____

- _____

- _____

List two examples of applications that use TCP.

_____

Briefly explain what is meant by best-effort delivery and give an example.

_____

_____

_____

TCP and UDP Overview

TCP is a _____-oriented protocol that negotiates and establishes a permanent _____ between source and destination. The _____ is terminated only after all communication is completed.

In networking terms, _____ means ensuring that each piece of data that the source sends arrives at the destination.

Why might data arrive at the destination in the wrong order?

_____

_____

How does TCP ensure data is reassembled in order?

_____

Explain the purpose of flow control.

_____

_____

_____

Why is TCP called a stateful protocol?

_____

_____

Each TCP segment has 20 bytes of overhead in the header encapsulating the application layer data. The TCP header is shown in Figure 9-1. Fill in the missing fields. Include the number of bits for each field.

Figure 9-1   The TCP Header

Bit 0	Bit 8	Bit 16	Bit 24
Header Length (4)	Reserved (6)	Control Bits (6)	
Checksum (16)		Urgent (16)	
Options (0 or 32 if any)			
Application Layer Data (Size Varies)			

UDP is a lightweight transport protocol that offers the same data segmentation and reassembly as TCP, but without TCP reliability and flow control.

Why is UDP called a stateless protocol?

_____

Each UDP datagram has 8 bytes of overhead in the header encapsulating the application layer data. The UDP header is shown in Figure 9-2. Fill in the missing fields. Include the number of bits for each field.

Figure 9-2   The UDP Header

Bit 0	Bit 8	Bit 16	Bit 24
Checksum (16)		Urgent (16)	
Application Layer Data (Size Varies)			

In Table 9-1, indicate which transport layer protocol is described by the characteristic.

Table 9-1   TCP and UDP Characteristics

Characteristic	TCP	UDP
Flow control		
Ordered delivery		
No ordered delivery		
Sequenced message segments		
Session establishment		
Less overhead		
Fast transmission requirements		
Guaranteed delivery		
No acknowledgment of receipt		
Connectionless		

TCP and UDP use port numbers to track different conversations. In Table 9-2, fill in the values for the port number ranges.

Table 9-2   Port Number Groups

Port Number Range	Port Group
	Well-known ports
	Registered ports
	Private and/or dynamic ports

Memorizing the well-known port numbers is important for networking students. These port numbers are used in some configurations and are displayed in the output of some commands. In Table 9-3, fill in the port numbers and whether the application uses TCP, UDP, or both.

Table 9-3   Port Number Groups

Port Number	Protocol	Application	Acronym
		File Transfer Protocol (data)	FTP
		File Transfer Protocol (control)	FTP
		Secure Shell	SSH
		Telnet	—
		Simple Mail Transfer Protocol	SMTP
		Domain Name Service	DNS
		Dynamic Host Configuration Protocol (server)	DHCP

continued

Port Number	Protocol	Application	Acronym
		Dynamic Host Configuration Protocol (client)	DHCP
		Trivial File Transfer Protocol	TFTP
		Hypertext Transfer Protocol	HTTP
		Post Office Protocol version 3	POP3
		Internet Message Access Protocol	IMAP
		Simple Network Management Protocol	SNMP
		Hypertext Transfer Protocol Secure	HTTPS

TCP and UDP

The key distinction between TCP and UDP is reliability. TCP uses connection-oriented sessions. The main purpose of these sessions is to ensure that the destination receives all the data intact. UDP, in contrast, is a simple protocol that provides the basic transport layer functions without all the overhead of TCP because it is not connection oriented and does not offer the sophisticated retransmission, sequencing, and flow-control mechanisms that provide reliability.

TCP Communication

To establish a TCP connection, the source and destination perform a three-way handshake, which does the following:

- Establishes that the destination device is present on the network

- Verifies that the destination device has an active service and is accepting requests on the port number that the source intends to use for the session

- Informs the destination device that the source client intends to establish a communication session on that port number

In Figure 9-3, fill in the four blanks with one of the following options. Not all options are used:

- Send ACK

- Send SYN

- SYN received

- Established, ACK

- ACK received

- SYN, ACK received

- Send SYN, ACK

Figure 9-3   The TCP Three-Way Handshake

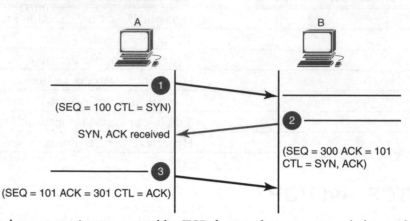

To terminate a single conversation supported by TCP, four exchanges are needed to end both sessions, as shown in Figure 9-4. Fill in the eight blanks with one of the following options. Not all options are used. Options may be used more than once:

- Send ACK

- Send FIN

- Send SYN

- ACK received

- FIN received

- SYN received

Figure 9-4   The TCP Session-Termination Process

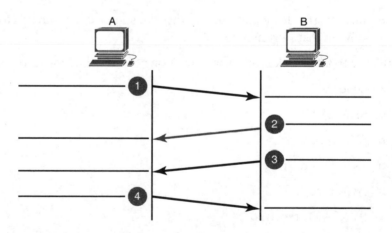

UDP Communication

Directions: In the following paragraphs, circle the correct answer.

UDP is a [simple/complex] protocol that provides the basic transport layer functions. It has much [higher/lower] overhead than TCP because it is does not offer the sophisticated retransmission, sequencing, and flow-control mechanisms that provide reliability. UDP makes it very desirable for applications that are [sensitive/not sensitive] to delays in the transmission of data.

Because UDP is [connectionless/connection oriented], sessions are [established/not established] before communication takes place.

When multiple datagrams are sent to a destination, they may take different paths and arrive in the wrong order. UDP [has no way to reorder/reorders] datagrams into their transmission order because it [does not track/tracks] sequence numbers.

TCP or UDP, That Is the Question

In Table 9-4, indicate which transport protocol is used by each of the application layer protocols.

Table 9-4   Classifying Transport Layer Protocols

Application	TCP	UDP	Both
SNMP			
FTP			
IPTV			
HTTP			
DNS			
DHCP			
Telnet			
VoIP			
TFTP			
SMTP			

Labs and Activities

Command Reference

In Table 9-5, record the command, including the correct router or switch prompt, that fits the description. Fill in any blanks with the appropriate missing information.

Table 9-5   Commands for Chapter 9, Transport Layer

Command	Description
	Lists the protocols in use, the local address and port numbers, the foreign address and port numbers, and the connection state.

9.0.1.2 Class Activity–We Need to Talk

Objectives

Explain how transport layer protocols and services support communications across data networks.

Background/Scenario

Note: This activity works best with medium-sized groups of 6 to 8 students per group.

This chapter helps you understand how transport layer protocols and services support network data communications.

The instructor will whisper a complex message to the first student in a group. An example of the message might be "Our final exam will be given next Tuesday, February 5th, at 2 p.m. in Room 1151."

That student whispers the message to the next student in the group. Each group follows this process until all members of each group have heard the whispered message. Here are the rules you are to follow:

- You can whisper the message only once to your neighbor.

- The message must keep moving from one person to the other with no skipping of participants. The instructor should ask a student to keep time of the full message activity from first participant to last participant stating the messages. The first or last person would mostly likely be the best one to keep this time.

- The last student will say aloud exactly what she heard.

The instructor will then restate the original message so that the group can compare it to the message that was delivered by the last student in the group.

Required Resources

- Timer for the student who is keeping a record of the conversation's duration.

Reflection

1. Would the contents of this message need to be fully correct when you received them if you were depending on this message to drive your personal/business calendar, studying schedule, and so on?

_____

_____

2. Would the length of time taken to deliver the message be an important factor to the sender and recipient?

_____

_____

9.2.1.6 Lab–Using Wireshark to Observe the TCP 3-Way Handshake

Topology

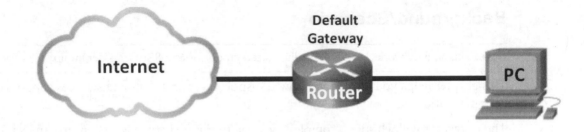

Default Gateway

Internet

Router

PC

Objectives

Part 1: Prepare Wireshark to Capture Packets

Part 2: Capture, Locate, and Examine Packets

Background/Scenario

In this lab, you will use Wireshark to capture and examine packets generated between the PC browser using the HyperText Transfer Protocol (HTTP) and a web server, such as www.google.com. When an application such as HTTP or File Transfer Protocol (FTP) first starts on a host, TCP uses the three-way handshake to establish a reliable TCP session between the two hosts. For example, when a PC uses a web browser to surf the Internet, a three-way handshake is initiated, and a session is established between the PC host and web server. A PC can have multiple, simultaneous, active TCP sessions with various web sites.

Note: This lab cannot be completed using Netlab. This lab assumes that you have Internet access.

Required Resources

1 PC (Windows 7 or 8 with command prompt access, Internet access, and Wireshark installed)

Part 1: Prepare Wireshark to Capture Packets

In Part 1, you will start the Wireshark program and select the appropriate interface to begin capturing packets.

Step 1:   Retrieve the PC interface addresses.

For this lab, you need to retrieve your PC's IP address and its network interface card (NIC) physical address, also called the MAC address.

a.   Open a command prompt window, type **ipconfig /all**, and press Enter.

```
Physical Address. . . . . . . . . : 00-1A-73-EA-63-8C
DHCP Enabled. . . . . . . . . . . : Yes
Autoconfiguration Enabled . . . . : Yes
Link-local IPv6 Address . . . . . : fe80::a858:5f3e:35e2:d38f%14(Preferred)
IPv4 Address. . . . . . . . . . . : 192.168.1.130(Preferred)
Subnet Mask . . . . . . . . . . . : 255.255.255.0
```

b. Write down the IP and MAC addresses associated with the selected Ethernet adapter. That is the source address to look for when examining captured packets.

The PC host IP address: _____

The PC host MAC address: _____

Step 2:   Start Wireshark and select the appropriate interface.

a. Click the Windows **Start** button. In the pop-up menu, double-click **Wireshark**.

b. After Wireshark starts, click **Interface List**.

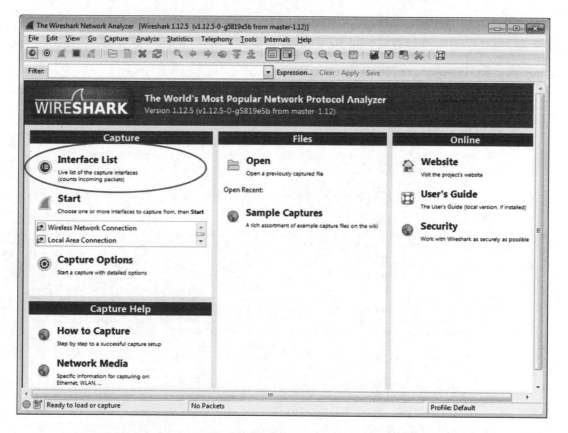

c. In the **Wireshark: Capture Interfaces** window, click the check box next to the interface that is connected to your LAN.

Note: If multiple interfaces are listed and you are unsure which interface to select, click **Details**. Click the **802.3 (Ethernet)** tab, and verify that the MAC address matches what you wrote down in Step 1b. Close the Interface Details window after verification.

Part 2: Capture, Locate, and Examine Packets

Step 1: Capture the data.

    a. Click the **Start** button to start the data capture.

    b. Navigate to www.google.com. Minimize the browser and return to Wireshark. Stop the data capture.

Note: Your instructor may provide you with a different website. If so, enter the website name or address here:

_____

The capture window is now active. Locate the **Source**, **Destination**, and **Protocol** columns.

Step 2: Locate appropriate packets for the web session.

If the computer was recently started and there has been no activity in accessing the Internet, you can see the entire process in the captured output, including the Address Resolution Protocol (ARP), Domain Name System (DNS), and the TCP three-way handshake. If the PC already had an ARP entry for the default gateway, it started with the DNS query to resolve www.google.com.

    a. Frame 11 shows the DNS query from the PC to the DNS server, which is attempting to resolve the domain name www.google.com to the IP address of the web server. The PC must have the IP address before it can send the first packet to the web server.

What is the IP address of the DNS server that the computer queried?

_____

b. Frame 13 is the response from the DNS server. It contains the IP address of www. google.com.

c. Find the appropriate packet for the start of your three-way handshake. In the example, frame 14 is the start of the TCP three-way handshake.

What is the IP address of the Google web server? _____

d. If you have many packets that are unrelated to the TCP connection, it may be necessary to use the Wireshark filter tool. Type **tcp** in the filter entry area within Wireshark and press **Enter**.

Step 3: Examine the information within packets including IP addresses, TCP port numbers, and TCP control flags.

a. In our example, frame 14 is the start of the three-way handshake between the PC and the Google web server. In the packet list pane (top section of the main window), select the frame. This highlights the line and displays the decoded information from that packet in the two lower panes. Examine the TCP information in the packet details pane (middle section of the main window).

b. Click the **+** icon to the left of the Transmission Control Protocol in the packet details pane to expand the view of the TCP information.

c. Click the **+** icon to the left of the Flags. Look at the source and destination ports and the flags that are set.

Note: You may have to adjust the top and middle window sizes within Wireshark to display the necessary information.

```
File  Edit  View  Go  Capture  Analyze  Statistics  Telephony  Tools  Internals  Help

Filter: tcp                                        ▼  Expression...  Clear  Apply  Save

No.      Time          Source              Destination         Protocol  Length   Info
      8 1.747681000  173.194.115.178     192.168.1.130       TCP        60 80→49382 [ACK] Seq=1 Ack=685 Win=3
      9 2.149995000  173.194.115.178     192.168.1.130       HTTP      583 HTTP/1.1 302 Found  (text/html)
     10 2.159742000  192.168.1.130       216.58.216.35       TCP        66 49386→443 [SYN] Seq=0 Win=8192 Ler
     12 2.163473000  192.168.1.130       173.194.115.178     TLSv1.2   116 Application Data
     14 2.181706000  192.168.1.130       216.58.216.46       TCP        66 49387→443 [SYN] Seq=0 Win=8192 Ler
     15 2.206406000  216.58.216.46       192.168.1.130       TCP        66 443→49387 [SYN, ACK] Seq=0 Ack=1 W
     16 2.206555000  192.168.1.130       216.58.216.46       TCP        54 49387→443 [ACK] Seq=1 Ack=1 Win=17
     17 2.206900000  192.168.1.130       216.58.216.46       TLSv1.2   266 Client Hello

⊞ Frame 14: 66 bytes on wire (528 bits), 66 bytes captured (528 bits) on interface 0
⊞ Ethernet II, Src: GemtekTe_ea:63:8c (00:1a:73:ea:63:8c), Dst: Netgear_ea:b1:7a (80:37:73:ea:b1:7a)
⊞ Internet Protocol Version 4, Src: 192.168.1.130 (192.168.1.130), Dst: 216.58.216.46 (216.58.216.46)
⊟ Transmission Control Protocol, Src Port: 49387 (49387), Dst Port: 443 (443), Seq: 0, Len: 0
      Source Port: 49387 (49387)
      Destination Port: 443 (443)
      [Stream index: 3]
      [TCP Segment Len: 0]
      Sequence number: 0     (relative sequence number)
      Acknowledgment number: 0
      Header Length: 32 bytes
   ⊟ .... 0000 0000 0010 = Flags: 0x002 (SYN)
         000. .... .... = Reserved: Not set
         ...0 .... .... = Nonce: Not set
         .... 0... .... = Congestion Window Reduced (CWR): Not set
         .... .0.. .... = ECN-Echo: Not set
         .... ..0. .... = Urgent: Not set
         .... ...0 .... = Acknowledgment: Not set
         .... .... 0... = Push: Not set
         .... .... .0.. = Reset: Not set
      ⊞ .... .... ..1. = Syn: Set
         .... .... ...0 = Fin: Not set
      Window size value: 8192
      [Calculated window size: 8192]
   ⊞ Checksum: 0x5c37 [validation disabled]
      Urgent pointer: 0
```

What is the TCP source port number? _____

How would you classify the source port? _____

What is the TCP destination port number? _____

How would you classify the destination port? _____

Which flag (or flags) is set? _____

What is the relative sequence number set to? _____

d. To select the next frame in the three-way handshake, select **Go** on the Wireshark menu and select **Next Packet In Conversation.** In this example, this is frame **15.** This is the Google web server reply to the initial request to start a session.

File Edit View Go Capture Analyze Statistics Telephony Tools Internals Help

Filter: tcp   ▼ Expression... Clear Apply Save

No.	Time	Source	Destination	Protocol	Length	Info
10	2.159742000	192.168.1.130	216.58.216.35	TCP	66	49386→443 [SYN] Seq=0 Win=8192 Len
12	2.163473000	192.168.1.130	173.194.115.178	TLSv1.2	116	Application Data
14	2.181706000	192.168.1.130	216.58.216.46	TCP	66	49387→443 [SYN] Seq=0 Win=8192 Len
15	2.206406000	216.58.216.46	192.168.1.130	TCP	66	443→49387 [SYN, ACK] Seq=0 Ack=1 W
16	2.206555000	192.168.1.130	216.58.216.46	TCP	54	49387→443 [ACK] Seq=1 Ack=1 Win=17
17	2.206900000	192.168.1.130	216.58.216.46	TLSv1.2	266	Client Hello
18	2.232820000	216.58.216.46	192.168.1.130	TCP	54	443→49387 [ACK] Seq=1 Ack=213 Win=

⊞ Frame 15: 66 bytes on wire (528 bits), 66 bytes captured (528 bits) on interface 0
⊞ Ethernet II, Src: Netgear_ea:b1:7a (80:37:73:ea:b1:7a), Dst: GemtekTe_ea:63:8c (00:1a:73:ea:63:8c)
⊞ Internet Protocol Version 4, Src: 216.58.216.46 (216.58.216.46), Dst: 192.168.1.130 (192.168.1.130)
⊟ Transmission Control Protocol, Src Port: 443 (443), Dst Port: 49387 (49387), Seq: 0, Ack: 1, Len: 0
       Source Port: 443 (443)
       Destination Port: 49387 (49387)
       [Stream index: 3]
       [TCP Segment Len: 0]
       Sequence number: 0   (relative sequence number)
       Acknowledgment number: 1   (relative ack number)
       Header Length: 32 bytes
  ⊟ .... 0000 0001 0010 = Flags: 0x012 (SYN, ACK)
       000. .... = Reserved: Not set
       ...0 .... = Nonce: Not set
       .... 0... .... = Congestion Window Reduced (CWR): Not set
       .... .0.. .... = ECN-Echo: Not set
       .... ..0. .... = Urgent: Not set
       ....1 .... = Acknowledgment: Set
       .... 0... = Push: Not set
       .... .0.. = Reset: Not set
     ⊞ ....1. = Syn: Set
       ....0 = Fin: Not set
       Window size value: 42900
       [Calculated window size: 42900]
  ⊞ Checksum: 0xf159 [validation disabled]
       Urgent pointer: 0

What are the values of the source and destination ports? _____

Which flags are set? _____

What are the relative sequence and acknowledgment numbers set to?

_____

e. Finally, examine the third packet of the three-way handshake in the example. Click frame 16 in the top window to display the following information in this example:

```
File  Edit  View  Go  Capture  Analyze  Statistics  Telephony  Tools  Internals  Help

Filter: tcp                                    ▼  Expression... Clear  Apply  Save

No.      Time          Source               Destination          Protocol  Length  Info
      12 2.163473000 192.168.1.130        173.194.115.178      TLSv1.2   116 Application Data
      14 2.181706000 192.168.1.130        216.58.216.46        TCP        66 49387→443 [SYN] Seq=0 Win=8192 Len
      15 2.206406000 216.58.216.46        192.168.1.130        TCP        66 443→49387 [SYN, ACK] Seq=0 Ack=1 W
      16 2.206555000 192.168.1.130        216.58.216.46        TCP        54 49387→443 [ACK] Seq=1 Ack=1 Win=17
      17 2.206900000 192.168.1.130        216.58.216.46        TLSv1.2   266 Client Hello
      18 2.232820000 216.58.216.46        192.168.1.130        TCP        54 443→49387 [ACK] Seq=1 Ack=213 win=
      19 2.235597000 216.58.216.46        192.168.1.130        TLSv1.2  1314 Server Hello

⊞ Frame 16: 54 bytes on wire (432 bits), 54 bytes captured (432 bits) on interface 0
⊞ Ethernet II, Src: GemtekTe_ea:63:8c (00:1a:73:ea:63:8c), Dst: Netgear_ea:b1:7a (80:37:73:ea:b1:7a)
⊞ Internet Protocol Version 4, Src: 192.168.1.130 (192.168.1.130), Dst: 216.58.216.46 (216.58.216.46)
⊟ Transmission Control Protocol, Src Port: 49387 (49387), Dst Port: 443 (443), Seq: 1, Ack: 1, Len: 0
    Source Port: 49387 (49387)
    Destination Port: 443 (443)
    [Stream index: 3]
    [TCP Segment Len: 0]
    Sequence number: 1     (relative sequence number)
    Acknowledgment number: 1     (relative ack number)
    Header Length: 20 bytes
  ⊟ .... 0000 0001 0000 = Flags: 0x010 (ACK)
      000. .... .... = Reserved: Not set
      ...0 .... .... = Nonce: Not set
      .... 0... .... = Congestion Window Reduced (CWR): Not set
      .... .0.. .... = ECN-Echo: Not set
      .... ..0. .... = Urgent: Not set
      .... ...1 .... = Acknowledgment: Set
      .... .... 0... = Push: Not set
      .... .... .0.. = Reset: Not set
      .... .... ..0. = Syn: Not set
      .... .... ...0 = Fin: Not set
    Window size value: 68
    [Calculated window size: 17408]
    [Window size scaling factor: 256]
  ⊞ Checksum: 0xd95e [validation disabled]
```

Examine the third and final packet of the handshake.

Which flag (or flags) is set? _____

The relative sequence and acknowledgment numbers are set to 1 as a starting point. The TCP connection is established and communication between the source computer and the web server can begin.

f. Close the Wireshark program.

Reflection

1. There are hundreds of filters available in Wireshark. A large network could have numerous filters and many different types of traffic. List three filters that might be useful to a network administrator.

_____

2. What other ways could Wireshark be used in a production network?

_____

9.2.3.5 Lab–Using Wireshark to Examine a UDP DNS Capture

Topology

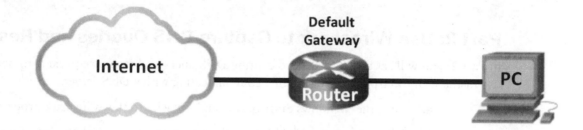

Objectives

Part 1: Record a PC's IP Configuration Information

Part 2: Use Wireshark to Capture DNS Queries and Responses

Part 3: Analyze Captured DNS or UDP Packets

Background/Scenario

If you have ever used the Internet, you have used the Domain Name System (DNS). DNS is a distributed network of servers that translates user-friendly domain names like www.google.com to an IP address. When you type a website URL into your browser, your PC performs a DNS query to the DNS server's IP address. Your PC's DNS server query and the DNS server's response make use of the User Datagram Protocol (UDP) as the transport layer protocol. UDP is connectionless and does not require a session setup as does TCP. DNS queries and responses are very small and do not require the overhead of TCP.

In this lab, you will communicate with a DNS server by sending a DNS query using the UDP transport protocol. You will use Wireshark to examine the DNS query and response exchanges with the same server.

Note: This lab cannot be completed using Netlab. This lab assumes that you have Internet access.

Required Resources

1 PC (Windows 7 or 8 with command prompt access, Internet access, and Wireshark installed)

Part 1: Record a PC's IP Configuration Information

In Part 1, you will use the **ipconfig /all** command on your local PC to find and record the MAC and IP addresses of your PC's network interface card (NIC), the IP address of the specified default gateway, and the DNS server IP address specified for the PC. Record this information in the table provided. The information will be used in parts of this lab with packet analysis.

IP address	10.140.17.29
MAC address	34-17-EB-A1-C9-E8
Default gateway IP address	10.140.17.1
DNS server IP address	10.140.110.2

Part 2: Use Wireshark to Capture DNS Queries and Responses

In Part 2, you will set up Wireshark to capture DNS query and response packets to demonstrate the use of the UDP transport protocol while communicating with a DNS server.

   a.   Click the Windows **Start** button and navigate to the Wireshark program.

   b.   Select an interface for Wireshark to capture packets. Use the **Interface List** to choose the interface that is associated with the recorded PC's IP and MAC addresses in Part 1.

   c.   After selecting the desired interface, click **Start** to capture the packets.

   d.   Open a web browser and type **www.google.com**. Press **Enter** to continue.

   e.   Click **Stop** to stop the Wireshark capture when you see Google's home page.

Part 3: Analyze Captured DNS or UDP Packets

In Part 3, you will examine the UDP packets that were generated when communicating with a DNS server for the IP addresses for www.google.com.

Step 1:   Filter DNS packets.

   a.   In the Wireshark main window, type **dns** in the entry area of the **Filter** toolbar. Click **Apply** or press **Enter**.

Note: If you do not see any results after the DNS filter was applied, close the web browser. In the command prompt window, type **ipconfig /flushdns** to remove all previous DNS results. Restart the Wireshark capture and repeat the instructions in Part 2b –2e. If this does not resolve the issue, type **nslookup www.google.com** in the command prompt window as an alternative to the web browser.

---

b. In the packet list pane (top section) of the main window, locate the packet that includes **Standard query** and **A www.google.com**. See frame 5 as an example.

Step 2: Examine a UDP segment using DNS query.

Examine the UDP by using a DNS query for www.google.com as captured by Wireshark. In this example, Wireshark capture frame 5 in the packet list pane is selected for analysis. The protocols in this query are displayed in the packet details pane (middle section) of the main window. The protocol entries are highlighted in gray.

```
⊞ Frame 5: 74 bytes on wire (592 bits), 74 bytes captured (592 bits) on interface 0
⊞ Ethernet II, Src: GemtekTe_ea:63:8c (00:1a:73:ea:63:8c), Dst: Netgear_ea:b1:7a (80:37:73:ea:b1:7a)
⊞ Internet Protocol Version 4, Src: 192.168.1.11 (192.168.1.11), Dst: 192.168.1.1 (192.168.1.1)
⊟ User Datagram Protocol, Src Port: 60868 (60868), Dst Port: 53 (53)
     Source Port: 60868 (60868)
     Destination Port: 53 (53)
     Length: 40
  ⊞ Checksum: 0xd7c4 [validation disabled]
     [Stream index: 2]
⊞ Domain Name System (query)
```

a. In the first line in the packet details pane, frame 5 had 74 bytes of data on the wire. This is the number of bytes to send a DNS query to a named server requesting the IP addresses of www.google.com.

b. The Ethernet II line displays the source and destination MAC addresses. The source MAC address is from your local PC because your local PC originated the DNS query. The destination MAC address is from the default gateway because this is the last stop before this query exits the local network.

Is the source MAC address the same as the one recorded from Part 1 for the local PC?

_____

c. In the Internet Protocol Version 4 line, the IP packet Wireshark capture indicates that the source IP address of this DNS query is 192.168.1.11 and the destination IP address is 192.168.1.1. In this example, the destination address is the default gateway. The router is the default gateway in this network.

Can you identify the IP and MAC addresses for the source and destination devices?

Device	IP Address	MAC Address
Local PC		
Default Gateway		

The IP packet and header encapsulates the UDP segment. The UDP segment contains the DNS query as the data.

d. A UDP header only has four fields: source port, destination port, length, and checksum. Each field in a UDP header is only 16 bits as depicted on the next page.

UDP Segment

```
0                          16                          31
┌───────────────────────────┬───────────────────────────┐
│      UDP Source Port       │    UDP Destination Port    │
├───────────────────────────┼───────────────────────────┤
│     UDP Message Length     │       UDP Checksum         │
├───────────────────────────┴───────────────────────────┤
│                         Data                           │
├────────────────────────────────────────────────────────┤
│                        Data...                         │
└────────────────────────────────────────────────────────┘
```

Expand the User Datagram Protocol in the packet details pane by clicking the plus (+) sign. Notice that there are only four fields. The source port number in this example is 60868. The source port was randomly generated by the local PC using port numbers that are not reserved. The destination port is 53. Port 53 is a well-known port reserved for use with DNS. DNS servers listen on port 53 for DNS queries from clients.

```
⊟ User Datagram Protocol, Src Port: 60868 (60868), Dst Port: 53 (53)
      Source Port: 60868 (60868)
      Destination Port: 53 (53)
      Length: 40
  ⊟ Checksum: 0xd7c4 [validation disabled]
        [Good Checksum: False]
        [Bad Checksum: False]
      [Stream index: 2]
```

In this example, the length of the UDP segment is 40 bytes. Out of 40 bytes, 8 bytes are used as the header. The other 32 bytes are used by DNS query data. The 32 bytes of DNS query data are highlighted in the following illustration in the packet bytes pane (lower section) of the Wireshark main window.

```
⊟ Domain Name System (query)
      [Response In: 6]
      Transaction ID: 0x27db
  ⊞ Flags: 0x0100 Standard query
      Questions: 1
      Answer RRs: 0
      Authority RRs: 0
      Additional RRs: 0
  ⊟ Queries
    ⊟ www.google.com: type A, class IN
        Name: www.google.com
        [Name Length: 14]
        [Label Count: 3]
        Type: A (Host Address) (1)
        Class: IN (0x0001)
```

The checksum is used to determine the integrity of the packet after it has traversed the Internet.

The UDP header has low overhead because UDP does not have fields that are associated with the three-way handshake in TCP. Any data transfer reliability issues that occur must be handled by the application layer.

Record your Wireshark results in the table below:

Frame size	
Source MAC address	
Destination MAC address	
Source IP address	
Destination IP address	
Source port	
Destination port	

Is the source IP address the same as the local PC's IP address you recorded in Part 1?

_____

Is the destination IP address the same as the default gateway noted in Part 1?

_____

Step 3:   Examine a UDP using DNS response.

In this step, you will examine the DNS response packet and verify that the DNS response packet also uses the UDP.

a.   In this example, frame 6 is the corresponding DNS response packet. Notice the number of bytes on the wire is 170. It is a larger packet compared to the DNS query packet.

b.   In the Ethernet II frame for the DNS response, what device is the source MAC address and what device is the destination MAC address?

_____

c.   Notice the source and destination IP addresses in the IP packet. What is the destination IP address? What is the source IP address?

Destination IP address: _____ Source IP address: _____

What happened to the roles of source and destination for the local host and default gateway?

_____

d.   In the UDP segment, the role of the port numbers has also reversed. The destination port number is 60868. Port number 60868 is the same port that was generated by the local PC when the DNS query was sent to the DNS server. Your local PC listens for a DNS response on this port.

The source port number is 53. The DNS server listens for a DNS query on port 53 and then sends a DNS response with a source port number of 53 back to the originator of the DNS query.

When the DNS response is expanded, notice the resolved IP addresses for www.google. com in the **Answers** section.

```
☐ User Datagram Protocol, Src Port: 53 (53), Dst Port: 60868 (60868)
     Source Port: 53 (53)
     Destination Port: 60868 (60868)
     Length: 136
  ☐ Checksum: 0x8764 [validation disabled]
       [Good Checksum: False]
       [Bad Checksum: False]
     [Stream index: 2]
☐ Domain Name System (response)
     [Request In: 5]
     [Time: 0.017090000 seconds]
     Transaction ID: 0x27db
  ⊞ Flags: 0x8180 Standard query response, No error
     Questions: 1
     Answer RRs: 6
     Authority RRs: 0
     Additional RRs: 0
  ⊞ Queries
  ☐ Answers
     ☐ www.google.com: type A, class IN, addr 64.233.160.99
          Name: www.google.com
          Type: A (Host Address) (1)
          Class: IN (0x0001)
          Time to live: 281
          Data length: 4
          Address: 64.233.160.99 (64.233.160.99)
     ☐ www.google.com: type A, class IN, addr 64.233.160.104
          Name: www.google.com
          Type: A (Host Address) (1)
          Class: IN (0x0001)
          Time to live: 281
          Data length: 4
          Address: 64.233.160.104 (64.233.160.104)
```

Reflection

What are the benefits of using UDP instead of TCP as a transport protocol for DNS?

9.2.4.3 Lab–Using Wireshark to Examine TCP and UDP Captures

Topology–Part 1 (FTP)

Part 1 will highlight a TCP capture of an FTP session. This topology consists of a PC with Internet access.

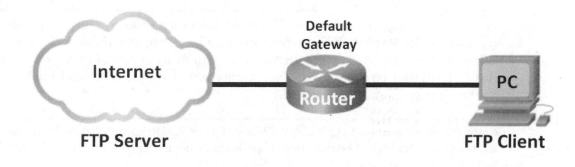

Topology–Part 2 (TFTP)

Part 2 will highlight a UDP capture of a TFTP session. The PC must have both an Ethernet connection and a console connection to Switch S1.

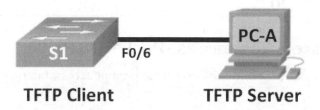

Addressing Table (Part 2)

Device	Interface	IP Address	Subnet Mask	Default Gateway
S1	VLAN 1	192.168.1.1	255.255.255.0	N/A
PC-A	NIC	192.168.1.3	255.255.255.0	192.168.1.1

Objectives

Part 1: Identify TCP Header Fields and Operation Using a Wireshark FTP Session Capture

Part 2: Identify UDP Header Fields and Operation Using a Wireshark TFTP Session Capture

Background/Scenario

Two protocols in the TCP/IP transport layer are TCP (defined in RFC 761) and UDP (defined in RFC 768). Both protocols support upper-layer protocol communication. For example, TCP is used to provide transport layer support for the HyperText Transfer Protocol (HTTP) and FTP protocols, among others. UDP provides transport layer support for the Domain Name System (DNS) and TFTP, among others.

Note: Understanding the parts of the TCP and UDP headers and operation are a critical skill for network engineers.

In Part 1 of this lab, you will use the Wireshark open source tool to capture and analyze TCP protocol header fields for FTP file transfers between the host computer and an anonymous FTP server. The Windows command line utility is used to connect to an anonymous FTP server and download a file. In Part 2 of this lab, you will use Wireshark to capture and analyze UDP header fields for TFTP file transfers between the host computer and S1.

Note: The switch used is a Cisco Catalyst 2960s with Cisco IOS Release 15.0(2) (lanbasek9 image). Other switches and Cisco IOS versions can be used. Depending on the model and Cisco IOS version, the available commands and the output produced might vary from what displays in the labs.

Note: Make sure that the switch has been erased and has no startup configurations. If you are unsure, contact your instructor.

Note: Part 1 assumes the PC has Internet access and cannot be performed using Netlab. Part 2 is Netlab compatible.

Required Resources–Part 1 (FTP)

1 PC (Windows 7 or 8 with command prompt access, Internet access, and Wireshark installed)

Required Resources–Part 2 (TFTP)

- 1 Switch (Cisco 2960 with Cisco IOS Release 15.0(2) lanbasek9 image or comparable)
- 1 PC (Windows 7 or 8 with Wireshark and a TFTP server, such as tftpd32 installed)
- Console cable to configure the Cisco IOS devices via the console port
- Ethernet cable as shown in the topology

Part 1: Identify TCP Header Fields and Operation Using a Wireshark FTP Session Capture

In Part 1, you use Wireshark to capture an FTP session and inspect TCP header fields.

Step 1: Start a Wireshark capture.

   a. Close all unnecessary network traffic, such as the web browser, to limit the amount of traffic during the Wireshark capture.

   b. Start the Wireshark capture.

Step 2: Download the Readme file.

    a. From the command prompt, enter **ftp ftp.cdc.gov**.

    b. Log into the FTP site for Centers for Disease Control and Prevention (CDC) with user **anonymous** and no password.

```
C:\Users\user1>ftp ftp.cdc.gov
Connected to ftp.cdc.gov.
220 Microsoft FTP Service
User (ftp.cdc.gov:(none)): anonymous
331 Anonymous access allowed, send identity (e-mail name) as password.
Password:
230 Anonymous user logged in.
```

    c. Locate and download the Readme file by entering the **ls** command to list the files.

```
ftp> ls
200 PORT command successful.
150 Opening ASCII mode data connection for file list.
aspnet_client
pub
Readme
Siteinfo
up.htm
w3c
web.config
welcome.msg
226 Transfer complete.
ftp: 76 bytes received in 0.00Seconds 19.00Kbytes/sec.
```

    d. Enter the command **get Readme** to download the file. When the download is complete, enter the command **quit** to exit.

```
ftp> get Readme
200 PORT command successful.
150 Opening ASCII mode data connection for Readme(1428 bytes).
226 Transfer complete.
ftp: 1428 bytes received in 0.01Seconds 204.00Kbytes/sec.
ftp> quit
221
```

Step 3: Stop the Wireshark capture.

Step 4: View the Wireshark main window.

Wireshark captured many packets during the FTP session to ftp.cdc.gov. To limit the amount of data for analysis, type **tcp and ip.addr == 198.246.117.106** in the **Filter: entry** area and click **Apply**. The IP address, 198.246.117.106, is the address for ftp.cdc.gov at this time.

Step 5:   Analyze the TCP fields.

After the TCP filter has been applied, the first three frames in the packet list pane (top section) display the transport layer protocol TCP creating a reliable session. The sequence of [SYN], [SYN, ACK], and [ACK] illustrates the three-way handshake.

TCP is routinely used during a session to control datagram delivery, verify datagram arrival, and manage window size. For each data exchange between the FTP client and FTP server, a new TCP session is started. At the conclusion of the data transfer, the TCP session is closed. When the FTP session is finished, TCP performs an orderly shutdown and termination.

In Wireshark, detailed TCP information is available in the packet details pane (middle section). Highlight the first TCP datagram from the host computer, and expand the TCP datagram. The expanded TCP datagram appears similar to the packet detail pane shown on the next page.

```
⊞ Frame 20: 66 bytes on wire (528 bits), 66 bytes captured (528 bits) on interface 0
⊞ Ethernet II, Src: GemtekTe_ea:63:8c (00:1a:73:ea:63:8c), Dst: Netgear_ea:b1:7a (80:37:73:ea:b1:7a)
⊞ Internet Protocol Version 4, Src: 192.168.1.17 (192.168.1.17), Dst: 198.246.117.106 (198.246.117.106)
⊟ Transmission Control Protocol, Src Port: 49411 (49411), Dst Port: 21 (21), Seq: 0, Len: 0
     Source Port: 49411 (49411)
     Destination Port: 21 (21)
     [Stream index: 1]
     [TCP Segment Len: 0]
     Sequence number: 0     (relative sequence number)
     Acknowledgment number: 0
     Header Length: 32 bytes
  ⊟ .... 0000 0000 0010 = Flags: 0x002 (SYN)
        000. .... .... = Reserved: Not set
        ...0 .... .... = Nonce: Not set
        .... 0... .... = Congestion Window Reduced (CWR): Not set
        .... .0.. .... = ECN-Echo: Not set
        .... ..0. .... = Urgent: Not set
        .... ...0 .... = Acknowledgment: Not set
        .... .... 0... = Push: Not set
        .... .... .0.. = Reset: Not set
     ⊞ .... .... ..1. = Syn: Set
        .... .... ...0 = Fin: Not set
     Window size value: 8192
     [Calculated window size: 8192]
  ⊞ Checksum: 0x5bba [validation disabled]
     Urgent pointer: 0
  ⊞ Options: (12 bytes), Maximum segment size, No-Operation (NOP), Window scale, No-Operation (NOP), No-O|
```

```
                             TCP SEGMENT
   0      4        10            16           24        31
  ┌─────────────────────────────┬──────────────────────────┐
  │   TCP SOURCE PORT NUMBER     │ TCP DESTINATION PORT NUMBER│
  ├─────────────────────────────┴──────────────────────────┤
  │                    SEQUENCE NUMBER                       │
  ├────────────────────────────────────────────────────────┤
  │                ACKNOWLEDGEMENT NUMBER                    │
  ├────────┬──────────┬──────────┬──────────────────────────┤
  │  HLEN  │ RESERVED │ CODE BITS│         WINDOW           │
  ├────────┴──────────┴──────────┼──────────────────────────┤
  │      TCP CHECKSUM            │     URGENT POINTER        │
  ├─────────────────────────────┼────────────┬─────────────┤
  │      OPTIONS (IF ANY)       │            │   PADDING    │
  ├─────────────────────────────┴────────────┴─────────────┤
  │                         DATA                            │
  ├────────────────────────────────────────────────────────┤
  │                        DATA ...                         │
  └────────────────────────────────────────────────────────┘

        CODE BITS:  ┌──┬──┬──┬──┬──┬──┐
                    │U │A │R │P │S │F │
                    │R │C │S │S │Y │I │
                    │G │K │T │H │N │N │
                    └──┴──┴──┴──┴──┴──┘
```

The image above is a TCP datagram diagram. An explanation of each field is provided for reference:

- The **TCP source port number** belongs to the TCP session host that opened a connection. The value is normally a random value above 1,023.

- The **TCP destination port number** is used to identify the upper layer protocol or application on the remote site. The values in the range 0–1,023 represent the "well-known ports" and are associated with popular services and applications (as described in RFC 1700), such as Telnet, FTP, and HTTP. The combination of the source IP address, source port, destination IP address, and destination port uniquely identifies the session to the sender and receiver.

Note: In the Wireshark capture above, the destination port is 21, which is FTP. FTP servers listen on port 21 for FTP client connections.

- The **Sequence number** specifies the number of the last octet in a segment.

- The **Acknowledgment number** specifies the next octet expected by the receiver.

- The **Code bits** have a special meaning in session management and in the treatment of segments. Among interesting values are:

  - ACK—Acknowledgment of a segment receipt.

  - SYN—Synchronize, only set when a new TCP session is negotiated during the TCP three-way handshake.

  - FIN—Finish, the request to close the TCP session.

- The **Window size** is the value of the sliding window. It determines how many octets can be sent before waiting for an acknowledgment.

- The **Urgent pointer** is only used with an Urgent (URG) flag when the sender needs to send urgent data to the receiver.

- The **Options** has only one option currently, and it is defined as the maximum TCP segment size (optional value).

Using the Wireshark capture of the first TCP session startup (SYN bit set to 1), fill in information about the TCP header.

From the PC to CDC server (only the SYN bit is set to 1):

Source IP address	
Destination IP address	
Source port number	
Destination port number	
Sequence number	
Acknowledgment number	
Header length	
Window size	

In the second Wireshark filtered capture, the CDC FTP server acknowledges the request from the PC. Note the values of the SYN and ACK bits.

```
⊞ Frame 21: 66 bytes on wire (528 bits), 66 bytes captured (528 bits) on interface 0
⊞ Ethernet II, Src: Netgear_ea:b1:7a (80:37:73:ea:b1:7a), Dst: GemtekTe_ea:63:8c (00:1a:73:ea:63:8c)
⊞ Internet Protocol Version 4, Src: 198.246.117.106 (198.246.117.106), Dst: 192.168.1.17 (192.168.1.17)
⊟ Transmission Control Protocol, Src Port: 21 (21), Dst Port: 49411 (49411), Seq: 0, Ack: 1, Len: 0
     Source Port: 21 (21)
     Destination Port: 49411 (49411)
     [Stream index: 1]
     [TCP Segment Len: 0]
     Sequence number: 0     (relative sequence number)
     Acknowledgment number: 1    (relative ack number)
     Header Length: 32 bytes
  ⊟ .... 0000 0001 0010 = Flags: 0x012 (SYN, ACK)
       000. .... .... = Reserved: Not set
       ...0 .... .... = Nonce: Not set
       .... 0... .... = Congestion Window Reduced (CWR): Not set
       .... .0.. .... = ECN-Echo: Not set
       .... ..0. .... = Urgent: Not set
       .... ...1 .... = Acknowledgment: Set
       .... .... 0... = Push: Not set
       .... .... .0.. = Reset: Not set
    ⊞ .... .... ..1. = Syn: Set
       .... .... ...0 = Fin: Not set
     Window size value: 8192
     [Calculated window size: 8192]
  ⊞ Checksum: 0x0ee7 [validation disabled]
     Urgent pointer: 0
  ⊞ Options: (12 bytes), Maximum segment size, No-Operation (NOP), Window scale, No-Operation (NOP), No
⊞ [SEQ/ACK analysis]
```

Fill in the following information regarding the SYN-ACK message.

Source IP address	
Destination IP address	
Source port number	
Destination port number	
Sequence number	
Acknowledgment number	
Header length	
Window size	

In the final stage of the negotiation to establish communications, the PC sends an acknowledgment message to the server. Notice only the ACK bit is set to 1, and the Sequence number has been incremented to 1.

```
⊞ Frame 22: 54 bytes on wire (432 bits), 54 bytes captured (432 bits) on interface 0
⊞ Ethernet II, Src: GemtekTe_ea:63:8c (00:1a:73:ea:63:8c), Dst: Netgear_ea:b1:7a (80:37:73:ea:b1:7a)
⊞ Internet Protocol Version 4, Src: 192.168.1.17 (192.168.1.17), Dst: 198.246.117.106 (198.246.117.106)
⊟ Transmission Control Protocol, Src Port: 49411 (49411), Dst Port: 21 (21), Seq: 1, Ack: 1, Len: 0
     Source Port: 49411 (49411)
     Destination Port: 21 (21)
     [Stream index: 1]
     [TCP Segment Len: 0]
     Sequence number: 1    (relative sequence number)
     Acknowledgment number: 1    (relative ack number)
     Header Length: 20 bytes
  ⊟ .... 0000 0001 0000 = Flags: 0x010 (ACK)
       000. .... .... = Reserved: Not set
       ...0 .... .... = Nonce: Not set
       .... 0... .... = Congestion Window Reduced (CWR): Not set
       .... .0.. .... = ECN-Echo: Not set
       .... ..0. .... = Urgent: Not set
       .... ...1 .... = Acknowledgment: Set
       .... .... 0... = Push: Not set
       .... .... .0.. = Reset: Not set
       .... .... ..0. = Syn: Not set
       .... .... ...0 = Fin: Not set
     Window size value: 8192
     [Calculated window size: 8192]
     [Window size scaling factor: 1]
  ⊞ Checksum: 0x4f6a [validation disabled]
     Urgent pointer: 0
  ⊞ [SEQ/ACK analysis]
```

Fill in the following information regarding the ACK message.

Source IP address	
Destination IP address	
Source port number	
Destination port number	
Sequence number	
Acknowledgment number	
Header length	
Window size	

How many other TCP datagrams contained a SYN bit?

_____

After a TCP session is established, FTP traffic can occur between the PC and FTP server. The FTP client and server communicate with each other, unaware that TCP has control and management over the session. When the FTP server sends a *Response: 220* to the FTP client, the TCP session on the FTP client sends an acknowledgment to the TCP session on the server. This sequence is visible in the Wireshark capture below.

```
23 4.742303000 198.246.117.106 192.168.1.17    FTP     81 Response: 220 Microsoft FTP Service
24 4.951371000 192.168.1.17    198.246.117.106 TCP     54 49411→21 [ACK] Seq=1 Ack=28 Win=8165 Len
40 11.78808800(192.168.1.17    198.246.117.106 FTP     70 Request: USER anonymous
41 11.87052800(198.246.117.106 192.168.1.17    FTP    126 Response: 331 Anonymous access allowed,
```

```
⊞ Frame 23: 81 bytes on wire (648 bits), 81 bytes captured (648 bits) on interface 0
⊞ Ethernet II, Src: Netgear_ea:b1:7a (80:37:73:ea:b1:7a), Dst: GemtekTe_ea:63:8c (00:1a:73:ea:63:8c)
⊞ Internet Protocol Version 4, Src: 198.246.117.106 (198.246.117.106), Dst: 192.168.1.17 (192.168.1.17)
⊞ Transmission Control Protocol, Src Port: 21 (21), Dst Port: 49411 (49411), Seq: 1, Ack: 1, Len: 27
⊟ File Transfer Protocol (FTP)
  ⊟ 220 Microsoft FTP Service\r\n
       Response code: Service ready for new user (220)
       Response arg: Microsoft FTP Service
```

When the FTP session has finished, the FTP client sends a command to "quit." The FTP server acknowledges the FTP termination with a *Response: 221 Goodbye*. At this time, the FTP server TCP session sends a TCP datagram to the FTP client, announcing the termination of the TCP session. The FTP client TCP session acknowledges receipt of the termination datagram, and then sends its own TCP session termination. When the originator of the TCP termination (the FTP server) receives a duplicate termination, an ACK datagram is sent to acknowledge the termination and the TCP session is closed. This sequence is visible in the diagram and capture below.

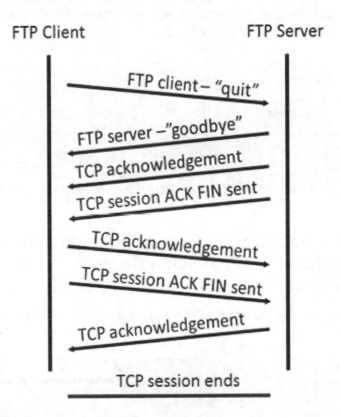

By applying an **ftp** filter, the entire sequence of the FTP traffic can be examined in Wireshark. Notice the sequence of the events during this FTP session. The username **anonymous** was used to retrieve the Readme file. After the file transfer completed, the user ended the FTP session.

No.	Time	Source	Destination	Protocol	Length	Info
23	4.742303000	198.246.117.106	192.168.1.17	FTP	81	Response: 220 Microsoft FTP Service
40	11.78808800	192.168.1.17	198.246.117.106	FTP	70	Request: USER anonymous
41	11.87052800	198.246.117.106	192.168.1.17	FTP	126	Response: 331 Anonymous access allowed, ser
44	13.13486100	192.168.1.17	198.246.117.106	FTP	61	Request: PASS
46	13.32829400	198.246.117.106	192.168.1.17	FTP	75	Response: 230 User logged in.
51	16.35224800	192.168.1.17	198.246.117.106	FTP	79	Request: PORT 192,168,1,17,193,4
52	16.68268000	192.168.1.17	198.246.117.106	FTP	79	[TCP Retransmission] Request: PORT 192,168
54	17.35453800	198.246.117.106	192.168.1.17	FTP	84	[TCP Retransmission] Response: 200 PORT con
55	17.36344200	192.168.1.17	198.246.117.106	FTP	60	Request: NLST
56	17.44263500	198.246.117.106	192.168.1.17	FTP	95	Response: 150 Opening ASCII mode data conne
62	19.89744100	198.246.117.106	192.168.1.17	FTP	78	Response: 226 Transfer complete.
73	24.29718100	192.168.1.17	198.246.117.106	FTP	79	Request: PORT 192,168,1,17,193,5
75	24.60749800	192.168.1.17	198.246.117.106	FTP	79	[TCP Retransmission] Request: PORT 192,168
82	25.13688600	198.246.117.106	192.168.1.17	FTP	84	[TCP Retransmission] Response: 200 PORT con
83	25.14232900	192.168.1.17	198.246.117.106	FTP	67	Request: RETR Readme
101	25.27018500	198.246.117.106	192.168.1.17	FTP	95	Response: 150 Opening ASCII mode data conne
127	27.78452300	192.168.1.17	198.246.117.106	FTP	78	Response: 226 Transfer complete.
147	30.48299200	192.168.1.17	198.246.117.106	FTP	60	Request: QUIT
148	30.56511700	198.246.117.106	192.168.1.17	FTP	68	Response: 221 Goodbye.

Apply the TCP filter again in Wireshark to examine the termination of the TCP session. Four packets are transmitted for the termination of the TCP session. Because TCP connection is full-duplex, each direction must terminate independently. Examine the source and destination addresses.

In this example, the FTP server has no more data to send in the stream. It sends a segment with the FIN flag set in frame 149. The PC sends an ACK to acknowledge the receipt of the FIN to terminate the session from the server to the client in frame 150.

In frame 151, the PC sends a FIN to the FTP server to terminate the TCP session. The FTP server responds with an ACK to acknowledge the FIN from the PC in frame 152. Now the TCP session terminated between the FTP server and PC.

```
147 30.48299200(192.168.1.17      198.246.117.106 FTP      60 Request: QUIT
148 30.56511700(198.246.117.106 192.168.1.17      FTP      68 Response: 221 Goodbye.
149 30.56646700(198.246.117.106 192.168.1.17      TCP      54 21→49411 [FIN, ACK] Seq=325 Ack=99 Win=1
150 30.56653200(192.168.1.17      198.246.117.106 TCP      54 49411→21 [ACK] Seq=99 Ack=326 Win=7868 L
151 30.56679900(192.168.1.17      198.246.117.106 TCP      54 49411→21 [FIN, ACK] Seq=99 Ack=326 Win=7
152 30.66777000(198.246.117.106 192.168.1.17      TCP      54 21→49411 [ACK] Seq=326 Ack=100 Win=13209

⊞ Frame 149: 54 bytes on wire (432 bits), 54 bytes captured (432 bits) on interface 0
⊞ Ethernet II, Src: Netgear_ea:b1:7a (80:37:73:ea:b1:7a), Dst: GemtekTe_ea:63:8c (00:1a:73:ea:63:8c)
⊞ Internet Protocol Version 4, Src: 198.246.117.106 (198.246.117.106), Dst: 192.168.1.17 (192.168.1.17)
⊞ Transmission Control Protocol, Src Port: 21 (21), Dst Port: 49411 (49411), Seq: 325, Ack: 99, Len: 0
```

Part 2: Identify UDP Header Fields and Operation Using a Wireshark TFTP Session Capture

In Part 2, you use Wireshark to capture a TFTP session and inspect the UDP header fields.

Step 1: Set up this physical topology and prepare for TFTP capture.

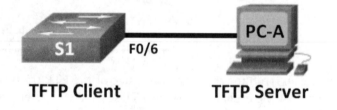

S1 F0/6   **PC-A**

TFTP Client   **TFTP Server**

a. Establish a console and Ethernet connection between PC-A and S1.

b. Manually configure the IP address on the PC to 192.168.1.3. It is not required to set the default gateway.

c. Configure the switch. Assign an IP address of 192.168.1.1 to VLAN 1. Verify connectivity with the PC by pinging 192.168.1.3. Troubleshoot as necessary.

```
Switch> enable
Switch# conf t
Enter configuration commands, one per line.  End with CNTL/Z.
Switch(config)# host S1
S1(config)# interface vlan 1
S1(config-if)# ip address 192.168.1.1 255.255.255.0
S1(config-if)# no shut
*Mar  1 00:37:50.166: %LINK-3-UPDOWN: Interface Vlan1, changed state to up
*Mar  1 00:37:50.175: %LINEPROTO-5-UPDOWN: Line protocol on Interface Vlan1,
changed state to up
```

```
S1(config-if)# end
S1# ping 192.168.1.3
Type escape sequence to abort.
Sending 5, 100-byte ICMP Echos to 192.168.1.3, timeout is 2 seconds:
!!!!!
Success rate is 100 percent (5/5), round-trip min/avg/max = 1/203/1007 ms
```

    d. Save the running configuration to NVRAM.

```
S1# copy run start
```

Step 2:   Prepare the TFTP server on the PC.

    a. If it does not already exist, create a folder on the PC desktop called **TFTP**. The files from the switch will be copied to this location.

    b. Start **tftpd32** on the PC.

    c. Click **Browse** and change the current directory to **C:\Users\user1\Desktop\TFTP** by replacing user1 with your username.

    The TFTP server should look like this:

    Notice that in Current Directory, it lists the user and the Server (PC-A) interface with the IP address of **192.168.1.3**.

    d. Test the ability to copy a file using TFTP from the switch to the PC. Troubleshoot as necessary.

```
S1# copy start tftp
Address or name of remote host []? 192.168.1.3
Destination filename [s1-confg]?
!!
1638 bytes copied in 0.026 secs (63000 bytes/sec)
```

    If you see that the file has been copied, and then you are ready to go on to the next step. If the file has not been copied, troubleshoot as needed. If you get the `%Error opening tftp (Permission denied)` error, determine whether your firewall is blocking TFTP and whether you are copying the file to a location where your username has adequate permission, such as the desktop.

Step 3:   Capture a TFTP session in Wireshark.

    a. Open Wireshark. From the **Edit** menu, choose **Preferences** and click the (+) sign to expand **Protocols**. Scroll down and select **UDP**. Click the **Validate the UDP checksum if possible** check box and click **Apply**. Then click **OK**.

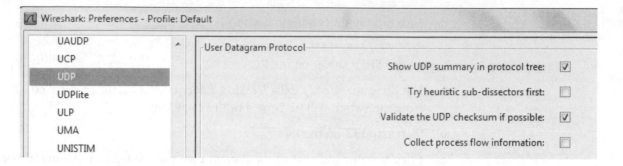

    b. Start a Wireshark capture.

    c. Run the **copy start tftp** command on the switch.

    d. Stop the Wireshark capture.

No.	Time	Source	Destination	Protocol	Length	Info
12	9.75564700	192.168.1.1	192.168.1.3	TFTP	60	Write Request, File: s1-confg, Transfer type: octet
13	9.75668700	192.168.1.3	192.168.1.1	TFTP	46	Acknowledgement, Block: 0
14	9.75794800	192.168.1.1	192.168.1.3	TFTP	558	Data Packet, Block: 1
15	9.75804400	192.168.1.3	192.168.1.1	TFTP	46	Acknowledgement, Block: 1
16	9.75905100	192.168.1.1	192.168.1.3	TFTP	558	Data Packet, Block: 2
17	9.75911700	192.168.1.3	192.168.1.1	TFTP	46	Acknowledgement, Block: 2
18	9.76013200	192.168.1.1	192.168.1.3	TFTP	558	Data Packet, Block: 3
19	9.76018700	192.168.1.3	192.168.1.1	TFTP	46	Acknowledgement, Block: 3
20	9.76227300	192.168.1.1	192.168.1.3	TFTP	148	Data Packet, Block: 4 (last)
21	9.76240000	192.168.1.3	192.168.1.1	TFTP	46	Acknowledgement, Block: 4

    e. Set the filter to **tftp**. Your output should look similar to the output shown above. This TFTP transfer is used to analyze transport layer UDP operations.

Detailed UDP information is available in the Wireshark packet details pane. Highlight the first UDP datagram from the host computer and move the mouse pointer to the packet details pane. It may be necessary to adjust the packet details pane and expand the UDP record by clicking the protocol expand box. The expanded UDP datagram should look similar to the diagram below.

UDP Header

```
⊟ User Datagram Protocol, Src Port: 62513 (62513), Dst Port: tftp (69)
    Source port: 62513 (62513)
    Destination port: tftp (69)
    Length: 25
  ⊞ Checksum: 0x482c [correct]
```

UDP Data

```
⊟ Trivial File Transfer Protocol
    [DESTINATION File: s1-confg]
    Opcode: Write Request (2)
    DESTINATION File: s1-confg
    Type: octet
```

The figure on the next page is a UDP datagram diagram. Header information is sparse, compared to the TCP datagram. Similar to TCP, each UDP datagram is identified by the UDP source port and UDP destination port.

UDP SEGMENT

0	16	31
UDP SOURCE PORT	UDP DESTINATION PORT	
UDP MESSAGE LENGTH	UDP CHECKSUM	
DATA		
DATA ...		

Using the Wireshark capture of the first UDP datagram, fill in information about the UDP header. The checksum value is a hexadecimal (base 16) value, denoted by the preceding 0x code:

Source IP address _____

Destination IP address _____

Source port number _____

Destination port number _____

UDP message length _____

UDP checksum _____

How does UDP verify datagram integrity?

_____

_____

Examine the first frame returned from the tftpd server. Fill in the information about the UDP header:

Source IP address _____

Destination IP address _____

Source port number _____

Destination port number _____

UDP message length _____

UDP checksum _____


```
⊟ User Datagram Protocol, Src Port: 58565 (58565), Dst Port: 62513 (62513)
     Source port: 58565 (58565)
     Destination port: 62513 (62513)
     Length: 12
   ⊞ Checksum: 0x8372 [incorrect, should be 0xa385 (maybe caused by "UDP checksum offload"?)]
⊟ Trivial File Transfer Protocol
     [DESTINATION File: s1-confg]
     Opcode: Acknowledgement (4)
     Block: 0
```

Notice that the return UDP datagram has a different UDP source port, but this source port is used for the remainder of the TFTP transfer. Because there is no reliable connection, only the original source port used to begin the TFTP session is used to maintain the TFTP transfer.

Also, notice that the UDP Checksum is incorrect. This is most likely caused by UDP checksum offload. You can learn more about why this happens by searching for "UDP checksum offload."

Reflection

This lab provided the opportunity to analyze TCP and UDP protocol operations from captured FTP and TFTP sessions. How does TCP manage communication differently than UDP?

_____

_____

Challenge

Because neither FTP or TFTP are secure protocols, all transferred data is sent in clear text. This includes any user IDs, passwords, or clear-text file contents. Analyzing the upper-layer FTP session will quickly identify the user ID, password, and configuration file passwords. Upper-layer TFTP data examination is more complicated, but the data field can be examined, and the configuration's user ID and password information extracted.

Cleanup

Unless directed otherwise by your instructor:

1) Remove the files that were copied to your PC.

2) Erase the configurations on S1.

3) Remove the manual IP address from the PC and restore Internet connectivity.

9.3.1.1 Class Activity–We Need to Talk, Again

Objectives

Explain how transport layer protocols and services support communications across data networks.

Background/Scenario

Note: It is important that the students have completed the Introductory MA for this chapter. This activity works best in medium-sized groups of 6 to 8 students.

The instructor will whisper a complex message to the first student in a group. An example of the message might be "We are expecting a blizzard tomorrow. It should be arriving in the morning and school will be delayed two hours so bring your homework."

That student whispers the message to the next student in the group. Each group follows this process until all members of each group have heard the whispered message.

Here are the rules you are to follow:

- You can whisper the message in short parts to your neighbor AND you can repeat the message parts after verifying your neighbor heard the correct message.

- Small parts of the message may be checked and repeated again (clockwise OR counter-clockwise to ensure accuracy of the message parts) by whispering. A student will be assigned to time the entire activity.

- When the message has reached the end of the group, the last student will say aloud what she heard. Small parts of the message may be repeated (i.e., re-sent), and the process can be restarted to ensure that ALL parts of the message are fully delivered and correct.

- The Instructor will restate the original message to check for quality delivery.

Reflection

1. Would the contents of this message need to be clear and correct when you received them if you were depending on this message to drive your personal/business calendar, studying schedule, and so on?

2. Would the length of time taken to deliver the message be an important factor to the sender and recipient?

3. Compare the Introductory MA of this chapter to this activity. What differences do you notice about the delivery of the message?

9.3.1.2 Packet Tracer Simulation–Exploration of TCP and UDP Communication

Topology

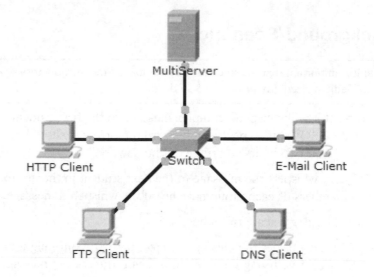

Objectives

Part 1: Generate Network Traffic in Simulation Mode

Part 2: Examine the Functionality of the TCP and UDP Protocols

Background

This simulation activity is intended to provide a foundation for understanding TCP and UDP in detail. Simulation mode provides the ability to view the functionality of the different protocols.

As data moves through the network, it is broken down into smaller pieces and identified in some fashion so that the pieces can be put back together. Each of these pieces is assigned a specific name (protocol data unit [PDU]) and associated with a specific layer. Packet Tracer Simulation mode enables the user to view each of the protocols and the associated PDU. The steps outlined below lead the user through the process of requesting services using various applications available on a client PC.

This activity provides an opportunity to explore the functionality of the TCP and UDP protocols, multiplexing, and the function of port numbers in determining which local application requested the data or is sending the data.

Part 1: Generate Network Traffic in Simulation Mode

Step 1:   Generate traffic to populate Address Resolution Protocol (ARP) tables.

Perform the following tasks to reduce the amount of network traffic viewed in the simulation.

  a.   Click **MultiServer** and click the **Desktop** tab > **Command Prompt**.

  b.   Enter the **ping 192.168.1.255** command. This will take a few seconds as every device on the network responds to **MultiServer**.

  c.   Close the **MultiServer** window.

Step 2: Generate web (HTTP) traffic.

    a. Switch to Simulation mode.

    b. Click **HTTP Client** and click the **Desktop** tab > **Web Browser**.

    c. In the URL field, enter **192.168.1.254** and click **Go**. Envelopes (PDUs) will appear in the simulation window.

    d. Minimize, but do not close, the **HTTP Client** configuration window.

Step 3: Generate FTP traffic.

    a. Click **FTP Client** and click the **Desktop** tab > **Command Prompt**.

    b. Enter the **ftp 192.168.1.254** command. PDUs will appear in the simulation window.

    c. Minimize, but do not close, the **FTP Client** configuration window.

Step 4: Generate DNS traffic.

    a. Click **DNS Client** and click the **Desktop** tab > **Command Prompt**.

    b. Enter the **nslookup multiserver.pt.ptu** command. A PDU will appear in the simulation window.

    c. Minimize, but do not close, the **DNS Client** configuration window.

Step 5: Generate Email traffic.

    a. Click **E-Mail Client** and click the **Desktop** tab > **E Mail** tool.

    b. Click **Compose** and enter the following information:

        To: user@multiserver.pt.ptu

        Subject: Personalize the subject line

        E-Mail Body: Personalize the Email

    c. Click **Send**.

    d. Minimize, but do not close, the **E-Mail Client** configuration window.

Step 6: Verify that the traffic is generated and ready for simulation.

Every client computer should have PDUs listed in the Simulation Panel.

Part 2: Examine Functionality of the TCP and UDP Protocols

Step 1: Examine multiplexing as all of the traffic crosses the network.

You will now use the **Capture/Forward button** and the **Back** button in the Simulation Panel.

    a. Click **Capture/Forward** once. All of the PDUs are transferred to the switch.

    b. Click **Capture/Forward** again. Some of the PDUs disappear. What do you think happened to them?

---

    c. Click **Capture/Forward** six times. All clients should have received a reply. Note that only one PDU can cross a wire in each direction at any given time. What is this called?

---

d. A variety of PDUs appears in the event list in the upper right pane of the simulation window. Why are they so many different colors?

_____

e. Click **Back** eight times. This should reset the simulation.

_____

Note: Do not click **Reset Simulation** any time during this activity; if you do, you will need to repeat the steps in Part 1.

Step 2: Examine HTTP traffic as the clients communicate with the server.

a. Filter the traffic that is currently displayed to display only **HTTP** and **TCP** PDUs filter the traffic that is currently displayed:

1) Click **Edit Filters** and toggle the **Show All/None** check box.

2) Select **HTTP** and **TCP**. Click anywhere outside of the Edit Filters box to hide it. The Visible Events should now display only **HTTP** and **TCP** PDUs.

b. Click **Capture/Forward**. Hold your mouse above each PDU until you find one that originates from **HTTP Client**. Click the PDU envelope to open it.

c. Click the **Inbound PDU Details** tab and scroll down to the last section. What is the section labeled?

_____

Are these communications considered to be reliable?

_____

d. Record the **SRC PORT, DEST PORT, SEQUENCE NUM**, and **ACK NUM** values. What is written in the field to the left of the **WINDOW** field?

_____

e. Close the PDU and click **Capture/Forward** until a PDU returns to the **HTTP Client** with a checkmark.

f. Click the PDU envelope and select **Inbound PDU Details**. How are the port and sequence numbers different than before?

_____

_____

g. There is a second **PDU** of a different color, which **HTTP Client** has prepared to send to **MultiServer**. This is the beginning of the HTTP communication. Click this second PDU envelope and select **Outbound PDU Details.**

h. What information is now listed in the TCP section? How are the port and sequence numbers different from the previous two PDUs?

_____

_____

i. Click **Back** until the simulation is reset.

Step 3:   Examine FTP traffic as the clients communicate with the server.

    a. In the Simulation Panel, change **Edit Filters** to display only **FTP** and **TCP**.

    b. Click **Capture/Forward**. Hold your cursor above each PDU until you find one that originates from **FTP Client**. Click that PDU envelope to open it.

    c. Click the **Inbound PDU Details** tab and scroll down to the last section. What is the section labeled?

_____

       Are these communications considered to be reliable?

_____

    d. Record the **SRC PORT, DEST PORT, SEQUENCE NUM,** and **ACK NUM** values. What is written in the field to the left of the **WINDOW** field?

_____

    e. Close the PDU and click **Capture/Forward** until a PDU returns to the **FTP Client** with a checkmark.

    f. Click the PDU envelope and select **Inbound PDU Details**. How are the port and sequence numbers different than before?

_____

_____

    g. Click the **Outbound PDU Details** tab. How are the port and sequence numbers different from the previous two results?

_____

_____

    h. Close the PDU and click **Capture/Forward** until a second PDU returns to the **FTP Client**. The PDU is a different color.

    i. Open the PDU and select **Inbound PDU Details**. Scroll down past the TCP section. What is the message from the server?

_____

    j. Click **Back** until the simulation is reset.

Step 4:   Examine DNS traffic as the clients communicate with the server.

    a. In the Simulation Panel, change **Edit Filters** to display only **DNS** and **UDP**.

    b. Click the PDU envelope to open it.

    c. Click the **Inbound PDU Details** tab and scroll down to the last section. What is the section labeled?

_____

       Are these communications considered to be reliable?

_____

   d. Record the **SRC PORT** and **DEST PORT** values. Why is there no sequence and acknowledgment number?

_____

   e. Close the **PDU** and click **Capture/Forward** until a PDU returns to the **DNS Client** with a checkmark.

   f. Click the PDU envelope and select **Inbound PDU Details.** How are the port and sequence numbers different than before?

_____

   g. What is the last section of the **PDU** called?

_____

   h. Click **Back** until the simulation is reset.

Step 5: Examine email traffic as the clients communicate with the server.

   a. In the Simulation Panel, change **Edit Filters** to display only **POP3**, **SMTP**, and **TCP**.

   b. Click **Capture/Forward.** Hold your cursor above each PDU until you find one that originates from **E-mail Client.** Click that PDU envelope to open it.

   c. Click the **Inbound PDU Details** tab and scroll down to the last section. What transport layer protocol does email traffic use?

_____

Are these communications considered to be reliable?

_____

   d. Record the **SRC PORT**, **DEST PORT**, **SEQUENCE NUM**, and **ACK NUM** values. What is written in the field to the left of the **WINDOW** field?

_____

   e. Close the **PDU** and click **Capture/Forward** until a PDU returns to the **E-Mail Client** with a checkmark.

   f. Click the PDU envelope and select **Inbound PDU Details.** How are the port and sequence numbers different than before?

_____

_____

   g. Click the **Outbound PDU Details** tab. How are the port and sequence numbers different from the previous two results?

_____

_____

   h. There is a second **PDU** of a different color that **HTTP Client** has prepared to send to **MultiServer.** This is the beginning of the email communication. Click this second PDU envelope and select **Outbound PDU Details.**

    i. How are the port and sequence numbers different from the previous two **PDU**s?

    _____

    _____

    j. What email protocol is associated with TCP port 25? What protocol is associated with TCP port 110?

    _____

    k. Click **Back** until the simulation is reset.

Step 6: Examine the use of port numbers from the server.

    a. To see TCP active sessions, perform the following steps in quick succession:

      1) Switch back to **Realtime** mode.

      2) Click **MultiServer** and click the **Desktop** tab > **Command Prompt**.

    b. Enter the **netstat** command. What protocols are listed in the left column? _____

    What port numbers are being used by the server? _____

    c. What states are the sessions in?

    _____

    d. Repeat the **netstat** command several times until you see only one session still ESTABLISHED. For which service is this connection still open? _____

    Why doesn't this session close like the other three? (Hint: Check the minimized clients)

    _____

Suggested Scoring Rubric

Activity Section	Question Location	Possible Points	Earned Points
Part 2: Examine Functionality of the TCP and UDP Protocols	Step 1	15	
	Step 2	15	
	Step 3	15	
	Step 4	15	
	Step 5	15	
	Step 6	25	
	Total Score	**100**	

CHAPTER 10

Application Layer

The Study Guide portion of this chapter uses a combination of matching, fill-in-the-blank, multiple-choice, and open-ended question exercises to test your knowledge and skills of basic router concepts and configuration. The Lab and Activities portion of this chapter includes all the online curriculum labs and Packet Tracer activities to ensure that you have mastered the hands-on skills needed to understand basic IP addressing and router configuration.

As you work through this chapter, use Chapter 10 in *Introduction to Networks v6 Companion Guide* or use the corresponding Chapter 10 in the Introduction to Networks online curriculum for assistance.

Study Guide

Applications, such as HTTP, video streaming, online gaming, and chat, provide the human interface to the underlying network. They enable us to send and receive data with relative ease. In this chapter, we review the role of the application layer.

Application Layer Protocols

By now, you should be familiar with both the OSI and TCP/IP models. The TCP/IP application layer includes a number of protocols that provide specific functionality to a variety of end-user applications.

OSI and TCP/IP Model Comparison

To review the structure of the OSI and TCP/IP models, label Figure 10-1 with the layers for each model.

Figure 10-1   The OSI and TCP/IP Models

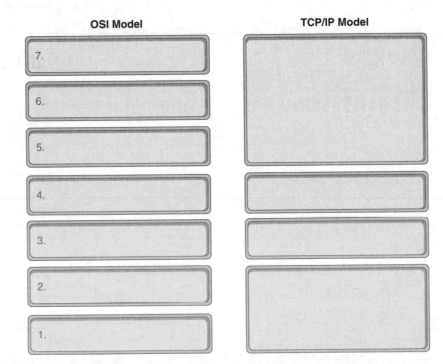

Application and Presentation Protocols and Standards

Provide the missing information in Table 10-1. Write in the full name for each acronym and indicate whether the protocol or standard belongs to the application layer or the presentation layer. You may not have seen some of these acronyms. If needed, search the Internet for answers.

Table 10-1 Application and Presentation Protocols and Standards

Acronym	Full Name	OSI Application Layer	OSI Presentation Layer
IMAP			
MPEG			
TFTP			

Acronym	Full Name	OSI Application Layer	OSI Presentation Layer
ASCII			
PNG			
XML			
POP			
FTP			
SMTP			
HTML			
GIF			
HTTP			
SSH			
DHCP			
SNMP			
DNS			
JPEG			

How Application Protocols Interact with End-User Applications

Describe the client/server model.

_____

_____

_____

_____

_____

Describe the peer-to-peer model.

_____

_____

_____

List at least four common peer-to-peer applications.

_____

_____

_____

_____

_____

Well-Known Application Layer Protocols and Services

There are dozens of well-known application layer protocols and services. In this section, we review the more important ones to your networking studies.

Web and Email Services

Web services primarily use HTTP. Email services use SMTP, POP, and IMAP.

Web Services

A web address or _____ (URL), such as http://www.cisco.com/index.html, can be broken down into three basic parts:

- http://: _____

- www.cisco.com: _____

- index.html: _____

Briefly explain how HTTP works. Include the three common HTTP message types in your explanation.

_____

_____

_____

What is the difference between HTTP and HTTPS?

_____

_____

Email Services

Email supports three separate protocols for operation:

- _____

- _____

- _____

The application layer process that sends mail uses _____. When a client sends email, the client process connects with a server process on well-known port _____. A client retrieves email, however, using one of two application layer protocols: _____ or _____. With _____, mail is downloaded from the server to the client and then deleted on the server. The server starts the _____ service by passively listening on TCP port _____ for client connection requests. However, when a client connects to a server running _____, copies of the messages are downloaded to the client application. The original messages are kept on the server until manually deleted.

IP Addressing Services

IP addressing services include dynamically assigning IP addresses to end devices and resolving URLs to the destination's IP address.

Domain Names

The _____ (DNS) was created for domain name to address resolution. DNS uses a distributed set of servers to resolve the names associated with _____.

The DNS server stores different types of resource records used to resolve names. These records contain the name, address, and type of record.

Some of these record types are as follows:

- A: _____

- NS: _____

- AAAA: _____

- MX: _____

Briefly explain how a DNS server or end system can reduce bandwidth and upstream server processing required for DNS queries.

_____

_____

_____

_____

What is the command to display all the cached DNS entries on a Windows PC?

_____

Briefly explain the DNS hierarchical system.

_____

_____

_____

_____

Computer operating systems have a utility called _____ that allows the user to manually query the name servers to resolve a given hostname. This utility can also be used to trouble-shoot name resolution issues and to verify the current status of the name servers.

DHCPv4

The _____ (DHCPv4) automates the assignment of

- _____

- _____

- _____

- Other IP networking parameters (such as a domain name and DNS server)

What is the alternative to using DHCPv4?

_____

What are some common situations where you would use DHCP and where you would use static addressing?

_____

_____

Label Figure 10-2 with the four DHCPv4 messages.

Figure 10-2   DHCPv4 Messages

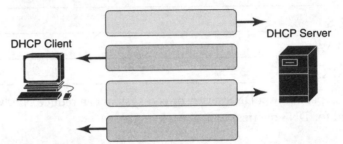

When a DHCPv4-configured device boots or connects to the network, the client broadcasts a
_____ message to identify any available DHCPv4 servers on the network.
A DHCPv4 server replies with a _____ message, which offers a lease to the
client. The message contains the IPv4 address and subnet mask to be assigned, the IPv4 address of
the DNS server, and the IPv4 address of the default gateway. The lease offer also includes the duration
of the lease. The client may receive multiple _____ messages if there is more
than one DHCPv4 server on the local network; therefore, it must choose between them, and sends a
_____ message that identifies the explicit server and lease offer that the client
is accepting. Assuming that the IPv4 address requested by the client, or offered by the server, is still
available, the server returns a _____ message that acknowledges to the client that
the lease is finalized. If the offer is no longer valid, perhaps because of a timeout or another client taking
the lease, the selected server responds with a _____ message. If a DHCPNAK
message is returned, the selection process must begin again with a new DHCPDISCOVER message being
transmitted.

File Sharing Services

The _____ (FTP) was developed to allow for data transfers between a client and a
server. An FTP client is an application that runs on a computer that is used to push and pull data from a
server running an _____ (FTPd).

In Figure 10-3, label and describe the two connections required between the client and server.

Figure 10-3   FTP Connection Process

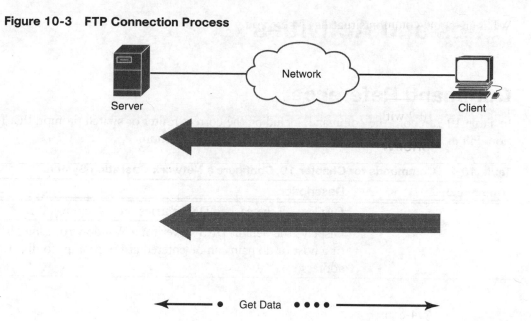

Labs and Activities

Command Reference

In Table 10-2, record the command, including the correct router or switch prompt, that fits the description. Fill in any blanks with the appropriate missing information.

Table 10-2   Commands for Chapter 10, Configure a Network Operating System

Command	Description
	Displays all the cached DNS entries on a Windows PC.
	Displays the default DNS server for a Windows or Linux host. The name of a host or domain can be entered at the prompt to discover the IP address(es)

10.0.1.2 Class Activity–Application Investigation

Objective

Explain how the application layer provides support to end-user applications.

Background/Scenario

It is the beginning of your work week. Your employer has decided to install IP telephones in your workplace, which results in the network being inoperable until next week.

However, your work must continue. You have emails to send and quotes to write for your manager's approval. Due to possible security issues, you are not allowed to use personal or external computer systems, equipment, or off-site equipment and systems.

Your instructor may ask you to complete the questions from both scenarios below. Answer the questions fully for the scenario(s). Be prepared to discuss your answers in class.

Emails

- What method(s) can you use to send email communication?

- How can you send the same email to multiple recipients?

- How can you get a large attachment to multiple recipients?

- Are these methods cost-effective to your corporation?

- Do these methods violate any security policies of your corporation?

Quote for Manager's Approval

- You have a desktop application software package installed on your computer. Will it be relatively easy to produce the quote your manager needs for the new contract due by the end of the week? What limitations will be experienced while trying to complete the quote?

- How will you present the quote to your manager for approval? How do you think she will send the quote to the client for her approval?

- Are these methods cost-effective to your corporation? Justify your answer.

Reflection

What steps did you identify as important to communicating without network applications available to you for a week in your workplace? Which steps were not important? Justify your answer.

_____

_____

_____

_____

_____

10.1.2.5 Lab–Researching Peer-to-Peer File Sharing

Objectives

Part 1: Identify P2P Networks, File Sharing Protocols, and Applications

Part 2: Research P2P File Sharing Issues

Part 3: Research P2P Copyright Litigations

Background/Scenario

Peer-to-peer (P2P) computing is a powerful technology that has many uses. P2P networks can be used to share and exchange files, and other electronic materials.

The use of P2P networks to upload, download, or share copyrighted material, such as movies, music, and software, can violate the rights of copyright owners. In the P2P file-sharing context, infringement may occur when one person purchases an authorized copy and then uploads it to a P2P network to share with others. Both the individual who makes the file available and those making copies may be found to have infringed the rights of the copyright owners and may be violating copyright law.

Another problem with P2P file sharing is that very little protection is in place to ensure that the files exchanged in these networks are not malicious. P2P networks are an ideal medium for spreading malware, such as computer viruses, worms, Trojan horses, spyware, adware, and other malicious programs.

In this lab, you will research available P2P file sharing software and identify issues that can arise from the use of this technology.

Required Resources

Device with Internet access

Part 1: Identify P2P Networks, File Sharing Protocols, and Applications

In Part 1, you will research P2P networks and identify popular P2P protocols and applications.

Step 1.   Define P2P networking.

    a.   What is a P2P network?

       _____

       _____

    b.   Identify at least two advantages that P2P provides over client-server architecture.

       _____

       _____

       _____

       _____

       _____

       _____

    c.   Identify at least two disadvantages of P2P networks.

_____

_____

Step 2.   Identify P2P file sharing protocols and applications.

    a.   Identify at least two P2P file sharing protocols used today.

_____

_____

    b.   Identify at least two popular P2P file sharing applications available today.

_____

_____

    c.   What P2P file sharing protocol is attributed to producing the most P2P traffic on the Internet today?

_____

Part 2: Research P2P File Sharing Issues

In Part 2, you will research P2P copyright infringement and identify other issues that can occur with P2P file sharing.

Step 1.   Research P2P copyright infringement.

    a.   What does the acronym DMCA stand for and what is it?

_____

_____

    b.   Name two associations that actively pursue P2P copyright infringement.

_____

_____

    c.   What are the penalties for copyright infringement?

_____

_____

    d.   What are the file sharing copyright laws in your area? Are they more strict or less strict than those in other areas of the world? How aggressively do enforcement agencies in your area pursue those who share copyrighted material?

_____

_____

Step 2.   Research other P2P issues.

    a.   What types of malware can be transported through P2P file sharing?

       _____

       _____

    b.   What is Torrent poisoning?

       _____

       _____

    c.   How could identity theft occur through the use of P2P file sharing?

       _____

       _____

Part 3: Research P2P Copyright Litigations

In Part 3, you will research and identify historical legal actions that have occurred as a result of P2P copyright infringement.

    a.   What was the first well-known P2P application that specialized in MP3 file sharing and was closed by court order?

       _____

    b.   What was one of the largest P2P file sharing lawsuits ever?

       _____

       _____

Reflection

How can you be sure that the files you are downloading from P2P networks are not copyrighted and are safe from malware?

_____

10.2.1.7 Packet Tracer–Web and Email

Topology

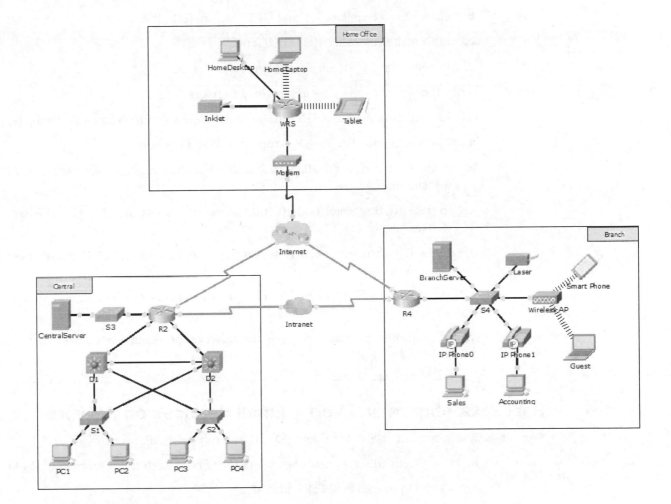

Objectives

Part 1: Configure and Verify Web Services

Part 2: Configure and Verify Email Services

Background

In this activity, you will configure web and email services using the simulated server in Packet Tracer. You will then configure clients to access the web and email services.

Note: Packet Tracer only simulates the process for configuring these services. Web and email software packages each have their own unique installation and configuration instructions.

Part 1: Configure and Verify Web Services

Step 1.   Configure web services on CentralServer and BranchServer.

    a.   Click **CentralServer** and click the **Services** tab > **HTTP**.

    b.   Click **On** to enable HTTP and HTTP Secure (HTTPS).

    c.   Optional. Personalize the HTML code.

    d.   Repeat Step 1a – 1c on **BranchServer**.

Step 2.   Verify the web servers by accessing the web pages.

There are many endpoint devices in this network, but for the purposes of this step, use PC3.

    a.   Click **PC3** and click the **Desktop** tab > **Web Browser**.

    b.   In the URL box, enter **10.10.10.2** as the IP address and click **Go**. The **CentralServer** website displays.

    c.   In the URL box, enter **64.100.200.1** as the IP address and click **Go**. The **BranchServer** website displays.

    d.   In the URL box, enter **centralserver.pt.pka** and click **Go**. The **CentralServer** website displays.

    e.   In the URL box, enter **branchserver.pt.pka** and click **Go**. The **BranchServer** website displays.

    f.   What protocol is translating the **centralserver.pt.pka** and **branchserver.pt.pka** names to IP addresses?

Part 2: Configure and Verify Email Services on Servers

Step 1.   Configure CentralServer to send (SMTP) and receive (POP3) Email.

    a.   Click **CentralServer**, and then select the **Services** tab followed by the **EMAIL** button.

    b.   Click **On** to enable SMTP and POP3.

    c.   Set the domain name to **centralserver.pt.pka** and click **Set**.

    d.   Create a user named **central-user** with password **cisco**. Click + to add the user.

Step 2.   Configure BranchServer to send (SMTP) and receive (POP3) Email.

    a.   Click **BranchServer** and click the **Services** tab > **EMAIL**.

    b.   Click **On** to enable SMTP and POP3.

    c.   Set the domain name to **branchserver.pt.pka** and click **Set**.

    d.   Create a user named **branch-user** with password **cisco**. Click + to add the user.

Step 3.   Configure PC3 to use the CentralServer email service.

    a.   Click **PC3** and click the **Desktop** tab > **E Mail**.

    b.   Enter the following values into their respective fields:

        1)   Your Name: **Central User**

        2)   Email Address: **central-user@centralserver.pt.pka**

       3) Incoming Mail Server: **10.10.10.2**

       4) Outgoing Mail Server: **10.10.10.2**

       5) User Name: **central-user**

       6) Password: **cisco**

   c. Click **Save.** The Mail Browser window displays.

   d. Click **Receive.** If everything has been set up correctly on both the client and server, the Mail Browser window displays the `Receive Mail Success` message confirmation.

Step 4. Configure Sales to use the Email service of BranchServer.

   a. Click **Sales** and click the **Desktop** tab > **E Mail**.

   b. Enter the following values into their respective fields:

       1) Your Name: **Branch User**

       2) Email Address: **branch-user@branchserver.pt.pka**

       3) Incoming Mail Server: **172.16.0.3**

       4) Outgoing Mail Server: **172.16.0.3**

       5) User Name: **branch-user**

       6) Password: **cisco**

   c. Click **Save.** The Mail Browser window displays.

   d. Click **Receive.** If everything has been set up correctly on both the client and server, the Mail Browser window displays the `Receive Mail Success` message confirmation.

   e. The activity should be 100% complete. Do not close the Sales configuration window or the Mail Browser window.

Step 5. Send an Email from the Sales client and the PC3 client.

   a. From the **Sales Mail Browser** window, click **Compose**.

   b. Enter the following values into their respective fields:

       1) To: **central-user@centralserver.pt.pka**

       2) Subject: *Personalize the subject line.*

       3) Email Body: *Personalize the email.*

   c. Click **Send.**

   d. Verify that **PC3** received the email. Click **PC3.** If the Mail Browser window is closed, click **E Mail.**

   e. Click **Receive.** An email from Sales displays. Double-click the email.

   f. Click **Reply**, personalize a response, and click **Send.**

   g. Verify that **Sales** received the reply.

10.2.2.7 Packet Tracer–DHCP and DNS Servers

Topology

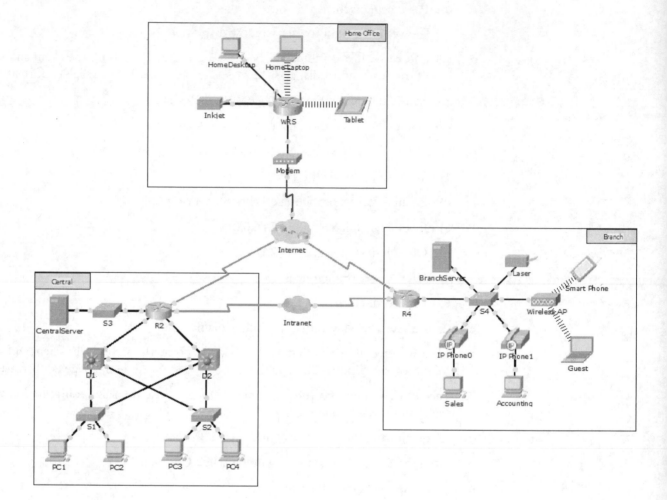

Objectives

Part 1: Configure Static IPv4 Addressing

Part 2: Configure and Verify DNS Records

Background

In this activity, you will configure and verify static IP addressing and DHCP addressing. You will then configure a DNS server to map IP addresses to the website names.

Note: Packet Tracer only simulates the process for configuring these services. DHCP and DNS software packages each have their own unique installation and configuration instructions.

Part 1: Configure Static IPv4 Addressing

Step 1.   Configure the Inkjet printer with static IPv4 addressing.

The home office computers need to know the printer's IPv4 address to send information to it. The printer, therefore, must use a static (unchanging) IPv4 address.

a.   Click **Inkjet** and click the **Config** tab, which displays the Global Settings.

b.   Statically assign the Gateway address as **192.168.0.1** and the DNS Server address as **64.100.8.8**.

c.   Click **FastEthernet0** and statically assign the IP address as **192.168.0.2** and the Subnet Mask address as **255.255.255.0**.

d.   Close the Inkjet window.

Step 2.   Configure WRS to provide DHCP services.

a.   Click **WRS** and click the **GUI** tab, and maximize the window.

b.   The Basic Setup window displays, by default. Configure the following settings in the Network Setup section:

1)   Change the IP Address to **192.168.0.1**.

2)   Set the Subnet Mask to **255.255.255.0**.

3)   Enable the DHCP Server.

4)   Set the Static DNS 1 address to **64.100.8.8**.

5)   Scroll to the bottom and click **Save**.

c.   Close the **WRS** window.

Step 3.   Request DHCP addressing for the home laptop.

This activity focuses on the home office. The clients that you will configure with DHCP are **Home Laptop** and **Tablet**.

a.   Click **Home Laptop** and click the **Desktop** tab > **IP Configuration**.

b.   Click **DHCP** and wait until the DHCP request is successful.

c.   **Home Laptop** should now have a full IP configuration. If not, return to Step 2 and verify your configurations on **WRS**.

d.   Close the IP Configuration window and then close the **Home Laptop** window.

Step 4.   Request DHCP addressing for the tablet.

a.   Click **Tablet** and click the **Desktop** tab > **IP Configuration**.

b.   Click **DHCP** and wait until the DHCP request is successful.

c.   **Tablet** should now have a full IP configuration. If not, return to Step 2 and verify your configurations on **WRS**.

Step 5.   Test access to websites.

a.   Close the **IP Configuration** window, and then click Web Browser.

b.   In the URL box, type **10.10.10.2** (for the **CentralServer** website) or **64.100.200.1** (for the **BranchServer** website) and click **Go**. Both websites should appear.

     c.   Reopen the web browser. Test the names for those same websites by entering **centralserver.pt.pka** and **branchserver.pt.pka**. Click on **Fast Forward Time** on the yellow bar below the topology to speed the process.

Part 2: Configure Records on the DNS Server

Step 1.   Configure famous.dns.pka with records for CentralServer and BranchServer.

Typically, DNS records are registered with companies, but for the purposes of this activity you control the famous.dns.pka server on the Internet.

     a.   Click the **Internet** cloud. A new network displays.

     b.   Click **famous.dns.pka** and click the **Services** tab > **DNS**.

     c.   Add the following resource records:

Resource Record Name	Address
centralserver.pt.pka	10.10.10.2
branchserver.pt.pka	64.100.200.1

Close the famous.dns.pka window.

     d.   Click **Back** to exit the **Internet** cloud.

Step 2.   Verify the ability of client computers to use DNS.

Now that you have configured DNS records, **Home Laptop** and **Tablet** should be able to access the websites by using the names instead of the IP addresses. First, check that the DNS client is working properly and then verify access to the website.

     a.   Click **Home Laptop** or **Tablet**.

     b.   If the web browser is open, close it and select **Command Prompt**.

Verify the IPv4 addressing by entering the command **ipconfig /all**. You should see the IP address for the DNS server.

     c.   Ping the DNS server at **64.100.8.8** to verify connectivity.

Note: The first two or three pings may fail as Packet Tracer simulates all the various processes that must occur for successful connectivity to a remote resource.

Test the functionality of the DNS server by entering the commands **nslookup centralserver.pt.pka** and **nslookup branchserver.pt.pka**. You should get a name resolution showing the IP address for each.

     d.   Close the Command Prompt window and click **Web Browser**. Verify that **Home Laptop** or **Tablet** can now access the web pages for **CentralServer** and **BranchServer**.

10.2.2.8 Lab–Observing DNS Resolution

Objectives

Part 1: Observe the DNS Conversion of a URL to an IP Address

Part 2: Observe DNS Lookup Using the nslookup Command on a Web Site

Part 3: Observe DNS Lookup Using the nslookup Command on Mail Servers

Background/Scenario

The Domain Name System (DNS) is invoked when you type a Uniform Resource Locator (URL), such as http://www.cisco.com, into a web browser. The first part of the URL describes which protocol is used. Common protocols are Hypertext Transfer Protocol (HTTP), Hypertext Transfer Protocol over Secure Socket Layer (HTTPS), and File Transfer Protocol (FTP).

DNS uses the second part of the URL, which in this example is www.cisco.com. DNS translates the domain name (www.cisco.com) to an IP address to allow the source host to reach the destination host. In this lab, you will observe DNS in action and use the **nslookup** (name server lookup) command to obtain additional DNS information. Work with a partner to complete this lab.

Required Resources

1 PC (Windows 7 or 8 with Internet and command prompt access)

Part 1: Observe the DNS Conversion of a URL to an IP Address

a. Click the **Windows Start** button, type **cmd** into the search field, and press **Enter**. The command prompt window appears.

b. At the command prompt, ping the URL for the Internet Corporation for Assigned Names and Numbers (ICANN) at **www.icann.org**. ICANN coordinates the DNS, IP addresses, top-level domain name system management, and root server system management functions. The computer must translate www.icann.org into an IP address to know where to send the Internet Control Message Protocol (ICMP) packets.

The first line of the output displays www.icann.org converted to an IP address by DNS. You should be able to see the effect of DNS, even if your institution has a firewall that prevents pinging, or if the destination server has prevented you from pinging its web server.

Note: If the domain name is resolved to an IPv6 address, use the command **ping -4 www.icann.org** to translate into an IPv4 address if desired.

```
C:\>ping www.icann.org

Pinging www.vip.icann.org [192.0.32.7] with 32 bytes of data:
Reply from 192.0.32.7: bytes=32 time=23ms TTL=246
Reply from 192.0.32.7: bytes=32 time=23ms TTL=246
Reply from 192.0.32.7: bytes=32 time=24ms TTL=246
Reply from 192.0.32.7: bytes=32 time=28ms TTL=246

Ping statistics for 192.0.32.7:
    Packets: Sent = 4, Received = 4, Lost = 0 (0% loss),
Approximate round trip times in milli-seconds:
    Minimum = 23ms, Maximum = 28ms, Average = 24ms
```

Record the IP address of www.icann.org. _____

c. Type the IP address from **Step b** into a web browser, instead of the URL. Click **Continue to this website (not recommended).** to proceed.

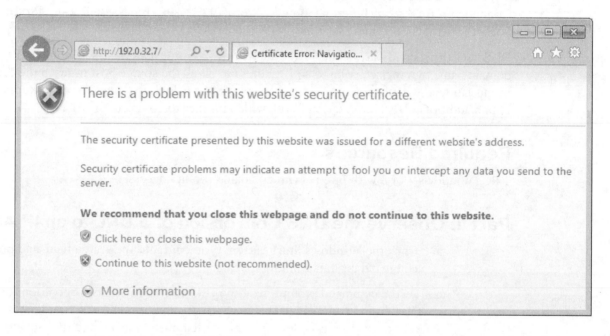

d. Notice that the ICANN home web page is displayed.

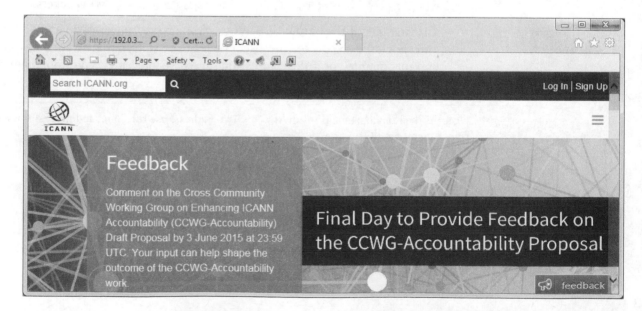

Most humans find it easier to remember words, rather than numbers. If you tell someone to go to **www.icann.org**, they can probably remember that. If you told them to go to 192.0.32.7, they would have a difficult time remembering an IP address. Computers process in numbers. DNS is the process of translating words into numbers. There is a second translation that takes place. Humans think in Base 10 numbers. Computers process in Base 2 numbers. The Base 10 IP address 192.0.32.7 in Base 2 numbers is 1100 0000.00000000.00100000.00000111. What happens if you cut and paste these Base 2 numbers into a browser?

_____

_____

_____

e. Now type **ping** www.cisco.com.

Note: If the domain name is resolved to an IPv6 address, use the command **ping -4 www.cisco.com** to translate into an IPv4 address if desired.

```
C:\>ping www.cisco.com

Pinging e144.dscb.akamaiedge.net [23.1.144.170] with 32 bytes of data:
Reply from 23.1.144.170: bytes=32 time=51ms TTL=58
Reply from 23.1.144.170: bytes=32 time=50ms TTL=58
Reply from 23.1.144.170: bytes=32 time=50ms TTL=58
Reply from 23.1.144.170: bytes=32 time=50ms TTL=58

Ping statistics for 23.1.144.170:
    Packets: Sent = 4, Received = 4, Lost = 0 (0% loss),
Approximate round trip times in milli-seconds:
    Minimum = 50ms, Maximum = 51ms, Average = 50ms
```

f. When you ping www.cisco.com, do you get the same IP address as the example? Explain.

_____

_____

_____

g. Type the IP address that you obtained when you pinged www.cisco.com into a browser. Does the web site display? Explain.

_____

_____

_____

Part 2: Observe DNS Lookup Using the nslookup Command on a Web Site

a. At the command prompt, type the **nslookup** command.

```
C:\>nslookup
Default Server:  dslrouter.westell.com
Address:  192.168.1.1

>
```

What is the default DNS server used? _____

Notice how the command prompt changed to a greater than (>) symbol. This is the **nslookup** prompt. From this prompt, you can enter commands related to DNS.

At the prompt, type **?** to see a list of all the available commands that you can use in **nslookup** mode.

b. At the prompt, type **www.cisco.com**.

```
> www.cisco.com
Server:  dslrouter.westell.com
Address:  192.168.1.1

Non-authoritative answer:
Name:    e144.dscb.akamaiedge.net
Addresses:  2600:1408:7:1:9300::90
            2600:1408:7:1:8000::90
            2600:1408:7:1:9800::90
            23.1.144.170
Aliases:  www.cisco.com
          www.cisco.com.akadns.net
          wwwds.cisco.com.edgekey.net
          wwwds.cisco.com.edgekey.net.globalredir.akadns.net
```

What is the translated IP address? _____

Note: The IP address from your location will most likely be different because Cisco uses mirrored servers in various locations around the world.

Is it the same as the IP address shown with the **ping** command? _____

Under addresses, in addition to the 23.1.144.170 IP address, there are the following numbers: 2600:1408:7:1:9300::90, 2600:1408:7:1:8000::90, 2600:1408:7:1:9800::90. What are these?

_____

c. At the prompt, type the IP address of the Cisco web server that you just found. You can use **nslookup** to get the domain name of an IP address if you do not know the URL.

```
> 23.1.144.170
Server:  dslrouter.westell.com
Address:  192.168.1.1

Name:    a23-1-144-170.deploy.akamaitechnologies.com
Address:  23.1.144.170
```

You can use the **nslookup** tool to translate domain names into IP addresses. You can also use it to translate IP addresses into domain names.

Using the **nslookup** tool, record the IP addresses associated with www.google.com.

```
> www.google.com
Server:  dslrouter.westell.com
Address:  192.168.1.1

Non-authoritative answer:
Name:    www.google.com
Addresses:  2607:f8b0:400c:c01::93
           173.194.75.147
           173.194.75.105
           173.194.75.99
           173.194.75.103
           173.194.75.106
           173.194.75.104
```

Part 3: Observe DNS Lookup Using the nslookup Command on Mail Servers

a. At the prompt, type **set type=mx** to use **nslookup** to identify mail servers.

```
> set type=mx
```

b. At the prompt, type cisco.com.

```
> cisco.com
Server:  dslrouter.westell.com
Address:  192.168.1.1

Non-authoritative answer:
cisco.com        MX preference = 10, mail exchanger = rcdn-mx-01.cisco.com
cisco.com        MX preference = 15, mail exchanger = alln-mx-01.cisco.com
cisco.com        MX preference = 15, mail exchanger = ams-mx-01.cisco.com
cisco.com        MX preference = 15, mail exchanger = rtp-mx-01.cisco.com

ams-mx-01.cisco.com     internet address = 64.103.36.169
rcdn-mx-01.cisco.com    internet address = 72.163.7.166
```

A fundamental principle of network design is redundancy (more than one mail server is configured). In this way, if one of the mail servers is unreachable, then the computer making the query tries the second mail server. Email administrators determine which mail server is contacted first by using **MX preference** (see above image). The mail server with the lowest **MX preference** is contacted first. Based upon the output above, which mail server will be contacted first when the email is sent to cisco.com?

_____

   c. At the nslookup prompt, type **exit** to return to the regular PC command prompt.

   d. At the PC command prompt, type **ipconfig /all**.

   e. Write the IP addresses of all the DNS servers that your school uses.

_____

Reflection

What is the fundamental purpose of DNS?

_____

_____

_____

10.2.3.3 Packet Tracer–FTP Servers

Topology

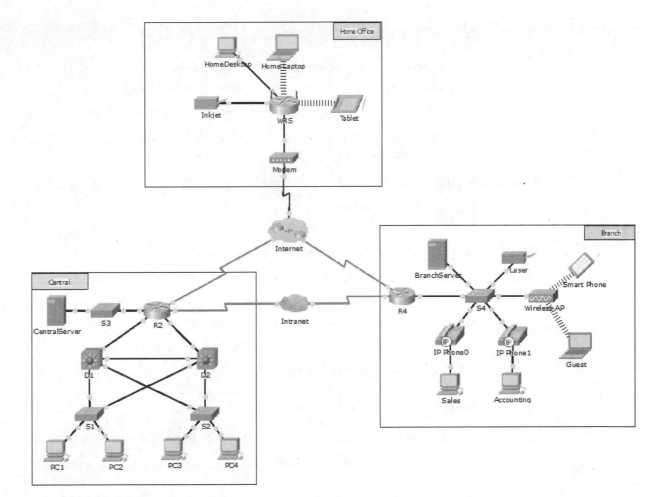

Objectives

Part 1: Configure FTP Services on Servers

Part 2: Upload a File to the FTP Server

Part 3: Download a File from the FTP Server

Background

In this activity, you will configure FTP services. You will then use the FTP services to transfer files between clients and the server.

Note: Packet Tracer only simulates the process for configuring these services. FTP server and client software packages each have their own unique installation and configuration instructions. The first time you attempt to connect to a web address, Packet Tracer takes several seconds to simulate the DNS name resolution process.

Part 1: Configure FTP Services on Servers

Step 1. Configure the FTP service on **CentralServer**.

    a. Click **CentralServer > Services** tab **> FTP**.

    b. Click **On** to enable FTP service.

    c. In **User Setup**, create the following user accounts. Click **Add** to add the account:

Username	Password	Permissions
anonymous	anonymous	limited to **Read** and **List**
administrator	cisco	full permission

    Click the default **cisco** user account and click **Remove** to delete it. Close the CentralServer configuration window.

Step 2. Configure the FTP service on **BranchServer**.

Repeat Step 1 on **BranchServer**.

Part 2: Upload a File to the FTP Server

Step 1. Transfer the README.txt file from the home laptop to CentralServer.

As network administrator, you must place a notice on the FTP servers. The document has been created on the home laptop and must be uploaded to the FTP servers.

    a. Click **Home Laptop** and click the **Desktop** tab **> Text Editor**.

    b. Open the **README.txt** file and review it. Close the **Text Editor** when done.

Note: Do not change the file because this affects scoring.

---

    c. In the **Desktop** tab, open the Command Prompt window and perform the following steps:

        1) Type **ftp centralserver.pt.pka**. Wait several seconds while the client connects.

Note: Because Packet Tracer is a simulation, it can take up to 30 seconds for FTP to connect the first time.

---

        2) The server prompts for a username and password. Use the credentials for the **administrator** account.

        3) The prompt changes to `ftp>`. List the contents of the directory by typing **dir**. The file directory on **CentralServer** displays.

        4) Transfer the README.txt file: at the `ftp>` prompt, type **put README.txt**. The README.txt file is transferred from the home laptop to **CentralServer**.

        5) Verify the transfer of the file by typing **dir**. The README.txt file is now listed in the file directory.

        6) Close the FTP client by typing **quit**. The prompt will return to `PC>`.

Step 2. Transfer the README.txt file from the home laptop to BranchServer.

    a. Repeat Step 1c to transfer the README.txt file to **branchserver.pt.pka**.

    b. Close the Command Prompt and Home Laptop windows, respectively.

Part 3: Download a File from the FTP Server

Step 1.   Transfer README.txt from CentralServer to PC2.

    a.   Click **PC2** and click the **Desktop** tab > **Command Prompt**.

        1)   Type **ftp centralserver.pt.pka.**

        2)   The server prompts for a username and password. Use the credentials for the **anonymous** account.

        3)   The prompt changes to `ftp>`. List the contents of the directory by typing **dir**. The README.txt file is listed at the top of the directory list.

        4)   Download the README.txt file: at the ftp> prompt, type **get README.txt**. The README.txt file is transferred to **PC2**.

        5)   Verify that the **anonymous** account does not have the permission to write files to **CentralServer** by typing **put sampleFile.txt**. The following error message displays:

```
Writing file sampleFile.txt to centralserver.pt.pka:
File transfer in progress...


%Error ftp://centralserver.pt.pka/sampleFile.txt (No such file or directory
Or Permission denied)
550-Requested action not taken. permission denied).
```

        6)   Close the FTP client by typing **quit**. The prompt returns to the `PC>` prompt.

        7)   Verify the transfer of the file to PC2 by typing **dir**. README.txt is listed in the directory.

        8)   Close the command line window.

    b.   In the **Desktop** tab, open the **Text Editor** and then the **README.txt** file to verify the integrity of the file.

    c.   Close the **Text Editor** and then the PC2 configuration window.

Step 2.   Transfer the README.txt file from BranchServer to the Smart Phone.

Repeat Step 1 for **Smart Phone**, except download the README.txt file from **branchserver. pt.pka.**

10.2.3.4 Lab–Exploring FTP

Objectives

Part 1: Use FTP from a Command Prompt

Part 2: Use FTP in a Browser

Part 3: Download an FTP File Using WS_FTP LE (Optional)

Background/Scenario

The File Transfer Protocol (FTP) is part of the TCP/IP suite. FTP is used to transfer files from one network device to another network device. Windows includes an FTP client application that you can execute from the command prompt. There are also free graphical user interface (GUI) versions of FTP that you can download. The GUI versions are easier to use than typing from a command prompt. FTP is frequently used for the transfer of files that may be too large to send using email.

When using FTP, one computer is normally the server and the other computer is the client. When accessing the server from the client, you need to provide a username and password. Some FTP servers have a user named **anonymous**. You can access these types of sites by simply typing "anonymous" for the user, without a password. Usually, the site administrator has files that can be copied but does not allow files to be posted with the anonymous user. Furthermore, FTP is not a secure protocol because the data is not encrypted during transmission.

In this lab, you will learn how to use anonymous FTP from the Windows command-line C:\> prompt. You will access an anonymous FTP server using your browser. Finally, you will use the GUI-based FTP program, WS_FTP LE.

Required Resources

1 PC (Windows 7 or 8 with access to the command prompt, Internet access, and WS_FTP LE installed (optional))

Part 1: Use FTP from a Command Prompt

a. Click the **Windows Start** button, type **cmd** in the search field, and press **Enter** to open a command window.

b. At the C:\> prompt type **ftp ftp.cdc.gov**. At the prompt that says **User (ftp.cdc.gov:(none)):** type **anonymous**. For the password, do not type anything. Press **Enter** to be logged in as an anonymous user.

```
Microsoft Windows [Version 6.1.7600]
Copyright (c) 2009 Microsoft Corporation.  All rights reserved.

C:\Users\User1>ftp ftp.cdc.gov
Connected to ftp.cdc.gov.
220 Microsoft FTP Service
User (ftp.cdc.gov:(none)): anonymous
331 Anonymous access allowed, send identity (e-mail name) as password.
Password:
230 Anonymous user logged in.
ftp>
```

Notice that the C:\> prompt has been replaced with the ftp> prompt. Type **ls** to list the files and directories. At the time that this lab was authored, there was a Readme file.

```
ftp> ls
200 PORT command successful.
150 Opening ASCII mode data connection for file list.
aspnet_client
pub
Readme
```

c. At the prompt, type **get Readme**. This downloads the file to your local computer from the anonymous FTP server the Centers for Disease Control has set up. The file will be copied into the directory shown in the C:\> prompt (C:\Users\User1 in this case).

```
ftp> get Readme
200 PORT command successful.
150 Opening ASCII mode data connection for Readme(1428 bytes).
226 Transfer complete.
ftp: 1428 bytes received in 0.00Seconds 1428000.00Kbytes/sec.
ftp>
```

d. Type **quit** to leave FTP and return to the C:\> prompt. Type **more Readme** to see the contents of the document.

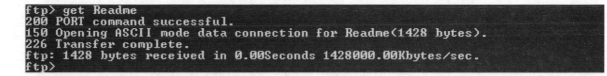

```
ftp> quit
221 Goodbye.

C:\Users\User1>more Readme

Welcome to the Centers for Disease Control and Prevention and Agency for
Toxic Substances and Disease Registry FTP server.  Information maintained on
this server is in the public domain and is available at anytime for your use.
CDC/ATSDR requests that you provide a valid e-mail address when responding to
the FTP server's password prompt.

FTP POLICY

CDC/ATSDR's file structure is designed to make information easily accessible
for faster response.  All FTP directories and sub-directories should contain
the following files:

        README.TXT        Contains general information and Disclaimer text.
                          (ASCII)
```

e. What is a drawback of using the FTP from the command line?

Part 2: Use FTP in a Browser

It is possible to use a browser as an anonymous FTP client.

a. In a browser, type **ftp://ftp.cdc.gov/**.

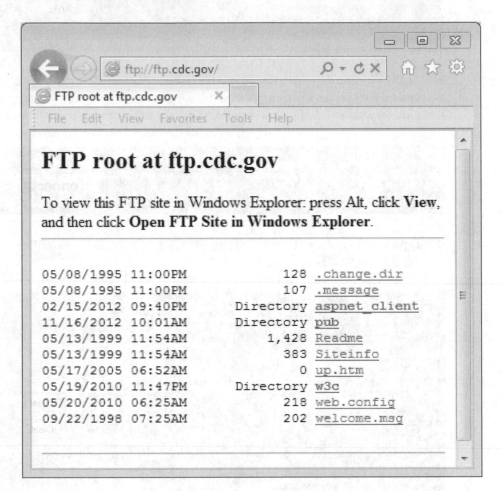

b. Click the **Readme** file.

ftp://ftp.cdc.gov/Read ×

ftp://ftp.cdc.gov/Readme

```
Welcome to the Centers for Disease Control and Prevention and Agency for
Toxic Substances and Disease Registry FTP server.  Information maintained on
this server is in the public domain and is available at anytime for your use.
CDC/ATSDR requests that you provide a valid e-mail address when responding to
the FTP server's password prompt.
```

c. Close the browser to disconnect the FTP connection.

Part 3: Download an FTP File Using WS_FTP LE (Optional)

In Part 3, you will download a file using WS_FTP LE (a free FTP transfer tool).

a. Start **WS_FTP LE**. If the Ipswitch WS_FTP LE window displays, click **Next** to continue and skip to step c. Otherwise, click the **Open a Remote Connection** link.

b. Click **Create Site....**

c. In the **Site Name** field, type **Center for Disease Control** and click **Next** to continue.

d. Click the **Connection Type** drop-down list, select **FTP** (the default connection type), and click **Next**.

e. In the **Server Address** field, type **ftp.cdc.gov,** and click **Next.**

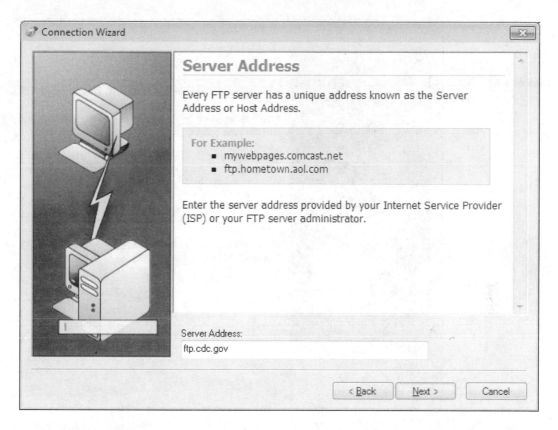

f. In the **User Name** field, type **anonymous,** and leave the password field blank. Click **Next.**

g.   Click **Finish**.

Connection Wizard

Finish

If the following information is correct, click Finish to create the **site**.

If you do not want to connect to this FTP server, clear the **Connect to this site** option.

- **Connection name:** Center for Disease Control
- **Server address:** ftp.cdc.gov
- **User name:** anonymous
- **Password:** Not Entered

REMEMBER: You can open this site from now on using the **Connect** button on the main application toolbar.

☑ Connect to this site   Advanced...

< Back   Finish   Cancel

h.   When the Login Information Missing dialog box displays, click **OK**. Do not type a password in the **Password** field.

Login

Login Information Missing

WS_FTP needs login information in order to start the connection process. Enter the missing login information below.

Enable the **Save login information** option to update and save your site login information.

User Name

anonymous

Password

☑ Save login information

OK   Cancel

i. You are now anonymously connected to the Centers for Disease Control FTP site.

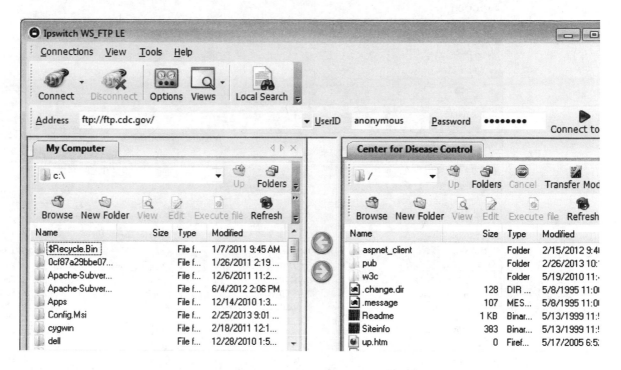

j. On the WS_FTP LE toolbar menu under My Computer, click **New Folder** to create a folder on your local C:\ drive.

k. In the Make Directory dialog box, name the folder as **CDC** and click **OK**.

Note: If the folder already exists, you can use the same folder or create another folder with a different name. If using the same CDC folder, you can replace the existing Readme file with the downloaded Readme file.

l. After the directory is created, in the **My Computer** tab page, double-click the directory to open it.

m. Drag the **Readme** file from the right side of the application (the remote CDC FTP server) into the CDC folder on to the local **C:** drive.

n. Double-click the **Readme** file in the **C:\CDC** folder on your local **C:** drive. If prompted for an application to open the document, choose any word processing software. You should see a message that looks something like this:

```
Welcome to the Centers for Disease Control and Prevention and
Agency for Toxic Substances and Disease Registry FTP server.
Information maintained on this server is in the public domain
and is available at anytime for your use.
```

o. Which was easier, using FTP from the **cmd** prompt, or using WS_FTP LE? _____

_____

_____

p. Verify that the Centers for Disease Control window is highlighted. Click **Disconnect** to disconnect from the ftp.cdc.gov site when finished.

q. The remote site will be removed from the saved list of FTP sites. In the Ipswitch WS_FTP LE window, click the **Open a Remote Connection** link. Select the **Centers for Disease Control** site, and click **Delete** to remove the FTP site. Click **Yes** to confirm the deletion. Click **Close** to exit the Site Manager.

r. Remove the **C:\CDC** folder.

s. Close Ipswitch WS_FTP_LE.

Reflection

List the advantages for using FTP from the command prompt, the browser, and an FTP client, such as WS_FTP LE?

_____

_____

_____

10.3.1.1 Class Activity–Make It Happen!

Objectives

Explain the operation of the application layer in providing support to end-user applications.

Background/Scenario

Refer to the modeling activity from the beginning of this chapter as the basis for this activity.

Your IP telephones were installed in a half day versus the full week originally anticipated. Your network has been restored to full capacity and network applications are available for your use. You have the same emails to answer and quotes to write for your manager's approval.

Use the same scenario you completed in the introduction modeling activity to answer the following questions:

Emails

- What method(s) can you use to send email correspondence now that the network is working?
- What format will your emails be sent over the network?
- How can you now send the same message to multiple recipients?
- How can you send the large attachments to multiple recipients using network applications?
- Would using network applications prove to be a cost-effective communication method for your corporation?

Quote for Manager's Approval

- Because you have desktop application programs installed on your computer, will it be relatively easy to produce the quote your manager needs for the new contract due by the end of the week? Explain your answer.
- When you finish writing the quote, how will you present it to your manager for approval? How will he send the quote to the client for his approval?
- Is using network applications a cost-effective way to complete business transactions? Justify your answer.
- Save a hard copy or an electronic copy of your answers. Be prepared to discuss your answers in class.

Reflection

Having network applications and services available to you may increase production, decrease costs, and save time. Would this be true with the scenario you chose? Justify your answer.

_____

_____

_____

10.3.1.2 Packet Tracer–Explore a Network

Topology

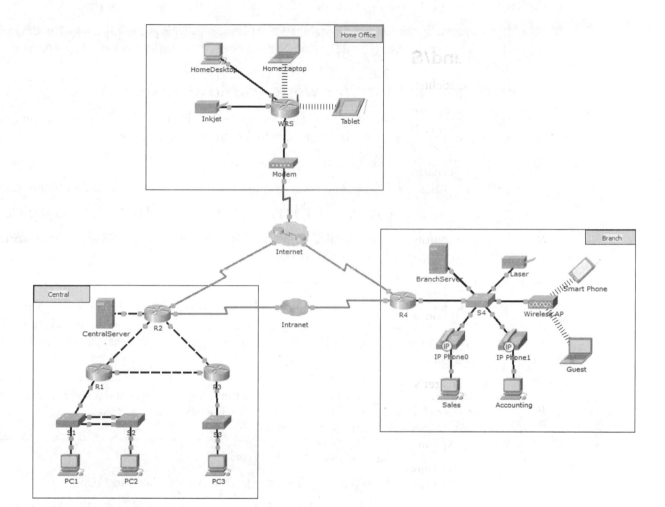

Objectives

Part 1: Examine Internetwork Traffic at Branch

Part 2: Examine Internetwork Traffic to Central

Part 3: Examine Internet Traffic from Branch

Background

This simulation activity is intended to help you understand the flow of traffic and the contents of data packets as they traverse a complex network. Communications will be examined at three different locations simulating typical business and home networks.

Take a few moments to study the topology displayed. The Central location has three routers and multiple networks possibly representing different buildings within a campus. The Branch location has only one router with a connection to both the Internet and a dedicated wide-area network (WAN) connection to the Central location. The Home Office makes use of a cable modem broadband connection to provide access to both the Internet and to corporate resources over the Internet.

The devices at each location use a combination of static and dynamic addressing. The devices are configured with default gateways and Domain Name System (DNS) information, as appropriate.

Part 1: Examine Internetwork Traffic at Branch

In Part 1 of this activity, you will use Simulation mode to generate web traffic and examine the HTTP protocol along with other protocols necessary for communications.

Step 1.   Switching from Realtime to Simulation mode.

    a.   Click the **Simulation** mode icon to switch from **Realtime** mode to **Simulation** mode.

    b.   Verify that **ARP**, **DNS**, **HTTP**, and **TCP** are selected from the **Event List Filters**.

    c.   Move the slider located below the **Play Controls** buttons (**Back**, **Auto Capture/Play**, **Capture/Forward**) all the way to the right.

Step 2.   Generate traffic using a web browser.

    Currently the Simulation Panel is empty. In the Event List at the top of the Simulation Panel there are six columns listed across the heading. As traffic is generated and stepped through, events display in the list. The **Info** column is used to inspect the contents of a particular event.

Note: The panel to the left of the Simulation Panel displays the topology. Use the scrollbars to bring the Branch location into the panel, if necessary. The panels can be adjusted in size by hovering next to the scrollbar and dragging left or right.

---

    a.   Click the **Sales PC** in the far left pane.

    b.   Click the **Desktop** tab and click the **Web Browser** icon to open it.

    c.   In the URL field, enter **http://branchserver.pt.pta** and click **Go**. Look in the Event List in the Simulation Panel. What is the first type of event listed?

---

    d.   Click the **DNS** info box. In the **Out Layers**, DNS is listed for Layer 7. Layer 4 is using UDP to contact the DNS server on port 53 (**Dst Port:**). Both the source and destination IP addresses are listed. What information is missing to communicate with the DNS server?

---

    e.   Click **Auto Capture/Play**. In approximately 30 to 40 seconds, a window displays, indicating the completion of the current simulation. (Or a window may display indicating that the buffer is full.) Click the **View Previous Events** button. Scroll back to the top of the list and note the number of **ARP** events. Looking at the Device column in Event list, how many of the devices in the Branch location does the **ARP** request pass through?

---

f. Scroll down the events in the list to the series of **DNS** events. Select the **DNS** event that has the "At Device" listed as **BranchServer**. Click the square box in the **Info** column. What can be determined by selecting Layer 7 in the **OSI Model?** (Look at the results displayed directly below **In Layers**.)

_____

g. Click the **Outbound PDU Details** tab. Scroll to the bottom of the window and locate the DNS Answer section. What is the address displayed?

_____

h. The next several events are **TCP** events enabling a communications channel to be established. Select the last **TCP** event at device **Sales** just prior to the **HTTP** event. Click the colored square Info box to display the PDU information. Highlight Layer 4 in the **In Layers** column. Looking at item 6 in the list directly below the In Layers column, what is the connection state?

_____

i. The next several events are **HTTP** events. Select any one of the **HTTP** events at an intermediary device (IP Phone or Switch). How many layers are active at one of these devices, and why?

_____

j. Select the last **HTTP** event at the Sales PC. Select the uppermost layer from the **OSI Model** tab. What is the result listed below the **In Layers** column?

_____

_____

Part 2: Examine Internetwork Traffic to Central

In Part 2 of this activity, you will use Packet Tracer (PT) Simulation mode to view and examine how traffic leaving the local network is handled.

Step 1.   Set up for traffic capture to the Central web server.

a. Close any open PDU Information windows.

b. Click **Reset Simulation** (located near the middle of the Simulation Panel).

c. Type **http://centralserver.pt.pta** in the web browser of the Sales PC.

d. Click **Auto Capture/Play**; in approximately 75 seconds, a window displays, indicating the completion of the current simulation. Click **View Previous Events**. Scroll back to the top of the list; note that the first series of events are DNS and there are no **ARP** entries prior to contacting the **BranchServer**. Based on what you have learned so far, why is this the case?

_____

e. Click the last DNS event in the **Info** column. Select **Layer 7** in the **OSI Model** tab.

By looking at the information provided, what can be determined about the DNS results? _____

f. Click the **Inbound PDU Details** tab. Scroll down to the **DNS ANSWER** section. What is the address listed for centralserver.pt.pta? _____

g. The next several events are **ARP** events. Click the colored square Info box of the last **ARP** event. Click the **Inbound PDU Details** tab and note the MAC address. Based on the information in the ARP section, what device is providing the ARP reply?

_____

h. The next several events are **TCP** events, once again preparing to set up a communications channel. Find the first **HTTP** event in the Event List. Click the colored square box of the **HTTP** event. Highlight Layer 2 in the **OSI Model** tab. What can be determined about the destination MAC address?

_____

i. Click the **HTTP** event at device **R4**. Notice that Layer 2 contains an Ethernet II header. Click the **HTTP** event at device **Intranet**. What is the Layer 2 listed at this device?

_____

Notice that there are only two active layers, as opposed to three active layers when moving through the router. This is a WAN connection, which will be discussed in a later course.

Part 3: Examine Internet Traffic from Branch

In Part 3 of this activity, you will clear the events and start a new web request that will make use of the Internet.

Step 1.   Set up for traffic capture to an Internet web server.

a. Close any open PDU information windows.

b. Click **Reset Simulation** near the middle of the Simulation Panel. Type **http://www.netacad.pta** in the web browser of the Sales PC.

c. Click **Auto Capture/Play**; in approximately 75 seconds, a window displays, indicating the completion of the current simulation. Click **View Previous Events**. Scroll back to the top of the list; notice that the first series of events are **DNS**. What do you notice about the number of **DNS** events?

_____

_____

d. Observe some of the devices that the **DNS** events travel through on the way to a DNS server. Where are these devices located? _____

_____

_____

e. Click the last **DNS** event. Click the **Inbound PDU Details** tab and scroll down to the last DNS Answer section. What is the address listed for **www.netacad.pta**?

_____

f. When routers move the **HTTP** event through the network, there are three layers active in both the **In Layers** and **Out Layers** in the **OSI Model** tab. Based on that information, how many routers are passed through?

_____

g. Click the **TCP** event just prior to the last **HTTP** event. Based on the information displayed, what is the purpose of this event? _____

h. There are several more **TCP** events listed. Locate the **TCP** event where the *Last Device* is **IP Phone** and the *Device At* is **Sales**. Click the colored square Info box and select **Layer 4** in the **OSI Model** tab. Based on the information from the output, what is the connection state set to? _____

Suggested Scoring Rubric

Activity Section	Question Location	Possible Points	Earned Points
Part 1: Examine Internetwork Traffic at Branch	Step 2c	5	
	Step 2d	5	
	Step 2e	5	
	Step 2f	5	
	Step 2g	5	
	Step 2h	5	
	Step 2i	5	
	Step 2j	5	
	Part 1 Total	40	
Part 2: Examine Internetwork Traffic to Central	Step 1c	5	
	Step 1d	5	
	Step 1e	5	
	Step 1f	5	
	Step 1g	5	
	Step 1h	5	
	Part 2 Total	30	
Part 3: Examine Internet Traffic from Branch	Step 1c	5	
	Step 1d	5	
	Step 1e	5	
	Step 1f	5	
	Step 1g	5	
	Step 1h	5	
	Part 3 Total	30	
	Total Score	100	

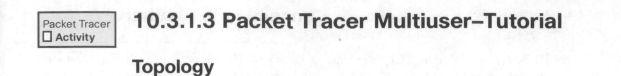

10.3.1.3 Packet Tracer Multiuser–Tutorial

Topology

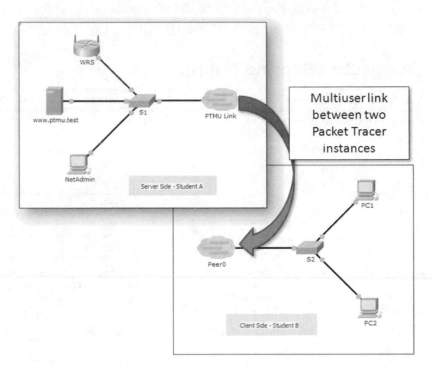

Addressing Table

Device	IP Address	Subnet Mask	DNS Server
www.ptmu.test	10.10.10.1	255.0.0.0	10.10.10.1
PC	10.10.10.10	255.0.0.0	10.10.10.1

Objectives

Part 1: Establish a Local Multiuser Connection to Another Instance of Packet Tracer

Part 2: Verify Connectivity Across a Local Multiuser Connection

Background

The multiuser feature in Packet Tracer allows multiple point-to-point connections between multiple instances of Packet Tracer. This first Packet Tracer Multiuser (PTMU) activity is a quick tutorial demonstrating the steps to establish and verify a multiuser connection to another instance of Packet Tracer within the same LAN. Ideally, this activity is meant for two students. However, it can also be completed as a solo activity simply by opening the two separate files to create two separate instances of Packet Tracer on your local machine.

Part 1: Establish a Local Multiuser Connection to Another Instance of Packet Tracer

Step 1.   Select a partner and determine the role for each student.

a.   Find a fellow classmate with whom you will cooperate to complete this activity. Your computers must both be connected to the same LAN.

b.   Determine which of you will play the server side and which of you will play the client side in this activity.

- The server side player opens **Packet Tracer Multiuser - Tutorial - Server Side.pka**.

- The client side player opens **Packet Tracer Multiuser - Tutorial - Client Side.pka**.

Note: Solo players can open both files and complete the steps for both sides.

Step 2.   Server Side Player - Configure the server side of the PTMU link.

The client side player must have the IP address, port number, and password used by the server side player before the client side player can create a connection to the server side player.

a.   Configure Packet Tracer to be ready for an incoming connection by completing the following steps:

1)   Click the **Extensions** menu, then **Multiuser**, then **Listen**.

2)   You have two Local Listening Addresses. If there are more than two listed, refer to the first two only. The first one is the real IP address of the server side player's local machine. It is the IP address your computer uses to send and receive data. The other IP address (127.0.0.1) can only be used for communications within your own computer's environment.

3)   The port number is listed next to your IP addresses and in the Port Number field. If this is the first instance of Packet Tracer you opened on your computer, then the port number will be 38000. However, if you have multiple instances open, it will increment by 1 for each instance (38001, 38002, etc.). The port number is required by the client side player to configure the multiuser connection.

4)   The password is set to cisco, by default. You can change it, but it is not necessary for this activity.

5)   Tell the client side player your IP address, port number, and password. The client side player will need these three pieces of information to connect to your Packet Tracer instance in Step 3.

6)   In the **Existing Remote Networks** section, you must click **Always Accept** or **Prompt** radio button for the client side player to successfully connect.

7)   In the **New Remote Networks** section, confirm that the **Always Deny** radio button is enabled. This will prevent the client side player from creating a new link that is not specified in this activity.

8)   Click **OK**.

b.   Click the **Multiuser Connection** icon (represented as a cloud with three lines). Then click the **Remote Network** icon and add a **Remote Network** to the topology.

c.   Click the **Peer0** name and change it to **PTMU Link** (it is case-sensitive).

      d. Click the **PTMU Link** cloud and verify that the Connection Type is **Incoming** and that the **Use Global Multiuser Password** check box is enabled.

      e. Click the **Connections** icon and choose the solid-black **Copper Straight-Through** connection.

      f. Click **S1** and choose the GigabitEthernet0/1 connection. Then click **PTMU Link > Create New Link.**

Step 3. Client Side Player - Configure the client side of the PTMU link.

      a. Record the following information supplied to you by the server side player:

IP Address: _____

Port Number: _____

Password (**cisco**, by default) _____

      b. The client side player must add a **Remote Network** to the topology using the following directions: Click the **Multiuser Connection** icon (represented as a cloud with three lines). Then click the **Remote Network** icon and add a **Remote Network** to the topology.

      c. Click the **Peer0** cloud and change the Connection Type to **Outgoing.**

         1) In the Peer Address field, enter the server side IP address you recorded in Step 3a.

         2) In the Peer Port Number field, enter the server side port number you recorded in Step 3a.

         3) In the Peer Network Name field, enter **PTMU Link**. This is case-sensitive.

         4) In the Password field, enter **cisco** or the password configured by the server side player.

         5) Click **Connect.**

      d. The **Peer0** cloud should now be yellow, indicating that the two instances of Packet Tracer are connected.

      e. Click the **Connections** icon and choose the solid-black **Copper Straight-Through** connection.

      f. Click **S2** and choose the **GigabitEthernet0/1** connection. Then click **Peer0 > Link 0 (S1 GigabitEthernet 0/1).**

The **Peer0** cloud on the client side player and the **PTMU Link** cloud on the server side player should now both be blue. After a short period, the link light between the switch and the cloud will transition from amber to green.

The multiuser link is now established and ready for testing.

Part 2: Verify Connectivity Across a Local Multiuser Connection

Step 1.   Configure IP addressing.

    a.   The server side player configures the **www.ptmu.test** server with the IP address **10.10.10.1**, the subnet mask **255.0.0.0**, and the DNS server address **10.10.10.1**.

    b.   The client side player configures the PC with the IP address **10.10.10.10**, the subnet mask **255.0.0.0**, and the DNS server address **10.10.10.1**.

Step 2.   Verify connectivity and access a web page on the server side.

    a.   The server side player should now be able to ping the PC in the client side player instance of Packet Tracer.

    b.   The client side player should now be able to ping the **www.ptmu.test** server.

    c.   The client side player should also be able to open the web browser and access the web page at **www.ptmu.test**. What is displayed on the web page? _____

_____

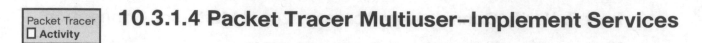

10.3.1.4 Packet Tracer Multiuser–Implement Services

Topology

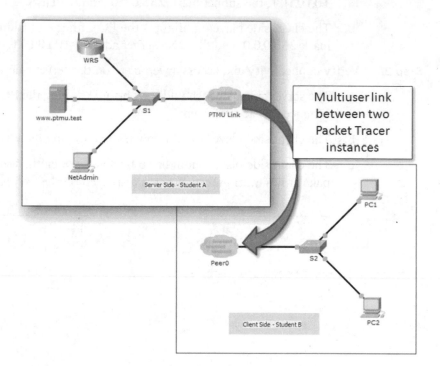

Addressing Table

Device	IP Address	Subnet Mask
Server Side Player		
WRS	172.16.1.254	255.255.255.0
S1	172.16.1.1	255.255.255.0
www.ptmu.test	172.16.1.5	255.255.255.0
NetAdmin	DHCP Assigned	DHCP Assigned
Client Side Player		
S2	172.16.1.2	255.255.255.0
PC1	DHCP Assigned	DHCP Assigned
PC2	DHCP Assigned	DHCP Assigned

Objectives

Part 1: Establish a Local Multiuser Connection to another Instance of Packet Tracer

Part 2: Server Side Player - Implement and Verify Services

Part 3: Client Side Player - Configure and Verify Access to Services

Background

Note: Completing the prior activities in this chapter, including the **Packet Tracer Multiuser - Tutorial**, are prerequisites to completing this activity.

In this multiuser activity, two students (players) cooperate to implement and verify services including DHCP, HTTP, Email, DNS, and FTP. The server side player will implement and verify services on one server. The client side player will configure two clients and verify access to services.

Part 1: Establish a Local Multiuser Connection to Another Instance of Packet Tracer

Step 1.   Select a partner and determine the role for each student.

  a.   Find a fellow classmate with whom you will cooperate to complete this activity. Your computers must both be connected to the same LAN.

  b.   Determine which of you will play the server side and which of you will play the client side in this activity.

  ▪   The server side player opens **Packet Tracer Multiuser - Implement Services - Server Side.pka.**

  ▪   The client side player opens **Packet Tracer Multiuser - Implement Services - Client Side.pka.**

Note: Solo players can open both files and complete the steps for both sides.

Step 2.   Configure the switches with initial configurations.

  Each player: configure your respective switch with the following:

  a.   Hostname using the name in the addressing tables (**S1** for the switch in the Server Side Player or **S2** for the switch in the Client Side Player). Change the Display Name of each switch to match the new hostname using the **Config** tab.

  b.   An appropriate message-of-the-day (MOTD) banner.

  c.   Privileged EXEC mode and line passwords.

  d.   Correct IP addressing, according to the Addressing Table.

  e.   Scoring should be 8/33 for the client side player and 8/44 for the server side player.

Step 3.   Server Side Player - Configure the **PTMU link** and communicate addressing.

  a.   Complete the steps necessary to verify that the **PTMU Link** is ready to receive an incoming connection.

  b.   Communicate the necessary configuration information to the client side player.

Step 4.   Client Side Player - Configure the outgoing multiuser connection.

  a.   Client side player: Record the following information supplied to you by the server side player:

  IP Address: _____

  Port Number: _____

  Password (cisco, by default) _____

      b.   Configure **Peer0** to connect to the server side player's **PTMU Link**.

      c.   Connect the **S2 GigabitEthernet0/1** to **Link0** on **Peer0**.

Step 5.   Verify connectivity across the local multiuser connection.

      a.   The server side player should be able to ping S2 in the client side player's instance of Packet Tracer.

      b.   The client side player should be able to ping S1 in the server side player's instance of Packet Tracer.

      c.   Scoring should be 11/33 for the client side player and 9/44 for the server side player.

Part 2: Server Side Player - Implement and Verify Services

Step 1.   Configure WRS as the DHCP server.

      WRS provides DHCP services. Configure DHCP Server Settings with the following:

      a.   Starting IP address is **172.16.1.11**.

      b.   Maximum number of users is **100**.

      c.   **Static DNS 1** is 172.16.1.5.

      d.   Verify **NetAdmin** received IP addressing through DHCP.

      e.   From **NetAdmin**, access the User Account Information web page at **172.16.1.5**. You will use this information to configure user accounts in Step 2.

      f.   Scoring should be 17/44 for the server side player.

Step 2.   Configure services on www.ptmu.test.

      The **www.ptmu.test** server provides the rest of the services and should be configured with the following:

      a.   Enable the DNS service and create a DNS record associating the IP address for **www.ptmu.test** server to the name www.ptmu.test.

      b.   Enable the Email services and create user accounts using the user list from Part 2 Step 1e. The Domain Name is **ptmu.test**.

      c.   Enable the FTP service and create user accounts using the user list from Part 2 Step 1e. Give each user permission to write, read, and list.

      d.   Scoring should be 38/44 for the server side player.

Step 3.   Verify that all services are implemented according to the requirements.

      From **NetAdmin**, complete the following:

      a.   Configure the email client for the NetAdmin user account. (Hint: Use www.ptmu.test for both the incoming and outgoing mail server.)

      b.   Send an email to the user at **PC1**.

      c.   Upload the **secret.txt** file to the FTP server. Do not change the file.

Note: The score for the server side player will be **43/44** until the client side player successfully downloads the **secret.txt** file, modifies the file, and then uploads it to the **www.ptmu.test** FTP server.

Part 3: Client Side Player - Configure and Verify Access to Services

Step 1.   Configure and verify PC addressing.

    a.   Configure **PC1** and **PC2** to automatically obtain addressing.

    b.   PC1 and PC2 should be able to access the web page using the IP address, **http://172.16.1.5**, as well as the domain name, **http://www.ptmu.test**.

    c.   The score for the client side player should be 21/33.

Step 2.   Configure and verify PC email accounts.

    a.   Configure email accounts according to the requirements at **www.ptmu.test/user.html**.

    b.   Verify that PC1 received an email from NetAdmin and send a reply.

    c.   Send an email from PC1 to PC2. Note: Scoring will not change.

    d.   Verify that PC2 received an email from PC1.

    e.   The score for the client side player should be 31/33.

Step 3.   Upload and download a file from the FTP server.

    a.   From PC2, access the FTP server and download the **secret.txt** file.

    b.   Open the **secret.txt** file, change only the secret word to **apple**, and upload the file.

    c.   The server side player score should be **44/44** and the client side player score should be **33/33**.

CHAPTER 11

Build a Small Network

The Study Guide portion of this chapter uses a combination of matching, fill-in-the-blank, multiple-choice, and open-ended question exercises to test your knowledge and skills of basic router concepts and configuration. The Lab and Activities portion of this chapter includes all the online curriculum labs and Packet Tracer activities to ensure that you have mastered the hands-on skills needed to understand basic IP addressing and router configuration.

As you work through this chapter, use Chapter 11 in *Introduction to Networks v6 Companion Guide* or use the corresponding Chapter 11 in the Introduction to Networks online curriculum for assistance.

Study Guide

So far, you have learned about the services that a data network can provide to the human network, examined the features of each layer of the OSI model and the operations of TCP/IP protocols, and looked in detail at Ethernet. In this chapter, we step back and see how to assemble these elements together in a functioning network that can be maintained.

Network Design

Growth is a natural process for many small businesses, and their networks must grow accordingly. Ideally, the network administrator has enough lead time to make intelligent decisions about growing the network in line with the growth of the company.

Devices in a Small Network

To meet user requirements, even small networks require planning and design. Planning ensures that all requirements, cost factors, and deployment options are given due consideration. When selecting the type of intermediate devices, a number of factors need to be considered.

Match the definition on the left with a design term on the right.

Definition

_____ Helps administrators track devices and control access to resources on the network

_____ Devices should be configured to prioritize real-time traffic, such as voice and video.

_____ Reliability can be increased by eliminating single points of failure.

_____ Small networks normally use DSL or cable

_____ A device that includes expansion slots that can be used to add new features and capabilities.

_____ A design factor that is impacted by things such as device capacity, management capability, and security features.

_____ A device with a specific number and type of ports or interfaces.

Term

a. WAN connection

b. IP addressing scheme

c. Modular configuration

d. Traffic management

e. Redundancy

f. Fixed configuration

g. Cost

Protocols in a Small Network

Match the services or protocols on the left with a server on the right.

Services and Protocols

    a. Uses SMTP, POP3, and/or IMAP

    b. Service that provides the IP address of a website or domain name so a host can connect to it

    c. Service that allows administrators to log in to a host from a remote location and control the host as if they were logged in locally

    d. Uses HTTP

    e. Service that allows for the download and upload of files between a client and server

    f. Service that assigns the IP address, subnet mask, default gateway, and other information to clients

Servers

_____ web server

_____ Telnet/SSH server

_____ FTP server

_____ DNS server

_____ email server

_____ DHCPv4 server

Scale to Larger Networks

List and briefly describe four elements required to scale a network.

_____

_____

_____

_____

What tool do network administrators use to capture traffic for evaluation purposes?

_____

Network Security

Attacks to a network can be devastating and can result in a loss of time and money due to damage or theft of important information or assets. Even in small networks, it is necessary to consider security threats and vulnerabilities when planning a network implementation.

Security Threats and Vulnerabilities

In Table 11-1, indicate which security threat applies to each scenario.

Table 11-1   Identify the Type of Security Threat

Scenario	Information Theft	Identity Theft	Data Loss/ Manipulation	Disruption of Service
Preventing legal users from accessing data services				
Making illegal online purchases				
Sending a virus to reformat a hard drive				

Scenario	Information Theft	Identity Theft	Data Loss/ Manipulation	Disruption of Service
Stealing a company's user database				
Overloading a network to keep users out				
Impersonating someone to obtain credit				
Altering data records				
Accessing scientific research reports				

Network Attacks

Match the scenario on the left with the type of security attack on the right.

Scenario

a. Sharon works for the finance department in her company. Her network administrator has given the finance department employees public IP addresses to access the Internet bank account. After an hour of work, the finance department members are told that the company bank account has been compromised.

b. Jeremiah downloaded some software from the Internet. He opened the file and his hard drive crashed immediately. He lost all information on his computer.

c. Angela receives an email with a link to her favorite online store, which is having a sale. She uses the link provided and is directed to a site that looks like her favorite online store. She orders from the web page using her credit card. Later, Angela discovers that her credit card has been used to pay for additional merchandise that she did not order.

d. Eli opened an email sent to him by a friend. Later in the day, Eli received telephone calls from his friends saying they received emails from him that he did not knowingly send.

e. George is ordering a pair of shoes from a bidding site. There are 20 seconds left in the bidding cycle. George decides to ping the bidding site, over and over again, to stop anyone else from bidding on his shoes. The 20 seconds pass, and George wins the bid.

f. Arianna was working on the Internet. A pop-up appeared stating that she needed to update her operating system by clicking the link. When she clicked the link, a program was installed on her computer (unknown to Arianna).

Type of Security Attack

_____ Trojan horse

_____ Denial of Service

_____ Access

_____ Worm

_____ Reconnaissance

_____ Virus

Network Attack Mitigation

Mitigating network attacks requires a comprehensive policy that includes regular data backups, installing upgrades, patching antivirus software, controlling access to the network, implementing firewalls, and maintaining endpoint security.

Match the description on the left to the attack mitigation techniques listed on the right.

Description

a. A network security service that provides the primary framework to set up access control on a network device.

b. The most effective way to mitigate a worm attack on host systems.

c. Determines who is allowed to access a network.

d. Determines what a user can do while accessing a network.

e. Monitors the actions a user performs while accessing the network.

f. A technique implemented by many firewall products to monitor incoming and outgoing traffic.

g. Depends on well-documented policies in place and includes employee training on the proper use of the network.

Attack Mitigation Technique

_____ AAA

_____ Accounting

_____ Endpoint security

_____ Patches

_____ Stateful packet inspection

_____ Authorize

_____ Authenticate

Device Security

In the space provided, record the commands to implement the following security policy on a router or switch:

- Encrypt all plain-text passwords.

- Enforce minimum password length of ten characters.

- Allow up to five attempts within 1 minute, after which additional attempts are blocked for 5 minutes.

- Enforce a 20-minute timeout on Telnet lines.

- Set **example.com** as the domain.

- Create a user named **admin** with **OnlyCisco1** as the password. Use the secret parameter.

- Allow only Secure Shell (SSH) access that uses a 2048-bit key and enforces local logins.

Script (include prompt):

_____

_____

_____

_____

_____

_____

_____

_____

_____

_____

_____

_____

Packet Tracer
☐ Activity

Packet Tracer Exercise 11-1: SSH Configuration and Verification

Now you are ready to use Packet Tracer to apply your documented configuration. Download and open the file LSG01-1101.pka found at the companion website for this book. Refer to the Introduction of this book for specifics on accessing files.

Note: The following instructions are also contained within the Packet Tracer Exercise.

In this Packet Tracer activity, you will configure a router for SSH access. Use the commands you documented in the section "Device Security." You will then verify that you can remotely connect to the router using an SSH connection.

Requirements

R1 is already configured with basic device settings. Use the password **LSG01only!** to access the privileged EXEC mode.

Configure R1 for SSH access using your script based on the following security policy:

- Encrypt all plain-text passwords.
- Enforce minimum password length of ten characters.
- Allow up to five attempts within 1 minute, after which additional attempts are blocked for **5** minutes.
- Enforce a 20-minute timeout on Telnet lines.
- Set **example.com** as the domain.
- Create a user named **admin** with **OnlyCisco1** as the password. Use the secret parameter.
- Allow only Secure Shell (SSH) access that uses a 2048-bit key and enforces local logins.

You should be able to connect to R1 from the PC1 using the command **ssh -l admin 10.1.1.1**. The **-l** is a lowercase "L," not a one.

Your completion percentage should be 100%. If it's not, click **Check Results** to see which required components are not yet completed.

Basic Network Performance

After the network has been implemented, a network administrator must be able to test the network connectivity to ensure that it is operating appropriately. In addition, it is a good idea for the network administrator to document the network.

Using the ping Command

In Table 11-2, match the symbol with the correct ping reply message description.

Table 11-2   Identify the Meaning of a Cisco Router Ping Message

Description	!	.	U
An ICMP unreachable message was received.			
Indicates receipt of an ICMP echo reply message.			
Indicates time expired while waiting for an ICMP echo reply message.			

Refer to Figure 11-1. You need to test routing to make sure that R2 can route to end devices attached to the R1 LAN. In the command output that follows the figure, complete the commands to do an extended ping, testing connectivity to the R2 LAN interface.

Figure 11-1   Extended ping Topology

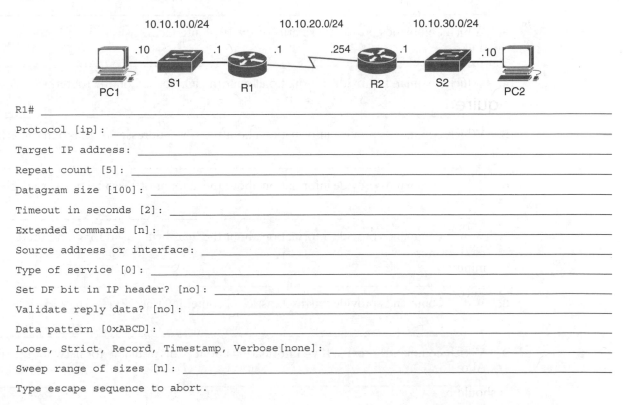

```
R1# _____

Protocol [ip]: _____

Target IP address: _____

Repeat count [5]: _____

Datagram size [100]: _____

Timeout in seconds [2]: _____

Extended commands [n]: _____

Source address or interface: _____

Type of service [0]: _____

Set DF bit in IP header? [no]: _____

Validate reply data? [no]: _____

Data pattern [0xABCD]: _____

Loose, Strict, Record, Timestamp, Verbose[none]: _____

Sweep range of sizes [n]: _____

Type escape sequence to abort.
```

```
Sending 5, 100-byte ICMP Echos to 10.10.30.1, timeout is 2 seconds:
Packet sent with a source address of 10.10.10.1
!!!!!
Success rate is 100 percent (5/5), round-trip min/avg/max = 2/3/4 ms
```

Tracing a Route

Refer to Figure 11-1. What command would you use, including the prompt, to trace a route from PC1 to PC2?

_____

What command would you use to trace a route from R1 to PC2?

_____

Show Commands

Network technicians use **show** commands extensively for viewing configuration files, checking the status of device interfaces and processes, and verifying the device operational status. Answer the following questions related to **show** commands.

1. Which commands would provide the IP address, network prefix, and interface?

   _____

   _____

2. Which commands provide the IPv4 address and interface assignment, but not the network prefix?

   _____

3. Which commands provide the status of the IPv4 interfaces?

   _____

4. Which commands provide information about the IOS loaded on the router?

   _____

5. Which commands provide information about the IPv4 addresses of the router interfaces?

   _____

6. Which commands provide information about the amount of Flash memory available?

   _____

7. Which commands provide information about the lines being used for configuration or device monitoring?

   _____

8. Which commands provide traffic statistics of router interfaces?

   _____

9. Which commands provide IPv4 information about paths available for network traffic?

   _____

Match the **show** command description on the left with the **show** command on the right.

Show Command Description

a. You are on a call with the Cisco Technical Assistance personnel. They ask you for the switch IOS name, RAM, NVRAM, and flash available. They also ask for the hexadecimal boot location.

b. You suspect there is a problem with the current switch configuration. You want to see the saved configuration so that you can compare it to what is currently running.

c. Your network documentation really needs to be updated. A quick listing of the IPv4 addresses of your routers in relation to their MAC addresses would help finish the task for recording purposes.

d. You are running the EIGRP routing protocol and need to know the update intervals and what active interfaces and networks are being advertised by your router.

e. You cannot get to the Internet. You need to find out whether your router has a path to the Internet and which protocols are being used to provide the paths.

f. A switch is the closest intermediary device to you. It has 24 ports. You want to see a simple list of the ports being used, their status, and the VLAN IPv4 address of the switch.

Show Command

_____ show ip protocol

_____ show arp

_____ show ip route

_____ show version

_____ show ip interface brief

_____ show startup-config

Network Troubleshooting

Network problems can be simple or complex, and can result from a combination of hardware, software, and connectivity issues.

Troubleshooting Methodology

Whether four steps or fifteen steps, efficient troubleshooting methodologies are usually based on the scientific method. Order the following troubleshooting steps by numbering them from one to six.

Step	Description
_____	Document Findings, Actions, and Outcomes
_____	Verify Full System Functionality and Implement Preventive Measures
_____	Test the Theory to Determine Cause
_____	Establish a Theory of Probable Causes
_____	Establish a Plan of Action to Resolve the Problem and Implement the Solution
_____	Identify the Problem

Packet Tracer Exercise 11-2: Troubleshooting Scenario

At this stage in your networking studies, you should be able to effectively troubleshoot small network connectivity issues. If you have had an opportunity to work with real equipment, either in a lab setting or on a production network, you know that the physical layer can often be the cause of connectivity issues. All the devices in the network must be correctly connected in accordance with the physical topology. Devices must be powered on and the NIC link lights should be active. If there are still physical layer issues, they are usually due to using the wrong cable, a faulty cable, or a bad NIC.

After you are sure the physical layer is operational and all interfaces are active, check the IP address settings for the devices involved in the connectivity issue. Devices could have the wrong IP address, the wrong subnet mask, or the wrong default gateway.

Now you are ready to use Packet Tracer to apply your troubleshooting skills. Download and open the file LSG01-1102.pka found at the companion website for this book. Refer to the Introduction of this book for specifics on accessing files.

Note: The following instructions are also contained in the Packet Tracer Exercise.

In this Packet Tracer activity, you will resolve several connectivity issues that prevent PC1 from accessing the LSG Web Server.

Requirements

All devices are already configured, although there are errors. Routers should have the first IP address in the network. R2 should have the second IP address for the network it shares with R1. Troubleshoot the connectivity issues until PC1 can access the web page on the LSG Web Server. Helpful tools include **ping**, **trace**, and **show** commands.

Your completion percentage should be 100%. **Check Results** is disabled.

Labs and Activities

Command Reference

In Table 11-3, record the command, including the correct router or switch prompt, that fits the description. Fill in any blanks with the appropriate missing information.

Table 11-3   Commands for Chapter 11, Build a Small Network

Command	Description
	Cisco security feature that can assist a network administrator in securing a system.
	Prevents unauthorized individuals from viewing passwords in plain text in the configuration file.
	Sets the minimum length of all passwords to 8 characters.
	After 5 login attempts within 60 seconds, this command will block further login attempts for 120 seconds.
	After 10 minutes of idle time, the user will be logged out of VTY or console lines.
	Configures the router to use the local database to authenticate remote users.
	Configures the lines to only use SSH as the remote access protocol.
	Sets the domain as example.com on the router.
	Configures **admin** as a user with the password **cisco**.
	Tests connectivity to a remote host at 10.1.1.1.
	On a router, this command returns a list of hops from the source to the destination at 10.1.1.1.
	On a Windows PC, this command returns a list of hops from the source to the destination at 10.1.1.1.
	Displays the current router configuration stored in RAM.
	Displays all the interface information on the router.
	Displays the ARP cache on the router.
	Displays the IPv4 routing table on the router.
	Displays a short listing of the interfaces with the protocol status and IP address/subnet mask configuration.
	Displays a variety of information about the router hardware and software including model, number and type of interfaces, and IOS version.
	Displays the IP address configuration on a Windows PC.

Command	Description
	Displays IP addressing information and the MAC address on a Windows PC.
	Displays all the cached DNS entries on a Windows PC.
	Lists all devices currently in the ARP cache on a Windows PC.
	Clears the ARP cache on a Windows PC.
	Displays a summary of all directly connected Cisco devices.
	Displays all directly connected Cisco devices including the IP address and IOS version.
	Displays abbreviated output of the **show ip interface** command.
	Used to monitor the status of ICMP messages on a Cisco router.
	Turns off all debugging on a Cisco router.
	Sends log messages to the terminal when accessing a Cisco router remotely.

11.0.1.2 Class Activity–Did You Notice?

Objectives

Explain how a small network of directly connected segments is created, configured, and verified.

Topology

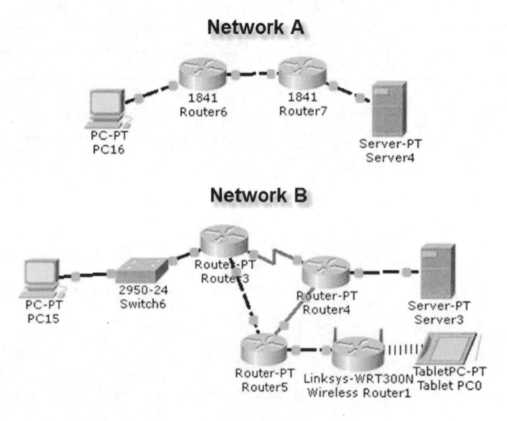

Background/Scenario

Take a look at the two networks in the topology diagram. Answer the following questions and record your answers in the Reflection section to share with the class.

- Visually compare and contrast Network A and Network B. How are the two networks the same?

- Make note of the devices used in each network design. Because the devices are labeled, you already know what types of end and intermediary devices they are. How are the two networks different? Is the number of devices present in one network the only differentiating factor? Justify your answer.

- Which network would you select if you owned a small- to medium-sized business? Justify your selected network based on cost, speed, ports, expandability, and manageability.

Required Resources

- Recording capabilities (paper, tablet, and so on) for reflective comments to be shared with the class.

Reflection

Reflect upon your comparisons of the two network scenarios. What are some things you noted as points of interest?

_____

_____

_____

11.2.2.6 Lab–Researching Network Security Threats

Objectives

Part 1: Explore the SANS Website

Part 2: Identify Recent Network Security Threats

Part 3: Detail a Specific Network Security Threat

Background/Scenario

To defend a network against attacks, an administrator must identify external threats that pose a danger to the network. Security websites can be used to identify emerging threats and provide mitigation options for defending a network.

One of the most popular and trusted sites for defending against computer and network security threats is SysAdmin, Audit, Network, Security (SANS). The SANS site provides multiple resources, including a list of the top 20 Critical Security Controls for Effective Cyber Defense and the weekly @Risk: The Consensus Security Alert newsletter. This newsletter details new network attacks and vulnerabilities.

In this lab, you will navigate to and explore the SANS site, use the SANS site to identify recent network security threats, research other websites that identify threats, and research and present the details about a specific network attack.

Required Resources

- Device with Internet access
- Presentation computer with PowerPoint or other presentation software installed

Part 1: Exploring the SANS Website

In Part 1, navigate to the SANS website and explore the available resources.

Step 1.   Locate SANS resources.

Navigate to www.SANS.org. From the home page, highlight the **Resources** menu.

List three available resources.

_____

_____

Step 2.   Locate the Top 20 Critical Controls.

The **Twenty Critical Security Controls for Effective Cyber Defense** listed on the SANS website are the culmination of a public-private partnership involving the Department of Defense (DoD), National Security Association, Center for Internet Security (CIS), and the SANS Institute. The list was developed to prioritize the cyber security controls and spending for DoD. It has become the centerpiece for effective security programs for the United States government. From the **Resources** menu, select **Top 20 Critical Controls**.

Select one of the 20 Critical Controls and list three of the implementation suggestions for this control.

_____

_____

_____

_____

_____

Step 3.   Locate the Newsletters menu.

Highlight the **Resources** menu, select **Newsletters**. Briefly describe each of the three newsletters available.

_____

_____

_____

_____

_____

Part 2: Identify Recent Network Security Threats

In Part 2, you will research recent network security threats using the SANS site and identify other sites containing security threat information.

Step 1.   Locate the @Risk: Consensus Security Alert Newsletter Archive.

From the **Newsletters** page, select **Archive** for the @RISK: The Consensus Security Alert. Scroll down to **Archives Volumes** and select a recent weekly newsletter. Review the **Notable Recent Security Issues and Most Popular Malware Files** sections.

List some recent attacks. Browse multiple recent newsletters, if necessary.

_____

_____

_____

Step 2.   Identify sites providing recent security threat information.

Besides the SANS site, identify some other websites that provide recent security threat information.

_____

_____

_____

List some of the recent security threats detailed on these websites.

_____

_____

_____

Part 3: Detail a Specific Network Security Attack

In Part 3, you will research a specific network attack that has occurred and create a presentation based on your findings. Complete the form below based on your findings.

Step 1. Complete the following form for the selected network attack.

Name of attack:	
Type of attack:	
Dates of attacks:	
Computers/Organizations affected:	
How it works and what it did:	

Mitigation options:	
References and info links:	

Follow the instructor's guidelines to complete the presentation.

Reflection

1. What steps can you take to protect your own computer?

   _____

   _____

   _____

2. What are some important steps that organizations can take to protect their resources?

   _____

   _____

   _____

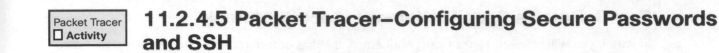

11.2.4.5 Packet Tracer–Configuring Secure Passwords and SSH

Topology

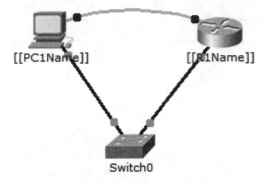

[[PC1Name]]   [[R1Name]]

Switch0

Addressing Table

Device	Interface	IP Address	Subnet Mask	Default Gateway
[[R1Name]]	G0/0	[[R1Add]]	255.255.255.0	N/A
[[PC1Name]]	NIC	[[PC1Add]]	255.255.255.0	[[R1Add]]

Scenario

The network administrator has asked you to prepare [[R1Name]] for deployment. Before it can be connected to the network, security measures must be enabled.

Requirements

- Configure IP addressing on [[PC1Name]] according to the Addressing Table.
- Console into [[R1Name]] from the Terminal on PC-A.
- Configure IP addressing on [[R1Name]] and enable the interface.
- Configure the hostname as [[R1Name]].
- Encrypt all plaintext passwords.

  `[[R1Name]](config)# service password-encryption`
- Set a strong secret password of your choosing.
- Set the domain name to [[R1Name]].com (case-sensitive for scoring in PT).

  `[[R1Name]](config)# ip domain-name [[R1Name]].com`
- Create a user of your choosing with a strong password.

  `[[R1Name]](config)# username any_user password any_password`
- Generate 1024-bit RSA keys.

Note: In Packet Tracer, enter the **crypto key generate rsa** command and press Enter to continue.

```
[[R1Name]](config)# crypto key generate rsa
```

- Block anyone for three minutes who fails to log in after four attempts within a two-minute period.

```
[[R1Name]](config)# login block-for 180 attempts 4 within 120
```

- Configure the VTY lines for SSH access and use the local user profiles for authentication.

```
[[R1Name]](config)# line vty 0 4
[[R1Name]](config-line)# transport input ssh
[[R1Name]](config-line)# login local
```

- Save the configuration to NVRAM.

- Be prepared to demonstrate to your instructor that you have established SSH access from **[[PC1Name]]** to **[[R1Name]]**.

11.2.4.6 Lab–Accessing Network Devices with SSH

Topology

Addressing Table

Device	Interface	IP Address	Subnet Mask	Default Gateway
R1	G0/1	192.168.1.1	255.255.255.0	N/A
S1	VLAN 1	192.168.1.11	255.255.255.0	192.168.1.1
PC-A	NIC	192.168.1.3	255.255.255.0	192.168.1.1

Objectives

Part 1: Configure Basic Device Settings

Part 2: Configure the Router for SSH Access

Part 3: Configure the Switch for SSH Access

Part 4: SSH from the CLI on the Switch

Background/Scenario

In the past, Telnet was the most common network protocol used to remotely configure network devices. Telnet does not encrypt the information between the client and server. This allows a network sniffer to intercept passwords and configuration information.

Secure Shell (SSH) is a network protocol that establishes a secure terminal emulation connection to a router or other networking device. SSH encrypts all information that passes over the network link and provides authentication of the remote computer. SSH is rapidly replacing Telnet as the remote login tool of choice for network professionals. SSH is most often used to log in to a remote device and execute commands; however, it can also transfer files using the associated Secure FTP (SFTP) or Secure Copy (SCP) protocols.

The network devices that are communicating must be configured to support SSH in order for SSH to function. In this lab, you will enable the SSH server on a router and then connect to that router using a PC with an SSH client installed. On a local network, the connection is normally made using Ethernet and IP.

Note: The routers used with CCNA hands-on labs are Cisco 1941 Integrated Services Routers (ISRs) with Cisco IOS Release 15.2(4)M3 (universalk9 image). The switches used are Cisco Catalyst 2960s with Cisco IOS Release 15.0(2) (lanbasek9 image). Other routers, switches, and Cisco IOS versions can be used. Depending on the model and Cisco IOS version, the commands available and the output produced might vary from what is shown in the labs. Refer to the Router Interface Summary Table at the end of this lab for the correct interface identifiers.

Note: Make sure that the routers and switches have been erased and have no startup configurations. If you are unsure, contact your instructor.

Required Resources

- 1 Router (Cisco 1941 with Cisco IOS Release 15.2(4)M3 universal image or comparable)

- 1 Switch (Cisco 2960 with Cisco IOS Release 15.0(2) lanbasek9 image or comparable)

- 1 PC (Windows 7 or 8 with terminal emulation program, such as Tera Term, and Wireshark installed)

- Console cables to configure the Cisco IOS devices via the console ports

- Ethernet cables as shown in the topology

Part 1: Configure Basic Device Settings

In Part 1, you will set up the network topology and configure basic settings, such as the interface IP addresses, device access, and passwords on the router.

Step 1. Cable the network as shown in the topology.

Step 2. Initialize and reload the router and switch.

Step 3. Configure the router.

   a. Console into the router and enable privileged EXEC mode.

   b. Enter configuration mode.

   c. Disable DNS lookup to prevent the router from attempting to translate incorrectly entered commands as though they were hostnames.

   d. Assign **class** as the privileged EXEC encrypted password.

   e. Assign **cisco** as the console password and enable login.

   f. Assign **cisco** as the VTY password and enable login.

   g. Encrypt the plaintext passwords.

   h. Create a banner that will warn anyone accessing the device that unauthorized access is prohibited.

   i. Configure and activate the G0/1 interface on the router using the information contained in the Addressing Table.

   j. Save the running configuration to the startup configuration file.

Step 4. Configure PC-A.

   a. Configure PC-A with an IP address and subnet mask.

   b. Configure a default gateway for PC-A.

Step 5. Verify network connectivity.

   Ping R1 from PC-A. If the ping fails, troubleshoot the connection.

Part 2: Configure the Router for SSH Access

Using Telnet to connect to a network device is a security risk because all information is transmitted in a clear text format. SSH encrypts the session data and provides device authentication, which is why SSH is recommended for remote connections. In Part 2, you will configure the router to accept SSH connections over the VTY lines.

Step 1.   Configure device authentication.

The device name and domain are used as part of the crypto key when it is generated. Therefore, these names must be entered prior to issuing the **crypto key** command.

a.   Configure the device name.

```
Router(config)# hostname R1
```

b.   Configure the domain for the device.

```
R1(config)# ip domain-name ccna-lab.com
```

Step 2.   Configure the encryption key method.

```
R1(config)# crypto key generate rsa modulus 1024
The name for the keys will be: R1.ccna-lab.com

% The key modulus size is 1024 bits
% Generating 1024 bit RSA keys, keys will be non-exportable...
[OK] (elapsed time was 1 seconds)

R1(config)#
*Jan 28 21:09:29.867: %SSH-5-ENABLED: SSH 1.99 has been enabled
```

Step 3.   Configure a local database username.

```
R1(config)# username admin privilege 15 secret adminpass
```

Note: A privilege level of 15 gives the user administrator rights.

Step 4.   Enable SSH on the VTY lines.

a.   Enable Telnet and SSH on the inbound VTY lines using the **transport input** command.

```
R1(config)# line vty 0 4
R1(config-line)# transport input telnet ssh
```

b.   Change the login method to use the local database for user verification.

```
R1(config-line)# login local
R1(config-line)# end
R1#
```

Step 5.   Save the running configuration to the startup configuration file.

```
R1# copy running-config startup-config
Destination filename [startup-config]?
Building configuration...
[OK]
R1#
```

Step 6.   Establish an SSH connection to the router.

    a.   Start Tera Term from PC-A.

    b.   Establish an SSH session to R1. Use the username **admin** and password **adminpass**. You should be able to establish an SSH session with R1.

Part 3: Configure the Switch for SSH Access

In Part 3, you will configure the switch in the topology to accept SSH connections. After the switch has been configured, establish an SSH session using Tera Term.

Step 1.   Configure the basic settings on the switch.

    a.   Console into the switch and enable privileged EXEC mode.

    b.   Enter configuration mode.

    c.   Disable DNS lookup to prevent the router from attempting to translate incorrectly entered commands as though they were hostnames.

    d.   Assign **class** as the privileged EXEC encrypted password.

    e.   Assign **cisco** as the console password and enable login.

    f.   Assign **cisco** as the VTY password and enable login.

    g.   Encrypt the plain text passwords.

    h.   Create a banner that will warn anyone accessing the device that unauthorized access is prohibited.

    i.   Configure and activate the VLAN 1 interface on the switch according to the Addressing Table.

    j.   Save the running configuration to the startup configuration file.

Step 2.   Configure the switch for SSH connectivity.

Use the same commands that you used to configure SSH on the router in Part 2 to configure SSH for the switch.

    a.   Configure the device name as listed in the Addressing Table.

    b.   Configure the domain for the device.

```
S1(config)# ip domain-name ccna-lab.com
```

    c.   Configure the encryption key method.

```
S1(config)# crypto key generate rsa modulus 1024
```

    d.   Configure a local database username.

```
S1(config)# username admin privilege 15 secret adminpass
```

    e.   Enable Telnet and SSH on the VTY lines.

```
S1(config)# line vty 0 15
S1(config-line)# transport input telnet ssh
```

    f.   Change the login method to use the local database for user verification.

```
S1(config-line)# login local
S1(config-line)# end
```

Step 3.   Establish an SSH connection to the switch.

Start Tera Term from PC-A, and then SSH to the SVI interface on S1.

Are you able to establish an SSH session with the switch? _____

Part 4: SSH from the CLI on the Switch

The SSH client is built into the Cisco IOS and can be run from the CLI. In Part 4, you will SSH to the router from the CLI on the switch.

Step 1.   View the parameters available for the Cisco IOS SSH client.

Use the question mark (**?**) to display the parameter options available with the **ssh** command.

```
S1# ssh ?
  -c    Select encryption algorithm
  -l    Log in using this user name
  -m    Select HMAC algorithm
  -o    Specify options
  -p    Connect to this port
  -v    Specify SSH Protocol Version
  -vrf  Specify vrf name
  WORD  IP address or hostname of a remote system
```

Step 2.   SSH to R1 from S1.

a.   You must use the **–l admin** option when you SSH to R1. This allows you to log in as user **admin**. When prompted, enter **adminpass** for the password.

```
S1# ssh -l admin 192.168.1.1
Password:
*************************************************
   Warning: Unauthorized Access is Prohibited!
*************************************************

R1#
```

b.   You can return to S1 without closing the SSH session to R1 by pressing **Ctrl+Shift+6**. Release the **Ctrl+Shift+6** keys and press **x**. The switch privileged EXEC prompt displays.

```
R1#
S1#
```

c.   To return to the SSH session on R1, press Enter on a blank CLI line. You may need to press Enter a second time to see the router CLI prompt.

```
S1#
[Resuming connection 1 to 192.168.1.1 ... ]

R1#
```

d. To end the SSH session on R1, type **exit** at the router prompt.

```
R1# exit

[Connection to 192.168.1.1 closed by foreign host]
S1#
```

What versions of SSH are supported from the CLI?

Reflection

How would you provide multiple users, each with their own username, access to a network device?

Router Interface Summary Table

	Router Interface Summary			
Router Model	Ethernet Interface #1	Ethernet Interface #2	Serial Interface #1	Serial Interface #2
1800	Fast Ethernet 0/0 (F0/0)	Fast Ethernet 0/1 (F0/1)	Serial 0/0/0 (S0/0/0)	Serial 0/0/1 (S0/0/1)
1900	Gigabit Ethernet 0/0 (G0/0)	Gigabit Ethernet 0/1 (G0/1)	Serial 0/0/0 (S0/0/0)	Serial 0/0/1 (S0/0/1)
2801	Fast Ethernet 0/0 (F0/0)	Fast Ethernet 0/1 (F0/1)	Serial 0/1/0 (S0/1/0)	Serial 0/1/1 (S0/1/1)
2811	Fast Ethernet 0/0 (F0/0)	Fast Ethernet 0/1 (F0/1)	Serial 0/0/0 (S0/0/0)	Serial 0/0/1 (S0/0/1)
2900	Gigabit Ethernet 0/0 (G0/0)	Gigabit Ethernet 0/1 (G0/1)	Serial 0/0/0 (S0/0/0)	Serial 0/0/1 (S0/0/1)

Note: To find out how the router is configured, look at the interfaces to identify the type of router and how many interfaces the router has. There is no way to effectively list all the combinations of configurations for each router class. This table includes identifiers for the possible combinations of Ethernet and Serial interfaces in the device. The table does not include any other type of interface, even though a specific router may contain one. An example of this might be an ISDN BRI interface. The string in parentheses is the legal abbreviation that can be used in Cisco IOS commands to represent the interface.

11.2.4.7 Lab–Examining Telnet and SSH in Wireshark

Topology

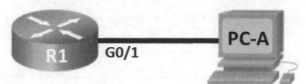

Addressing Table

Device	Interface	IP Address	Subnet Mask	Default Gateway
R1	G0/1	192.168.1.1	255.255.255.0	N/A
PC-A	NIC	192.168.1.3	255.255.255.0	192.168.1.1

Objectives

Part 1: Configure the Devices for SSH Access

Part 2: Examine a Telnet Session with Wireshark

Part 3: Examine an SSH Session with Wireshark

Background/Scenario

In this lab, you will configure a router to accept SSH connectivity, and use Wireshark to capture and view Telnet and SSH sessions. This will demonstrate the importance of encryption with SSH.

Note: The routers used with CCNA hands-on labs are Cisco 1941 Integrated Services Routers (ISRs) with Cisco IOS Release 15.2(4)M3 (universalk9 image). The switches used are Cisco Catalyst 2960s with Cisco IOS Release 15.0(2) (lanbasek9 image). Other routers, switches, and Cisco IOS versions can be used. Depending on the model and Cisco IOS version, the commands available and output produced might vary from what is shown in the labs. Refer to the Router Interface Summary Table at the end of this lab for the correct interface identifiers.

Note: Make sure that the routers and switches have been erased and have no startup configurations. If you are unsure, contact your instructor.

Required Resources

- 1 Router (Cisco 1941 with Cisco IOS Release 15.2(4)M3 universal image or comparable)
- 1 PC (Windows 7 or 8 with terminal emulation program, such as Tera Term, and Wireshark installed)
- Console cables to configure the Cisco IOS devices via the console ports
- Ethernet cables as shown in the topology

Part 1: Configure the Devices for SSH Access

In Part 1, you will set up the network topology and configure basic settings, such as the interface IP addresses, device access, and passwords on the router.

Step 1.   Cable the network as shown in the topology.

Step 2.   Initialize and reload the router.

Step 3.   Configure the basic settings on the router.

    a.   Console into the router and enable privileged EXEC mode.

    b.   Enter configuration mode.

    c.   Configure device name as listed in the Addressing Table.

    d.   Disable DNS lookup to prevent the router from attempting to translate incorrectly entered commands as though they were hostnames.

    e.   Assign **class** as the privileged EXEC encrypted password.

    f.   Assign **cisco** as the console password and enable login.

    g.   Assign **cisco** as the VTY password and enable login.

    h.   Encrypt the plain text passwords.

    i.   Create a banner that will warn anyone accessing the device that unauthorized access is prohibited.

    j.   Configure and activate the G0/1 interface using the information contained in the Addressing Table.

Step 4.   Configure R1 for SSH access.

    a.   Configure the domain for the device.

```
R1(config)# ip domain-name ccna-lab.com
```

    b.   Configure the encryption key method.

```
R1(config)# crypto key generate rsa modulus 1024
```

    c.   Configure a local database username.

```
R1(config)# username admin privilege 15 secret adminpass
```

    d.   Enable Telnet and SSH on the VTY lines.

```
R1(config)# line vty 0 4
R1(config-line)# transport input telnet ssh
```

    e.   Change the login method to use the local database for user verification.

```
R1(config-line)# login local
R1(config-line)# end
```

Step 5.   Save the running configuration to the startup configuration file.

Step 6.   Configure PC-A.

    a.   Configure PC-A with an IP address and subnet mask.

    b.   Configure a default gateway for PC-A.

Step 7.   Verify network connectivity.

    Ping R1 from PC-A. If the ping fails, troubleshoot the connection.

Part 2: Examine a Telnet Session with Wireshark

In Part 2, you will use Wireshark to capture and view the transmitted data of a Telnet session on the router. You will use Tera Term to telnet to R1, sign in, and then issue the **show run** command on the router.

Note: If a Telnet/SSH client software package is not installed on your PC, you must install one before continuing. Two popular freeware Telnet/SSH packages are Tera Term (http://download.cnet.com/Tera-Term/3000-20432_4-75766675.html) and PuTTY (www.putty.org).

Note: Telnet is not available from the command prompt in Windows 7, by default. To enable Telnet for use in the command prompt window, click **Start** > **Control Panel** > **Programs** > **Programs and Features** > **Turn Windows features on or off**. Click the **Telnet Client** check box, and then click **OK**.

Step 1.   Capture data.

    a.   Start Wireshark.

    b.   Start capturing data on the LAN interface.

Note: If you are unable to start the capture on the LAN interface, you may need to open Wireshark using the **Run as Administrator** option.

Step 2.   Start a Telnet session to the router.

    a.   Open Tera Term and select the **Telnet** Service radio button and in the Host field, enter **192.168.1.1**.

    What is the default TCP port for Telnet sessions? _____

    b.   At the Username: prompt, enter **admin** and at the Password: prompt, enter **adminpass**. These prompts are generated because you configured the VTY lines to use the local database with the **login local** command.

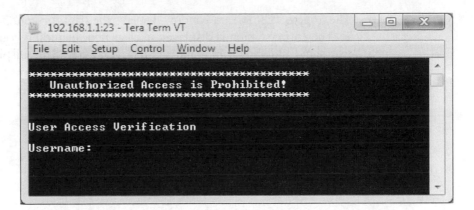

c. Issue the **show run** command.

```
R1# show run
```

d. Enter **exit** to exit the Telnet session and out of Tera Term.

```
R1# exit
```

Step 3. Stop the Wireshark capture.

Step 4. Apply a Telnet filter on the Wireshark capture data.

Step 5. Use the Follow TCP Stream feature in Wireshark to view the Telnet session.

a. Right-click one of the **Telnet** lines in the **Packet list** section of Wireshark, and from the drop-down list, select **Follow TCP Stream**.

b. The Follow TCP Stream window displays the data for your Telnet session with the router. The entire session is displayed in clear text, including your password. Notice that the username and **show run** command that you entered are displayed with duplicate characters. This is caused by the echo setting in Telnet to allow you to view the characters that you type on the screen.

c. After you have finished reviewing your Telnet session in the **Follow TCP Stream** window, click **Close**.

Part 3: Examine an SSH Session with Wireshark

In Part 3, you will use the Tera Term software to establish an SSH session with the router. Wireshark will be used to capture and view the data of this SSH session.

Step 1.   Open Wireshark and start capturing data on the LAN interface.

Step 2.   Start an SSH session on the router.

a. Open Tera Term and enter the G0/1 interface IP address of R1 in the Host: field of the Tera Term: New Connection window. Ensure that the **SSH** radio button is selected and then click **OK** to connect to the router.

What is the default TCP port used for SSH sessions? _____

b. The first time you establish an SSH session to a device, a **SECURITY WARNING** is generated to let you know that you have not connected to this device before. This message is part of the authentication process. Read the security warning and click **Continue.**

c. In the SSH Authentication window, enter **admin** for the username and **adminpass** for the passphrase. Click **OK** to sign into the router.

SSH Authentication

Logging in to 192.168.1.1

Authentication required.

User name: admin

Passphrase: •••••••••

☑ Remember password in memory

☐ Forward agent

◉ Use plain password to log in

◯ Use RSA/DSA/ECDSA/ED25519 key to log in   Private key file:

◯ Use rhosts to log in (SSH1)   Local user name:

Host private key file:

◯ Use challenge/response to log in(keyboard-interactive)

◯ Use Pageant to log in

OK   Disconnect

d.   You have established an SSH session on the router. The Tera Term software looks very similar to a command window. At the command prompt, issue the **show run** command.

192.168.1.1:22 - Tera Term VT

File   Edit   Setup   Control   Window   Help

```
************************************************
   Unauthorized Access is Prohibited!
************************************************

R1#show run
```

e.   Exit the SSH session by issuing the **exit** command.

```
R1# exit
```

Step 3.   Stop the Wireshark capture.

Step 4.   Apply an SSH filter on the Wireshark Capture data.

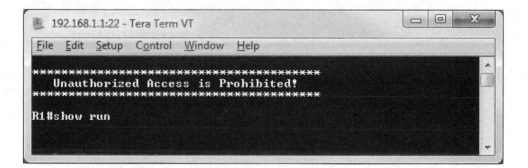

Filter: ssh   ▼   Expression...   Clear   Apply

Step 5.   Use the Follow TCP Stream feature in Wireshark to view the SSH session.

a.   Right-click one of the **SSHv2** lines in the **Packet list** section of Wireshark, and in the drop-down list, select the **Follow TCP Stream** option.

b. Examine the **Follow TCP Stream** window of your SSH session. The data has been encrypted and is unreadable. Compare the data in your SSH session to the data of your Telnet session.

```
Follow TCP Stream (tcp.stream eq 0)

Stream Content
SSH-1.99-Cisco-1.25
SSH-2.0-TTSSH/2.69 Win32
...l..../.....h(${.`.....Ydiffie-hellman-group-exchange-sha1,diffie-
hellman-group14-sha1,diffie-hellman-group1-sha1....ssh-
rsa...Jaes128-ctr,aes192-ctr,aes256-ctr,aes128-cbc,3des-cbc,aes192-
cbc,aes256-cbc...Jaes128-ctr,aes192-ctr,aes256-ctr,aes128-cbc,3des-
cbc,aes192-cbc,aes256-cbc....hmac-sha1,hmac-sha1-96....hmac-
sha1,hmac-
sha1-96....none....none........................j._..@..?
u.7....ecdh-sha2-nistp256,ecdh-sha2-nistp384,ecdh-sha2-
nistp521,diffie-hellman-group-exchange-sha256,diffie-hellman-group-
exchange-sha1,diffie-hellman-group14-sha1,diffie-hellman-group1-
sha1...Wecdsa-sha2-nistp256,ecdsa-sha2-nistp384,ecdsa-sha2-
nistp521,ssh-ed25519,ssh-rsa,ssh-dss....camellia256-ctr,aes256-

Entire conversation (9318 bytes)

Find    Save As    Print    ○ ASCII    ○ EBCDIC    ○ Hex Dump    ○ C Arrays    ◉ Raw

Help                          Filter Out This Stream         Close
```

Why is SSH preferred over Telnet for remote connections?

_____

_____

c. After examining your SSH session, click **Close**.

d. Close Wireshark.

Reflection

How would you provide multiple users, each with their own username, access to a network device?

_____

Router Interface Summary Table

Router Interface Summary			
Router Model	Ethernet Interface #1	Ethernet Interface #2	Serial Interface #1	Serial Interface #2
---	---	---	---	---
1800	Fast Ethernet 0/0 (F0/0)	Fast Ethernet 0/1 (F0/1)	Serial 0/0/0 (S0/0/0)	Serial 0/0/1 (S0/0/1)
1900	Gigabit Ethernet 0/0 (G0/0)	Gigabit Ethernet 0/1 (G0/1)	Serial 0/0/0 (S0/0/0)	Serial 0/0/1 (S0/0/1)
2801	Fast Ethernet 0/0 (F0/0)	Fast Ethernet 0/1 (F0/1)	Serial 0/1/0 (S0/1/0)	Serial 0/1/1 (S0/1/1)
2811	Fast Ethernet 0/0 (F0/0)	Fast Ethernet 0/1 (F0/1)	Serial 0/0/0 (S0/0/0)	Serial 0/0/1 (S0/0/1)
2900	Gigabit Ethernet 0/0 (G0/0)	Gigabit Ethernet 0/1 (G0/1)	Serial 0/0/0 (S0/0/0)	Serial 0/0/1 (S0/0/1)

Note: To find out how the router is configured, look at the interfaces to identify the type of router and how many interfaces the router has. There is no way to effectively list all the combinations of configurations for each router class. This table includes identifiers for the possible combinations of Ethernet and Serial interfaces in the device. The table does not include any other type of interface, even though a specific router may contain one. An example of this might be an ISDN BRI interface. The string in parentheses is the legal abbreviation that can be used in Cisco IOS commands to represent the interface.

11.2.4.8 Lab–Securing Network Devices

Topology

Addressing Table

Device	Interface	IP Address	Subnet Mask	Default Gateway
R1	G0/1	192.168.1.1	255.255.255.0	N/A
S1	VLAN 1	192.168.1.11	255.255.255.0	192.168.1.1
PC-A	NIC	192.168.1.3	255.255.255.0	192.168.1.1

Objectives

Part 1: Configure Basic Device Settings

Part 2: Configure Basic Security Measures on the Router

Part 3: Configure Basic Security Measures on the Switch

Background/Scenario

It is recommended that all network devices be configured with at least a minimum set of best practice security commands. This includes end user devices, servers, and network devices, such as routers and switches.

In this lab, you will configure the network devices in the topology to accept SSH sessions for remote management. You will also use the IOS CLI to configure common, basic best practice security measures. You will then test the security measures to verify that they are properly implemented and working correctly.

Note: The routers used with CCNA hands-on labs are Cisco 1941 ISRs with Cisco IOS Release 15.2(4)M3 (universalk9 image). The switches used are Cisco Catalyst 2960s with Cisco IOS Release 15.0(2) (lanbasek9 image). Other routers, switches, and Cisco IOS versions can be used. Depending on the model and Cisco IOS version, the commands available and output produced might vary from what is shown in the labs. Refer to the Router Interface Summary table at the end of the lab for the correct interface identifiers.

Note: Make sure that the routers and switches have been erased and have no startup configurations. If you are unsure, contact your instructor.

Required Resources

- 1 Router (Cisco 1941 with Cisco IOS software, release 15.2(4)M3 universal image or comparable)

- 1 Switch (Cisco 2960 with Cisco IOS Release 15.0(2) lanbasek9 image or comparable)

- 1 PC (Windows 7 or 8 with terminal emulation program, such as Tera Term)

- Console cables to configure the Cisco IOS devices via the console ports

- Ethernet cables as shown in the topology

Part 1: Configure Basic Device Settings

In Part 1, you will set up the network topology and configure basic settings, such as the interface IP addresses, device access, and passwords on the devices.

Step 1. Cable the network as shown in the topology.

Attach the devices shown in the topology and cable as necessary.

Step 2. Initialize and reload the router and switch.

Step 3. Configure the router and switch.

    a. Console into the device and enable privileged EXEC mode.

    b. Assign the device name according to the Addressing Table.

    c. Disable DNS lookup to prevent the router from attempting to translate incorrectly entered commands as though they were hostnames.

    d. Assign **class** as the privileged EXEC encrypted password.

    e. Assign **cisco** as the console password and enable login.

    f. Assign **cisco** as the VTY password and enable login.

    g. Create a banner that warns anyone accessing the device that unauthorized access is prohibited.

    h. Configure and activate the G0/1 interface on the router using the information contained in the Addressing Table.

    i. Configure the default SVI on the switch with the IP address information according to the Addressing Table.

    j. Save the running configuration to the startup configuration file.

Part 2: Configure Basic Security Measures on the Router

Step 1. Encrypt the clear text passwords.

```
R1(config)# service password-encryption
```

Step 2. Strengthen passwords.

An administrator should ensure that passwords meet the standard guidelines for strong passwords. These guidelines could include combining letters, numbers, and special characters in the password and setting a minimum length.

Note: Best practice guidelines require the use of strong passwords, such as those shown here, in a production environment. However, the other labs in this course use the cisco and class passwords for ease in performing the labs.

    a. Change the privileged EXEC encrypted password to meet guidelines.

```
R1(config)# enable secret Enablep@55
```

    b. Require that a minimum of 10 characters be used for all passwords.

```
R1(config)# security passwords min-length 10
```

Step 3. Enable SSH connections.

    a. Assign the domain name as CCNA-lab.com.

```
R1(config)# ip domain-name CCNA-lab.com
```

    b. Create a local user database entry to use when connecting to the router via SSH. The password should meet strong password standards, and the user should have user EXEC access. If privilege level is not specified in the command, the user will have user EXEC (level 15) access by default.

```
R1(config)# username SSHadmin privilege 15 secret Admin1p@55
```

    c. Configure the transport input for the VTY lines so that they accept SSH connections, but do not allow Telnet connections.

```
R1(config)# line vty 0 4
R1(config-line)# transport input ssh
```

    d. The VTY lines should use the local user database for authentication.

```
R1(config-line)# login local
R1(config-line)# exit
```

    e. Generate an RSA crypto key using a modulus of 1024 bits.

```
R1(config)# crypto key generate rsa modulus 1024
```

Step 4. Secure the console and VTY lines.

    a. You can set the router to log out of a connection that has been idle for a specified time. If a network administrator was logged into a networking device and was suddenly called away, this command automatically logs the user out after the specified time. The following commands cause the line to log out after 5 minutes of inactivity.

```
R1(config)# line console 0
R1(config-line)# exec-timeout 5 0
R1(config-line)# line vty 0 4
R1(config-line)# exec-timeout 5 0
R1(config-line)# exit
R1(config)#
```

    b. The following command impedes brute force login attempts. The router blocks login attempts for 30 seconds if someone fails two attempts within 120 seconds. This timer is set especially low for the purpose of this lab.

```
R1(config)# login block-for 30 attempts 2 within 120
```

What does the **2 within 120** mean in the above command?

_____

What does the **block-for 30** mean in the above command?

_____

Step 5.   Verify that all unused ports are disabled.

Router ports are disabled by default, but it is always prudent to verify that all unused ports are in an administratively down state. This can be quickly checked by issuing the **show ip interface brief** command. Any unused ports that are not in an administratively down state should be disabled using the **shutdown** command in interface configuration mode.

```
R1# show ip interface brief
Interface                 IP-Address      OK? Method Status                 Protocol
Embedded-Service-Engine0/0 unassigned     YES NVRAM  administratively down down
GigabitEthernet0/0        unassigned      YES NVRAM  administratively down down
GigabitEthernet0/1        192.168.1.1     YES manual up                     up
Serial0/0/0               unassigned      YES NVRAM  administratively down down
Serial0/0/1               unassigned      YES NVRAM  administratively down down
R1#
```

Step 6.   Verify that your security measures have been implemented correctly.

a.   Use Tera Term to Telnet to R1.

Does R1 accept the Telnet connection? Explain.

_____

_____

b.   Use Tera Term to SSH to R1.

Does R1 accept the SSH connection? _____

c.   Intentionally mistype the user and password information to see if login access is blocked after two attempts.

What happened after you failed to log in the second time?

_____

_____

d.   From your console session on the router, issue the **show login** command to view the login status. In the example below, the **show login** command was issued within the 30-second login blocking period and shows that the router is in Quiet-Mode. The router will not accept any login attempts for 14 more seconds.

```
R1# show login
    A default login delay of 1 second is applied.
    No Quiet-Mode access list has been configured.

    Router enabled to watch for login Attacks.
    If more than 2 login failures occur in 120 seconds or less,
    logins will be disabled for 30 seconds.

    Router presently in Quiet-Mode.
    Will remain in Quiet-Mode for 14 seconds.
    Denying logins from all sources.
    R1#
```

e. After the 30 seconds has expired, SSH to R1 again and log in using the **SSHadmin** username and **Admin1p@55** for the password.

After you successfully logged in, what was displayed? _____

f. Enter privileged EXEC mode and use **Enablep@55** for the password.

If you mistype this password, are you disconnected from your SSH session after two failed attempts within 120 seconds? Explain.

_____

_____

g. Issue the **show running-config** command at the privileged EXEC prompt to view the security settings you have applied.

Part 3: Configure Basic Security Measures on the Switch

Step 1. Encrypt the clear text passwords.

```
S1(config)# service password-encryption
```

Step 2. Strengthen passwords on the switch.

Change the privileged EXEC encrypted password to meet strong password guidelines.

```
S1(config)# enable secret Enablep@55
```

Note: The security **password min-length** command is not available on the 2960 switch.

Step 3. Enable SSH Connections.

a. Assign the domain-name as **CCNA-lab.com**

```
S1(config)# ip domain-name CCNA-lab.com
```

b. Create a local user database entry for use when connecting to the switch via SSH. The password should meet strong password standards, and the user should have user EXEC access. If privilege level is not specified in the command, the user will have user EXEC (level 1) access by default.

```
S1(config)# username SSHadmin privilege 1 secret Admin1p@55
```

c. Configure the transport input for the VTY lines to allow SSH connections but not allow Telnet connections.

```
S1(config)# line vty 0 15
S1(config-line)# transport input ssh
```

d. The VTY lines should use the local user database for authentication.

```
S1(config-line)# login local
S1(config-line)# exit
```

e. Generate an RSA crypto key using a modulus of 1024 bits.

```
S1(config)# crypto key generate rsa modulus 1024
```

Step 4.   Secure the console and VTY lines.

a.   Configure the switch to log out a line that has been idle for 10 minutes.

```
S1(config)# line console 0
S1(config-line)# exec-timeout 10 0
S1(config-line)# line vty 0 15
S1(config-line)# exec-timeout 10 0
S1(config-line)# exit
S1(config)#
```

b.   To impede brute force login attempts, configure the switch to block login access for 30 seconds if there are 2 failed attempts within 120 seconds. This timer is set especially low for the purpose of this lab.

```
S1(config)# login block-for 30 attempts 2 within 120
S1(config)# end
```

Step 5.   Verify all unused ports are disabled.

Switch ports are enabled, by default. Shut down all ports that are not in use on the switch.

a.   You can verify the switch port status using the **show ip interface brief** command.

```
S1# show ip interface brief
Interface            IP-Address      OK? Method Status              Protocol
Vlan1                192.168.1.11    YES manual up                  up
FastEthernet0/1      unassigned      YES unset  down                down
FastEthernet0/2      unassigned      YES unset  down                down
FastEthernet0/3      unassigned      YES unset  down                down
FastEthernet0/4      unassigned      YES unset  down                down
FastEthernet0/5      unassigned      YES unset  up                  up
FastEthernet0/6      unassigned      YES unset  up                  up
FastEthernet0/7      unassigned      YES unset  down                down
FastEthernet0/8      unassigned      YES unset  down                down
FastEthernet0/9      unassigned      YES unset  down                down
FastEthernet0/10     unassigned      YES unset  down                down
FastEthernet0/11     unassigned      YES unset  down                down
FastEthernet0/12     unassigned      YES unset  down                down
FastEthernet0/13     unassigned      YES unset  down                down
FastEthernet0/14     unassigned      YES unset  down                down
FastEthernet0/15     unassigned      YES unset  down                down
FastEthernet0/16     unassigned      YES unset  down                down
FastEthernet0/17     unassigned      YES unset  down                down
FastEthernet0/18     unassigned      YES unset  down                down
FastEthernet0/19     unassigned      YES unset  down                down
FastEthernet0/20     unassigned      YES unset  down                down
FastEthernet0/21     unassigned      YES unset  down                down
FastEthernet0/22     unassigned      YES unset  down                down
FastEthernet0/23     unassigned      YES unset  down                down
FastEthernet0/24     unassigned      YES unset  down                down
GigabitEthernet0/1   unassigned      YES unset  down                down
GigabitEthernet0/2   unassigned      YES unset  down                down
S1#
```

b. Use the **interface range** command to shut down multiple interfaces at a time.

```
S1(config)# interface range f0/1-4 , f0/7-24 , g0/1-2
S1(config-if-range)# shutdown
S1(config-if-range)# end
S1#
```

c. Verify that all inactive interfaces have been administratively shut down.

```
S1# show ip interface brief
Interface              IP-Address      OK? Method Status
Protocol
Vlan1                  192.168.1.11    YES manual up                          up
FastEthernet0/1        unassigned      YES unset  administratively down down
FastEthernet0/2        unassigned      YES unset  administratively down down
FastEthernet0/3        unassigned      YES unset  administratively down down
FastEthernet0/4        unassigned      YES unset  administratively down down
FastEthernet0/5        unassigned      YES unset  up                          up
FastEthernet0/6        unassigned      YES unset  up                          up
FastEthernet0/7        unassigned      YES unset  administratively down down
FastEthernet0/8        unassigned      YES unset  administratively down down
FastEthernet0/9        unassigned      YES unset  administratively down down
FastEthernet0/10       unassigned      YES unset  administratively down down
FastEthernet0/11       unassigned      YES unset  administratively down down
FastEthernet0/12       unassigned      YES unset  administratively down down
FastEthernet0/13       unassigned      YES unset  administratively down down
FastEthernet0/14       unassigned      YES unset  administratively down down
FastEthernet0/15       unassigned      YES unset  administratively down down
FastEthernet0/16       unassigned      YES unset  administratively down down
FastEthernet0/17       unassigned      YES unset  administratively down down
FastEthernet0/18       unassigned      YES unset  administratively down down
FastEthernet0/19       unassigned      YES unset  administratively down down
FastEthernet0/20       unassigned      YES unset  administratively down down
FastEthernet0/21       unassigned      YES unset  administratively down down
FastEthernet0/22       unassigned      YES unset  administratively down down
FastEthernet0/23       unassigned      YES unset  administratively down down
FastEthernet0/24       unassigned      YES unset  administratively down down
GigabitEthernet0/1     unassigned      YES unset  administratively down down
GigabitEthernet0/2     unassigned      YES unset  administratively down down
S1#
```

Step 6. Verify that your security measures have been implemented correctly.

a. Verify that Telnet has been disabled on the switch.

b. SSH to the switch and intentionally mistype the user and password information to see if login access is blocked.

c. After the 30 seconds has expired, SSH to S1 again and log in using the **SSHadmin** username and **Admin1p@55** for the password.

Did the banner appear after you successfully logged in? _____

d. Enter privileged EXEC mode using **Enablep@55** as the password.

e. Issue the **show running-config** command at the privileged EXEC prompt to view the security settings you have applied.

Reflection

1. The **password cisco** command was entered for the console and VTY lines in your basic configuration in Part 1. When is this password used after the best practice security measures have been applied?

    _____

    _____

    _____

2. Are preconfigured passwords shorter than 10 characters affected by the **security passwords minlength 10** command?

    _____

    _____

    _____

Router Interface Summary Table

	Router Interface Summary			
Router Model	Ethernet Interface #1	Ethernet Interface #2	Serial Interface #1	Serial Interface #2
1800	Fast Ethernet 0/0 (F0/0)	Fast Ethernet 0/1 (F0/1)	Serial 0/0/0 (S0/0/0)	Serial 0/0/1 (S0/0/1)
1900	Gigabit Ethernet 0/0 (G0/0)	Gigabit Ethernet 0/1 (G0/1)	Serial 0/0/0 (S0/0/0)	Serial 0/0/1 (S0/0/1)
2801	Fast Ethernet 0/0 (F0/0)	Fast Ethernet 0/1 (F0/1)	Serial 0/1/0 (S0/0/0)	Serial 0/1/1 (S0/0/1)
2811	Fast Ethernet 0/0 (F0/0)	Fast Ethernet 0/1 (F0/1)	Serial 0/0/0 (S0/0/0)	Serial 0/0/1 (S0/0/1)
2900	Gigabit Ethernet 0/0 (G0/0)	Gigabit Ethernet 0/1 (G0/1)	Serial 0/0/0 (S0/0/0)	Serial 0/0/1 (S0/0/1)

Note: To find out how the router is configured, look at the interfaces to identify the type of router and how many interfaces the router has. There is no way to effectively list all the combinations of configurations for each router class. This table includes identifiers for the possible combinations of Ethernet and Serial interfaces in the device. The table does not include any other type of interface, even though a specific router may contain one. An example of this might be an ISDN BRI interface. The string in parenthesis is the legal abbreviation that can be used in Cisco IOS commands to represent the interface.

11.3.2.3 Packet Tracer–Testing Connectivity with Traceroute

Topology

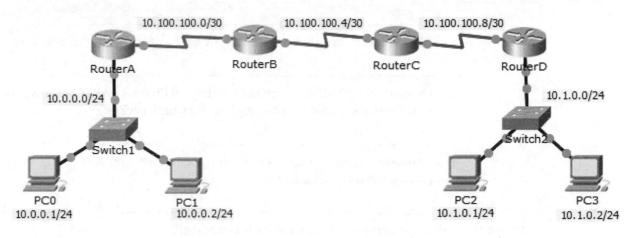

Objectives

Part 1: Test End-to-End Connectivity with the tracert Command

Part 2: Compare to the traceroute Command on a Router

Background

This activity is designed to help you troubleshoot network connectivity issues using commands to trace the route from source to destination. You are required to examine the output of **tracert** (the Windows command) and **traceroute** (the IOS command) as packets traverse the network and determine the cause of a network issue. After the issue is corrected, use the **tracert** and **traceroute** commands to verify the completion.

Part 1: Test End-to-End Connectivity with the tracert Command

Step 1.   Send a ping from one end of the network to the other end.

Click **PC1** and open the **Command Prompt**. Ping **PC3** at **10.1.0.2**. What message is displayed as a result of the ping?

_____

Step 2.   Trace the route from PC1 to determine where in the path connectivity fails.

   a.   From the **Command Prompt** of **PC1**, enter the **tracert 10.1.0.2** command.

   b.   When you receive the **Request timed out** message, press **Ctrl+C**. What was the first IP address listed in the **tracert** output?

_____

   c.   Observe the results of the **tracert** command. What is the last address reached with the **tracert** command?

_____

Step 3.   Correct the network problem.

    a.   Compare the last address reached with the **tracert** command with the network addresses listed on the topology. The furthest device from the host 10.0.0.2 with an address in the network range found is the point of failure. What devices have addresses configured for the network where the failure occurred?

---

    b.   Click **RouterC** and then the **CLI** tab. What is the status of the interfaces?

---

    c.   Compare the IP addresses on the interfaces with the network addresses on the topology. Does there appear to be anything extraordinary?

---

    d.   Make the necessary changes to restore connectivity; however, do not change the subnets. What is the solution?

Step 4.   Verify that end-to-end connectivity is established.

    a.   From the **PC1 Command Prompt**, enter the **tracert 10.1.0.2** command.

    b.   Observe the output from the **tracert** command. Was the command successful?

Part 2: Compare to the traceroute Command on a Router

    a.   Click **RouterA** and then the **CLI** tab.

    b.   Enter the **traceroute 10.1.0.2** command. Did the command complete successfully?

---

    c.   Compare the output from the router **traceroute** command with the PC **tracert** command. What is noticeably different about the list of addresses returned?

Part 3: Using Extended Traceroute

In addition to **traceroute**, Cisco IOS also includes extended traceroute. Extended traceroute allows the administrator to adjust minor traceroute operation parameters by asking simple questions.

As part of the verification process, use extended traceroute on **RouterA** to increase the number of ICMP packets traceroute sends to each hop.

Note: Windows **tracert** also allows the user to adjust a few aspects through the use of command line options.

a. Click **RouterA** and then the **CLI** tab.

b. Enter the **traceroute** and press **ENTER**. Notice that just the **traceroute** command should be entered.

c. Answer the questions asked by extended traceroute as follows. Extended **traceroute** should run right after the last question is answered.

```
Protocol [ip]: ip
Target IP address: 10.1.0.2
Source address: 10.100.100.1
Numeric display [n]: n
Timeout in seconds [3]: 3
Probe count [3]: 5
Minimum Time to Live [1]: 1
Maximum Time to Live [30]: 30
```

Note: the value displayed in brackets is the default value and will be used by **traceroute** if no value is entered. Simply press **ENTER** to use the default value.

How many questions were answered with non-default values? What was the new value?

_____

How many ICMP packets were sent by **RouterA**?

_____

Note: Probe count specifies the number of ICMP packets sent to each hop by **traceroute**. A higher number of probes allows for a more accurate average round trip time for the packets.

d. Still on **RouterA**, run extended **traceroute** again but this time change the timeout value to 7 seconds.

What happened? How does the different timeout value affect **traceroute**?

_____

Can you think of a use for the timeout parameter?

_____

Suggested Scoring Rubric

Activity Section	Question Location	Possible Points	Earned Points
Part 1: Test End-to-End Connectivity with the **tracert** Command	Step 1	10	
	Step 2b	10	
	Step 2c	10	
	Step 3a	10	
	Step 3c	10	
	Step 3d	5	
	Step 3e	5	
	Step 4b	10	
	Part 1 Total	70	
Part 2: Compare to the **traceroute** Command on a Router	a	2	
	b	3	
	c	5	
	Part 2 Total	10	
Part 3: Extended Traceroute	a	2	
	b	3	
	c	2	
	d	3	
	Part 3 Total	10	
	Packet Tracer Score	10	
	Total Score	100	

11.3.2.4 Lab–Testing Network Latency with Ping and Traceroute

Topology

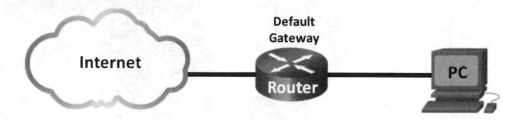

Objectives

Part 1: Use Ping to Document Network Latency

Part 2: Use Traceroute to Document Network Latency

Background/Scenario

To obtain realistic network latency statistics, this activity must be performed on a live network. Be sure to check with your instructor for any local security restrictions against using the **ping** command on the network.

The purpose of this lab is to measure and evaluate network latency over time, and during different periods of the day to capture a representative sample of typical network activity. This will be accomplished by analyzing the return delay from a distant computer with the **ping** command. Return delay times, measured in milliseconds, will be summarized by computing the average latency (mean) and the range (maximum and minimum) of the delay times.

Required Resources

- 1 PC (Windows 7 or 8 with Internet access)

Part 1: Use Ping to Document Network Latency

In Part 1, you will examine network latency of several websites in different parts of the globe. This process can be used in an enterprise production network to create a performance baseline.

Step 1. Verify connectivity.

Ping the following Regional Internet Registry (RIR) websites to verify connectivity:

```
C:\Users\User1> ping www.arin.net
C:\Users\User1> ping www.lacnic.net
C:\Users\User1> ping www.afrinic.net
C:\Users\User1> ping www.apnic.net
```

Note: Because www.ripe.net does not reply to ICMP requests, it cannot be used for this lab.

Note: If the websites are resolved to IPv6 addresses, the option -4 can be used to resolve to IPv4 addresses if desired. The command becomes **ping -4 www.arin.net.**

Step 2.   Collect network data.

You will collect a sufficient amount of data to compute statistics on the **ping** output by sending out 25 echo requests to each address listed in Step 1. Record the results for each website to text files.

a. At the command prompt, type **ping** to list the available options.

```
C:\Users\User1> ping

Usage: ping [-t] [-a] [-n count] [-l size] [-f] [-i TTL] [-v TOS]
            [-r count] [-s count] [[-j host-list] | [-k host-list]]
            [-w timeout] [-R] [-S srcaddr] [-4] [-6] target_name

Options:
    -t              Ping the specified host until stopped.
                    To see statistics and continue - type Control-Break;
                    To stop - type Control-C.
    -a              Resolve addresses to hostnames.
    -n count        Number of echo requests to send.
    -l size         Send buffer size.
    -f              Set Don't Fragment flag in packet (IPv4-only).
    -i TTL          Time To Live.
    -v TOS          Type Of Service (IPv4-only. This setting has been deprecated
<output omitted>
```

b. Using the **ping** command with the count option, you can send 25 echo requests to the destination as illustrated below. Furthermore, it will create a text file with a filename of **arin.txt** in the current directory. This text file will contain the results of the echo requests.

```
C:\Users\User1> ping -n 25 www.arin.net > arin.txt
```

Note: The terminal remains blank until the command has finished, because the output has been redirected to a text file, **arin.txt**, in this example. The **>** symbol is used to redirect the screen output to the file and overwrite the file if it already exists. If appending more results to the file is desired, replace **>** with **>>** in the command.

c. Repeat the **ping** command for the other websites.

```
C:\Users\User1> ping -n 25 www.afrinic.net > afrinic.txt
C:\Users\User1> ping -n 25 www.apnic.net > apnic.txt
C:\Users\User1> ping -n 25 www.lacnic.net > lacnic.txt
```

Step 3. Verify data collection.

To see the results in the file created, use the **more** command at the command prompt.

```
C:\Users\User1> more arin.txt

Pinging www.arin.net [192.149.252.76] with 32 bytes of data:
Reply from 192.149.252.76: bytes=32 time=108ms TTL=45
Reply from 192.149.252.76: bytes=32 time=114ms TTL=45
Reply from 192.149.252.76: bytes=32 time=112ms TTL=45
<output omitted>
Reply from 192.149.252.75: bytes=32 time=111ms TTL=45
Reply from 192.149.252.75: bytes=32 time=112ms TTL=45
Reply from 192.149.252.75: bytes=32 time=112ms TTL=45

Ping statistics for 192.149.252.75:
    Packets: Sent = 25, Received = 25, Lost = 0 (0% loss),
Approximate round trip times in milli-seconds:
    Minimum = 107ms, Maximum = 121ms, Average = 111ms
```

Note: Press the Spacebar to display the rest of the file or press **q** to exit.

To verify that the files have been created, use the **dir** command to list the files in the directory. Also the wildcard * can be used to filter only the text files.

```
C:\Users\User1> dir *.txt
Volume in drive C is OS
 Volume Serial Number is 0A97-D265

 Directory of C:\Users\User1

02/07/2013  12:59 PM             1,642 afrinic.txt
02/07/2013  01:00 PM             1,615 apnic.txt
02/07/2013  12:40 PM             1,641 arin.txt
02/07/2013  12:58 PM             1,589 lacnic.txt
               4 File(s)          6,487 bytes
               0 Dir(s)  34,391,453,696 bytes free
```

Record your results in the following table.

	Minimum	Maximum	Average
www.afrinic.net			
www.apnic.net			
www.arin.net			
www.lacnic.net			

Compare the delay results. How is delay affected by geographical location?

_____

_____

Part 2: Use Traceroute to Document Network Latency

The routes traced may go through many hops and a number of different ISPs depending on the size of the ISPs and the location of the source and destination hosts. The **traceroute** commands can also be used to observe network latency. In Part 2, the **tracert** command is used to trace the path to the same destinations in Part 1. The command **tracert** is the Windows version of the **traceroute** command.

The **tracert** command uses ICMP TTL Exceed packets and ICMP echo replies to trace the path.

Step 1.   Use the **tracert** command and record the output to text files.

Copy the following commands to create the traceroute files:

```
C:\Users\User1> tracert www.arin.net > traceroute_arin.txt

C:\Users\User1> tracert www.lacnic.net > traceroute_lacnic.txt

C:\Users\User1> tracert www.afrinic.net > traceroute_afrinic.txt

C:\Users\User1> tracert www.apnic.net > traceroute_apnic.txt
```

Note: If the websites are resolved to IPv6 addresses, the option -4 can be used to resolve to IPv4 addresses if desired. The command becomes **tracert -4** www.arin.net **> traceroute_arin.txt**.

Step 2.   Use the more command to examine the traced path.

   a.   Use the **more** command to access the content of these files:

```
C:\Users\User1> more traceroute_arin.txt


Tracing route to www.arin.net [192.149.252.75]
over a maximum of 30 hops:


  1     <1 ms     <1 ms     <1 ms    192.168.1.1
  2     11 ms     12 ms     11 ms    10.39.0.1
  3     10 ms     15 ms     11 ms    172.21.0.116
  4     19 ms     10 ms     11 ms    70.169.73.90
  5     13 ms     10 ms     11 ms    chnddsrj01-ae2.0.rd.ph.cox.net [70.169.76.229]
  6     72 ms     71 ms     70 ms    mrfddsrj02-ae0.0.rd.dc.cox.net [68.1.1.7]
  7     72 ms     71 ms     72 ms    68.100.0.146
  8     74 ms     83 ms     73 ms    172.22.66.29
  9     75 ms     71 ms     73 ms    172.22.66.29
 10     74 ms     75 ms     73 ms    wsip-98-172-152-14.dc.dc.cox.net
[98.172.152.14]
 11     71 ms     71 ms     71 ms    host-252-131.arin.net [192.149.252.131]
 12     73 ms     71 ms     71 ms    www.arin.net [192.149.252.75]


Trace complete.
```

In this example, it took less than 1 ms to receive a reply from the default gateway (192.168.1.1). In hop count 6, the round trip to 68.1.1.7 took an average of 71 ms. For the round trip to the final destination at www.arin.net took an average of 72 ms.

Between lines 5 and 6, there is more network delay as indicated by the round trip time increase from an average of 11 ms to 71 ms

b. Perform the same analysis with the rest of the tracert results.

What can you conclude regarding the relationship between the roundtrip time and geographical location?

_____

_____

Reflection

1. The **tracert** and **ping** results can provide important network latency information. What do you need to do if you want an accurate baseline picture regarding network latency for your network?

_____

2. How can you use the baseline information?

_____

11.3.3.3 Packet Tracer–Using Show Commands

Objectives

Part 1: Analyze Show Command Output

Part 2: Reflection Questions

Background

This activity is designed to reinforce the use of router **show** commands. You are not required to configure, but rather examine the output of several **show** commands.

Part 1: Analyze Show Command Output

Step 1. Connect to ISPRouter

    a. Click **ISP PC**, then the **Desktop** tab, followed by **Terminal**.

    b. Enter privileged EXEC mode.

    c. Use the following **show** commands to answer the Reflection Questions in Part 2:

```
show arp
show flash:
show ip route
show interfaces
show ip interface brief
show protocols
show users
show version
```

Part 2: Reflection Questions

1. Which commands would provide the IP address, network prefix, and interface? _____

   _____

2. Which commands provide the IP address and interface assignment, but not the network prefix?

   _____

3. Which commands provide the status of the interfaces? _____

4. Which commands provide information about the IOS loaded on the router? _____

5. Which commands provide information about the addresses of the router interfaces? _____

   _____

6. Which commands provide information about the amount of Flash memory available? _____

   _____

7. Which commands provide information about the lines being used for configuration or device monitoring?_____

8. Which commands provide traffic statistics of router interfaces? _____

9. Which commands provide information about paths available for network traffic? _____

10. Which interfaces are currently active on the router? _____

Suggested Scoring Rubric

Each question is worth 10 points for a total score of 100.

11.3.4.6 Lab–Using the CLI to Gather Network Device Information

Topology

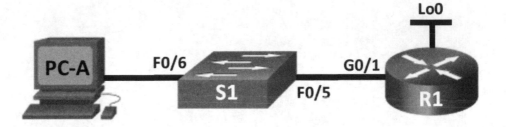

Addressing Table

Device	Interface	IP Address	Subnet Mask	Default Gateway
R1	G0/1	192.168.1.1	255.255.255.0	N/A
	Lo0	209.165.200.225	255.255.255.224	N/A
S1	VLAN 1	192.168.1.11	255.255.255.0	192.168.1.1
PC-A	NIC	192.168.1.3	255.255.255.0	192.168.1.1

Objectives

Part 1: Set Up Topology and Initialize Devices

Part 2: Configure Devices and Verify Connectivity

Part 3: Gather Network Device Information

Background/Scenario

Documenting a working network is one of the most important tasks a network professional can perform. Having proper documentation of IP addresses, model numbers, IOS versions, ports used, and testing security, can go a long way in helping to troubleshoot a network.

In this lab, you will build a small network, configure the devices, add some basic security, and then document the configurations by issuing various commands on the router, switch, and PC to gather your information.

Note: The routers used with CCNA hands-on labs are Cisco 1941 Integrated Services Routers (ISRs) with Cisco IOS Release 15.2(4)M3 (universalk9 image). The switches used are Cisco Catalyst 2960s with Cisco IOS Release 15.0(2) (lanbasek9 image). Other routers, switches, and Cisco IOS versions can be used. Depending on the model and Cisco IOS version, the commands available and output produced might vary from what is shown in the labs. Refer to the Router Interface Summary Table at the end of this lab for the correct interface identifiers.

Note: Make sure that the routers and switches have been erased and have no startup configurations. If you are unsure, contact your instructor.

Required Resources

- 1 Router (Cisco 1941 with Cisco IOS Release 15.2(4)M3 universal image or comparable)

- 1 Switch (Cisco 2960 with Cisco IOS Release 15.0(2) lanbasek9 image or comparable)

- 1 PC (Windows 7 or 8 with terminal emulation program, such as Tera Term)

- Console cables to configure the Cisco IOS devices via the console ports

- Ethernet cables as shown in the topology

Part 1: Set Up the Topology and Initialize Devices

In Part 1, you will set up the network topology, clear any configurations if necessary, and configure basic settings on the router and switch.

Step 1.   Cable the network as shown in the topology.

    a.   Attach the devices as shown in the topology and cable as necessary.

    b.   Power on all devices in the topology.

Step 2.   Initialize and reload the router and the switch.

Part 2: Configure Devices and Verify Connectivity

In Part 2, you will set up the network topology and configure basic settings on the router and switch. Refer to the topology and Addressing Table at the beginning of this lab for device names and address information.

Step 1.   Configure the IPv4 address for the PC.

    Configure the IPv4 address, subnet mask, and default gateway address for PC-A based on the Addressing Table.

Step 2.   Configure the router.

    a.   Console into the router and enter privileged EXEC mode.

    b.   Set the correct time on the router.

    c.   Enter global configuration mode.

        1)   Assign a device name to the router based on the topology and Addressing Table.

        2)   Disable DNS lookup.

        3)   Create an MOTD banner that warns anyone accessing the device that unauthorized access is prohibited.

        4)   Assign **class** as the privileged EXEC encrypted password.

        5)   Assign **cisco** as the console password and enable console login access.

        6)   Encrypt clear text passwords.

        7)   Create a domain name of **cisco.com** for SSH access.

        8)   Create a user named **admin** with a secret password of **cisco** for SSH access.

        9)   Generate an RSA modulus key. Use **1024** for the number of bits.

d. Configure VTY line access.

    1) Use the local database for authentication for SSH.

    2) Enable SSH only for login access.

e. Return to global configuration mode.

    1) Create the Loopback 0 interface and assign the IP address based on the Addressing Table.

    2) Configure and activate interface G0/1 on the router.

    3) Configure interface descriptions for G0/1 and L0.

    4) Save the running configuration file to the startup configuration file.

Step 3. Configure the switch.

a. Console into the switch and enter privileged EXEC mode.

b. Set the correct time on the switch.

c. Enter global configuration mode.

    1) Assign a device name on the switch based on the topology and Addressing Table.

    2) Disable DNS lookup.

    3) Create an MOTD banner that warns anyone accessing the device that unauthorized access is prohibited.

    4) Assign **class** as the privileged EXEC encrypted password.

    5) Encrypt the clear text passwords.

    6) Create a domain name of **cisco.com** for SSH access.

    7) Create a user named **admin** with a secret password of **cisco** for SSH access.

    8) Generate an RSA key. Use **1024** for the number of bits.

    9) Create and activate an IP address on the switch based on the topology and Addressing Table.

    10) Set the default gateway on the switch.

    11) Assign **cisco** as the console password and enable console login access.

d. Configure VTY line access.

    1) Use local database for authentication for SSH.

    2) Enable SSH only for login access.

    3) Save the running configuration file to the startup configuration file.

e. Enter proper mode to configure interface descriptions for F0/5 and F0/6.

Step 4. Verify network connectivity.

a. From a command prompt on PC-A, ping the S1 VLAN 1 IP address. Troubleshoot your physical and logical configurations if the pings were not successful.

b. _____ Troubleshoot your physical and logical configurations if the pings were not successful.

    c. _____ Troubleshoot
your physical and logical configurations if the pings were not successful.

    d. _____ Troubleshoot
your physical and logical configurations if the pings were not successful.

Part 3: Gather Network Device Information

In Part 3, you will use a variety of commands to gather information about the devices on your network, as well as some performance characteristics. Network documentation is a very important component of managing your network. Documentation of both physical and logical topologies is important, as is verifying platform models and IOS versions of your network devices. Having knowledge of the proper commands to gather this information is essential for a network professional.

Step 1.   Gather information on R1 using IOS commands.

One of the most basic steps is to gather information on the physical device, as well as information on the operating system.

    a. Issue the appropriate command to discover the following information:

    Router Model: _____

    IOS Version: _____

    Total RAM: _____

    Total NVRAM: _____

    Total Flash Memory: _____

    IOS Image File: _____

    Configuration Register: _____

    Technology Package: _____

    What command did you issue to gather the information?

    _____

    b. Issue the appropriate command to display a summary of important information about the router interfaces. Write down the command and record your results below.

_____

    Note: Only record interfaces that have IP addresses.

_____

_____

_____

_____

_____

c. Issue the appropriate command to display the routing table. Write down the command and record your results below.

_____

_____

_____

_____

_____

_____

_____

d. What command would you use to display the Layer 2 to Layer 3 mapping of addresses on the router? Write down the command and record your results below.

_____

_____

_____

_____

e. What command would you use to see detailed information about all the interfaces on the router or about a specific interface? Write down the command below.

_____

f. Cisco has a very powerful protocol that operates at Layer 2 of the OSI model. This protocol can help you map out how Cisco devices are connected physically, as well as determining model numbers and even IOS versions and IP addressing. What command or commands would you use on router R1 to find out information about switch S1 to help you complete the table below?

Device ID	Local Interface	Capability	Model #	Remote Port ID	IP Address	IOS Version

g. A very elementary test of your network devices is to see if you can telnet into them. Remember, Telnet is not a secure protocol. It should not be enabled in most cases. Using a Telnet client, such as Tera Term or PuTTY, try to telnet to R1 using the default gateway IP address. Record your results below.

_____

h. From PC-A, test to ensure that SSH is working properly. Using an SSH client, such as Tera Term or PuTTY, SSH into R1 from PC-A. If you get a warning message regarding a different key, click **Continue**. Log in with the appropriate username and password you created in Part 2. Were you successful?

_____

Note: The passwords used for our lab (cisco and class) do not follow the best practices needed for strong passwords. These passwords are used merely for the convenience of performing the labs. By default, the console password and any vty passwords configured would display in clear text in your configuration file.

    i. Verify that all of your passwords in the configuration file are encrypted. Write down the command and record your results below.

Command: _____

Is the console password encrypted? _____

Is the SSH password encrypted? _____

Step 2.   Gather information on S1 using IOS commands.

Many of the commands that you used on R1 can also be used with the switch. However, there are some differences with some of the commands.

    a. Issue the appropriate command to discover the following information:

Switch Model: _____

IOS Version: _____

Total NVRAM: _____

IOS Image File: _____

What command did you issue to gather the information?

_____

    b. Issue the appropriate command to display a summary of status information about the switch interfaces. Write down the command and record your results below.

Note: Only record active interfaces.

_____

_____

_____

_____

_____

    c. Issue the appropriate command to display the switch MAC address table. Record the dynamic type MAC addresses only in the space below.

_____

_____

_____

    d. Verify that Telnet VTY access is disabled on S1. Using a Telnet client, such as Tera Term or PuTTY, try to telnet to S1 using the 192.168.1.11 address. Record your results below.

_____

e. From PC-A, test to ensure that SSH is working properly. Using an SSH client, such as Tera Term or PuTTY, SSH into S1 from PC-A. If you get a warning message regarding a different key, click Continue. Log in with an appropriate username and password. Were you successful?

_____

f. Complete the table below with information about router R1 using the appropriate command or commands necessary on S1.

Device Id	Local Interface	Capability	Model #	Remote Port ID	IP Address	IOS Version

g. Verify that all of your passwords in the configuration file are encrypted. Write down the command and record your results below.

Command: _____

Is the console password encrypted? _____

Step 3.   Gather information on PC-A.

Using various Windows utility commands, you will gather information on PC-A.

a. From the PC-A command prompt, issue the **ipconfig /all** command and record your answers below.

What is the PC-A IP address?

_____

What is the PC-A subnet mask?

_____

What is the PC-A default gateway address?

_____

What is the PC-A MAC address?

_____

b. Issue the appropriate command to test the TCP/IP protocol stack with the NIC. What command did you use?

_____

c. Ping the loopback interface of R1 from the PC-A command prompt. Was the ping successful?

_____

d. Issue the appropriate command on PC-A to trace the list of router hops for packets originating from PC-A to the loopback interface on R1. Record the command and output below. What command did you use?

_____

_____

e. Issue the appropriate command on PC-A to find the Layer 2 to Layer 3 address mappings held on your NIC. Record your answers below. Only record answers for the 192.168.1.0/24 network. What command did you use?

_____

_____

_____

_____

Reflection

Why is it important to document your network devices?

_____

_____

_____

_____

Router Interface Summary Table

	Router Interface Summary			
Router Model	Ethernet Interface #1	Ethernet Interface #2	Serial Interface #1	Serial Interface #2
1800	Fast Ethernet 0/0 (F0/0)	Fast Ethernet 0/1 (F0/1)	Serial 0/0/0 (S0/0/0)	Serial 0/0/1 (S0/0/1)
1900	Gigabit Ethernet 0/0 (G0/0)	Gigabit Ethernet 0/1 (G0/1)	Serial 0/0/0 (S0/0/0)	Serial 0/0/1 (S0/0/1)
2801	Fast Ethernet 0/0 (F0/0)	Fast Ethernet 0/1 (F0/1)	Serial 0/1/0 (S0/1/0)	Serial 0/1/1 (S0/1/1)
2811	Fast Ethernet 0/0 (F0/0)	Fast Ethernet 0/1 (F0/1)	Serial 0/0/0 (S0/0/0)	Serial 0/0/1 (S0/0/1)
2900	Gigabit Ethernet 0/0 (G0/0)	Gigabit Ethernet 0/1 (G0/1)	Serial 0/0/0 (S0/0/0)	Serial 0/0/1 (S0/0/1)

Note: To find out how the router is configured, look at the interfaces to identify the type of router and how many interfaces the router has. There is no way to effectively list all the combinations of configurations for each router class. This table includes identifiers for the possible combinations of Ethernet and Serial interfaces in the device. The table does not include any other type of interface, even though a specific router may contain one. An example of this might be an ISDN BRI interface. The string in parentheses is the legal abbreviation that can be used in Cisco IOS commands to represent the interface.

11.4.3.5 Lab–Troubleshooting Connectivity Issues

Topology

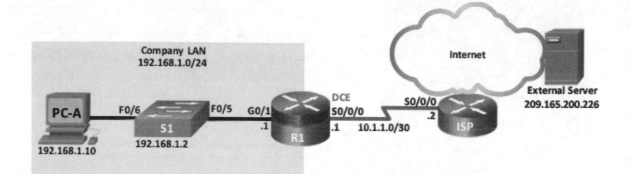

Addressing Table

Device	Interface	IP Address	Subnet Mask	Default Gateway
R1	G0/1	192.168.1.1	255.255.255.0	N/A
	S0/0/0	10.1.1.1	255.255.255.252	N/A
ISP	S0/0/0	10.1.1.2	255.255.255.252	N/A
	Lo0	209.165.200.226	255.255.255.255	N/A
S1	VLAN 1	192.168.1.2	255.255.255.0	192.168.1.1
PC-A	NIC	192.168.1.10	255.255.255.0	192.168.1.1

Objectives

Part 1: Identify the Problem

Part 2: Implement Network Changes

Part 3: Verify Full Functionality

Part 4: Document Findings and Configuration Changes

Background/Scenario

In this lab, the company that you work for is experiencing problems with their Local-Area Network (LAN). You have been asked to troubleshoot and resolve the network issues. In Part 1, you will connect to devices on the LAN and use troubleshooting tools to identify the network issues, establish a theory of probable cause, and test that theory. In Part 2, you will establish a plan of action to resolve and implement a solution. In Part 3, you will verify full functionality has been restored. Part 4 provides space for you to document your troubleshooting findings along with the configuration changes that you made to the LAN devices.

Note: The routers used with CCNA hands-on labs are Cisco 1941 Integrated Services Routers (ISRs) with Cisco IOS Release 15.2(4)M3 (universalk9 image). The switches used are Cisco Catalyst 2960s with Cisco IOS Release 15.0(2) (lanbasek9 image). Other routers, switches, and Cisco IOS versions may be used. Depending on the model and Cisco IOS version, the commands available and the output produced might vary from what is shown in the labs. Refer to the Router Interface Summary Table at the end of this lab for the correct interface identifiers.

Required Resources

- 2 Routers (Cisco 1941 with Cisco IOS Release 15.2(4)M3 universal image or comparable)
- 1 Switch (Cisco 2960 with Cisco IOS Release 15.0(2) lanbasek9 image or comparable)
- 1 PC (Windows 7 or 8 with terminal emulation program, such as Tera Term)
- Ethernet and Serial cables as shown in the topology

Troubleshooting Configurations

The following settings must be configured on the devices shown in the topology. Paste the configurations onto the specified devices prior to starting the lab.

S1:

```
no ip domain-lookup
hostname S1
ip domain-name ccna-lab.com
username admin01 privilege 15 secret 9 $9$lJgfiLCHj.Xp/q$hA2w.oyQPTMhBGPeR.FZo3NZR-
J9T1FdqvgRCFyBYnNs
interface FastEthernet0/1
 shutdown
interface FastEthernet0/2
 shutdown
interface FastEthernet0/3
 shutdown
interface FastEthernet0/4
 shutdown
interface FastEthernet0/5
 duplex full
interface Vlan1
 ip address 192.168.1.2 255.255.255.0
line vty 0 4
 login local
 transport input ssh
line vty 5 15
 login local
 transport input ssh
crypto key generate rsa general-keys modulus 1024
end
```

R1:

```
hostname R1
no ip domain-lookup
ip domain-name ccna-lab.com
username admin01 privilege 15 secret 9 $9$8a4jGjbPPpeeoE$WyPsIiOaYT4ATlJzrR6T9E6vIdESOGF.NYX-
53arPmtA
interface GigabitEthernet0/0
 shutdown
interface GigabitEthernet0/1
 ip address 192.168.1.1 255.255.255.0
 duplex half
 speed auto
 no shutdown
interface Serial0/0/0
 ip address 10.1.2.1 255.255.255.252
 no shutdown
interface Serial0/0/1
 no ip address
 shutdown
line vty 0 4
 login local
 transport input ssh
crypto key generate rsa general-keys modulus 1024
end
```

ISP:

```
hostname ISP
no ip domain-lookup
interface Serial0/0/0
 ip address 10.1.1.2 255.255.255.252
 no shut
interface Lo0
 ip address 209.165.200.226 255.255.255.255
ip route 0.0.0.0 0.0.0.0 10.1.1.1
end
```

Part 1: Identify the Problem.

The only available information about the network problem is that the users are experiencing slow response times and that they are not able to reach an external device on the Internet at IP address 209.165.200.226. To determine probable cause(s) for these network issues, you will need to utilize network commands and tools on the LAN equipment shown in the topology.

Note: The user name **admin01** with a password of **cisco12345** will be required to log into the network equipment.

Step 1. Troubleshoot from the PC.

    a. From the PC command prompt, **ping** the external server IP Address **209.165.200.226**.

```
C:\Windows\system32\cmd.exe

C:\Users\NetAcad>ping 209.165.200.226

Pinging 209.165.200.226 with 32 bytes of data:
PING: transmit failed. General failure.
PING: transmit failed. General failure.
PING: transmit failed. General failure.
PING: transmit failed. General failure.

Ping statistics for 209.165.200.226:
    Packets: Sent = 4, Received = 0, Lost = 4 (100% loss),

C:\Users\NetAcad>
```

    b. Use the **ipconfig** command to determine the network settings on the PC.

```
C:\Windows\system32\cmd.exe

C:\Users\NetAcad>ipconfig

Windows IP Configuration


Ethernet adapter Local Area Connection:

   Connection-specific DNS Suffix  . :
   Link-local IPv6 Address . . . . . : fe80::e9f5:e056:806:f9a0%11
   IPv4 Address. . . . . . . . . . . : 192.168.1.10
   Subnet Mask . . . . . . . . . . . : 255.255.255.0
   Default Gateway . . . . . . . . . :

Tunnel adapter isatap.{E2FC1866-B195-460A-BF40-F04F42A38FFE}:

   Media State . . . . . . . . . . . : Media disconnected
   Connection-specific DNS Suffix  . :

Tunnel adapter Local Area Connection* 11:

   Media State . . . . . . . . . . . : Media disconnected
   Connection-specific DNS Suffix  . :

C:\Users\NetAcad>_
```

Step 2. Troubleshoot from S1 using a SSH client session.

Note: Any SSH client software can be used. Tera Term is used in the examples in this lab.

---

    a. SSH to S1 using its IP Address of 192.168.1.2 and log into the switch using **admin01** for the user name and **cisco12345** for the password.

b. Issue the **terminal monitor** command on S1 to allow log messages to be sent to the VTY line of your SSH session. After a few seconds you notice the following error message being displayed in your SSH window.

```
S1# terminal monitor
S1#
*Mar  1 02:08:11.338: %CDP-4-DUPLEX_MISMATCH: duplex mismatch discovered on
FastEthernet0/5 (not half duplex), with R1.ccna-lab.com GigabitEthernet0/1
(half duplex).
S1#
```

c. On S1, issue the **show interface f0/5** command to view the duplex setting of the interface.

```
S1# show interface f0/5
FastEthernet0/5 is up, line protocol is up (connected)
  Hardware is Fast Ethernet, address is 0cd9.96e8.8a05 (bia 0cd9.96e8.8a05)
  MTU 1500 bytes, BW 100000 Kbit/sec, DLY 100 usec,
     reliability 255/255, txload 1/255, rxload 1/255
  Encapsulation ARPA, loopback not set
  Keepalive set (10 sec)
  Full-duplex, 100Mb/s, media type is 10/100BaseTX
  input flow-control is off, output flow-control is unsupported
  ARP type: ARPA, ARP Timeout 04:00:00
  Last input 00:00:35, output 00:00:01, output hang never
  Last clearing of "show interface" counters never
  Input queue: 0/75/0/0 (size/max/drops/flushes); Total output drops: 0
  Queueing strategy: fifo
  Output queue: 0/40 (size/max)
  5 minute input rate 0 bits/sec, 0 packets/sec
  5 minute output rate 0 bits/sec, 0 packets/sec
     849 packets input, 104642 bytes, 0 no buffer
     Received 123 broadcasts (122 multicasts)
     0 runts, 0 giants, 0 throttles
     0 input errors, 0 CRC, 0 frame, 0 overrun, 0 ignored
     0 watchdog, 122 multicast, 0 pause input
     0 input packets with dribble condition detected
     4489 packets output, 361270 bytes, 0 underruns
```

```
            0 output errors, 0 collisions, 1 interface resets
            0 unknown protocol drops
            0 babbles, 0 late collision, 0 deferred
            0 lost carrier, 0 no carrier, 0 pause output
            0 output buffer failures, 0 output buffers swapped out
    S1#
```

Step 3.   Troubleshoot on R1 using an SSH client.

    a.   SSH to R1's LAN interface and log in using **admin01** for the user name and **cisco12345** as the password.

    b.   Issue the **terminal monitor** command on R1 to allow log messages to be sent to the VTY line of your SSH session for R1. After a few seconds the duplex mismatch message appears on R1's SSH session.

```
R1# terminal monitor
R1#
*Nov 23 16:12:36.623: %CDP-4-DUPLEX_MISMATCH: duplex mismatch discovered on
GigabitEthernet0/1 (not full duplex), with S1.ccna-lab.com FastEthernet0/5
(full duplex).
R1#
```

    c.   Issue the **show interface G0/1** command on R1 to display the duplex setting.

```
R1# show interfaces g0/1
GigabitEthernet0/1 is up, line protocol is up
  Hardware is CN Gigabit Ethernet, address is d48c.b5ce.a0c1 (bia d48c.b5ce.
a0c1)
  Internet address is 192.168.1.1/24
  MTU 1500 bytes, BW 100000 Kbit/sec, DLY 100 usec,
     reliability 255/255, txload 1/255, rxload 1/255
  Encapsulation ARPA, loopback not set
  Keepalive set (10 sec)
  Half Duplex, 100Mbps, media type is RJ45
  output flow-control is unsupported, input flow-control is unsupported
  ARP type: ARPA, ARP Timeout 04:00:00
  Last input 00:00:15, output 00:00:05, output hang never
  Last clearing of "show interface" counters never
  Input queue: 0/75/0/0 (size/max/drops/flushes); Total output drops: 0
```

```
        Queueing strategy: fifo
        Output queue: 0/40 (size/max)
        5 minute input rate 0 bits/sec, 0 packets/sec
        5 minute output rate 0 bits/sec, 0 packets/sec
           641 packets input, 101892 bytes, 0 no buffer
           Received 453 broadcasts (0 IP multicasts)
           0 runts, 0 giants, 0 throttles
           0 input errors, 0 CRC, 0 frame, 0 overrun, 0 ignored
           0 watchdog, 361 multicast, 0 pause input
           1043 packets output, 123698 bytes, 0 underruns
           0 output errors, 0 collisions, 1 interface resets
           235 unknown protocol drops
           0 babbles, 0 late collision, 0 deferred
           0 lost carrier, 0 no carrier, 0 pause output
           0 output buffer failures, 0 output buffers swapped out
    R1#
```

d. Issue the **ping 209.165.200.226** command on R1 to test connectivity to the external server.

```
R1# ping 209.165.200.226
Type escape sequence to abort.
Sending 5, 100-byte ICMP Echos to 209.165.200.226, timeout is 2 seconds:
.....
Success rate is 0 percent (0/5)
R1#
```

e. Issue the **show ip interface brief** command on R1 to verify interface IP Address settings.

```
R1# show ip interface brief
Interface                  IP-Address      OK? Method Status                Protocol
Embedded-Service-Engine0/0 unassigned      YES unset  administratively down down
GigabitEthernet0/0         unassigned      YES unset  administratively down down
GigabitEthernet0/1         192.168.1.1     YES manual up                    up
Serial0/0/0                10.1.2.1        YES manual up                    up
Serial0/0/1                unassigned      YES unset  administratively down down
R1#
```

f. Issue the **show ip route** command on R1 to verify the router's default gateway setting.

```
R1# show ip route
Codes: L - local, C - connected, S - static, R - RIP, M - mobile, B - BGP
       D - EIGRP, EX - EIGRP external, O - OSPF, IA - OSPF inter area
       N1 - OSPF NSSA external type 1, N2 - OSPF NSSA external type 2
       E1 - OSPF external type 1, E2 - OSPF external type 2
       i - IS-IS, su - IS-IS summary, L1 - IS-IS level-1, L2 - IS-IS level-2
       ia - IS-IS inter area, * - candidate default, U - per-user static route
       o - ODR, P - periodic downloaded static route, H - NHRP, l - LISP
       a - application route
       + - replicated route, % - next hop override


Gateway of last resort is not set


      10.0.0.0/8 is variably subnetted, 2 subnets, 2 masks
```

```
C        10.1.2.0/30 is directly connected, Serial0/0/0
L        10.1.2.1/32 is directly connected, Serial0/0/0
      192.168.1.0/24 is variably subnetted, 2 subnets, 2 masks
C        192.168.1.0/24 is directly connected, GigabitEthernet0/1
L        192.168.1.1/32 is directly connected, GigabitEthernet0/1
R1#
```

List the probable causes for the network problems that employees are experiencing.

_____

_____

_____

_____

Part 2: Implement Network Changes

You have communicated the problems that you discovered in Part 1 to your supervisor. She has approved these changes and has requested that you implement them.

Step 1.   Set the Default Gateway on the PC to 192.168.1.1.

Step 2.   Set the duplex setting for interface G0/1 on R1 to full duplex.

```
R1# conf t
Enter configuration commands, one per line.  End with CNTL/Z.
R1(config)#
```

```
*Nov 23 17:23:36.879: %CDP-4-DUPLEX_MISMATCH: duplex mismatch discovered on
GigabitEthernet0/1 (not full duplex), with S1.ccna-lab.com FastEthernet0/5 (full
duplex).
R1(config)#
R1(config)# interface g0/1
R1(config-if)# duplex full
R1(config-if)# exit
*Nov 23 17:24:08.039: %LINK-3-UPDOWN: Interface GigabitEthernet0/1, changed state to
down
R1(config)#
*Nov 23 17:24:10.363: %LINK-3-UPDOWN: Interface GigabitEthernet0/1, changed state to
up
*Nov 23 17:24:10.459: %SYS-5-CONFIG_I: Configured from console by console
R1(config)#
```

Step 3. Reconfigure the IP address for S0/0/0 to IP Address 10.1.1.1/30 on R1.

```
R1(config)# interface s0/0/0
R1(config-if)# ip address 10.1.1.1 255.255.255.252
R1(config-if)# exit
```

Step 4. Configure the Gateway of last resort on R1 with a 10.1.1.2 default route.

```
R1(config)# ip route 0.0.0.0 0.0.0.0 10.1.1.2
R1(config)# end
```

Part 3: Verify Full Functionality

Verify that full functionality has been restored.

Step 1. Verify that all interfaces and routes have been set correctly and that routing has been restored on R1.

    a. Issue the **show ip route** command to verify that the default gateway has been set correctly.

```
R1# show ip route
Codes: L - local, C - connected, S - static, R - RIP, M - mobile, B - BGP
       D - EIGRP, EX - EIGRP external, O - OSPF, IA - OSPF inter area
       N1 - OSPF NSSA external type 1, N2 - OSPF NSSA external type 2
       E1 - OSPF external type 1, E2 - OSPF external type 2
       i - IS-IS, su - IS-IS summary, L1 - IS-IS level-1, L2 - IS-IS level-2
       ia - IS-IS inter area, * - candidate default, U - per-user static route
       o - ODR, P - periodic downloaded static route, H - NHRP, l - LISP
       a - application route
       + - replicated route, % - next hop override


Gateway of last resort is 10.1.1.2 to network 0.0.0.0


S*      0.0.0.0/0 [1/0] via 10.1.1.2
        10.0.0.0/8 is variably subnetted, 2 subnets, 2 masks
C          10.1.1.0/30 is directly connected, Serial0/0/0
L          10.1.1.1/32 is directly connected, Serial0/0/0
        192.168.1.0/24 is variably subnetted, 2 subnets, 2 masks
```

```
C        192.168.1.0/24 is directly connected, GigabitEthernet0/1
L        192.168.1.1/32 is directly connected, GigabitEthernet0/1
R1#
```

b. Issue the **show ip interface s0/0/0** command to verify that the IP Address on S0/0/0 is set correctly.

```
R1# show ip interface s0/0/0
Serial0/0/0 is up, line protocol is up
  Internet address is 10.1.1.1/30
  Broadcast address is 255.255.255.255
  Address determined by setup command
  MTU is 1500 bytes
  <output omitted>
  IPv4 WCCP Redirect exclude is disabled
R1#
```

c. Issue the **ping 209.165.200.226** command to verify that the external server is reachable now.

```
R1# ping 209.165.200.226
Type escape sequence to abort.
Sending 5, 100-byte ICMP Echos to 209.165.200.226, timeout is 2 seconds:
!!!!!
Success rate is 100 percent (5/5), round-trip min/avg/max = 1/2/4 ms
R1#
```

d. Issue the **show interface g0/1** command to verify that the duplex setting is full duplex.

```
R1# show interface g0/1
GigabitEthernet0/1 is up, line protocol is up
  Hardware is CN Gigabit Ethernet, address is d48c.b5ce.a0c1 (bia d48c.b5ce.
a0c1)
  Internet address is 192.168.1.1/24
  MTU 1500 bytes, BW 100000 Kbit/sec, DLY 100 usec,
     reliability 255/255, txload 1/255, rxload 1/255
  Encapsulation ARPA, loopback not set
  Keepalive set (10 sec)
  Full Duplex, 100Mbps, media type is RJ45
  output flow-control is unsupported, input flow-control is unsupported
  ARP type: ARPA, ARP Timeout 04:00:00
  Last input 00:00:04, output 00:00:04, output hang never
  Last clearing of "show interface" counters never
  Input queue: 0/75/0/0 (size/max/drops/flushes); Total output drops: 0
  Queueing strategy: fifo
  Output queue: 0/40 (size/max)
  5 minute input rate 0 bits/sec, 0 packets/sec
  5 minute output rate 0 bits/sec, 0 packets/sec
     559 packets input, 74066 bytes, 0 no buffer
     Received 279 broadcasts (0 IP multicasts)
     0 runts, 0 giants, 0 throttles
```

```
        0 input errors, 0 CRC, 0 frame, 0 overrun, 0 ignored
        0 watchdog, 208 multicast, 0 pause input
        742 packets output, 81462 bytes, 0 underruns
        0 output errors, 0 collisions, 2 interface resets
        133 unknown protocol drops
        0 babbles, 0 late collision, 0 deferred
        1 lost carrier, 0 no carrier, 0 pause output
        0 output buffer failures, 0 output buffers swapped out
   R1#
```

Step 2.   Verify End-to-End connectivity from the LAN PC.

   a.   Issue the **ipconfig** command from the command prompt on the PC.

```
C:\Windows\system32\cmd.exe

C:\Users\NetAcad>ipconfig

Windows IP Configuration

Ethernet adapter Local Area Connection:

   Connection-specific DNS Suffix  . :
   Link-local IPv6 Address . . . . . : fe80::e9f5:e056:806:f9a0%11
   IPv4 Address. . . . . . . . . . . : 192.168.1.10
   Subnet Mask . . . . . . . . . . . : 255.255.255.0
   Default Gateway . . . . . . . . . : 192.168.1.1

Tunnel adapter isatap.{E2FC1866-B195-460A-BF40-F04F42A38FFE}:

   Media State . . . . . . . . . . . : Media disconnected
   Connection-specific DNS Suffix  . :

Tunnel adapter Local Area Connection* 11:

   Media State . . . . . . . . . . . : Media disconnected
   Connection-specific DNS Suffix  . :

C:\Users\NetAcad>
```

   b.   Issue the **ping 209.165.200.226** command from the CMD window on the PC

```
C:\Windows\system32\cmd.exe
C:\Users\NetAcad>ping 209.165.200.226

Pinging 209.165.200.226 with 32 bytes of data:
Reply from 209.165.200.226: bytes=32 time=1ms TTL=254
Reply from 209.165.200.226: bytes=32 time=1ms TTL=254
Reply from 209.165.200.226: bytes=32 time=1ms TTL=254
Reply from 209.165.200.226: bytes=32 time=1ms TTL=254

Ping statistics for 209.165.200.226:
    Packets: Sent = 4, Received = 4, Lost = 0 (0% loss),
Approximate round trip times in milli-seconds:
    Minimum = 1ms, Maximum = 1ms, Average = 1ms

C:\Users\NetAcad>
C:\Users\NetAcad>
```

Part 4: Document Findings and Configuration Changes

Use the space provided below to document the issues found during your troubleshooting and the configurations changes made to resolve those issues.

_____

_____

_____

_____

_____

_____

_____

_____

_____

_____

_____

_____

_____

_____

_____

_____

_____

Reflection

This lab had you troubleshoot all devices before making any changes. Is there another way to apply the troubleshooting methodology?

_____

_____

_____

_____

_____

_____

Router Interface Summary Table

Router Interface Summary				
Router Model	Ethernet Interface #1	Ethernet Interface #2	Serial Interface #1	Serial Interface #2
1800	Fast Ethernet 0/0 (F0/0)	Fast Ethernet 0/1 (F0/1)	Serial 0/0/0 (S0/0/0)	Serial 0/0/1 (S0/0/1)
1900	Gigabit Ethernet 0/0 (G0/0)	Gigabit Ethernet 0/1 (G0/1)	Serial 0/0/0 (S0/0/0)	Serial 0/0/1 (S0/0/1)
2801	Fast Ethernet 0/0 (F0/0)	Fast Ethernet 0/1 (F0/1)	Serial 0/1/0 (S0/1/0)	Serial 0/1/1 (S0/1/1)
2811	Fast Ethernet 0/0 (F0/0)	Fast Ethernet 0/1 (F0/1)	Serial 0/0/0 (S0/0/0)	Serial 0/0/1 (S0/0/1)
2900	Gigabit Ethernet 0/0 (G0/0)	Gigabit Ethernet 0/1 (G0/1)	Serial 0/0/0 (S0/0/0)	Serial 0/0/1 (S0/0/1)

Note: To find out how the router is configured, look at the interfaces to identify the type of router and how many interfaces the router has. There is no way to effectively list all the combinations of configurations for each router class. This table includes identifiers for the possible combinations of Ethernet and Serial interfaces in the device. The table does not include any other type of interface, even though a specific router may contain one. An example of this might be an ISDN BRI interface. The string in parentheses is the legal abbreviation that can be used in Cisco IOS commands to represent the interface.

Packet Tracer
☐ Activity

11.4.3.6 Packet Tracer–Troubleshooting Connectivity Issues

Topology

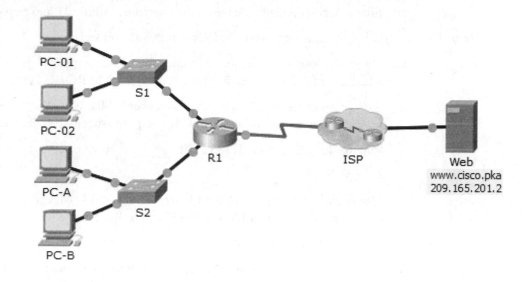

Addressing Table

Device	Interface	IP Address	Subnet Mask	Default Gateway
R1	G0/0	172.16.1.1	255.255.255.0	N/A
	G0/1	172.16.2.1	255.255.255.0	N/A
	S0/0/0	209.165.200.226	255.255.255.252	N/A
R2	G0/0	209.165.201.1	255.255.255.224	N/A
	S0/0/0 (DCE)	209.165.200.225	255.255.255.252	N/A
PC-01	NIC	172.16.1.3	255.255.255.0	172.16.1.1
PC-02	NIC	172.16.1.4	255.255.255.0	172.16.1.1
PC-A	NIC	172.16.2.3	255.255.255.0	172.16.2.1
PC-B	NIC	172.16.2.4	255.255.255.0	172.16.2.1
Web	NIC	209.165.201.2	255.255.255.224	209.165.201.1
DNS1	NIC	209.165.201.3	255.255.255.224	209.165.201.1
DNS2	NIC	209.165.201.4	255.255.255.224	209.165.201.1

Objectives

The objective of this Packet Tracer activity is to troubleshoot and resolve connectivity issues, if possible. Otherwise, the issues should be clearly documented so they can be escalated.

Background/Scenario

Users are reporting that they cannot access the web server, www.cisco.pka after a recent upgrade that included adding a second DNS server. You must determine the cause and attempt to resolve the issues for the users. Clearly document the issues and any solution(s). You do not have access to the devices in the cloud or the server www.cisco.pka. Escalate the problem if necessary.

Router R1 can only be accessed using SSH with the username **Admin01** and password **cisco12345**.

Step 1.   Determine the connectivity issue between PC-01 and web server.

    a.   On PC-01, open the command prompt. Enter the command **ipconfig** to verify what IP address and default gateway have been assigned to PC-01. Correct as necessary.

    b.   After correcting the IP addressing issues on PC-01, issue the pings to the default gateway, web server, and other PCs. Were the pings successful? Record the results.

        Ping to default gateway (172.16.1.1) _____   To web server (209.165.201.2) _____

        Ping to PC-02 _____   To PC-A _____   To PC-B _____

    c.   Use the web browser to access the web server on PC-01. Enter the URL www.cisco.pka and then using the IP address 209.165.201.2. Record the results.

        Can PC-01 access www.cisco.pka? _____   using the web server IP address? _____

    d.   Document the issues and provide the solution(s). Correct the issues if possible.

    _____

    _____

Step 2.   Determine the connectivity issue between PC-02 and web server.

    a.   On PC-02, open the command prompt. Enter the command **ipconfig** to verify the configuration for the IP address and default gateway. Correct as necessary.

    b.   After correcting the IP addressing issues on PC-02, issue the pings to the default gateway, web server, and other PCs. Were the pings successful? Record the results.

        Ping to default gateway (172.16.1.1) _____   To web server (209.165.201.2) _____

        Ping to PC-01 _____   To PC-A _____   To PC-B _____

    c.   Navigate to www.cisco.pka using the web browser on PC-02. Record the results.

        Can PC-01 access www.cisco.pka? _____   using the web server IP address _____

    d.   Document the issues and provide the solution(s). Correct the issues if possible.

    _____

    _____

Step 3.   Determine the connectivity issue between PC-A and web server.

    a.   On PC-A, open the command prompt. Enter the command **ipconfig** to verify the configuration for the IP address and default gateway. Correct as necessary.

    b.   After correcting the IP addressing issues on PC-A, issue the pings to the default gateway, web server, and other PCs. Were the pings successful? Record the results.

    Ping to default gateway (172.16.2.1) _____   To web server (209.165.201.2) _____

    Ping to PC-B _____   To PC-01 _____   To PC-02 _____

    c.   Navigate to www.cisco.pka.net using the web browser on PC-A. Record the results.

    Can PC-A access www.cisco.pka? _____   using the web server IP address _____

    d.   Document the issues and provide the solution(s). Correct the issues if possible.

    _____

    _____

Step 4.   Determine the connectivity issue between PC-B and web server.

    a.   On PC-B, open the command prompt. Enter the command **ipconfig** to verify the configuration for the IP address and default gateway. Correct as necessary.

    b.   After correcting the IP addressing issues on PC-B, issue the pings to the default gateway, web server, and other PCs. Were the pings successful? Record the results.

    Ping to default gateway (172.16.2.1) _____   To web server (209.165.201.2) _____

    Ping to PC-A _____   To PC-01 _____   To PC-02 _____

    c.   Navigate to www.cisco.pka using the web browser. Record the results.

    Can PC-B access www.cisco.pka? _____   using the web server IP address _____

    d.   Document the issues and provide the solution(s). Correct the issues if possible.

    _____

    _____

Step 5.   Verify connectivity.

Verify that all the PCs can access the web server www.cisco.pka.

Your completion percentage should be 100%. If not, click **Check Results** to see which required components are not yet completed.

Suggested Scoring Rubric

Activity Section	Possible Points	Earned Points
Step 1d	5	
Step 2d	5	
Step 3d	5	
Step 4d	5	
Packet Tracer	15	
Total Score	35	

11.5.1.1 Class Activity–Design and Build a Small Business Network (Capstone Project)

Objectives

Explain how a small network of directly connected segments is created, configured, and verified.

Background/Scenario

Note: This activity is best completed in groups of 2-3 students.

Design and build a network from scratch.

- Your design must include a minimum of one router, one switch, and one PC.
- Fully configure the network and use IPv4 or IPv6. (Subnetting must be included as a part of your addressing scheme.)
- Verify the network using at least five show commands.
- Secure the network using SSH, secure passwords, and console passwords (minimum).

Create a rubric to use for informal peer grading. Present your Capstone Project to the class and be able to answer questions from your peers and instructor!

Required Resources

- Packet Tracer
- Student/group-created rubric for assessment of the assignment

Reflection

1. What was the most difficult portion of this activity?

   _____

   _____

   _____

2. Why do you think network documentation is so important to this activity and in the real world?

   _____

   _____

   _____

11.5.1.2 Packet Tracer–Skills Integration Challenge

Packet Tracer
☐ Activity

Topology

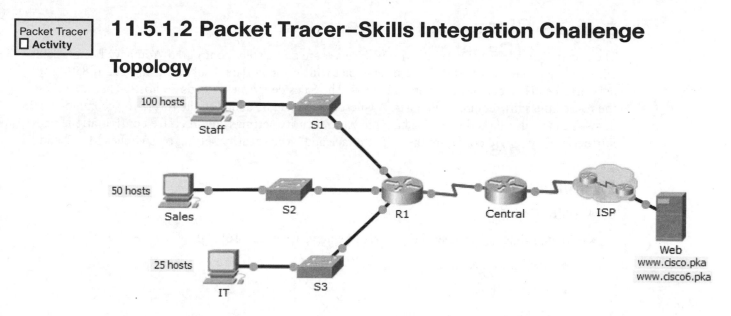

Addressing Table

Device	Interface	IPv4 Address	Subnet Mask	Default Gateway
		IPv6 Address/Prefix	IPv6 Link-local	
R1	G0/0			N/A
		2001:DB8:ACAD::1/64	FE80::1	N/A
	G0/1			N/A
		2001:DB8:ACAD:1::1/64	FE80::1	N/A
	G0/2			N/A
		2001:DB8:ACAD:2::1/64	FE80::1	N/A
	S0/0/1	172.16.1.2	255.255.255.252	N/A
		2001:DB8:2::1/64	FE80::1	N/A
Central	S0/0/0	209.165.200.226	255.255.255.252	N/A
		2001:DB8:1::1/64	FE80::2	N/A
	S0/0/1	172.16.1.1	255.255.255.252	N/A
		2001:DB8:2::2/64	FE80::2	N/A
S1	VLAN 1			
S2	VLAN 1			
S3	VLAN 1			
Staff	NIC			
		2001:DB8:ACAD::2/64	FE80::2	FE80::1
Sales	NIC			
		2001:DB8:ACAD:1::2/64	FE80::2	FE80::1
IT	NIC			
		2001:DB8:ACAD:2::2/64	FE80::2	FE80::1
Web	NIC	64.100.0.3	255.255.255.248	64.100.0.1
		2001:DB8:CAFE::3/64	FE80::2	FE80::1

Scenario/Background

The router Central, ISP cluster, and the Web server are completely configured. You have been tasked with creating a new IPv4 addressing scheme that will accommodate 4 subnets using 192.168.0.0/24 network. The IT department requires 25 hosts. The Sales department needs 50 hosts. The subnet for the rest of the staff requires 100 hosts. A Guest subnet will be added in the future to accommodate 25 hosts. You are also tasked with finishing the basic security settings and interface configurations on R1. Furthermore, you will configure the SVI interface and basic security setting on switches S1, S2, and S3.

Requirements

IPv4 Addressing

- Create subnets that meet the host requirements using 192.168.0.0/24.

    - Staff: 100 hosts

    - Sales: 50 hosts

    - IT: 25 hosts

    - Guest network to be added later: 25 hosts

- Document the assigned IPv4 addresses in the Addressing Table.

- Record the subnet for Guest network: _____

PC Configurations

- Configure the assigned IPv4 address, subnet mask, and default gateway settings on the Staff, Sales, and IT PCs using your addressing scheme.

- Assign IPv6 unicast and link local addresses and default gateway to the Staff, Sales, and IT networks according to the Addressing Table.

R1 Configurations

- Configure the device name according to the Addressing Table.

- Disable DNS lookup.

- Assign **Ciscoenpa55** as the encrypted privileged EXEC mode password.

- Assign **Ciscoconpa55** as the console password and enable login.

- Require that a minimum of 10 characters be used for all passwords.

- Encrypt all plaintext passwords.

- Create a banner that warns anyone accessing the device that unauthorized access is prohibited. Make sure to include the word **Warning** in the banner.

- Configure all the Gigabit Ethernet interfaces.

    - Configure the IPv4 addresses according to your addressing scheme.

    - Configure the IPv6 addresses according to the Addressing Table.

- Configure SSH on R1:

    - Set the domain name to **CCNA-lab.com**

    - Generate a **1024**-bit RSA key.

- Configure the VTY lines for SSH access.

- Use the local user profiles for authentication.

- Create a user **Admin1** with a privilege level of **15** using the encrypted password for **Admin1pa55**.

- Configure the console and VTY lines to log out after five minutes of inactivity.

- Block anyone for three minutes who fails to log in after four attempts within a two-minute period.

Switch Configurations

- Configure the device name according to the Addressing Table.

- Configure the SVI interface with the IPv4 address and subnet mask according to your addressing scheme.

- Configure the default gateway.

- Disable DNS lookup.

- Assign **Ciscoenpa55** as the encrypted privileged EXEC mode password.

- Assign **Ciscoconpa55** as the console password and enable login.

- Configure the console and VTY lines to log out after five minutes of inactivity.

- Encrypt all plaintext passwords.

Verify Connectivity

- Using the web browser from Staff, Sales, and IT PCs, navigate to **www.cisco.pka**.

- Using the web browser from Staff, Sales, and IT PCs, navigate to **www.cisco6.pka**.

- All PCs should be able to ping all the devices.

Packet Tracer
☐ Activity

11.5.1.3 Packet Tracer–Troubleshooting Challenge

Topology

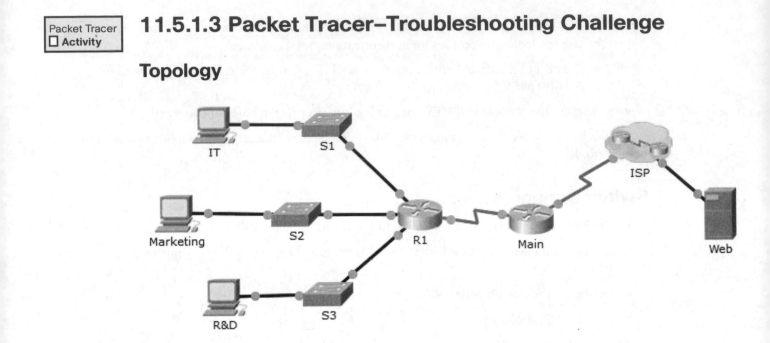

Addressing Table

Device	Interface	IPv4 Address	Subnet Mask	Default Gateway
		IPv6 Address/Prefix	IPv6 Link-local	
R1	G0/0	172.16.1.62	255.255.255.192	N/A
		2001:DB8:CAFE::1/64	FE80::1	N/A
	G0/1	172.16.1.126	255.255.255.192	N/A
		2001:DB8:CAFE:1::1/64	FE80::1	N/A
	G0/2	172.16.1.254	255.255.255.128	N/A
		2001:DB8:CAFE:2::1/64	FE80::1	N/A
	S0/0/1	10.0.0.2	255.255.255.252	N/A
		2001:DB8:2::1/64	FE80::1	N/A
Main	S0/0/0	209.165.200.226	255.255.255.252	N/A
		2001:DB8:1::1/64	FE80::2	N/A
	S0/0/1	10.0.0.1	255.255.255.252	N/A
		2001:DB8:2::2/64	FE80::2	N/A
S1	VLAN 1	172.16.1.61	255.255.255.192	172.16.1.62
S2	VLAN 1	172.16.1.125	255.255.255.192	172.16.1.126
S3	VLAN 1	172.16.1.253	255.255.255.128	172.16.1.254
IT	NIC	172.16.1.1	255.255.255.192	172.16.1.62
		2001:DB8:CAFE::2/64	FE80::2	FE80::1
Marketing	NIC	172.16.1.65	255.255.255.192	172.16.1.126
		2001:DB8:CAFE:1::2/64	FE80::2	FE80::1

Device	Interface	IPv4 Address	Subnet Mask	Default Gateway
		IPv6 Address/Prefix	IPv6 Link-local	
R&D	NIC	172.16.1.129	255.255.255.128	172.16.1.254
		2001:DB8:CAFE:2::2/64	FE80::2	FE80::1
Web	NIC	64.100.0.3	255.255.255.248	64.100.0.1
		2001:DB8:ACAD::3/64	FE80::2	FE80::1

Scenario/Background

After an update to the network, some devices were misconfigured. You have been tasked with correcting the configurations and verifying that all the PCs can access the websites, R1, switches, and other PCs can access R1 using SSH.

Router R1 and all the switches have been preconfigured with the following:

- Enable password: **Ciscoenpa55**

- Console password: **Ciscoconpa55**

- Admin username and password: **Admin1/Admin1pa55**

Required number of hosts per subnet:

- IT: 50 hosts

- Marketing: 50 hosts

- R&D: 100 hosts

Requirements

- IT, Marketing, and R&D PCs can navigate to **www.cisco.pka** and **www.cisco6.pka**.

- IT, Marketing, and R&D PCs can SSH into R1 with the username **Admin1** and encrypted password **Admin1pa55**.

- All PCs should be able to ping R1, S1, S2, S3, and other PCs.

Appendix Lab–Observing ARP with the Windows CLI, IOS CLI, and Wireshark

Topology

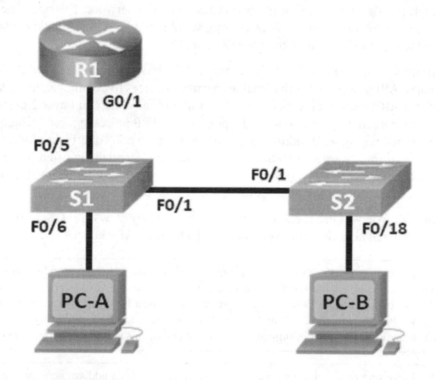

Addressing Table

Device	Interface	IP Address	Subnet Mask	Default Gateway
R1	G0/1	192.168.1.1	255.255.255.0	N/A
S1	VLAN 1	192.168.1.11	255.255.255.0	192.168.1.1
S2	VLAN 1	192.168.1.12	255.255.255.0	192.168.1.1
PC-A	NIC	192.168.1.3	255.255.255.0	192.168.1.1
PC-B	NIC	192.168.1.2	255.255.255.0	192.168.1.1

Objectives

Part 1: Build and Configure the Network

Part 2: Use the Windows ARP Command

Part 3: Use the IOS Show ARP Command

Part 4: Use Wireshark to Examine ARP Exchanges

Background/Scenario

The Address Resolution Protocol (ARP) is used by TCP/IP to map a Layer 3 IP address to a Layer 2 MAC address. When a frame is placed on the network, it must have a destination MAC address. To dynamically discover the MAC address for the destination device, an ARP request is broadcast on the LAN. The device that contains the destination IP address responds, and the MAC address is recorded in the ARP cache. Every device on the LAN keeps its own ARP cache, or small area in RAM that holds ARP results. An ARP cache timer removes ARP entries that have not been used for a certain period of time.

ARP is an excellent example of performance trade-off. With no cache, ARP must continually request address translations each time a frame is placed on the network. This adds latency to the communication and could congest the LAN. Conversely, unlimited hold times could cause errors with devices that leave the network or change the Layer 3 address.

A network administrator should be aware of ARP, but may not interact with the protocol on a regular basis. ARP is a protocol that enables network devices to communicate with the TCP/IP protocol. Without ARP, there is no efficient method to build the datagram Layer 2 destination address. Also, ARP is a potential security risk. ARP spoofing, or ARP poisoning, is a technique used by an attacker to inject the wrong MAC address association in a network. An attacker forges the MAC address of a device, and frames are sent to the wrong destination. Manually configuring static ARP associations is one way to prevent ARP spoofing. Finally, an authorized MAC address list may be configured on Cisco devices to restrict network access to only approved devices.

In this lab, you will use the ARP commands in both Windows and Cisco routers to display the ARP table. You will also clear the ARP cache and add static ARP entries.

Note: The routers used with CCNA hands-on labs are Cisco 1941 Integrated Services Routers (ISRs) with Cisco IOS Release 15.2(4)M3 (universalk9 image). The switches used are Cisco Catalyst 2960s with Cisco IOS Release 15.0(2) (lanbasek9 image). Other routers, switches, and Cisco IOS versions can be used. Depending on the model and Cisco IOS version, the commands available and output produced might vary from what is shown in the labs. Refer to the Router Interface Summary Table at the end of this lab for the correct interface identifiers.

Note: Make sure that the routers and switches have been erased and have no startup configurations. If you are unsure, contact your instructor.

Required Resources

- 1 Router (Cisco 1941 with Cisco IOS Release 15.2(4)M3 universal image or comparable)
- 2 Switches (Cisco 2960 with Cisco IOS Release 15.0(2) lanbasek9 image or comparable)
- 2 PCs (Windows 7, Vista, or XP with terminal emulation program, such as Tera Term and Wireshark installed)
- Console cables to configure the Cisco IOS devices via the console ports
- Ethernet cables as shown in the topology

Note: The Fast Ethernet interfaces on Cisco 2960 switches are autosensing and an Ethernet straight-through cable may be used between switches S1 and S2. If using another Cisco switch model, it may be necessary to use an Ethernet crossover cable.

Part 1: Build and Configure the Network

Step 1.   Cable the network according to the topology.

Step 2.   Configure the IP addresses for the devices according to the Addressing Table.

Step 3.   Verify network connectivity by pinging all the devices from PC-B.

Part 2: Use the Windows ARP Command

The **arp** command allows the user to view and modify the ARP cache in Windows. You access this command from the Windows command prompt.

Step 1.   Display the ARP cache.

    a.   Open a command window on PC-A and type **arp**.

```
C:\Users\User1> arp

Displays and modifies the IP-to-Physical address translation tables used by
address resolution protocol (ARP).

ARP -s inet_addr eth_addr [if_addr]
ARP -d inet_addr [if_addr]
ARP -a [inet_addr] [-N if_addr] [-v]

   -a            Displays current ARP entries by interrogating the current
                 protocol data.  If inet_addr is specified, the IP and Physical
                 addresses for only the specified computer are displayed.  If
                 more than one network interface uses ARP, entries for each ARP
                 table are displayed.
   -g            Same as -a.
   -v            Displays current ARP entries in verbose mode.  All invalid
                 entries and entries on the loop-back interface will be shown.
   inet_addr     Specifies an internet address.
   -N if_addr    Displays the ARP entries for the network interface specified
                 by if_addr.
   -d            Deletes the host specified by inet_addr. inet_addr may be
                 wildcarded with * to delete all hosts.
   -s            Adds the host and associates the Internet address inet_addr
                 with the Physical address eth_addr.  The Physical address is
                 given as 6 hexadecimal bytes separated by hyphens. The entry
                 is permanent.
   eth_addr      Specifies a physical address.
   if_addr       If present, this specifies the Internet address of the
                 interface whose address translation table should be modified.
                 If not present, the first applicable interface will be used.
Example:
   > arp -s 157.55.85.212   00-aa-00-62-c6-09  .... Adds a static entry.
   > arp -a                                    .... Displays the arp table.
```

b. Examine the output.

What command would be used to display all entries in the ARP cache?

_____

What command would be used to delete all ARP cache entries (flush ARP cache)?

_____

What command would be used to delete the ARP cache entry for 192.168.1.11?

_____

c. Type **arp –a** to display the ARP table.

```
C:\Users\User1> arp -a


Interface: 192.168.1.3 --- 0xb
  Internet Address       Physical Address      Type
  192.168.1.1            d4-8c-b5-ce-a0-c1     dynamic
  192.168.1.255          ff-ff-ff-ff-ff-ff     static
  224.0.0.22             01-00-5e-00-00-16     static
  224.0.0.252            01-00-5e-00-00-fc     static
  239.255.255.250        01-00-5e-7f-ff-fa     static
```

Note: The ARP table is empty if you use Windows XP (as displayed below).

```
C:\Documents and Settings\User1> arp -a
No ARP Entries Found.
```

d. Ping from PC-A to PC-B to dynamically add entries in the ARP cache.

```
C:\Documents and Settings\User1> ping 192.168.1.2


Interface: 192.168.1.3 --- 0xb
  Internet Address       Physical Address      Type
  192.168.1.2            00-50-56-be-f6-db     dynamic
```

What is the physical address for the host with IP address of 192.168.1.2?

_____

Step 2. Adjust entries in the ARP cache manually.

To delete entries in ARP cache, issue the command **arp –d {inet-addr | *}**. Addresses can be deleted individually by specifying the IP address, or all entries can be deleted with the wildcard *.

Verify that the ARP cache contains the following entries: the R1 G0/1 default gateway (192.168.1.1), PC-B (192.168.1.2), and both switches (192.168.1.11 and 192.168.1.12).

a. From PC-A, ping all the addresses in the Address Table.

b. Verify that all the addresses have been added to the ARP cache. If the address is not in ARP cache, ping the destination address and verify that the address was added to the ARP cache.

```
C:\Users\User1> arp -a

Interface: 192.168.1.3 --- 0xb
  Internet Address      Physical Address     Type
  192.168.1.1           d4-8c-b5-ce-a0-c1    dynamic
  192.168.1.2           00-50-56-be-f6-db    dynamic
  192.168.1.11          0c-d9-96-e8-8a-40    dynamic
  192.168.1.12          0c-d9-96-d2-40-40    dynamic
  192.168.1.255         ff-ff-ff-ff-ff-ff    static
  224.0.0.22            01-00-5e-00-00-16    static
  224.0.0.252           01-00-5e-00-00-fc    static
  239.255.255.250       01-00-5e-7f-ff-fa    static
```

c. As an administrator, access the command prompt. Click the **Start** icon, and in the Search programs and file box, type **cmd**. When the **cmd** icon appears, right-click the icon and select **Run as administrator**. Click **Yes** to allow this program to make changes.

Note: For Windows XP users, it is not necessary to have administrator privileges to modify ARP cache entries.

---

d. In the Administrator command prompt window, type **arp –d ***. This command deletes all the ARP cache entries. Verify that all the ARP cache entries are deleted by typing **arp –a** at the command prompt.

```
C:\windows\system32> arp -d *
C:\windows\system32> arp -a
No ARP Entries Found.
```

e. Wait a few minutes. The Neighbor Discovery protocol starts to populate the ARP cache again.

```
C:\Users\User1> arp -a


Interface: 192.168.1.3 --- 0xb
  Internet Address        Physical Address        Type
    192.168.1.255           ff-ff-ff-ff-ff-ff       static
```

Note: The Neighbor Discovery protocol is not implemented in Windows XP.

f. From PC-A, ping PC-B (192.168.1.2) and the switches (192.168.1.11 and 192.168.1.12) to add the ARP entries. Verify that the ARP entries have been added to the cache.

```
C:\Users\User1> arp -a


Interface: 192.168.1.3 --- 0xb
  Internet Address        Physical Address        Type
    192.168.1.2             00-50-56-be-f6-db       dynamic
    192.168.1.11            0c-d9-96-e8-8a-40       dynamic
    192.168.1.12            0c-d9-96-d2-40-40       dynamic
    192.168.1.255           ff-ff-ff-ff-ff-ff       static
```

g. Record the physical address for switch S2.

_____

h. Delete a specific ARP cache entry by typing **arp –d inet-addr**. At the command prompt, type **arp -d 192.168.1.12** to delete the ARP entry for S2.

```
C:\windows\system32> arp -d 192.168.1.12
```

i. Type **arp –a** to verify that the ARP entry for S2 has been removed from the ARP cache.

```
C:\Users\User1> arp -a


Interface: 192.168.1.3 --- 0xb
  Internet Address        Physical Address        Type
    192.168.1.2             00-50-56-be-f6-db       dynamic
    192.168.1.11            0c-d9-96-e8-8a-40       dynamic
    192.168.1.255           ff-ff-ff-ff-ff-ff       static
```

j. You can add a specific ARP cache entry by typing **arp –s inet_addr mac_addr**. The IP address and MAC address for S2 will be used in this example. Use the MAC address recorded in Step g.

```
C:\windows\system32> arp -s 192.168.1.12 0c-d9-96-d2-40-40
```

k. Verify that the ARP entry for S2 has been added to the cache.

Part 3: Use the IOS show arp Command

The Cisco IOS can also display the ARP cache on routers and switches with the **show arp** or **show ip arp** command.

Step 1.   Display ARP entries on router R1.

```
R1# show arp
Protocol  Address          Age (min)  Hardware Addr   Type  Interface
Internet  192.168.1.1              -  d48c.b5ce.a0c1  ARPA  GigabitEthernet0/1
Internet  192.168.1.2              0  0050.56be.f6db  ARPA  GigabitEthernet0/1
Internet  192.168.1.3              0  0050.56be.768c  ARPA  GigabitEthernet0/1
R1#
```

Notice there is no Age (-) for the first entry, router interface G0/1 (the LAN default gateway). The Age is the number of minutes (min) that the entry has been in ARP cache and is incremented for the other entries. The Neighbor Discovery protocol populates the PC-A and PC-B IP and MAC address ARP entries.

Step 2.   Add ARP entries on router R1.

You can add ARP entries to the ARP table of the router by pinging other devices.

   a. Ping switch S1.

```
R1# ping 192.168.1.11
Type escape sequence to abort.
Sending 5, 100-byte ICMP Echos to 192.168.1.11, timeout is 2 seconds:
.!!!!
Success rate is 80 percent (4/5), round-trip min/avg/max = 1/2/4 ms
```

   b. Verify that an ARP entry for switch S1 has been added to the ARP table of R1.

```
R1# show ip arp
Protocol  Address          Age (min)  Hardware Addr   Type  Interface
Internet  192.168.1.1              -  d48c.b5ce.a0c1  ARPA  GigabitEthernet0/1
Internet  192.168.1.2              6  0050.56be.f6db  ARPA  GigabitEthernet0/1
Internet  192.168.1.3              6  0050.56be.768c  ARPA  GigabitEthernet0/1
Internet  192.168.1.11             0  0cd9.96e8.8a40  ARPA  GigabitEthernet0/1
R1#
```

Step 3.   Display ARP entries on switch S1.

```
S1# show ip arp
Protocol  Address          Age (min)  Hardware Addr   Type  Interface
Internet  192.168.1.1             46  d48c.b5ce.a0c1  ARPA  Vlan1
Internet  192.168.1.2              8  0050.56be.f6db  ARPA  Vlan1
Internet  192.168.1.3              8  0050.56be.768c  ARPA  Vlan1
Internet  192.168.1.11             -  0cd9.96e8.8a40  ARPA  Vlan1
S1#
```

Step 4.   Add ARP entries on switch S1.

By pinging other devices, ARP entries can also be added to the ARP table of the switch.

a. From switch S1, ping switch S2.

```
S1# ping 192.168.1.12
Type escape sequence to abort.
Sending 5, 100-byte ICMP Echos to 192.168.1.12, timeout is 2 seconds:
.!!!!
Success rate is 80 percent (4/5), round-trip min/avg/max = 1/2/8 ms
```

b. Verify that the ARP entry for switch S2 has been added to ARP table of S1.

```
S1# show ip arp
Protocol  Address          Age (min)  Hardware Addr   Type   Interface
Internet  192.168.1.1              5  d48c.b5ce.a0c1  ARPA   Vlan1
Internet  192.168.1.2             11  0050.56be.f6db  ARPA   Vlan1
Internet  192.168.1.3             11  0050.56be.768c  ARPA   Vlan1
Internet  192.168.1.11             -  0cd9.96e8.8a40  ARPA   Vlan1
Internet  192.168.1.12             2  0cd9.96d2.4040  ARPA   Vlan1
S1#
```

Part 4: Use Wireshark to Examine ARP Exchanges

In Part 4, you will examine ARP exchanges by using Wireshark to capture and evaluate the ARP exchange. You will also examine network latency caused by ARP exchanges between devices.

Step 1.   Configure Wireshark for packet captures.

a. Start Wireshark.

b. Choose the network interface to use for capturing the ARP exchanges.

Step 2.   Capture and evaluate ARP communications.

a. Start capturing packets in Wireshark. Use the filter to display only ARP packets.

b. Flush the ARP cache by typing the **arp –d** * command at the command prompt.

c. Verify that the ARP cache has been cleared.

d. Send a ping to the default gateway, using the **ping 192.168.1.1** command.

e. Stop the Wireshark capture after pinging to the default gateway is finished.

f. Examine the Wireshark captures for the ARP exchanges in the packet details pane.

What was the first ARP packet? _____

```
File  Edit  View  Go  Capture  Analyze  Statistics  Telephony  Tools  Internals  Help
```

Filter: arp   ▼ Expression... Clear Apply Save

No.	Time	Source	Destination	Protocol	Length	Info
6	1.795609000	Dell_19:55:92	Broadcast	ARP	42	Who has 192.168.1.1? Tell 192.168.1.3
7	1.796075000	Cisco_45:73:a1	Dell_19:55:92	ARP	60	192.168.1.1 is at c4:71:fe:45:73:a1

```
⊞ Frame 6: 42 bytes on wire (336 bits), 42 bytes captured (336 bits) on interface 0
⊞ Ethernet II, Src: Dell_19:55:92 (5c:26:0a:19:55:92), Dst: Broadcast (ff:ff:ff:ff:ff:ff)
⊟ Address Resolution Protocol (request)
    Hardware type: Ethernet (1)
    Protocol type: IP (0x0800)
    Hardware size: 6
    Protocol size: 4
    Opcode: request (1)
    Sender MAC address: Dell_19:55:92 (5c:26:0a:19:55:92)
    Sender IP address: 192.168.1.3 (192.168.1.3)
    Target MAC address: 00:00:00_00:00:00 (00:00:00:00:00:00)
    Target IP address: 192.168.1.1 (192.168.1.1)
```

```
0000  ff ff ff ff ff ff 5c 26  0a 19 55 92 08 06 00 01   ......\& ..U.....
0010  08 00 06 04 00 01 5c 26  0a 19 55 92 c0 a8 01 03   ......\& ..U.....
0020  00 00 00 00 00 00 c0 a8  01 01                     ........ ..
```

Fill in the following table with information about your first captured ARP packet:

Field	Value
Sender MAC address	
Sender IP address	
Target MAC address	
Target IP address	

What was the second ARP packet? _____

```
File  Edit  View  Go  Capture  Analyze  Statistics  Telephony  Tools  Internals  Help
```

Filter: arp   ▼ Expression... Clear Apply Save

No.	Time	Source	Destination	Protocol	Length	Info
6	1.795609000	Dell_19:55:92	Broadcast	ARP	42	who has 192.168.1.1? Tell 192.168.1.3
7	1.796075000	Cisco_45:73:a1	Dell_19:55:92	ARP	60	192.168.1.1 is at c4:71:fe:45:73:a1

```
⊞ Frame 7: 60 bytes on wire (480 bits), 60 bytes captured (480 bits) on interface 0
⊞ Ethernet II, Src: Cisco_45:73:a1 (c4:71:fe:45:73:a1), Dst: Dell_19:55:92 (5c:26:0a:19:55:92)
⊟ Address Resolution Protocol (reply)
    Hardware type: Ethernet (1)
    Protocol type: IP (0x0800)
    Hardware size: 6
    Protocol size: 4
    Opcode: reply (2)
    Sender MAC address: Cisco_45:73:a1 (c4:71:fe:45:73:a1)
    Sender IP address: 192.168.1.1 (192.168.1.1)
    Target MAC address: Dell_19:55:92 (5c:26:0a:19:55:92)
    Target IP address: 192.168.1.3 (192.168.1.3)
```

```
0000  5c 26 0a 19 55 92 c4 71  fe 45 73 a1 08 06 00 01   \&..U..q .Es.....
0010  08 00 06 04 00 02 c4 71  fe 45 73 a1 c0 a8 01 01   .......q .Es.....
0020  5c 26 0a 19 55 92 c0 a8  01 03 00 00 00 00 00 00   \&..U... ........
0030  00 00 00 00 00 00 00 00  00 00 00 00               ........ ....
```

Fill in the following table with information about your second captured ARP packet:

Field	Value
Sender MAC address	
Sender IP address	
Target MAC address	
Target IP address	

Step 3.   Examine network latency caused by ARP.

    a.   Clear the ARP entries on PC-A.

    b.   Start a Wireshark capture.

    c.   Ping switch S2 (192.168.1.12). The ping should be successful after the first echo request.

Note: If all the pings were successful, S1 should be reloaded to observe network latency with ARP.

```
C:\Users\User1> ping 192.168.1.12
Request timed out.
Reply from 192.168.1.12: bytes=32 time=2ms TTL=255
Reply from 192.168.1.12: bytes=32 time=2ms TTL=255
Reply from 192.168.1.12: bytes=32 time=2ms TTL=255

Ping statistics for 192.168.1.12:
    Packets: Sent = 4, Received = 3, Lost = 1 (25% loss),
Approximate round trip times in milli-seconds:
    Minimum = 1ms, Maximum = 3ms, Average = 2ms
```

d. Stop the Wireshark capture after the pinging is finished. Use the Wireshark filter to display only ARP and ICMP outputs. In Wireshark, type **arp or icmp** in the **Filter:** entry area.

e. Examine the Wireshark capture. In this example, frame 10 is the first ICMP request sent by PC-A to S1. Because there is no ARP entry for S1, an ARP request was sent to the management IP address of S1 asking for the MAC address. During the ARP exchanges, the echo request did not receive a reply before the request was timed out. (frames 8–12)

After the ARP entry for S1 was added to the ARP cache, the last three ICMP exchanges were successful, as displayed in frames 26, 27, and 30–33.

As displayed in the Wireshark capture, ARP is an excellent example of performance trade-off. With no cache, ARP must continually request address translations each time a frame is placed on the network. This adds latency to the communication and could congest the LAN.

File   Edit   View   Go   Capture   Analyze   Statistics   Telephony   Tools   Internals   Help

Filter: arp or icmp   ▼   Expression...   Clear   Apply   Save

No.	Time	Source	Destination	Protocol	Length	Info
8	1.649929000	Dell_19:55:92	Broadcast	ARP	42	Who has 192.168.1.12? Tell 192.168.1.3
9	1.651202000	Cisco_59:91:c0	Dell_19:55:92	ARP	60	192.168.1.12 is at 00:23:5d:59:91:c0
10	1.651489000	192.168.1.3	192.168.1.12	ICMP	74	Echo (ping) request id=0x0001, seq=187:
11	1.653790000	Cisco_59:91:c0	Broadcast	ARP	60	Who has 192.168.1.3? Tell 192.168.1.12
12	1.653999000	Dell_19:55:92	Cisco_59:91:c0	ARP	42	192.168.1.3 is at 5c:26:0a:19:55:92
26	6.562409000	192.168.1.3	192.168.1.12	ICMP	74	Echo (ping) request id=0x0001, seq=1874
27	6.564426000	192.168.1.12	192.168.1.3	ICMP	74	Echo (ping) reply id=0x0001, seq=1874
30	7.560977000	192.168.1.3	192.168.1.12	ICMP	74	Echo (ping) request id=0x0001, seq=187!
31	7.563586000	192.168.1.12	192.168.1.3	ICMP	74	Echo (ping) reply id=0x0001, seq=187!
32	8.559352000	192.168.1.3	192.168.1.12	ICMP	74	Echo (ping) request id=0x0001, seq=187(
33	8.560466000	192.168.1.12	192.168.1.3	ICMP	74	Echo (ping) reply id=0x0001, seq=187(

⊞ Frame 8: 42 bytes on wire (336 bits), 42 bytes captured (336 bits) on interface 0
⊞ Ethernet II, Src: Dell_19:55:92 (5c:26:0a:19:55:92), Dst: Broadcast (ff:ff:ff:ff:ff:ff)
⊟ Address Resolution Protocol (request)
    Hardware type: Ethernet (1)
    Protocol type: IP (0x0800)
    Hardware size: 6
    Protocol size: 4
    Opcode: request (1)
    Sender MAC address: Dell_19:55:92 (5c:26:0a:19:55:92)
    Sender IP address: 192.168.1.3 (192.168.1.3)
    Target MAC address: 00:00:00_00:00:00 (00:00:00:00:00:00)
    Target IP address: 192.168.1.12 (192.168.1.12)

```
0000  ff ff ff ff ff ff 5c 26  0a 19 55 92 08 06 00 01   ......\& ..U.....
0010  08 00 06 04 00 01 5c 26  0a 19 55 92 c0 a8 01 03   ......\& ..U.....
0020  00 00 00 00 00 00 c0 a8  01 0c                      ........ ..
```

Reflection

1. How and when are static ARP entries removed?

_____

2. Why do you want to add static ARP entries in the cache?

_____

3. If ARP requests can cause network latency, why is it a bad idea to have unlimited hold times for ARP entries?

_____

Router Interface Summary Table

Router Interface Summary				
Router Model	Ethernet Interface #1	Ethernet Interface #2	Serial Interface #1	Serial Interface #2
1800	Fast Ethernet 0/0 (F0/0)	Fast Ethernet 0/1 (F0/1)	Serial 0/0/0 (S0/0/0)	Serial 0/0/1 (S0/0/1)
1900	Gigabit Ethernet 0/0 (G0/0)	Gigabit Ethernet 0/1 (G0/1)	Serial 0/0/0 (S0/0/0)	Serial 0/0/1 (S0/0/1)
2801	Fast Ethernet 0/0 (F0/0)	Fast Ethernet 0/1 (F0/1)	Serial 0/1/0 (S0/1/0)	Serial 0/1/1 (S0/1/1)
2811	Fast Ethernet 0/0 (F0/0)	Fast Ethernet 0/1 (F0/1)	Serial 0/0/0 (S0/0/0)	Serial 0/0/1 (S0/0/1)
2900	Gigabit Ethernet 0/0 (G0/0)	Gigabit Ethernet 0/1 (G0/1)	Serial 0/0/0 (S0/0/0)	Serial 0/0/1 (S0/0/1)

Note: To find out how the router is configured, look at the interfaces to identify the type of router and how many interfaces the router has. There is no way to effectively list all the combinations of configurations for each router class. This table includes identifiers for the possible combinations of Ethernet and Serial interfaces in the device. The table does not include any other type of interface, even though a specific router may contain one. An example of this might be an ISDN BRI interface. The string in parentheses is the legal abbreviation that can be used in Cisco IOS commands to represent the interface.

Appendix Lab–Researching Subnet Calculators

Objectives

Part 1: Review Available Subnet Calculators

Part 2: Perform Network Calculations Using a Subnet Calculator

Background/Scenario

While it is important to understand how to convert a decimal IP address to its binary format and apply the bitwise ANDing operation to determine the network address, it is also a tedious and mistake-prone process. To assist with these calculations, many network administrators make use of an IP subnet calculator utility program. A number of these types of programs have been developed that can be downloaded or run directly from the Internet.

In this lab, you will be introduced to a few of the free IP subnet calculators that are available. You will use a web-based IP subnet calculator to perform the network operations in this lab.

Required Resources

Device with Internet access

Part 1: Review Available Subnet Calculators

In Part 1, you are introduced to two types of subnet calculators: client-based (programs that are downloaded and installed) and web-based (utilities that are run from a browser).

Step 1.   Review client-based subnet calculators.

Solarwinds provides a free subnet calculator that can be downloaded and installed on a PC running a Windows operating system. You will be required to provide personal information (Name, Company, Location, Email Address, and Phone Number) to be able to download this program. You can download and install the Solarwinds Subnet Calculator at www.solarwinds.com.

If you have a PC running Linux, it is recommended that you use the **ipcalc** utility (available with most Linux distributions). Use the **apt-get install ipcalc** command to install ipcalc on a PC running Linux.

Step 2.   Use a web-based subnet calculator.

Web-based subnet calculators do not require installation, but you do need Internet access to use them. The following web-based subnet calculator is accessible from any device that has Internet access, including smartphones and tablets.

a.   From your browser, go to www.ipcalc.org and click the **IP Subnet Calculator** link.

Note: Several other useful utilities are also listed on the menu, such as MAC vendor lookup, whois lookup, and DNS lookup.

Note: At the time of this writing, a page formatting issue was encountered when viewing the www.ipcalc.org website using Internet Explorer (Version 9). While the site functioned correctly, you may want to consider using another browser (Firefox or Chrome) when accessing this site.

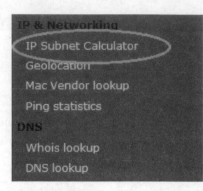

b. On the IP Subnet Calculator screen, enter an IP address and subnet mask or an IP address and CIDR prefix notation. Examples of how to enter each of these are shown in the Introduction area.

:: IP Subnet Calculator ::

Introduction:

A subnet is a logically visible subdivision of an IP network. The practice of dividing a network into subnetworks is called subnetting.

This application will help you to compute information about IP subnetting. It's easy to use.

In the following form you can enter differents address format:

Description	Format
IP & CIDR Netmask	10.0.0.1/22
IP & Netmask	10.0.0.1 255.255.252.0
IP & Wildcard Mask	10.0.0.1 0.0.3.255

The behavior of this application is the same that the *ipcalc* binary of GNU/Linux system's !

Application:

Enter IP & Mask or CIDR here !   Calc !

c. In the Application field, enter **192.168.50.50/27** and click **Calc!**. The next screen displays a table with network information in both decimal and binary formats.

Application:

192.168.50.50/27   Calc !

Description	Value		Extra
Address	192.168.50.50	11000000.10101000.00110010.00110010	
Netmask	255.255.255.224	11111111.11111111.11111111.11100000	/27
Network	192.168.50.32	11000000.10101000.00110010.00100000	
Broadcast	192.168.50.63		
Host min	192.168.50.33	11000000.10101000.00110010.00100001	
Host max	192.168.50.62	11000000.10101000.00110010.00111110	
Host/net	30	Class C, Private Internet	

d. Using the information provided in the example above, answer the following questions.

What is the network address? _____

What is the subnet mask? _____

How many hosts will this network support? _____

What is the lowest host address? _____

What is the highest host address? _____

What is the broadcast address? _____

Part 2: Perform Network Calculations Using a Subnet Calculator

In Part 2, use the www.ipcalc.org web-based subnet calculator to fill in the tables provided.

Step 1.   Fill in the following table for address 10.223.23.136/10:

Description	Decimal	Binary
Address	10.223.23.136	
Subnet mask		
Network address		
Broadcast address		
First host address		
Last host address		
Number of hosts available	N/A	

What is the type of address: public or private? _____

Step 2.   Fill in the following table for the 172.18.255.92 address with a subnet mask of 255.255.224.0:

Description	Decimal	Binary
Address	172.18.255.92	
Subnet mask	255.255.224.0	
Network address		
Broadcast address		
First host address		
Last host address		
Number of hosts available	N/A	

What is the CIDR prefix notation for this network? _____

What is the type of address: public or private? _____

Step 3.   Fill in the following table using the 192.168.184.78 address with a subnet mask of 255.255.255.252:

Description	Decimal	Binary
Address	192.168.184.78	
Subnet mask		
Network address		
Broadcast address		
First host address		
Last host address		
Number of hosts available	N/A	

What is the CIDR prefix notation for this network? _____

What is the type of address: public or private? _____

Where would you most likely find a network like this being used?

_____

Step 4.   Fill in the following table for the 209.165.200.225/27 address:

Description	Decimal	Binary
Address	209.165.200.225	
Subnet mask		
Network address		
Broadcast address		
First host address		
Last host address		
Number of hosts available	N/A	

What is the type of address: public or private? _____

Step 5.   Fill in the following table for address 64.104.110.7/20:

Description	Decimal	Binary
Address	64.104.110.7	
Subnet mask		
Network address		
Broadcast address		
First host address		
Last host address		
Number of hosts available	N/A	

What is the type of address: public or private? _____

Reflection

1. What is an advantage of using a client-based subnet calculator?

   _____

   _____

2. What is an advantage of using a web-based subnet calculator?

   _____

   _____

Appendix Lab–Subnetting Network Topologies

Objectives

Parts 1 to 5, for each network topology:

- Determine the number of subnets.
- Design an appropriate addressing scheme.
- Assign addresses and subnet mask pairs to device interfaces.
- Examine the use of the available network address space and future growth potential.

Background/Scenario

When given a network topology, it is important to be able to determine the number of subnets required. In this lab, several scenario topologies will be provided, along with a base network address and mask. You will subnet the network address and provide an IP addressing scheme that will accommodate the number of subnets displayed in the topology diagram. You must determine the number of bits to borrow, the number of hosts per subnet, and potential for growth as specified by the instructions.

Part 1: Network Topology A

In Part 1, you have been given the 192.168.10.0/24 network address to subnet, with the following topology. Determine the number of networks needed and then design an appropriate addressing scheme.

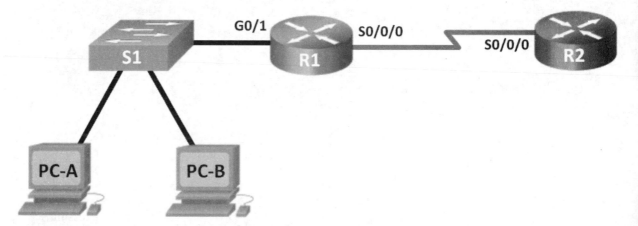

Step 1. Determine the number of subnets in Network Topology A.

    a. How many subnets are there? _____

    b. How many bits should you borrow to create the required number of subnets?

    _____

    c. How many usable host addresses per subnet are in this addressing scheme?

    _____

    d. What is the new subnet mask in dotted decimal format? _____

    e. How many subnets are available for future use? _____

Step 2.   Record the subnet information.

Fill in the following table with the subnet information:

Subnet Number	Subnet Address	First Usable Host Address	Last Usable Host Address	Broadcast Address
0				
1				
2				
3				
4				
5				

Part 2: Network Topology B

The network topology from Part 1 has expanded to accommodate the addition of router R3 and its accompanying network, as illustrated in the following topology. Use the 192.168.10.0/24 network address to provide addresses to the network devices, and then design a new addressing scheme to support the additional network requirement.

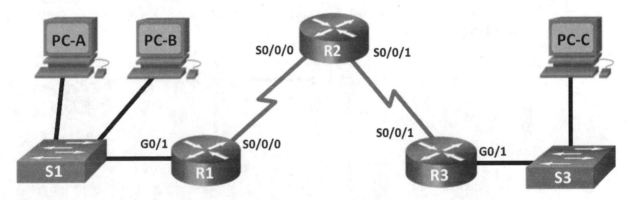

Step 1.   Determine the number of subnets in Network Topology B.

   a.   How many subnets are there? _____

   b.   How many bits should you borrow to create the required number of subnets? _____

   c.   How many usable host addresses per subnet are in this addressing scheme? _____

   d.   What is the new subnet mask in dotted decimal format? _____

   e.   How many subnets are available for future use? _____

Step 2. Record the subnet information.

Fill in the following table with the subnet information:

Subnet Number	Subnet Address	First Usable Host Address	Last Usable Host Address	Broadcast Address
0				
1				
2				
3				
4				
5				
6				
7				

Part 3: Network Topology C

The topology has changed again with a new LAN added to R2 and a redundant link between R1 and R3. Use the 192.168.10.0/24 network address to provide addresses to the network devices. Also provide an IP address scheme that will accommodate these additional devices. For this topology, assign a subnet to each network.

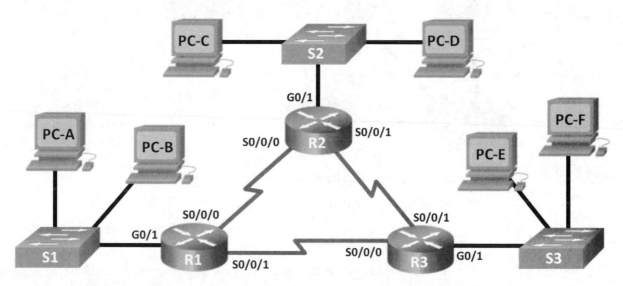

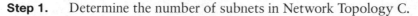

Step 1. Determine the number of subnets in Network Topology C.

    a. How many subnets are there? _____

    b. How many bits should you borrow to create the required number of subnets?

    _____

    c. How many usable host addresses per subnet are in this addressing scheme?

    _____

    d. What is the new subnet mask in dotted decimal format? _____

    e. How many subnets are available for future use? _____

Step 2. Record the subnet information.

Fill in the following table with the subnet information:

Subnet Number	Subnet Address	First Usable Host Address	Last Usable Host Address	Broadcast Address
0				
1				
2				
3				
4				
5				
6				
7				
8				
9				
10				

Step 3. Assign addresses to network devices in the subnets.

a. Fill in the following table with IP addresses and subnet masks for the router interfaces:

Device	Interface	IP Address	Subnet Mask
R1	GigabitEthernet 0/1		
	Serial 0/0/0		
	Serial 0/0/1		
R2	GigabitEthernet 0/1		
	Serial 0/0/0		
	Serial 0/0/1		
R3	GigabitEthernet 0/1		
	Serial 0/0/0		
	Serial 0/0/1		

b. Fill in the following table with the IP addresses and subnet masks for devices in the LAN as displayed in the topology.

Device	Interface	IP Address	Subnet Mask	Default Gateway
PC-A	NIC			
PC-B	NIC			
S1	VLAN 1			
PC-C	NIC			
PC-D	NIC			
S2	VLAN 1			
PC-E	NIC			
PC-F	NIC			
S3	VLAN 1			

Part 4: Network Topology D

The network was modified to accommodate changes in the organization. The 192.168.10.0/24 network address is used to provide the addresses in the network.

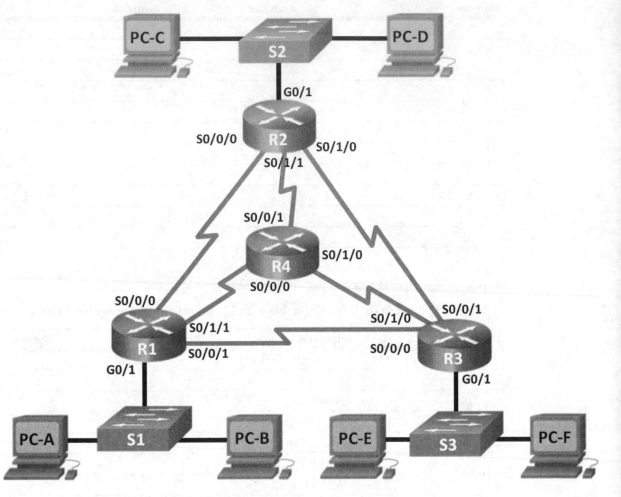

Step 1.   Determine the number of subnets in Network Topology D.

   a.   How many subnets are there? _____

   b.   How many bits should you borrow to create the required number of subnets?
   _____

   c.   How many usable host addresses per subnet are in this addressing scheme?
   _____

   d.   What is the new subnet mask in dotted decimal format? _____

   e.   How many subnets are available for future use? _____

Step 2.   Record the subnet information.

Fill in the following table with the subnet information.

Subnet Number	Subnet Address	First Usable Host Address	Last Usable Host Address	Broadcast Address
0				
1				
2				
3				
4				
5				
6				
7				
8				
9				
10				
11				
12				
13				
14				
15				
16				
17				

Part 5: Network Topology E

The organization has a network address of 172.16.128.0/17 to be divided as illustrated in the following topology. You must choose an addressing scheme that can accommodate the number of networks and hosts in the topology.

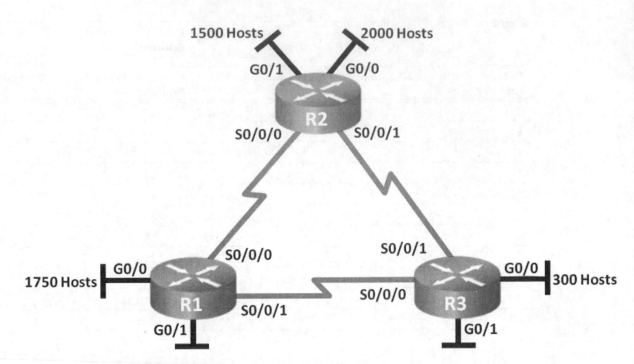

Step 1. Determine the number of subnets in Network Topology E.

    a. How many subnets are there? _____

    b. How many bits should you borrow to create the required number of subnets?

    _____

    c. How many usable host addresses per subnet are in this addressing scheme?

    _____

    d. What is the new subnet mask in dotted decimal format? _____

    e. How many subnets are available for future use? _____

Step 2. Record the subnet information.

Fill in the following table with the subnet information:

Subnet Number	Subnet Address	First Usable Host Address	Last Usable Host Address	Broadcast Address
0				
1				
2				
3				
4				
5				
6				
7				
8				
9				
10				
11				

Subnet Number	Subnet Address	First Usable Host Address	Last Usable Host Address	Broadcast Address
12				
13				
14				
15				
16				
17				

Step 3.   Assign addresses to network devices in the subnets.

    a.   Fill in the following table with IP addresses and subnet masks for the router interfaces:

Device	Interface	IP Address	Subnet Mask
R1	GigabitEthernet 0/0		
	GigabitEthernet 0/1		
	Serial 0/0/0		
	Serial 0/0/1		
R2	GigabitEthernet 0/0		
	GigabitEthernet 0/1		
	Serial 0/0/0		
	Serial 0/0/1		
R3	GigabitEthernet 0/0		
	GigabitEthernet 0/1		
	Serial 0/0/0		
	Serial 0/0/1		

Reflection

1. What information is needed when determining an appropriate addressing scheme for a network?

_____

_____

2. After the subnets are assigned, will all the host addresses be utilized in each subnet?

_____

_____

Appendix Lab–Viewing Host Routing Tables

Topology

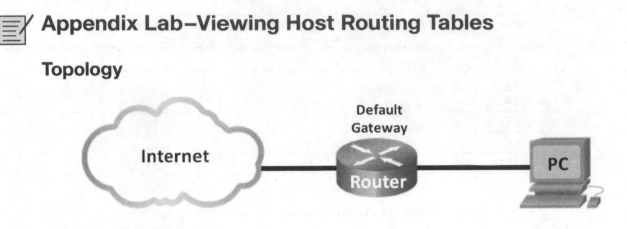

Objectives

Part 1: Access the Host Routing Table

Part 2: Examine IPv4 Host Routing Table Entries

Part 3: Examine IPv6 Host Routing Table Entries

Background/Scenario

To access a resource on a network, your host will determine the route to the destination host using its routing table. The host routing table is similar to that of a router but is specific to the local host and much less complex. For a packet to reach a local destination, the local host routing table is required. To reach a remote destination, both the local host routing table and the router routing table are required. The **netstat –r** and **route print** commands provide insight into how your local host routes packets to the destination.

In this lab, you will display and examine the information in the host routing table of your PC using the **netstat –r** and **route print** commands. You will determine how packets will be routed by your PC depending on the destination address.

Note: This lab cannot be completed using Netlab. This lab assumes that you have Internet access.

Required Resources

- 1 PC (Windows 7, Vista, or XP with Internet and command prompt access)

Part 1: Access the Host Routing Table

Step 1.   Record your PC information.

On your PC, open a command prompt window and type the **ipconfig /all** command to display the following information and record it:

IPv4 Address	
MAC Address	
Default Gateway	

Step 2.   Display the routing tables.

In a command prompt window type the **netstat –r** (or **route print**) command to display the host routing table.

```
C:\Users\user1>netstat -r
===========================================================================
Interface List
 13...90 4c e5 be 15 63 ......Atheros AR9285 802.11b/g/n WiFi Adapter
  1...........................Software Loopback Interface 1
 25...00 00 00 00 00 00 00 e0 Microsoft ISATAP Adapter
 12...00 00 00 00 00 00 00 e0 Microsoft 6to4 Adapter
 26...00 00 00 00 00 00 00 e0 Microsoft ISATAP Adapter #2
 14...00 00 00 00 00 00 00 e0 Teredo Tunneling Pseudo-Interface
===========================================================================

IPv4 Route Table
===========================================================================
Active Routes:
Network Destination        Netmask          Gateway       Interface  Metric
          0.0.0.0          0.0.0.0      192.168.1.1    192.168.1.11     25
        127.0.0.0        255.0.0.0         On-link         127.0.0.1    306
        127.0.0.1  255.255.255.255         On-link         127.0.0.1    306
  127.255.255.255  255.255.255.255         On-link         127.0.0.1    306
      192.168.1.0    255.255.255.0         On-link      192.168.1.11    281
     192.168.1.11  255.255.255.255         On-link      192.168.1.11    281
    192.168.1.255  255.255.255.255         On-link      192.168.1.11    281
        224.0.0.0        240.0.0.0         On-link         127.0.0.1    306
        224.0.0.0        240.0.0.0         On-link      192.168.1.11    281
  255.255.255.255  255.255.255.255         On-link         127.0.0.1    306
  255.255.255.255  255.255.255.255         On-link      192.168.1.11    281
===========================================================================
Persistent Routes:
  None

IPv6 Route Table
===========================================================================
Active Routes:
 If Metric Network Destination      Gateway
 14     58 ::/0                     On-link
  1    306 ::1/128                  On-link
 14     58 2001::/32                On-link
 14    306 2001:0:9d38:6ab8:1863:3bca:3f57:fef4/128
                                    On-link
 14    306 fe80::/64                On-link
 14    306 fe80::1863:3bca:3f57:fef4/128
                                    On-link
  1    306 ff00::/8                 On-link
 14    306 ff00::/8                 On-link
===========================================================================
Persistent Routes:
  None
```

What are the three sections displayed in the output?

_____

Step 3.   Examine the Interface List.

The first section, Interface List, displays the Media Access Control (MAC) addresses and assigned interface number of every network-capable interface on the host.

```
===========================================================================
Interface List
 13...90 4c e5 be 15 63 ......Atheros AR9285 802.11b/g/n WiFi Adapter
  1...........................Software Loopback Interface 1
 25...00 00 00 00 00 00 00 e0 Microsoft ISATAP Adapter
 12...00 00 00 00 00 00 00 e0 Microsoft 6to4 Adapter
 26...00 00 00 00 00 00 00 e0 Microsoft ISATAP Adapter #2
 14...00 00 00 00 00 00 00 e0 Teredo Tunneling Pseudo-Interface
===========================================================================
```

The first column is the interface number. The second column is the list of MAC addresses associated with the network-capable interfaces on the hosts. These interfaces can include Ethernet, Wi-Fi, and Bluetooth adapters. The third column shows the manufacturer and a description of the interface.

In this example, the first line displays the wireless interface that is connected to the local network.

Note: If you have a PC with an Ethernet interface and a Wireless adapter enabled, both interfaces would be listed in the Interface List.

What is the MAC address of the interface connected to your local network? How does the MAC address compare to the recorded MAC address in Step 1?

The second line is loopback interface. The loopback interface is automatically assigned an IP address of 127.0.0.1 when the Transmission Control Protocol/Internet Protocol (TCP/IP) is running on a host.

The last four lines represent transition technology that allows communication in a mixed environment and includes IPv4 and IPv6.

Part 2: Examine IPv4 Host Routing Table Entries

In Part 2, you will examine the IPv4 host routing table. This table is in the second section as a result of the **netstat –r** output. It lists all the known IPv4 routes, including direct connections, local network, and local default routes.

```
IPv4 Route Table
===========================================================================
Active Routes:
Network Destination        Netmask          Gateway       Interface  Metric
          0.0.0.0          0.0.0.0      192.168.1.1    192.168.1.11     25
        127.0.0.0        255.0.0.0         On-link        127.0.0.1    306
        127.0.0.1  255.255.255.255         On-link        127.0.0.1    306
  127.255.255.255  255.255.255.255         On-link        127.0.0.1    306
      192.168.1.0    255.255.255.0         On-link     192.168.1.11    281
     192.168.1.11  255.255.255.255         On-link     192.168.1.11    281
    192.168.1.255  255.255.255.255         On-link     192.168.1.11    281
        224.0.0.0        240.0.0.0         On-link        127.0.0.1    306
        224.0.0.0        240.0.0.0         On-link     192.168.1.11    281
  255.255.255.255  255.255.255.255         On-link        127.0.0.1    306
  255.255.255.255  255.255.255.255         On-link     192.168.1.11    281
===========================================================================
Persistent Routes:
  None
```

The output is divided in five columns: Network Destination, Netmask, Gateway, Interface, and Metric.

- The Network Destination column lists the reachable network. The Network Destination is used with Netmask to match the destination IP address.

- The Netmask lists the subnet mask that the host uses to determine the network and host portions of the IP address.

- The Gateway column lists the address that the host uses to send the packets to a remote network destination. If a destination is directly connected, the gateway is listed as On-link in the output.

- The Interface column lists the IP address that is configured on the local network adaptor. This is used to forward a packet on the network.

- The Metric column lists the cost of using a route. It is used to calculate the best route to a destination. A preferred route has a lower metric number than other routes listed.

The output displays five different types of active routes:

- The local default route 0.0.0.0 is used when the packet does not match other specified addresses in the routing table. The packet will be sent to the gateway from the PC for further processing. In this example, the packet will be sent to 192.168.1.1 from 192.168.1.11.

- The loopback addresses, 127.0.0.0–127.255.255.255, are related to the direct connection and provide services to the local host.

- The addresses for the subnet, 192.168.1.0–192.168.1.255, are all related to the host and the local network. If the final destination of the packet is in the local network, the packet will exit 192.168.1.11 interface.

    - The local route address 192.168.1.0 represents all devices on the 192.168.1.0/24 network.

    - The address of the local host is 192.168.1.11.

    - The network broadcast address 192.168.1.255 is used to send messages to all the hosts on the local network.

- The special multicast class D addresses 224.0.0.0 are reserved for use through either the loopback interface (127.0.0.1) or the host (192.168.1.11).

- The local broadcast address 255.255.255.255 can be used through either the loopback interface (127.0.0.1) or host (192.168.1.11).

Based on the contents of the IPv4 routing table, if the PC wanted to send a packet to 192.168.1.15, what would it do and where would it send the packet?

_____

_____

_____

_____

If the PC wanted to send a packet to a remote host located at 172.16.20.23, what would it do and where would it send the packet?

_____

_____

_____

_____

_____

Part 3: Examine IPv6 Host Routing Table Entries

In Part 3, you will examine the IPv6 routing table. This table is in the third section displayed in the **netstat –r** output. It lists all the known IPv6 routes including direct connections, local network, and local default routes.

```
IPv6 Route Table
===============================================================================
Active Routes:
 If Metric Network Destination          Gateway
 14     58 ::/0                          On-link
  1    306 ::1/128                       On-link
 14     58 2001::/32                     On-link
 14    306 2001:0:9d38:6ab8:1863:3bca:3f57:fef4/128
                                         On-link
 14    306 fe80::/64                     On-link
 14    306 fe80::1863:3bca:3f57:fef4/128
                                         On-link
  1    306 ff00::/8                      On-link
 14    306 ff00::/8                      On-link
===============================================================================
Persistent Routes:
  None
```

The output of the IPv6 Route Table differs in column headings and format because the IPv6 addresses are 128 bits versus only 32 bits for IPv4 addresses. The IPv6 Route Table section displays four columns:

- The If column lists the interface numbers of the IPv6-enabled network interfaces from the Interface List section of the **netstat –r** command.

- The Metric column lists the cost of each route to a destination. The lower cost is the preferred route, and the metric is used to select between multiple routes with the same prefix.

- The Network Destination column lists the address prefix for the route.

- The Gateway lists the next-hop IPv6 address to reach the destination. On-link is listed as the next-hop address if it is directly connected to the host.

In this example, the figure displays the IPv6 Route Table section generated by the **netstat –r** command to reveal the following network destinations:

- ::/0: This is the IPv6 equivalent of the local default route. The Gateway column provides the link-local address of the default router.

- ::1/128: This is equivalent to the IPv4 loopback address and provides services to the local host.

- 2001::/32: This is the global unicast network prefix.

- 2001:0:9d38:6ab8:1863:3bca:3f57:fef4/128: This is the global unicast IPv6 address of the local computer.

- fe80::/64: This is the local link network route address and represents all computers on the local-link IPv6 network.

- fe80::1863:3bca:3f57:fef4/128: This is the link-local IPv6 address of the local computer.

- ff00::/8: These are special reserved multicast class D addresses equivalent to the IPv4 224.x.x.x addresses.

The host routing table for IPv6 has similar information as the IPv4 routing table. What is the local default route for IPv4 and what is it for IPv6?

_____

What is the loopback address and subnet mask for IPv4? What is the loopback IP address for IPv6? ___

_____

How many IPv6 addresses have been assigned to this PC?

_____

How many broadcast addresses does the IPv6 routing table contain?

_____

Reflection

1. How is the number of bits for the network indicated for IPv4? How is it done for IPv6?

   _____

2. Why is there both IPv4 and IPv6 information in the host routing tables?

   _____

Packet Tracer–Configuring an Integrated Router

Topology

Host-A

WR   Laptop

Objectives

Part 1: Connect to an Integrated Router

Part 2: Enable Wireless Connectivity

Part 3: Configure and Verify Wireless Client Access

Background

In this activity, you will configure an integrated router, allowing remote access to wireless clients as well as connectivity with WPA security.

Part 1: Connect to an Integrated Router

Step 1.   Establish and verify connectivity to the integrated router.

    a.   Connect the appropriate cable from Host-A to the Ethernet 1 port on IR.

    b.   Wait for the link light to turn green. Open the command prompt for Host-A. Use the **ipconfig** command to verify host-received IP addressing information.

    c.   Enter the command **ping 192.168.0.1** to verify Host-A can access the default gateway.

Step 2.   Access the IR graphical user interface (GUI) using a web browser.

    a.   Open the web browser on Host-A to access the GUI on IR for configuration. Enter the default gateway address of Host-A in the URL field.

    b.   Enter **admin** as the default username and password to access IR.

Part 2: Enable Wireless Connectivity

Step 1.   Configure IR for Internet connectivity.

There is no Internet connectivity in this scenario, but you will still configure the settings for the Internet-facing interface. For **Internet Connection Type**, choose **Static IP** from the drop-down list. Then enter the following static IP information:

- Internet IP Address–**198.133.219.1**

- Subnet Mask–**255.255.255.0**

- Default Gateway–**198.133.219.254**

- DNS 1–**198.133.219.10**

Step 2.   Configure the inside network parameters.

Scroll down to the **Network Setup** section and configure the following information:

- IP Address–**172.31.1.1**

- Subnet Mask–**255.255.255.224**

- Starting IP Address–Enter **5** for the last octet.

- Maximum number of Users–**25**

Note: The IP address range of the DHCP pool will only reflect the changes after you click **Save Settings**.

Step 3.   Save the settings and reconnect to IR.

a.   Scroll to the bottom of the page and clicked **Save Settings**. If you move from one tab to another without saving, your configurations will be lost.

b.   You lost your connection when you clicked **Save Settings** because you changed the IP address of the router.

c.   Return to the command prompt of Host-A. Enter the command **ipconfig /renew** to renew the IP address.

d.   Use the Host-A web browser to reconnect to IR. You will need to use the new default gateway address. Verify the **Internet Connection** settings in the **Status** tab. The settings should match the values you configured in Part 2, Step 1. If not, repeat Part 2, Step 1 and Step 2.

Step 4.   Configure wireless connectivity for wireless devices.

a.   Click the **Wireless** tab and investigate the options in the drop-down list for **Network Mode**.

When would you choose the **Disable** option? _____

When would you choose the **Mixed** option? _____

---

b.   Set the network mode for **Wireless-N Only**.

c.   Change the SSID to **MyHomeNetwork**.

d.   When a wireless client surveys the area searching for wireless networks, it detects any SSID broadcasts. SSID broadcasts are enabled by default.

If the SSID of an access point is not being broadcast, how will devices connect to it?

_____

_____

    e.   For best performance in a network using Wireless-N, set the radio band to **Wide-40MHz.**

    f.   Click **Save Settings** and then click **Continue.**

Step 5.   Configure wireless security so that clients must authenticate to connect to the wireless network.

    a.   Click the **Wireless Security** option under the **Wireless** tab.

    b.   Set the **Security Mode** to **WPA2 Personal.**

       What is the difference between personal and enterprise? _____

_____

    c.   Leave the encryption mode set to AES and set the passphrase to **itsasecret.**

    d.   Click **Save Settings** and then click **Continue.**

Step 6.   Change the default password to access IR for configuration.

    a.   You should always change the default password. Click the **Administration** tab and change the **Router Access** password to **letmein.**

    b.   Click **Save Settings.** Enter the username **admin** and the new password.

Part 3: Configure and Verify Wireless Client Access

Step 1.   Configure Laptop to access the wireless network.

    a.   Click **Laptop** and click **Desktop > PC Wireless.** The window that opens is the client IR GUI.

    b.   Click the **Connect** tab and click **Refresh,** if necessary. You should see **MyHomeNetwork** listed under Wireless Network Name.

    c.   Click **MyHomeNetwork** and click **Connect.**

    d.   You should now see **MyHomeNetwork.** Click it and then click **Connect.**

    e.   The **Pre-shared Key** is the password you configured in Part 2, Step 5c. Enter the password and click **Connect.**

    f.   Close the IR GUI and click **Command Prompt.** Enter the command **ipconfig** to verify **Laptop** received IP addressing.

Step 2.   Verify connectivity between Laptop and Host-A.

    a.   Ping IR from the Laptop.

    b.   Ping Host-A from the Laptop.

Suggested Scoring Rubric

Activity Section	Question Location	Possible Points	Earned Points
Part 2: Enable Wireless Connectivity	Step 4	4	
	Step 5	1	
	Part 2 Total	5	
	Packet Tracer Score	95	
	Total Score	100	

Packet Tracer
☐ Activity

Packet Tracer–Subnet Scenario 2

Topology

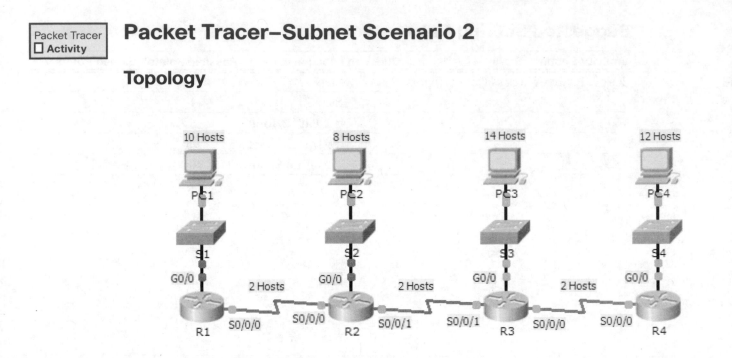

Addressing Table

Device	Interface	IP Address	Subnet Mask	Default Gateway
R1	G0/0			N/A
	S0/0/0			N/A
R2	G0/0			N/A
	S0/0/0			N/A
	S0/0/1			N/A
R3	G0/0			N/A
	S0/0/0			N/A
	S0/0/1			N/A
R4	G0/0			N/A
	S0/0/0			N/A
S1	VLAN 1			
S2	VLAN 1			
S3	VLAN 1			
S4	VLAN 1			
PC1	NIC			
PC2	NIC			
PC3	NIC			
PC4	NIC			

Objectives

Part 1: Design an IP Addressing Scheme

Part 2: Assign IP Addresses to Network Devices and Verify Connectivity

Scenario

In this activity, you are given the network address of 172.31.1.0 /24 to subnet and provide the IP addressing for the network shown in the topology. The required host addresses for each WAN and LAN link are labeled in the topology.

Part 1: Design an IP Addressing Scheme

Step 1.   Subnet the 172.31.1.0/24 network based on the maximum number of hosts required by the largest subnet.

    a.   Based on the topology, how many subnets are needed? _____

    b.   How many bits must be borrowed to support the number of subnets in the topology table?_____

    c.   How many subnets does this create? _____

    d.   How many usable host addresses does this create per subnet? _____

Note: If your answer is less than the 14 maximum hosts required for the R3 LAN, then you borrowed too many bits.

---

    e.   Calculate the binary value for the first five subnets. Subnet zero is already shown.

```
Net 0: 172 . 31 . 1 . 0  0  0  0  0  0  0  0
```

```
Net 1: 172 . 31 . 1 . __ __ __ __ __ __ __ __
```

```
Net 2: 172 . 31 . 1 . __ __ __ __ __ __ __ __
```

```
Net 3: 172 . 31 . 1 . __ __ __ __ __ __ __ __
```

```
Net 4: 172 . 31 . 1 . __ __ __ __ __ __ __ __
```

    f.   Calculate the binary and decimal value of the new subnet mask.

```
11111111.11111111.11111111. __ __ __ __ __ __ __ __
```

```
  255  .  255  .  255  . _____
```

    g.   Complete the **Subnet Table**, listing all available subnets, the first and last usable host address, and the broadcast address. The first subnet is done for you. Repeat until all addresses are listed.

Note: You may not need to use all rows.

Subnet Table

Subnet Number	Subnet IP	First Usable Host IP	Last Usable Host IP	Broadcast Address
0	172.31.1.0	172.31.1.1	172.31.1.14	172.31.1.15
1				
2				
3				
4				
5				
6				
7				
8				
9				
10				
11				
12				
13				
14				
15				

Step 2.   Assign the subnets to the network shown in the topology.

When assigning the subnets, keep in mind that routing is necessary to allow information to be sent throughout the network.

   a.   Assign Subnet 0 to the R1 LAN: _____

   b.   Assign Subnet 1 to the R2 LAN: _____

   c.   Assign Subnet 2 to the R3 LAN: _____

   d.   Assign Subnet 3 to the R4 LAN: _____

   e.   Assign Subnet 4 to the link between R1 and R2: _____

   f.   Assign Subnet 5 to the link between R2 and R3: _____

   g.   Assign Subnet 6 to the link between R3 and R4: _____

Step 3.   Document the addressing scheme.

Complete the **Addressing Table** using the following guidelines:

   a.   Assign the first usable IP addresses to routers for each of the LAN links.

   b.   Use the following method to assign WAN link IP addresses:

     ■   For the WAN link between R1 and R2, assign the first usable IP address to R1 and last usable IP address to R2.

     ■   For the WAN link between R2 and R3, assign the first usable IP address to R2 and last usable IP address to R3.

     ■   For the WAN link between R3 and R4, assign the first usable IP address to R3 and last usable IP address to R4.

c. Assign the second usable IP addresses to the switches.

d. Assign the last usable IP addresses to the hosts.

Part 2: Assign IP Addresses to Network Devices and Verify Connectivity

Most of the IP addressing is already configured on this network. Implement the following steps to complete the addressing configuration.

Step 1. Configure IP addressing on R1 and R2 LAN interfaces.

Step 2. Configure IP addressing on S3, including the default gateway.

Step 3. Configure IP addressing on PC4, including the default gateway.

Step 4. Verify connectivity.

You can only verify connectivity from R1, R2, S3, and PC4. However, you should be able to ping every IP address listed in the **Addressing Table**.

Suggested Scoring Rubric

Note: The majority of points are allocated to designing and documenting the addressing scheme. Implementation of the addresses in Packet Tracer is of minimal consideration.

Activity Section	Question Location	Possible Points	Earned Points
Part 1: Design an IP Addressing Scheme	Step 1a	1	
	Step 1b	1	
	Step 1c	1	
	Step 1d	1	
	Step 1e	4	
	Step 1f	2	
Complete Subnet Table	Step 1g	10	
Assign Subnets	Step 2	10	
Document Addressing	Step 3	40	
	Part 1 Total	70	
	Packet Tracer Score	30	
	Total Score	100	